Semiotic La

Advances in Sociolinguistics
Series Editors: Professor Sally Johnson, University of Leeds
Dr Tommaso M. Milani, University of the Witwatersrand

Since the emergence of sociolinguistics as a new field of enquiry in the late 1960s, research into the relationship between language and society has advanced almost beyond recognition. In particular, the past decade has witnessed the considerable influence of theories drawn from outside of sociolinguistics itself. Thus rather than see language as a mere reflection of society, recent work has been increasingly inspired by ideas drawn from social, cultural, and political theory that have emphasized the constitutive role played by language/discourse in all areas of social life. The Advances in Sociolinguistics series seeks to provide a snapshot of the current diversity of the field of sociolinguistics and the blurring of the boundaries between sociolinguistics and other domains of study concerned with the role of language in society.

Discourses of Endangerment: Ideology and Interest in the Defence of Languages
Edited by Alexandre Duchêne and Monica Heller

Globalization of Language and Culture in Asia
Edited by Viniti Vaish

Linguistic Minorities and Modernity, 2nd Edition: A Sociolinguistic Ethnography
Monica Heller

Language, Culture and Identity: An Ethnolinguistic Perspective
Philip Riley

Language Ideologies and Media Discourse: Texts, Practices, Politics
Edited by Sally Johnson and Tommaso M. Milani

Language in the Media: Representations, Identities, Ideologies
Edited by Sally Johnson and Astrid Ensslin

Language and Power: An Introduction to Institutional Discourse
Andrea Mayr

Language Testing, Migration and Citizenship
Edited by Guus Extra, Massimiliano Spotti and Piet Van Avermaet

Multilingualism: A Critical Perspective
Adrian Blackledge and Angela Creese

The Languages of Global Hip Hop
Edited by Marina Terkourafi

The Language of Newspapers: Socio-Historical Perspectives
Martin Conboy

The Languages of Urban Africa
Edited by Fiona Mc Laughlin

Semiotic Landscapes

Language, Image, Space

Edited by
Adam Jaworski and Crispin Thurlow

Continuum International Publishing Group
The Tower Building
11 York Road
London SE1 7NX

80 Maiden Lane
Suite 704
New York NY 10038

www.continuumbooks.com

First published 2010
Paperback edition first published 2011

British Library Cataloguing-in-Publication Data
A catalogue record for this book is available from the British Library.

ISBN: 978-1-8470-6182-9 (Hardback)
ISBN: 978-1-4411-2472-2 (Paperback)

Library of Congress Cataloging-in-Publication Data
A catalog record for this book is available from the Library of Congress.

Typeset by Newgen Imaging Systems Pvt Ltd, Chennai, India
Printed and bound in Great Britain

Contents

Acknowledgements

This book, like any other academic enterprise of this sort, is a result of many collaborations, and we are grateful to all who have provided us with input and inspiration. Most of all, we thank the chapter authors for sharing their work with us and for their patience. We also thank the editor of this book series, Sally Johnson, for her initial support for the project, and all at Continuum, especially Gurdeep Mattu and Colleen Coalter, for adding the book to their list and for their help at every stage.

At the University of Washington end of things, special thanks are due to Crispin's colleagues – and especially Jerry Baldasty – in the Department of Communication for their financial support towards two *indispensible* visits to the Helen R. Whiteley Center, a wonderful writing retreat on San Juan Island in the Puget Sound. We are incredibly grateful to Kathy Cowell and her colleagues at the Whiteley Center for their generous, friendly assistance. Thanks also to Chris Harihar, Crispin's research assistant, for his help with the preparation of our manuscript for publication.

Adam has enjoyed and benefited from numerous conversations about 'language in place' with Nik Coupland, Chris Hutton, Kasper Juffermans, Gerlinde Mautner, Aneta Pavlenko, Frances Rock and Simone Yeung, as well as the participants at the Linguistic Landscape Workshops in Tel Aviv (January, 2008) and Siena (January, 2009) organized by Elana Shohamy, Eliezer Ben-Rafael, Shoshi Waksman, Nira Trumper-Hecht and Efrat Marco (Tel Aviv), and Monica Barni and Carla Bagna (Siena). Adam is also grateful to all colleagues at the Department of English, University of Hong Kong, where some of the initial work on the book was carried out between January–March 2007, and to all colleagues at the Centre for Language and Communication Research, Cardiff University, for continuously providing the stimulating research environment.

As always, we are most indebted and grateful to our families for supporting us in our academic endeavours, tolerating extravagant working hours, long absences, taking endless photos of seemingly bizarre objects, and claiming to still like us as much as before we started work on this book (and the other two!). For Adam, this is Ania and Maja. For Crispin, this is Jürg, Joe and Jay.

At the planning stages, we were extremely privileged when Ron Scollon and Suzie Wong Scollon agreed to write an Epilogue for the book. Just as we were ready to send them the manuscript, however, we heard from Ron about his illness and, understandably, about their inability to write the epilogue. A little later, we were saddened to hear about Ron's passing away. Of course, this was far more than a blow to our modest project. Ron's work, largely in collaboration with Suzie, not only permeates all the pages of this book but also the fields of sociolinguistics, discourse analysis, social semiotics and visual communication more broadly. We are reminded of one of many inspiring pieces by Ron, the paper titled 'The machine stops: Silence in the metaphor of malfunction' published in the collection *Perspectives on Silence*, edited by Deborah Tannen and Muriel Saville-Troike (Ablex, 1995). Ron has fallen silent, but the machine of his work has not stopped, and will continue to hum away, informing and influencing generations of researchers to come.

List of Contributors

Gill Abousnnouga, University of Glamorgan, Wales
Giorgia Aiello, University of Leeds, England
Ella Chmielewska, University of Edinburgh, Scotland
Nikolas Coupland, Cardiff University, Wales
Susan Dray, Lancaster University, England
Irina Gendelman, Saint Martin's University, Olympia, USA
Adam Jaworski, Cardiff University, Wales
Rodney H. Jones, City University of Hong Kong, China
Jeffrey L. Kallen, Trinity College, Dublin, Ireland
David Machin, Cardiff University, Wales
Thomas D. Mitchell, Carnegie Mellon University, USA
Alastair Pennycook, University of Technology, Sydney, Australia
Ingrid Piller, Macquarie University, Sydney, Australia
Mark Sebba, Lancaster University, England
Elana Shohamy, Tel Aviv University, Israel
Crispin Thurlow, University of Washington, Seattle, USA
Shoshi Waksman, Levinsky College of Education, Tel Aviv, Israel

Introducing Semiotic Landscapes

Adam Jaworski and Crispin Thurlow

In the era of multimodality semiotic modes other than language are treated as fully capable of serving for representation and communication. Indeed, language, whether as speech or as writing, may now often be seen as ancillary to other semiotic modes: to the visual for instance. Language may now be 'extravisual'. The very facts of the new communicational landscape have made that inescapably the issue.

Kress and van Leeuwen, 2001: 46

The problem of the proper conceptualization of space is resolved through human practice with respect to it. In other words, there are no philosophical answers to philosophical questions that arise over the nature of space – the answers lie in human practice. The question 'what is space?' is therefore replaced by the question 'how is it that different human practices create and make use of different conceptualizations of space?'

Harvey, 2006: 125–126

As suggested by the subtitle of this book, we are concerned here with the interplay between language, visual discourse, and the spatial practices and dimensions of culture, especially the textual mediation or discursive construction of place and the use of space as a semiotic resource in its own right. The broader context which we are interested in is the extent to which these mutual processes are in turn shaped by the economic and political reorderings of post-industrial or advanced capitalism, intense patterns of human mobility, the mediatization of social life (Fairclough, 1999), and transnational flows of information, ideas and ideologies (Appadurai, 1990, 1996). This dual attention to the multimodality and political-economy of discourse is motivated by new ways of thinking within our own scholarly field (see, for example, Gunther Kress and Theo van Leeuwen quoted above) as well as the growing recognition of – and interest in – discourse beyond our field (see, for example, David Harvey also quoted above). Whether as a consequence of intellectual fashion or as a tangible experience of contemporary life, no self-respecting scholar these days can afford to overlook the discourse/s of place and the place/s of discourse.

The main title of the book is, in turn, meant to reflect this wide-ranging, yet – we believe – coherent scope. Although the focus of the majority of the chapters is on written language 'in place', we have choosen not to call this book 'Linguistic Landscapes', as some of our predecessors have (e.g. Ben-Rafael et al., 2004, 2006; Gorter, 2006a,b; Backhaus, 2007; Shohamy and Gorter, 2008; see also Spolsky and Cooper, 1991), because in this collection we are keen to emphasize the way written discourse interacts with other discursive modalities: visual images, nonverbal communication, architecture and the built environment. For this reason, 'linguistic' is only one, albeit extremely important, element for the construction and interpretation of place. Although potentially misleading – all landscape is semiotic, i.e. its meaning is always construed in the act of socio-cultural interpretation – we follow Scollon and Wong Scollon (2003) in making a qualified distinction between semiotic and non-semiotic spaces; we thus take *semiotic landscape* to mean, in the most general sense, any (public) space with visible inscription made through deliberate human intervention and meaning making. However, as is clear from its thematic and empirical scope (i.e. data sets oriented to by individual chapters) writing and image, broadly defined, are at the analytic centre for most part of the book. The interpretive frameworks range from sociolinguistic to discourse analytic, encompassing visual, multimodal and mediated approaches, to social semiotic and cultural/critical, and this 'progression' is reflected in the way we have sequenced the book's chapters.

Framing semiotic landscapes

The study of landscape has been traditionally a prerogative of art historians and geographers (see, for example, Andrews, 1999; Cosgrove, 1998; Wylie, 2007), although in recent years it has developed into a truly interdisciplinary project (e.g. DeLue and Elkins, 2008). The role of the human geographer Denis Cosgrove (e.g. 1984, 1998) in bringing these perspectives together as part of the 'humanist turn' in geography cannot be overestimated. Cosgrove departs from the narrow, mechanistic views of landscape as 'an artistic or literary response to the visible scene' (Cosgrove, 1984: 46) or as a lived environment examined and evaluated to facilitate local government aerial planning. In particular, Cosgrove rejects the utlitarian, perception-led studies of landscape in favour of theorizing the geographical environment as incorporating the individual, imaginative and creative aspects of human experience. However, Cosgrove does trace the (Western) idea of landscape to its roots in the scientific and artistic developments of the Italian Renaissance in the fifteenth and sixteenth centuries, when the combined work of mathematicians and artists (typically one and the same person), motivated equally by the pursuit of artistic and scientific knowledge, led to the formulation of the geometric principles for the creation of 'realistic illusion' to represent a three-dimensional space on a two-dimensional surface. The principles of the technique known as *linear perspective* were formulated by the Florentine artist and architect Leon

Battista Alberti in his *De Pictura* (On Painting, 1435) alongside the visual experiments of his close associate Filippo Brunelleschi; these principles were not only key for the subsequent compositional and aesthetic developments in painting, but were also applied to architecture, land survey, map-making, artillery science, and the measurement of distance, surface and volume, all pertinent to the early development of commerce, capitalist finance, agriculture, the land market, navigation and warfare, in sum, the early development of urban, bourgeois, rationalist conception of the world (Cosgrove, 1984; see also Panofsky, 1991 [1927]). Thus, landscape is defined by Cosgrove, borrowing John Berger's (1982) terminology, as a '*way of seeing* the external world' (1984: 46) and as 'a visual ideology' (47). This was evident both in art and other applications of linear perspective. 'The artist, through perspective, establishes the arrangement or composition, and thus the specific time, of the events described, determines – in both senses – the "point of view" to be taken by the observer, and controls through framing the scope of reality revealed' (Cosgrove, 1984: 48). In cartography, applications of geometrical principles led to the production of detailed survey maps of cities allowing accurate yet detached, distant and dominating views of vast urban areas, placing the human observer in the 'divine' position of creator and controller, not unlike in the vast panoramic landscapes by Titian and Bruegel which, for example, give the observer a sense of dominion and control over space (certainly a technique carried through to the later medium of photography and used widely in a range of commercial contexts, cf. Thurlow and Jaworski, this volume). These achievements in geometrical representation of space coincided with, or rather facilitated, the (colonial) appropriation of territory and of the production of (private) property:

> Surveyors' charts which located and measured individual estates, for example in England after the dissolution of monasteries; cartographers' maps which used the graticule to apportion global space, for example the line defined by Pope Alexander VI dividing the new world between Portugal and Spain; engineers' plans for fortresses and cannon trajectories to conquer or defend national territory, as for example Vauban's French work or Sorte's for the Venetian defences against Austria. (Cosgrove, 1984: 55)

But landscape as a way of seeing is not to be confined to the mediated representations of space in art and literature. It is a broader concept pertaining to how we view and interpret space in ways that are contingent on geographical, social, economic, legal, cultural and emotional circumstances, as well as our practical uses of the physical environment as nature and territory, aesthetic judgements, memory and myth, for example drawing on religious beliefs and references, historical discourses, politics of gender relations, class, ethnicity, and the imperial projects of colonization – all of which are still present today and consistently reproduced in, for example, contemporary tourist landscapes (Massey, 1994; Cosgrove, 2008 [1998]; Crouch, 1999; Cartier and Lew, 2005; Osborne, 2000).

Thus, Cosgrove and others position the idea of landscape within the sphere of social and cultural practice, as our ways of seeing are subject to a number of competing 'scopic regimes' or 'visual subcultures' (Jay, 1998: 4) shaped in part by the changes in the representation of space. For example, most tourists visiting the Yosemite Park 'see' it as mediated through Anselm Adams' famous photographs, which they attempt to recreate in their own holiday snaps (cf. DeLue and Elkins, 2008), just as William Hodges' idyllic paintings of Tahiti inspired by his journey accompanying Captain Cook on one of his voyages in the eighteenth century continue to provide a template for depicting the exotic and 'unspoilt' 'winter sun' destinations in tourist brochures (Khan, 2003; de Botton, 2003).

Defining landscape as a way of seeing underscores its historical volatility. Commenting on the 'photographic turn' in mediation of space, John Berger observes: 'Every drawing or painting that used perspective proposed to the spectator that he was the unique centre of the world. The camera – and more particularly the movie camera – demonstrated that there was no centre' (Berger, 1972: 18). Other technological developments, especially with regard to mobility, are equally significant here. Opening up of space for gazing or glancing from the moving train, motor car, or airplane afforded new modes of experiencing large vistas and 'passing' terrains, 'reaching an apogee in the 1968 photograph of the earth rising over the lunar surface' (Cosgrove, 2008 [1998]: 31; see also Schivelbusch, 1986). John Urry (1995, 2005, 2007) links the transformation of *land*, a tangible commodity to be toiled, bought and sold, and passed on from generation to generation, to *landscape*, a place of affect, contemplative looking, gazing, connoisseurship, and its particular significance marked by the increase in people's mobility, especially the rise of 'scenic tourism' in the eighteenth century. But being on the move has also turned landscape into a succession of decontextualized, passing images neatly framed by the rectangular of the train or the oval of the plane window (again, see Schivelbusch, 1986). As Urry observes, '[t]he Ford brochure of 1949 declared that "The 49 Ford is a living room on wheels" (Marsh and Collett, 1986: 11; the VW camper is described as a "Room with a View")' (Urry, 2004: 30–31). In this spirit, one of the major attractions of the Venice-Simplon Orient Express mentioned on its website for the Venice–Paris–London train service is 'gazing at the beautiful passing scenery of the Italian Dolomites and the Swiss Alps' on the first day of the journey. Perhaps understandably the website is silent on the dominant urban and industrial landscape the train will be passing through the next morning, with numerous commuters gazing at the anachronistic curiosity of a restored train and its 'high-end' passengers, making their way so slowly through the crowded transportation hubs in and around modern-day Paris. For all its juxtaposition, the Orient-Express attempts to recreate and reglamorize not only a mode of travel but also a way of consuming place/s.

Ironically, rather than opening up more space, speed may at times interfere with the landscape turning it into a blur, allowing only short glimpses of the passing scenery, and noticeable only when something 'meaningful' happens to come to our field of vision (cf. Bissell, 2009; and Schivelbusch, 1986, on 'panoramic travel'). And that's only if one is lucky enough not to have all the 'scenery' obscured by the reflected interior of a night train, or obliterated in a traffic jam stuck behind an SUV, or substituted for the black voids of the windows in an underground train. Nevertheless, mobility, and especially automobility, has undeniably altered rural and especially urban landscapes, with transport infrastructure (roads, car parks, railways), architecture (stations, out-of-town shopping centres, drive-through restaurants, petrol and service stations, motels, coach and train stations, and airports) (cf. Urry, 2004; Pascoe, 2001), traffic signs, signposting and billboards. And by adding another layer of semioticization, cars, trains, trams, buses, bicycles, motorbikes, rikshaws, ships, ferries, yachts, barges, aeroplanes, etc., are as much a means of accessing new scenery as part of the scenery itself (cf. Thurlow and Aiello, 2007; Sebba, this volume; Dray, this volume).

In recent decades, new technological developments have opened up new ways of representing, accessing and theorizing space/place. Especially with the rise of digital media and the omnipresence of screens in public and private lives such as television sets, computer monitors, CCTV, electronic billboards, information displays, screens in mobile phones, mp3 players, digital cameras and camcorders, and a whole range of 'interactive' screens attached to machines for drawing cash, 'fast' check-in at airports, making payment at car parks, and so on, social and material landscapes have become more multimodal and more mediatized than ever before (Jewitt and Triggs, 2006; Jones, this volume). This is, after all, the age of cyberspace. And it is by responding to the digital, virtual 'revolution' that Daniels and Cosgrove (1988: 8) venture their metaphor for the understanding of (contemporary) landscape as 'a flickering text displayed on the word-processor screen whose meaning can be created, extended, altered, elaborated and finally obliterated by the merest touch of a button'.

In human geography, the metaphor of landscape as text and spectacle, which is of particular relevance to the remit and methodological approaches represented in this volume, has a well-established position. Following their critique of mimetic, realist, universalizing interpretations of the surveyed world through 'descriptive fieldwork' or observation modelled on positivist science, Duncan and Ley (1993) align themselves with hermeneutic interpretations which posit an intersubjective and dialogic relationship between researchers embedded within particular intellectual and institutional contexts and their data – other people and places. This approach makes way for the view of landscape as 'the discursive terrain across which the struggle between the different, often hostile, codes of meaning construction has been engaged' (Daniels and Cosgrove, 1993: 59), and it is only one step away from forging links between landscape and identity, social order and power.

> Each society's 'moral order' is reflected in its particular spatial order and in the language and imagery by which that spatial order is represented.

> Conversely, the social is spatially constituted, and people make sense of their social identity in terms of their environment. Their place of residence offers a map of their place in society: we produce not housing but 'dwellings of definite sorts, as a peasant's hut or nobleman's castle . . . [in] a continuous process of social life in which men [sic] reciprocally define objects in terms of themselves and themselves in terms of objects' (Sahlins, 1976: 169), To 'place' someone, to 'know one's place': this language of social existence is unmistakably geographical. Cultural geography thus calls for a decoding of landscape imagery, a reading of the environmental 'maps of meaning' (Jackson, 1989) which reveal and reproduce – and sometimes resist – social order. (Mills, 1993: 150)

But landscape is not to be reduced 'to a mere social construction' (Cosgrove, 2008 [1988]: 34). In fact, the above quote emphasizes the dichotomous, dialectical nature of landscape both as physical (built) environment, a context for human action and socio-political activity, while at the same time a symbolic system of signifiers with wide-ranging affordances activated by social actors to position themselves and others in that context. This dichotomy is captured by John Wylie's metaphor of landscape as tension, when he asks whether landscape is 'the world we are living *in*, or a scene we are looking *at*, from afar?' (Wylie, 2007: 1). The answer is probably both, as suggested by Kenneth Olwig's (2008) distinction in the meaning of landscape as 'domain' and 'scenery', or neither, as suggested by John Urry: 'Landscape is . . . neither nature nor culture, neither mind nor matter. It is the world as known to those who have dwelt in that place, those who currently dwell there, those who will dwell there, and those whose practical activities take them through its many sites and journey along its multiple paths' (Urry, 2007: 32).

Making space, locating self

An imperceptible line seems to divide studies of 'landscape' from the cultural, social and political aspects of space more broadly. Within the confines of a brief overview, we cannot do justice to the vast literature on this topic in human geography, anthropology and sociology, but in this section we attempt to draw some points of contact between these traditions of work and the linguistic and semiotic approaches to the study of space represented in this book. As we started by noting above, space and spatiality are key topics of concern for a wide range of contemporary scholars, prompting Mike Crang and Nigel Thrift describe it as 'the everywhere of modern thought' (2000: 1). Central to this 'spatial turn' is the recognition that space is not only physically but also socially constructed, which necessarily shifts absolutist notions of space towards more communicative or discursive conceptualizations (e.g. Harvey, 1989, 2006; Lefebvre, 1991; Massey and Jess, 1995). As such, the focus of scholarly interest is nowadays often less on space *per se* as it is on *spatialization*, the different processes by which space comes to be represented, organized and experienced.

One of the central interests in this retheorizing of space is the notion of the social construction of place and people's 'sense of place'. In these terms, space is not regarded as something purely physical or neatly bounded. Rather, it is a 'multiplicity' (Massey, 2005). As people and cultures are located in space, it is particularly the idea of 'home' (understood as points of origin and belonging) that is inevitably bound up with specific geographical locations which we come to know and experience both sensually and intellectually through semiotic framing and various forms of discoursal construal (Entrikin, 1991; Johnstone, 2004). We create our identities in part through the process of geographical imagining, the locating of self in space, claiming the ownership of specific places, or by being excluded from them, by sharing space and interacting with others, however subtly and fleetingly, for example, as strangers in a large city (Simmel, 1997).

By the same token, our sense of national or regional identity is closely linked to the nation's collective gaze at the physical attributes of landscape, especially the pictorial, cartographic and textual representations of the countryside. The production of these landscapes in the construction of regional and national identity has been well recognized and extensively documented (e.g. Daniels, 1993; Matless, 1998; Rycroft and Cosgrove, 1995). Following on from the Industrial Revolution and into the twentieth century, the countryside, rural life, and the unspoiled wilderness of remote, uninhabited areas have been perceived as the sites of the 'soul' of the nation, national integrity, moral virtue, or freedom of spirit. The need to preserve the threatened countryside and iconic landscape from the spreading urbanization or such external threats as wars, has been considered a moral duty and vital for the protection of the nation (Cosgrove et al., 1995; Colls, 2002; Kumar, 2003). More recently, the iconic images of urban (capital) heartlands – buildings, statues, towers, gardens and so on (Lawson, 2001) – have themselves been landscaped and incorporated into popular and official imaginings of national identity.

The emergence of symbolic and mental landscapes as part of the regional and national identity building takes place through semioticizing processes referred to by Sörlin (1999) as the 'articulation of territory', whereby landscape features (such as mountains, rivers, coastal areas), alongside architectural (church spires, typical rural dwellings, bridges, etc.), and other, large-scale landscaping and engineering interventions (parks, dams, water reservoirs and so on), are described, reproduced and recreated in literary texts, art, models and maquettes in museums and so on, as well as through the social practice of tourism (cf. Cosgrove et al., 1995). The notion of territorial articulation intersects with Lefebvre's (1991) well-known dimensions of space which he calls *conceived* space, *perceived* space, and *lived* space. Briefly, conceived space corresponds to mental or represented images of space (e.g. those of advertising, Thurlow and Jaworski, this volume); perceived space is equivalent to material or physical space responsible for economic production and social reproduction; while lived space is produced through the experiential intersection and/or interaction of both conceived and perceived space. In all three modes of space, or processes of *spatialization,* we find linguistic and other semiotic markings (texts) which define or organize the meaning of these spatial practices as well as social practices enacted in the spaces. For example, signs that mark the 'turf' boundaries (experiential spaces), indexical signs identifying specific places (representational, perceptual spaces), and 'overlayed' signs such as graffiti (reimagining spaces), all interact with one another, with the spaces of their emplacement, and with the social actors inhabiting these spaces in creating complex networks of meaning, or 'semiotic aggregates' (Scollon and Wong Scollon, 2003).

Imagery of place is, of course, an important resource for diasporic communities in maintaining their sense of national or ethnic identity and through which to express their longing and nostalgia for the 'lost' homeland. Place facilitates and creates the 'collective memory' of diaspora (Harvey, 1989). As Garrett et al. (2005: 532) state for 'diasporic social groups . . . imagery of "home" has the potential to bridge across the physical space that separates "new communities" from their "roots of origin", linking past with present in the compression of time and space.' In their daily acts of identity, immigrant communities not only transpose images of 'home' into the mediated and mediatized spaces in which they live their diasporic subjectivities. They transform the typically urban areas of their concentration by (re)semioticizing these spaces, creating orders of indexicality which positions them in complex ways *vis-à-vis* their ancestral and host communities with the written and pictorial signs over shops, restaurants, travel agents, internet and telephone communications centres, cultural institutions and so on (cf. Collins and Slembrouck, 2004). Immigrant languages, national flags, colours, emblems, décor and architectural detail (e.g. gates marking the entrance to 'China towns' in European and North American cities) index these communities and allow them to claim these urban spaces as 'their own' – to make the foreign and distant, familiar and present.

Of course, leaving visible traces of human activity and social interactions within space is by no means the sole prerogative of migrant communities. Turning space into place, or creating a sense of place, is arguably a universal human need and an inevitable outcome of various (inter)actions involving the manipulation of 'nature' through agriculture, architecture, and landscaping, and symbolically, via such activities as depicting, narrating and remembering. Places thus come to be known both sensually and intellectually (Entrikin, 1991). They are also known discursively and only ever made meaningful in discourse. Speaking, writing, and other semiotic codes found *in* space index particular localities, orient us through different levels of territorial and societal stratification including identity claims, power relations, and their contestations (Johnstone, 2004). All of these practices involve territorial claims, spatial segregation or encroachment, and the categorization of social actors into ingroup and outgroup members, into Self and Other. For example, Edensor and Millington (2009) demonstrate how the British media engage in the vilifying criticism of prominent, often extravagantly bright and multi-coloured outdoor Christmas-light displays in many working-class areas in the United Kingdom, establishing and reinforcing negative stereotypes encapsulated in the disparaging term 'chavs' (i.e. 'lowly working-class "others"', ibid.: 104). Such displays, contrasting with the more 'understated' Christmas-light displays in middle-class areas, and the normative media discourses 'express different contemporary processes of class formation [which] operate within distinct circuits that provoke questions about social connectedness and the power to mobilize identity within different spatial contexts' (ibid.). Importantly, for our purposes, this is a story of space – spatialization – that is quintessentially semiotic (and meta-semiotic).

Although sociolinguists have long associated different ways of speaking with territorially-defined identities of speakers (through association of linguistic variables with neighbourhoods, cities, regions, or nations) it was not until recently that they became influenced by cultural geographers and started making more explicit connections between speech variation and place as a more dynamic, performative concept replacing the traditional view of place as a static, *a priori* 'location' of persons and objects in space. For example, Barbara Johnstone (2004) relates the idea of creating a sense of localness through the 'local' forms of speech, their development, cultivation, and folk-linguistic mythologies, particularly in response to the globalizing processes increasing contact between 'old' and 'new' ways of speaking. In her detailed ethnographic study of Mt. Pleasant, an area of Washington DC, Modan (2007) examines discourse as a form of spatial rather than social action, and demonstrates how the residents' spoken and written, private and public discourses and interactions create different conceptions of the neighbourhood and spatialized identities across ethnic, gender, socio-economic boundaries. Written from the position of language policy and planning, Mac Giolla Chríost's (2007) study takes a macro-sociolinguistic approach to theorizing urban spaces with regard to power relations and identity formation through the lens of place-naming, multilingualism, linguistic vitality, and language policy (cf. Shohamy, 2006).

'Linguistic landscapes'

Most (English-language) studies of linguistic landscape to date take as their starting point the definition proposed by Rodrigue Landry and Richard Bourhis (1997), which is recognized as the first major attempt to link publicly displayed – or *emplaced* – discourse to some aspects of the sociolinguistic reality of the place – in this case, the ethnolinguistic vitality of different communities sharing a particular territory. Building on the work of Jacques Leclerc (1989), Landry and Bourhis propose that:

> The language of public road signs, advertising billboards, street names, place names, commercial shop signs, and public signs on government buildings combines to form the linguistic landscape of a given territory, region, or urban agglomeration. (Landry and Bourhis, 1997: 25)

Landry and Bourhis go on to distinguish between 'private' and 'government' signs. The former include 'commercial signs on storefronts and business institutions (e.g. retail stores and banks), commercial advertising on billboards, and advertising signs displayed in public transport and on private vehicles' (p. 26). The latter include 'public signs used by national, regional, or municipal governments in the following domains: road signs, place names, street names, and inscriptions on state buildings including ministries, hospitals, universities, town halls, schools, metro stations, and public parks' (ibid.). The linguistic profile of the private and government signs may be similar or discordant; other things being equal, however, it usually appears to be more diverse in the private ones, reflecting more accurately the multilingual reality of a particular area or location (in this volume see chapters by Kallen; Coupland; Dray; Sebba; Mitchell). It is commonly believed that, apart from indexing a particular linguistic community, the act of displaying a language, especially on official, central or local government signage, carries the important symbolic function of increasing its value and status. Thus, the presence and dominance of one language over others (in frequency of occurrence or prominence of display) may indicate the relative demographic and institutional power of an ethnolinguistic group over others. In cases of conflict, repressed groups may be ideologically erased (Irvine and Gal, 2000) from public view (see Sebba, this volume). The meaning and power of language/s is/are thus dependent on, and derived from, space.

Working on aggregate, questionnaire data collected from among francophone high school students in different parts of Canada over a 10-year period, Landry and Bourhis concluded that, unsurprisingly, the presence of French in the linguistic landscape of the students' environment (as defined above) was most prominent in those parts of Canada where the perceived in-group, francophone ethnolinguistic identity of the students was the greatest. They also suggested, however tentatively, that 'the presence of private and government signs written in the in-group language might have acted as a stimulus for promoting the use of one's own language in a broad range of language domains' (p. 45), which is particularly salient in those areas where the in-group language is not dominant.

The more qualitative, ethnographically oriented studies of 'language in place' in our volume here (see Kallen; Sebba; Coupland; Dray; Pennycook; Piller; Mitchell) suggest a more subtle picture, where the degree of prominence of a language in a particular site is not necessarily the most accurate indicator of the ethnolinguistic vitality of its speakers. Rather, the presence or absence of a language on public signage, in combination with the type (or genre) of signs, their contents and style, are indicative of public and private language ideologies, i.e. '[r]epresentations, whether explicit or implicit, that construe the intersection of language and human beings in a social world' (Woolard, 1998: 3). The two core elements of this definition – the *linguistic* and the *social* – are certainly inseparable, but have been variously oriented to in different definitions of language ideology. We want to cite some of them here, relying on Woolard's useful summary:

> Linguistic or language ideologies have been defined most broadly as 'shared bodies of commonsense notions about the nature of language in the world' (Rumsey, 1990: 346). With more emphasis on linguistic structure and on the activist nature of ideology . . . Silverstein defines linguistic ideology as 'sets of beliefs about language articulated by users as a rationalization of justification of perceived language structure and use' (1979: 193). On the other hand, with a greater emphasis on the social facet, language ideology has been defined as 'self-evident ideas and objectives a group holds concerning roles of language in the social experiences of members as they contribute to the expression of the group' (Heath, 1989: 53) and as 'the cultural system of ideas about social and linguistic relationships, together with their loading of moral and political interests' (Irvine, 1989: 255). (Woolard, 1998: 3–4)

One key aspect of linguistic ideologies emerging from these definitions is that they are metalinguistic, or metadiscursive, in nature (cf. Coupland and Jaworski, 2004), i.e. they overlay, more or less explicitly, all language use with *value*, be it social, cultural, political, moral, economic or otherwise. The converse is equally valid; all metalinguistic commentary is ideological. By theorizing language ideologies as historical, Blommaert (1999a) positions them as debates which are 'more or less historically locatable periods in which a "struggle for authoritative entextualization" takes place' (Blommaert, 1999b: 9). He elaborates on this idea with reference to Silverstein and Urban's (1996: 11) notion of entextualization:

> 'Politics can be seen . . . as the struggle to entextualize authoritatively, and hence, in one relevant move, to fix certain metadiscursive perspectives on texts and discourse practices'. Metadiscursive entextualization – inserting texts into a chosen metadiscursive context and hence indicating the preferred way(s) of 'reading' these texts – is then a strategic practice often aimed at the 'acceptance of a metadiscourse by a community', a process that may be 'at the very center of a community's organizing social categories and their relationship, including political hierarchies' (1996: 12). (Blommaert, 1999b: 9)

If we agree, along with most contemporary geographers, to treat space as a discursive as well as physical formation (see above), it then follows that the emplacement, or entextualization, of linguistic signs is indeed a metadiscursive, and, of necessity, an ideological act (see also Coupland, this volume). In considering linguistic and other forms of semiotic inscription in space, Blommaert's and Silverstein and Urban's *preferred readings* of these inscriptions must be considered as part of Jay's 'scopic regime' (see above), not only affording a particular way of seeing but also subject to ideological dominance and contestation – as evidenced by a number of our contributors.

This growing recognition of the ideological implications of the language/space interplay – as well as the more widespread 'spatial turn' in the social sciences – which explains a recent surge of interest in the study of 'linguistic landscapes', with journal special issues, books and cyclical international conferences on the topic. Fuelled also by the spread and accessibility of digital photography, similar to developments in accessible, portable audio-recording technology which prompted the rise and expansion of sociolinguistics from the 1960s onwards (Gorter, 2006c), sociolinguists and other language scholars have turned to collecting samples of images of public signage, inscriptions, and various other texts 'in place'. The predominant focus of linguistic landscape studies to date has been on multilingual usage on commercial and place-name signs in urban areas (see Jaworski and Yeung [2010, in press]), on residential signage). One of the most popular approaches contrasts the presence and absence of different languages in 'official' and 'non-official' signs. For example, Backhaus (2006 citing Calvet, 1990, 1994; and Rosenbaum et al., 1977) suggests that the diversity of languages is greater on 'non-official'/'private' signs, in contrast to the more conservative, less plurilingual 'official' or 'government' signs. Backhaus makes a similar observation about his data collected in Tokyo: official multilingual signs are dominated by the use of Japanese with a considerable presence of English and a relatively low presence of Chinese and Korean, which he interprets as the manifestation of the state-induced, linguistic hegemony with a nod to a small number of linguistic minorities. The non-official multilingual signs in Tokyo display a wider array of languages (predominantly English), which Backhaus interprets as an expression of the sign-makers' solidarity with the foreign language community, and more generally with the Western (predominantly Anglo-American) cultural values and internationalism. These symbolic displays of English (and to a lesser degree other languages) are contrasted with the use of Korean in non-official signs, which is said to index the presence of a Korean minority living and working in a particular area of the city.

Along these lines, Eliezer Ben-Rafael and his colleagues (2006; see also 2004) examine Israel's linguistic landscape which they define as 'linguistic objects that mark the public space' (p. 7). They focus on the use of the three main languages of Israel: Hebrew, Arabic and English in predominantly Jewish, Israeli-Palestinian and non-Israeli Palestinian (East Jerusalem) areas. The theoretical backdrop to this study is the claim that the forces of modernity, globalization and multiculturalism create new personal, social and professional identities and relations in neighbourhoods and cities, and between public authority and civil society, all of which contribute to the reshaping of urban linguistic landscapes. Ben-Rafael et al. align themselves with Henri Lefebvre's (1991) notion of 'spatial practice' (see above) and the need to examine individual motivations and social circumstances for the way physical–geographical spaces are shaped. They also draw on Pierre Bourdieu's (1983, 1993) idea of different autonomous but interconnected 'fields' being structured by unequal power relations exemplified in the context of linguistic landscapes through the privileging of some codes over others. From Erving Goffman (1963, 1981), they then borrow the notion of the (linguistic) presentation of Self, and argue that the linguistic choices made on public signage are indicative of their producers' identities. Finally, following Raymond Boudon (1990), and in the spirit of Goffman, Ben-Rafael and his colleagues argue that the goal-oriented actions of social actors are based on their consideration of various options, and that these considerations motivate sign producers to create particular effects in their intended recipients; the idea known in sociolinguistics as 'audience design' (Bell, 1997).

Ben-Rafael et al. find the use and spread of the three languages reflecting, and maybe constituting, the complex power and allegiance relations within contemporary, urban Israeli society. The linguistic landscape of the Jewish areas is thus characterized by the dominance of Hebrew, the significant presence of English and only minimal Arabic. Israeli-Palestinian areas meanwhile are dominated by Arabic with significant use of Hebrew and insignificant use of English. Finally, non-Israeli-Palestinian areas are dominated by Arabic with significant presence of English and negligible Hebrew. Thus, while both Palestinian groups seem to construe themselves as predominantly and ethnolinguistically Arabic, they diverge in their orientation to their national identities; where the former leans towards the state of Israel, the other diverges from it and towards a more pan-Arabic, international or global position. Ben-Rafael et al. orient also to the privately vs. publicly motivated signs distinguishing between 'bottom-up' and 'top-down' flows of linguistic landscape elements. Not unlike in other localities (cf. Backhaus' study of Tokyo mentioned above), the private/bottom-up signs may display a greater variation of languages beyond those recognized officially. For example, in a number of Israeli Jewish areas populated by significant numbers of recent immigrants from the former Soviet Union, relatively frequent displays of Russian on private signs (but ignored on the official ones) index these communities. Private signs may also be a site of linguistic opposition and resistance to the official, bureaucratic language choice norms through omission. In the non-Israeli-Palestinian area of East Jerusalem, Hebrew does not feature at all in the bottom-up signs in contrast to the common trilingual (Arabic–English–Hebrew) displays of the top-down signs.

Other studies have found similar correlations between the use of specific languages and class, ethnicity or nationality. For example, with regard to urban

Bangladesh, Banu and Sussex (2001: 53) note the prevalence of English in 'shopping-cum-residential areas which are largely populated by middle-class and upper-middle-class educated Bengalis'. A similar role for English as a symbolic resource and marker of modernity, internationalism, globalization, 'high class', and so on, is found in the linguistic landscape of advertising (on billboards and in print media) documented by many (cf. Haarman, 1989; Cheshire and Moser, 1994; Piller, 2001; Friedrich, 2002; Thurlow and Jaworski, 2003; Kelly-Holmes, 2005).

The collection of studies on linguistic landscapes published in Gorter (2006a; reprinted as Gorter 2006b), some of which have been mentioned above, come with the subtitle 'A new approach to multilingualism' and position themselves as direct descendants of the Landry and Bourhis' view of linguistic landscapes cited above (see Gorter, 2006c). The novelty of their approach is most clearly seen in the use of site-specific data rather than questionnaire data, foregrounding the national (local) and international (global) orientation of the signs (predominantly through the presence or absence of English and other languages not indigenous to the area) (cf. Ben-Rafael et al., 2004, 2006; Backhaus, 2006, 2007; Cenoz and Gorter, 2006; Huebner, 2006; MacGregor, 2003; McArthur, 2000; Schlick, 2002). In this regard, all the contributions in our volume have likewise committed themselves to the analysis or discussion of situated text-space relationships in terms of their contexts of emplacement (or use). However, our goal in putting together *Semiotic Landscapes*, alongside a number of other, recent studies of linguistic landscapes, is to move on from the predominantly survey-based, quantitative approaches (cf. our reference above to Duncan and Ley's 1993 critique of mimetic 'descriptive fieldwork' in traditional geography) and also to complicate some of the taken-for-granted dichotomies in favour of more nuanced, genre- and context-specific analyses of language in 'landscape texts' (cf. Coupland, 2008). Jeffrey Kallen (2008) too is sceptical about any simplistic operationalizing of emplaced language as either 'top-down' or 'bottom-up', which conceals the actual effectiveness and power of the government-originated or 'official' signage, and the status of 'private' signs. 'A sign in a local shopkeeper's window . . . is not symmetrically "bottom-up": there is no necessary intention for the shopkeeper to communicate upwards to any governmental agent or agency. In terms of state authority, signs of this kind – being addressed to other private citizens – are best described as horizontal' (Kallen, 2008: 273). Instead, Kallen advocates Scollon and Wong Scollon's (2003) approach of sign emplacement and interpretation, social actors' motivations and communicative intents, and the indexicality of signs, i.e. 'the semiotic property of pointing to other things' (Kallen, 2008). Kallen examines the Irish linguistic landscape in the context of tourism, where language is part of the ideological work centred around the issues of authenticity of the tourist experience, security of tourist movement, tourist play, and memorability of the tourist experience. Thom Huebner (2008) advocates the study of 'artifacts' found in linguistic landscapes in terms of genre labels assigned to them by the local communities claiming their ownership, and in consideration of the immediate context of their emplacement (rather than relying on the broad categorization such as 'shopping district'). Huebner also places the study of linguistic landscape within the broader framework of the ethnography of communication (Hymes, 1972) dispelling the somewhat grandiose and misguided idea of treating 'linguistic landscapes' as a new *discipline*. Rather, Huebner argues, language in landscape provides 'an often overlooked source of data for the analysis of language in society' (2008: 71), and illustrates how Dell Hymes' SPEAKING mnemonic of the components of the speech event (setting or scene; participants; ends or goals; act sequences; key; instrumentalities; norms; and genre) is applicable to their study as a descriptive framework (see also Coupland's discussion in this volume of Welsh linguistic landscapes in terms of 'core/periphery' and 'from above/from below').

In this same vein, the implicit or hidden ideological positions of emplaced texts are explored in David Malinowski's (2008) multimodal analysis of signs on ethnic Korean business in Oakland, California (shopping centre, restaurants, gift shop) in parallel with the examination of interviews with the sign-owners, designers, clients (sign 'consumers'), as well as various media (newspaper and internet) comments on code and design choices, and the 'meaning' of signs (a version of a 'language ideological debate'). In the course of his study, Malinowski unravels a complex web of interaction between the form and materiality of the signs, their spatial position, relation to other signs, and the personal histories and motivations of individuals involved in the 'interpretation' of the sign. The emergent meaning of these commercial signs which frequently exceeds the 'intended' meaning of their authors is accounted for in terms of Judith Butler's (1997) notion of the performative (and transformative) nature of speech as embodied action, escaping the speaker's control and exceeding the propositional content of what is said. Thus, Malinowski nicely demonstrates the importance of a multi-faceted, in-depth ethnographic approach in the study of language and/in landscape in order to avoid the misleading one-sidedness of textual interpretation resulting from the researcher's own reading of his or her data (see Reh, 2004; Pennycook, 2008).

The ideologies of semiotic landscapes

Most studies of displayed language to date orient to globalization as a key underlying concept behind much ongoing change in the linguistic/semiotic landscapes. For example, in a sociolinguistic variationist study of the linguistic landscape in the Mexican border-city of Reynosa, Tamaulipas (bordering with McAllen, Texas), Glenn Martínez (2005) demonstrates how commercial signs show degrees of lexical borrowing from English to Spanish alongside certain syntactic and morphological innovations (e.g. compounding pattern modelled on the English where the head is on the right-hand side, the so-called 'head-last' construction, e.g. *Colorflex Pinturas, Duratex Uniformes, Foly Muebles*). Martínez notes how, other things being equal, morphological innovation in Reynosa's linguistic landscape seems socially salient (even more so than the choice of English words in the commercial signs he studied) in that innovative morphological patterns display a sharp socio-economic stratification: new morphological patterns appear on professional (affluent) signs rather than hand-painted ones, and in predominantly middle class (rather than working class) serving areas. This linguistic change in business names in Reynosa may be attributed to the spread of global consumerism since most linguistic/textual innovation is found to be highly localized in the areas where more affluent consumers live and where capital intense businesses tend to cluster. Following Friedman (2002), Martínez considers an explicit connection between consumption and self-identification, suggesting that:

> as the city becomes more diversified in the face of globalization processes such as mobile labor from the south, itinerant capital from the north, and roving commodities from all around, residents are continuously finding new and creative ways of self-identification. One way is through the social practices of global consumption. Innovative morphological patterning, in this way, comes to be a symbol of membership not so much in a global community of consumers uniting both sides of the border in greater ties of interdependence but rather in a local team of residents differentiating themselves from newcomers and staking their claim to specific geographic sites within the city. (Martínez, 2005: 114)

In a study of the changing commercial signage in St. Petersburg in the post-Soviet era (in the 1990s), Yurchak (2000) demonstrates how the new class of Russian entrepreneurs mark and symbolically enact (again, in the sense of Judith Butler's 1997 notion of performativity and creativity – subjects 'breaking' into new utterances) a shift from the Soviet centralized economy to the globalized, market-driven economy suffused with Western values. 'By inventing new names for privately owned public places their owners are *privatizing* public space not only legally (as legitimate owners) but also symbolically (as the authors and masters of the new meaning of this space) (Yurchak, 2000: 407; see also Gendelman and Aiello, this volume; Chmielewska, this volume).

As Yurchak also demonstrates, the creativity of the linguistic forms on commercial signs in 'new' Russia is a result of their authors and owners 'importing' English and other Western styles, phonetic combinations, letter fonts, morphological shapes, etc., and combining them with the 'local' (Russian) language forms. This linguistic intertextuality creates rupture in the traditional sociolinguistic panorama of Russian cities (not unlike performance artists' linguistic interventions in public spaces, see below), while at the same time presenting their authors and owners as the masters of social change. This is also how we see a 'global semioscape' (Thurlow and Aiello, 2007; cf. Appadurai, 1990, 1996) being manifested and produced – the informal 'flow' of symbolic material, textual practices and aesthetic values. The 'imported' cultural and language forms do not, however, remain unchanged; instead, they 'often become comprehensively and unpredictably reinterpreted and re-customized to serve very particular local purposes' (Yurchak, 2000: 412; see Malinowski, 2008, cited above; Pennycook, this volume).

A similar point on the interpretation and reinterpretation of language (and other semiotic) forms that become part of the global 'flows' is asserted by Jan Blommaert:

> Whenever discourses travel across the globe, what is carried with them is their shape, but their value, meaning, or function do not travel along. Value, meaning, and function are a matter of uptake, they have to be granted by others on the basis of the prevailing orders of indexicality, and increasingly also on the basis of their real or potential 'market value' as a cultural commodity. (Blommaert, 2005: 72)

However, as globalization has been theorized, among other issues, in terms of the increased economic inequalities (e.g. Bauman, 1998; Giddens, 1990, 2000; Harvey, 2006), Blommaert also draws our attention to the inequalities resulting from the flow of styles, genres and codes across the places of global inequality:

> This world system, as Immanuel Wallerstein has extensively argued, is a system built on inequality, on particular, asymmetric divisions of labor between 'core regions' and 'peripheries', with 'semiperipheries' in between . . . Inequality, not uniformity, organizes the flows and the particular nature of such flows across the 'globe'. Consequently, whenever sociolinguistic items travel across the globe, they travel across structurally different spaces, and will consequently be picked up differently in different places. (Blommaert, 2003: 612)

In our own study of linguistic landscapes in Gambian tourist spaces (in Thurlow and Jaworski, 2010), we examine the names on Gambian souvenir market-stall signs appropriating internationally known names of London/ British department stores and international supermarket chains such as 'Harrods', 'Selfridges', 'Liberty', 'John Lewis' and 'Safeway' (see Lanza and Woldemariam, 2008 on similar 'borrowing' of McDonald's and Starbucks logos in Mekele, Ethiopia). As examples of what we call 'discourses on the move', the recontextualization of these prestigious, dominant, hegemonic Western brand names in the economically and linguistically under-resourced social domain of a poor African country inevitably brings about changes to their value and status. Rather than indexing affluent retail outlets, their denotative meaning is reduced to single, small, often poorly constructed stalls selling relatively cheap (for the tourists) souvenirs. Rather than highly prestigious, these names act as familiar and parodic, if humorous and strategically effective, signifiers of a new and 'exotic' space experienced by the largely British tourists. Although the vendors may use the symbolic value of these signs connoting wealth, glamour and internationalism to style (Cameron, 2000; Coupland, 2007) themselves as citizens of the globalized world, the signs' materiality (wooden planks, torn out pieces of cardboard, rusting metal sheets and so on), and their DIY-like execution (uneven lettering, inaccurate copying of the original signs, spelling 'mistakes', and so on), make them unmistakably examples of 'grassroots literacy' (Blommaert, 2005; Juffermans, 2008) rather than elite commercial displays. The appropriated brand names become part of the imagery of international tourism, which depend on the construction of myths and fantasies for the consumption of fleeting masses of tourists. Like copies of the iconic buildings and monuments in Disneyland or Las Vegas, in the act of intertextual play (Bauman, 2004), these commercial signs become backdrops to tourist playgrounds which are quite alien to the identities and practices of the host community and set apart from their 'ordinary' world (Crick, 1989; Shaw and Williams, 2004). At the same time, strategically these signs ease tourists' need to organize their gaze around well-defined and well-recognizable markers of space (Culler, 1988; MacCannell, 1989; Rojek and Urry, 1997; Urry, 2002). It is thus, not only space-as-place which resemioticizes these particular textual practices but also their movement across space, their mobility.

In reviewing the literature on linguistic landscapes and the semiotics of space, it is noticeable how most studies draw their data from urban spaces (although see McCarthy, 2008 on 'globalizing the countryside'). It is indeed the rise of the industrial age, or the modern era, which led to the sudden growth of cities with their architectural functionalism and aesthetic subservient to the capitalist project of the production and accumulation of capital (Harvey, 1989). Especially in industrial and post-industrial urban contexts the self-conscious, strategic production of space reveals itself. Thus, while the work of Scollon and Wong Scollon (2003) and other authors mentioned already provides an important point of entry for sociolinguistics and discourse analysis, most contributors in this volume are concerned to engage more squarely with social theory and with the political-economies which shape the semiotic landscapes they discuss. Either explicitly or implicitly, this perspective is indebted to the likes of David Harvey who, for example, argues:

> when the landscape shaped in relation to a certain phase of development (capitalist or pre-capitalist) becomes a barrier to further accumulation . . . the geographical configuration of places must then be reshaped around new transport and communications systems and physical infrastructures, new centers and styles of production and consumption, new agglomerations of labor power, and modified social infrastructures (including, for example, systems of governance and regulation of places). Old places . . . have to be devalued, destroyed, and redeveloped while new places are created. The cathedral city becomes a heritage center, the mining community becomes a ghost town, the old industrial center is deindustrialized, speculative boom

> towns or gentrified neighbourhoods arise on the frontiers of capitalist development or out of the ashes of deindustrialized communities. The history of capitalism is, then, punctuated by intense phases of spatial reorganization. (1996: 296)

This invention and reinvention of places is an intensely complex social process, which includes but, according to Harvey, does not necessarily privilege language and discourse. Rather, in Harvey's view, the social process of place-making is marked by six 'moments' or 'activities' operating simultaneously at any given point in time and remaining in a dialectic relationship with one another: language/discourse; beliefs/values/desires; institutions/rituals; material practices; social relations; power (cf. Harvey, 1996: 78–79). Here is Harvey again:

> Places are constructed and experienced as material ecological artefacts and intricate networks of social relations. They are the focus of the imaginary, of beliefs, longings, and desires (most particularly with respect to the psychological pull and push of the idea of 'home'). They are an intense focus of discursive activity, filled with symbolic and representational meanings, and they are a distinctive product of institutionalized social and economic power. The dialectical interplay across these different moments of the social process . . . is intricate and confusing. But it is precisely the way in which all these moments are caught up in the common flow of the social process that in the end determines the conflictual (and oftentimes internally contradictory) process of place construction, sustenance, and deconstruction. (Harvey, 1996: 316)

Although to us Harvey's 'activities' of urban regeneration and change can be largely conceived of as forms of linguistic or discursive social practice (see Gendelman and Aiello, this volume), his framework does offer a useful heuristic for theorizing place-making. A demonstration of the connections between Harvey's different 'moments' in the construction of place, especially between the languistic and material practices of architecture, is Thomas Markus and Deborah Cameron's (2002) study of how texts and images influence the 'meaning' of built environment, with all its consequences for our perception, interpretation, use and construction (or not) of buildings. Markus and Cameron treat buildings as 'social objects' (p. 3) and discuss them as sites (re)producing particular social values (e.g. 'privacy' vs. 'community'), relations (e.g. dominant power structures), and encouraging particular types of activities and social encounters (the latter being also discussed by Scollon and Wong Scollon, 2003 with reference to Erving Goffman's 1971 interaction order and E. T. Hall's 1966 proxemics).

Echoing the sentiments of Kress and van Leeuwen quoted at the start of this chapter, Markus and Cameron argue that '[b]uildings themselves are not representations' (p. 15), but ways of organizing space for their users; in other words, the way buildings are used and the way people using them relate to one another, is largely dependent on the spoken, written and pictorial texts about these buildings. The architect's categorization of space within a building in the blueprint or manifesto, the investor's brief for the architect, the journalist's review of a building, or a tourist brochure about the building are among the many types of texts which may give aesthetic (e.g. press review) or historical (e.g. guidebook description) value to a building, impose and sanction power relations between its users (e.g. advising which spaces may be accessible to whom), or designate some spaces as 'communal' vs. 'private' (e.g. regulating patterns of behaviour). Of course, all of these discourses and functional uses of buildings are subject to contestation and subversion; however, it is only through the production of new, competing texts that architectural spaces may gain new meaning for their users (see Jones, this volume, on the 're-shaping' of home and classroom spaces by personal computers). Some of the texts about buildings may be invisible to most of their users, as is usually the case with descriptions in blueprints, correspondence between architects, developers, town planners and engineering consultants, etc; some texts, such as specialist and more popular, journalistic articles may be available publicly; while other texts may in fact be part of the architectural design of the building, or a part added to the building's environment. These may range from brief and functional labels on doors such as 'seminar room' or 'debating chamber', to more or less elaborate texts, for example, regulating the flow of people in case of emergencies, or museum plans for visitors. Other texts may be more symbolic, commemorative or aestheticizing, for example Latin inscriptions on government buildings, plaques commemorating the laying of foundation stones, postcards with the image of the building available in its souvenir shop, and so on. Architecture and language (spoken and written) may then form an even more complex, multilayered landscape (or cityscape) combining built environment, writing, images, as well as other semiotic modes, such as speech, music, photography, and movement (cf. Eco, 2003 [1973], and, in this volume, chapters by Abousnnouga and Machin; Shohamy and Waksman; Gendelman and Aiello; Chmielewska).

One linguistic genre that has extensively connected the study of language, discourse and built environment is graffiti. In discourse analysis, graffiti has long been recognized as a literary genre (Blume, 1985). In literacy studies, alongside other public displays of language, such as home-made banners commemorating birthdays, anniversaries or engagements, placards advertising local events, jumble or yard sales, advertisements in shop windows, and so on, graffiti has been included in the 'visual literacy environment' (Barton and Hamilton, 1998: 40), which is indicative of a community's vernacular literacy practices. Lynn and Lea (2005: 41) offer the following taxonomy of the main graffiti sub-genres: 'art' (including 'gang' and 'hip-hop'), 'slogans' (or 'public' graffiti), and 'latrinalia' (or 'private' graffiti). All can be offensive in their content promulgating racist, sexist or homophobic sentiments, although some, like hip-hop art graffiti (see Pennycook, this volume), despite their political meaning, tend to veer towards the manifestation of a certain aesthetic rather than focusing simply on linguistically encoded ideational messages (although see below for a conflated view of the political nature of aesthetics).

One of the reasons why graffiti may have received more scholarly attention than any other form of public visual discourse is that, as is argued by Lynn and Lea (2005), other forms of writing or signage have largely undergone the process of 'automatization' (Halliday, 1982). This means that 'the foregrounding of one [semiotic] is often accompanied (or achieved) by the backgrounding or "automatization" of other semiotics, to the point where they appear so normal and natural as to become "invisible"' (Iedema, 2003: 40, cited by Lynn and Lea, 2005: 43). Graffiti, on the other hand, as a largely outlawed art form, is often perceived by many as 'out-of-place', as iconoclastic in its content and style, and as creating a more immediate, direct form of engagement with the viewer. Consistent with the geosemiotic approach of Scollon and Wong Scollon cited above, Lynn and Lea note that the actual location, time of creation, and authorship of graffiti are as important for their interpretation as is their form and content.

In terms of the text–space relation, one of the central concerns of our current volume, the presence of graffiti in urban landscape has provided rich material for the study of the linguistic and discursive marking of the spatial identity of groups, or territoriality, turf hostilities, and other sorts of intergroup – racial or class – tensions. For example, singling hip-hop graffiti out of several other sub-genres (e.g. 'gang', 'neo-Nazi', or 'racial'), Jeff Ferrell (1993) echoes Hebdige's (1979) theorizing of subculture and discusses the legal, political and mediatized aspects of graffiti production and reception in Denver, Colorado. Ferrell argues that the 'battle' over graffiti is one over style, and consequently, the right to assert and give voice to one's identity.

> Legal or illegal, in the interest of preventing AIDS or promoting the reputation of a local crew, graffiti style disrupts the aesthetic of authority. It intrudes on the controlled 'beauty' of ordered environments, and compels those invested in these environments to respond to it as an ugly threat to their aesthetic domination. Graffiti may lower the economic value of property, or intrude on the maintenance of city politics, but perhaps more importantly to those who control property and politics, it diminishes the sense of ordered style which accompanies them. . . . In the battle over graffiti – as in battle over ethnicity, generational identity, or workplace control – symbolism and style cannot be relegated to epiphenomena, to products or representations of the 'real' conflict. (Ferrell, 1993: 184)

Ferrell's approach brings home a significant premise underlying all the chapters in this volume, namely that spatial and social 'realities' do not simply precede linguistic/discursive/semiotic practices; they are always co-equivalent and co-constituted (see Lefebvre, 1991, and others above).

Of course, graffiti is never limited to disempowered urbanites 'reclaiming the streets', buildings and other public spaces from the authorities, the affluent establishment; nor does it always attract the same amount of attention from officials. Lynn and Lea (2005) set out to study 'racist' graffiti in areas of Glasgow noted for their large population of asylum seekers. They report that overt racist graffiti is very rare ('conspicuous by its absence' p. 46), which may be partly due to the efficiency of the local authorities in removing them, or partly due to the changing tactics of the local racist youth gangs, spraying the bridges, paths, and walls of the estate with their 'tag' only, which to those who 'know the code' (p. 56) still sends an intimidating, racist message. Needless to say, Lynn and Lea found that *covertly* racist graffiti are removed by the authorities far less swiftly and efficiently than the overtly racist messages.

Nor is graffiti always directed 'outwardly' to intimidate out-group members or to (re)claim territory. Adams and Winter's (1997) study of gang graffiti in Phoenix, Arizona demonstrates that gang graffiti, apart from turf claiming and marking, is also used for individual gang members to advertise themselves as *respectable* gang members, to create allegiances within and across gangs, and more generally to create and demarcate social structures and hierarchies within gangs. Antagonistic exchanges between gangs are one of the means to assert power and superiority (alongside physical violence, for example), and they create patterns of allegiance and rivalry. Alongside code-switching, vernacular spellings, and displayed orientation to one's own gang and its way of life, these texts, Adams and Winter argue, are powerful assertions of gang members' ethnic and cultural identity, as well as status otherwise denied to them by the social and institutional structures.

To label all graffiti as 'transgressive' or 'illegal' is an oversimplification (see also Pennycook, this volume). As the above quote from Jeff Ferrell indicates, in a situation of conflict, what constitutes a violation of rights for one party, may be an affirming and legitimate reclamation of voice (and space) for another, and it can be an important literacy/identity resource as '[l]earning to read the multimodal tags and grafs (graffiti) of urban landscapes . . . is one part of a broader multimodal engagement of the hip-hop world (Pennycook, 2007: 10; see also Adams and Winter, 1997 quoted below). Graffiti can only be transgressive if one privileges the hegemonic order as the 'legitimate' order. This is something that the British graffiti artist Banksy certainly does not do, recognizing that the ideologies and political economies of space are far less easily resolved. In the introduction to a book chronicling his graffiti images and quotations, Banksy delegitimizes big business' advertisements on billboards. It's these companies, he claims, that have started the fight by defacing 'our neighbourhoods', and it's the 'vandals' who claim them back and make the world a better looking place (cf. Ferrell quoted above). In Banksy's words:

> The people who run our cities don't understand graffiti because they think nothing has the right to exist unless it makes a profit. But if you just value

> money then your opinion is worthless. . . . The people who truly deface our neighbourhoods are the companies that scrawl their giant slogans across buildings and buses trying to make us feel inadequate unless we buy their stuff. They expect to be able to shout their message in your face from every available surface but you're never allowed to answer back. (Banksy, 2004: 8)

Just as space is no longer experientially or epistemologically bounded, the meanings of emplaced texts are always beyond the control of an individual author, designer, speaker or artist (cf. Gastman, et al., 2007; Große, 2008; Lewishon, 2008; Manco, 2002; and many others). These meanings are also under the constant and rapaciously commodifying sway of post-industrial capital. It is, for example, somewhat ironic – but true to form – that Banksy, like Jean-Michel Basquiat and Keith Haring before him, and more recently the French artist JR, has now crossed over from the self-proclaimed position of the egalitarian 'vandal' to the mainstream 'artist' where his works sell for vast amounts of money and are to be found adorning walls in elite galleries and private collections. Spaces of exclusion have now opened up; the outsider has come inside.

This book's landscape

The arrangement of chapters in this book should reveal a progression of themes, data and methodologies touched upon in this introductory chapter so far. As is usually the case, the boundaries between individual approaches are not clear-cut, so we decided to abstain from arranging the chapters into separate sections.

The first four chapters by Kallen, Sebba, Coupland and Dray engage predominantly with visible language/writing as a form of social, situated practice. These authors orient to the sociolinguistic tradition of work known as 'linguistic landscapes' (see above), yet their problematization and critique of language displays offers novel ways for understating the relationship between language and space, different linguistic texts visible in the 'same' spaces, and issues of policy and ideology.

Jeff Kallen's chapter on the displayed languages in contemporary Dublin caught in the flux of globalization, challenges the traditional conceptualization of 'top-down' and 'bottom-up' signage as ideologically viable. Although they can be found occupying a single visual field, linguistic signs indexing different domains, institutions and activities are typically 'read' as belonging to different interpretive frames (Goffman, 1974), as they are typically not meant to be hierarchically embedded one within another. This may also apply to graffiti, which is often deliberately placed *outside* of other dominant texts (or frames), for example on railway bridges, abandoned warehouses, or back-streets. Although certainly some graffiti may be seen as 'parasitic' on other texts and spaces (and 'transgressive' in the narrow sense), its embedding in urban spaces can also be seen as creating new experienced spaces without breaking up the global conceived space of the city (cf. Lefebvre, 1991). Thus, Kallen's approach informed by frame analysis offers a possible resolution to the methodological quandary for isolating 'units of analysis' in linguistic landscapes research, and an analytic tool for analysing emplaced inscriptions in semiotically diverse spaces (cf. Scollon and Wong Scollon's 'semiotic aggregates', Blommaert's *simultaneous layering* of indexicalities and contexts). Frame analysis, together with Jones' notion of *sites of attention/ engagement*, resonates with earlier conceptualizations of (urban) spaces as texts whose reading is located somewhere between the spatial action of walking and the signifying practice of toponyms, triggering the emergence in the passer-by of the city's symbolic landscapes (de Certeau, 1984; see also Pennycook, 2008). Barthes (1994: 191) likewise asserts that 'human space (and not only urban space) has always been a signifying space', and invokes the work of Kevin Lynch, an urban planner, whose work aimed to operationalize the way urban spaces are perceived and organized into their users' mental maps. Lynch (1960) proposed a 'vocabulary of signification' (Barthes, 1994: 191) which includes five discrete units: *paths,* along which people travel such as streets, pavements, stairs, escalators; *edges,* which are perceived as boundaries, e.g. walls, enclosures, dead-ends, river banks; *districts,* distinguishable sections of the city with a specific identity or character; *nodes,* or intersections understood to be some focal points; and *landmarks,* readily identifiable objects serving as reference points. In a corresponding manner, Kallen's frames (or zones) include: the *civic frame,* the *marketplace, portals,* the *wall* and the *detritus zone.* As Kallen observes, this list is not exhaustive with other possible categories to include the *community,* the *school,* and so on.

Mark Sebba examines data from two sites: the Isle of Man and apartheid South Africa. One of his focal interests is the idea of a wide array of mobile public texts, such as newspapers, T-shirts, books, banknotes, stamps and bus tickets. These circulate in large volumes and hence are 'read' by many people on a daily basis even though their familiarity means that users may give them little more than a glance. Again, we are faced here with the issue of 'attention' and 'engagement', i.e. the extent and manner to which these frequently esoteric texts signify, how they are 'read' by consumers and onlookers, and what makes them noticeable beyond 'merely' providing part of the street's background (e.g. newspapers displayed for sale), or 'purely' utilitarian value (e.g. bus tickets bought from the driver and inserted into one's pocket with the change, without looking). Sebba also discusses some ideological and socio-historical aspects of the use of various languages in public documents, objects and displays, such as different design features aiming at the 'equal' representation of English and Afrikaans, two languages of the dominant White minority in apartheid South Africa, to the complete exclusion or erasure of the indigenous languages of the Black majority. He also discusses how public uses of written Manx in the Isle of Man have become largely relegated to symbolic and ceremonial displays (cf. Bishop et al., 2005), as part of creating an aestheticized (using traditional Celtic font) and 'exotic' *linguascape* for tourists (cf. Jaworski et al., 2003); here, language serves as another symbolic resource in creating 'the society of spectacle' (see above).

Nik Coupland's chapter on the politics of displayed bilingualism in Wales takes as a starting point Barbara Adam's (1998) idea that visible features of landscape in the natural world are often shaped by invisible or hidden forces, human or non-human, such as land erosion created by winds or tides. In the case of linguistic landscapes, such 'invisible constitutive activities' are certainly brought about by human activity and are profoundly ideological, encapsulating social actors' priorities and competing value systems. Coupland discusses a wide range of data such as place-names found on road signs, public documents, commercial signs and T-shirt texts. What the chapter demonstrates is that despite the rigidity and prescriptivism of key governmental institutions such as Bwrdd Yr Iaith (The Welsh Language Board) in their bilingual language policy insisting on absolute language parallelism there is much variation, creativity and blending of the two languages, escaping the easy 'parallelism' formula. (Coupland points out that the policy of parallelism is itself rooted in the standard language ideology as is well-documented in sociolinguistics.) This chapter then may be read as a warning against an unproblematic reading of bi- and multi-lingual signs as 'parallel' in many quantitatively oriented studies without recourse to the underlying politics of language planning, phonological, syntactic and orthographic analysis of displayed texts, visual design, historical contextualization, and attention to linguistic creativity and innovation.

Susan Dray continues the theme of ideological significance of public signage with reference to the use of English considered to be the 'standard' variety with a highly codified orthography and enjoying its high status as a written language, and Jamaican Creole (Patois) – spoken by a majority of Jamaicans but with little prestige, no codified orthography, and commonly assumed not to be used for any form of writing at all. Yet, Dray's data provide a rich source of examples in which Creole *is* used on customer notices, fly posters, advertisements, and bus logos for clearly strategic purposes, such as managing interpersonal relations between business owners and clients, and regulating behaviour in service encounters. Some uses of written Creole are typical of the identities of their authors/owners aligning themselves with local values and manifesting their allegiance with local culture. Interestingly, such accommodating practices may also be found on commercial signs produced by transnational companies (e.g. KFC) seemingly converging towards their potential Creole customers. Generally, the ecology of public signage runs against the official policy of the Government denying Creole the status of an official, written language. Whether monolingual, bilingual or diglossic, signs incorporate Creole as a vibrant and creative resource, for example to express and promote political beliefs, or for marketing purposes. From a methodological standpoint, Dray's chapter demonstrates the value of combining quantitative, survey-type analysis with a detailed qualitative ethnographic and semiotic analysis, which allows her to make important between the genre or text types in public signage and their content, style, materiality and participation frameworks involved in their production and consumption.

Ingrid Piller explores the semiotic processes underlying the gendering and sexualization of urban space in the context of the tourist-oriented sex industry in Basel. Drawing on data sources ranging from overtly public, such as billboards, shop fronts and advertisements in local newspapers, to less publicly displayed but publicly accessible such as prostitutes', nightclubs' and escort agencies' websites, and clients' blogs, Piller demonstrates how Basel's *travel spaces* (cf. Lynch's *paths*; Kallen's *portals*) are permeated by commercially driven sexual imagery. However, in order to negotiate the high-class, clean image of Switzerland as a business/tourist destination, the sex industry likewise positions itself as 'high class' and 'clean'. To this end, Piller argues, consistent with the late modern, globalist shift to information-based economies and the commodification of language, the Swiss sex trade is largely redefined as 'communication' drawing on the multilingualism and good educational background of its international prostitutes as 'excellent conversationalists'. The relatively recent phenomenon of the sex industry branding itself as 'conversational' is underscored by more traditional urban spaces, where sex was part of the trade. For example, McDonogh (2003) makes the following observation about 'prostitution bars' in his study of the *barrio chino* (Raval) area of Barcelona:

> Hours of these bars resembled those of the spectacle bars, built around night-time activities, although some opened from early morning onwards. All specialized in overpriced liquor; these were never places of conversation or group sociability. Outside working hours, when prostitutes would relax, they themselves would go to neighborhood bars instead. (McDonogh, 2003: 273)

In our next chapter, Alastair Pennycook considers another genre of publicly displayed texts found in urban travel spaces – graffiti, or graffscapes – part of the urban landscape that is both toured and touring, constituting alternative ways of imagining and narrating the city ('the living *visage*') in contrast to the sanitized image ('the buffed *paysage*') offered for tourist consumption by the hegemonic marketing institutions. The social significance of graffscapes lies in their performative transformations of middle-class, public spaces into contact and contest zones, the aesthetics of class identity and struggle, sense-making and control over space, local and global identities, and local and global styles of giving voice. These are just some of the themes explored by Pennycook, and it is important to bear in mind that semiotic landscapes are not shaped solely through the commercial exploits of space but also by artists' interventions in and representations of public spaces (see above), alongside other grass roots initiatives, interests and priorities (see also Coupland, this volume; Dray, this volume; Modan, 2007).

Rodney Jones adds another layer of theorizing space in relation to language and communication that has come about with the metaphorization of the internet as 'space' (cyberspace), and computer mediated communication (CMC) as taking place *in* cyberspace (Hunter, 2003 discusses the legal implication of this linguistic fact). However, as Jones (also 2005) demonstrates, virtual spaces do not 'exist' independent of physical spaces, and *vice versa*. In fact, social actors engaging in CMC mobilize and orient to several interdependent spaces with all their affordances and constraints at any one time. Jones invokes here Jan Blommaert's (2005) notion of 'layered simultaneity' (see also Sloboda, 2008), and Ron Scollon's (2001) notion of the 'site of engagement', as 'those moments in time and points in space where mediated actions happen' (Jones, 2005: 141). These are the *physical spaces* (including *body* spaces) in which the social actors operate their computers; *virtual spaces* created by the computer interfaces; *relational spaces* created between the participants by the instance of communication; *screen spaces* as the locus of their visible act of communication; and *third spaces* which may be talked about but not inhabited by the participants at the moment of communication. As these sites of engagement tend to be necessarily very rich and complex socio-cultural environments, Jones argues that they are 'made not just of the physical spaces we inhabit and the timescales and trajectories that flow into them, but also, and more to the point, those aspects of space and time that we are inclined to *pay attention to*. We construct *sites of engagement* through our attention' (Jones, 2005: 152; this volume). In other words, we create and interpret sites of engagement by orienting to specific texts, images and other semiotic resources residing in the physical or virtual spaces; noticing and finding relevance of some such signs while ignoring or filtering out others (we use the notion of relevance here in the sense of Sperber and Wilson, 1986).

In his chapter, Thomas Mitchell confronts the idea of ideology of linguistic landscape *and* soundscape away from the principles of production to the media metadiscursive commentary (cf. Jaworski et al., 2004; Johnson and Ensslin, 2007) on the apparent spread of Spanish as indicative of the growing at best and menacing at worst Mexican inward migration to Pittsburgh's Beechview area. The confrontation of the press reports with the presence of written Spanish as displayed on commercial and community signage, and of spoken Spanish as experienced during an ethnographic 'walk-about' of Beechview's business corridor, suggests these reports to be largely exaggerated in their reporting of the magnitude of Mexican presence. Mitchell's chapter illustrates well the disjuncture between Lefebvre's experiential, representational and imagined spaces due to recontextualization and mediatization of aspects of a specific semiotic landscape.

In our own contribution to this volume, we return to Pennycook's focus on the production and legitimation of socially unequal and contested spaces; however, in this case we look at the diametrically opposite end of highly privileged, 'enclavic' spaces constructed (in their mediatized representations) through the absence of visible language: written inscriptions and spoken interactions. The chapter undertakes a social semiotic analysis of magazine advertisements of elite (or super-elite) adopting 'silence' as the key metaphor for creating a sense of luxury, exclusivity and privilege. The exaggeration of silence in these promotional texts is not simply a matter of quietude. The absence in the data of people, of human interactions, of signage, etc. conforms well to the increasingly anti-communicational or anti-interactional ethos of super-elite mobility more generally (Thurlow and Jaworski, 2006). In this case, luxury is clearly predicated on being free of, or rather excluded from, both the 'babble' of local people and the 'drivel' of the masses. Travel and silence itself are thereby also reclassed in the process.

In this next chapter, Gill Abousnnouga and David Machin examine a sample of British war memorials from World War I to the present demonstrating how these ubiquitous yet silent and often unattended elements of urban and rural landscapes have been changing their shape to construct different discourses and legitimations of warfare, nationalism, heroism and sacrifice. Resting their analysis on several interdisciplinary areas such as Roland Barthes' semiotics, Kress and van Leeuwen's social semiotics and design feature analysis (derived from Prague School's linguistic structuralism), Panofsky's iconology, and Critical Discourse Analysis, Abousnnouga and Machin relate the iconography (objects, persons and poses), and formal features (height, size, solidity and angularity) of the monuments to the expression of the dominant political and social ideologies in different historical periods, conflict of interest between the ruling and working classes, international relations, and the personal relationship between viewers and the monuments. Alongside several other chapters in this volume (especially Coupland; Pennycook; Thurlow and Jaworski; Shohamy and Waksman), this chapter touches on the moral dimension of the landscape, placing moral values, ethical considerations, justice, equality and power at the heart of much of geographical theorization of space (e.g. Tuan, 1989, 1993; Harvey, 1996; Smith, 2000; for the discussion of aesthetic, moral, social and political aspects of outdoor sculptures, including the significance of their emplacement, from an art historical perspective, see Gombrich, 1999).

Elana Shohamy and Shoshi Waksman continue the exploration of public monuments as part of the urban landscape. In their case study of the Tel Aviv *Ha'apala* memorial commemorating Jewish migration to Palestine between 1934 and 1948, they focus on its emplacement, architectural features, accompanying texts and photographs, and visitors' engagement with the site in order to reveal a range of competing narratives of migration. As in the chapter by Abousnnouga and Machin, these 'stories' are imbued with the invisible ideological forces surrounding the debates of nation building, ethnicity, suffering, memory and exclusion. Shohamy and Waksman make it also clear how the dominant discourses of the *Ha'apala* memorial in the changing moral and political landscape of contemporary Israel, caught up between the forces of global tourism and the ongoing Arab–Israeli war, categorize, segregate and silence other voices and narratives.

Irina Gendelman and Giorgia Aiello examine the postmodern semiotic landscape of several East European cities undergoing transition from centralized, state-run economies under communism to market-driven economies under globalization. Their discussion focuses on building façades in some of the most central, representative city locations and their incorporation into the process of globalization, commodification of heritage, and aestheticization of social life and commercial activities (Featherstone, 1991; cf. Debord's 1995 'society of the spectacle' below). As in several other chapters, the growth of tourism is cited as one of the factors in the ideological shift of the displayed imagery on the buildings' façades from communist propaganda to neoliberal capitalist icons of consumption. What appears to be common to both ideologies and the resulting practices is that each creates unequal subject positions among local populations, alienating the underprivileged groups through the oppressive centralization of state politics of the communist era, or the relentless drive to commercialization in market economy.

Ella Chmielewska brings the volume nicely to a close with a theoretical (re)interpretation of her empirical data of urban signage and the city as the site of a semiotic spectacle grounded in a broader framework of social theory and cultural criticism. Like Gendelman and Aiello, her broad, comparative sweep across several, international cities leads her to view the city's iconosphere as a resource for 'reading the city'. Chmielewska problematizes several key terms for a semiotic analysis of landscape: *em-/implacement, gazing/glancing, object/image,* and suggests that signs be treated as *topo-sensitive,* requiring multi-sensory reading and subject's immersion in their materiality. Chmielewska continues her discussion by examining the subjective readings and responses of an individual moving through more or less familiar semiotic landscapes. It is this 'literary' perspective on semiotic landscapes which leads us to make one more general observation before leaving our contributors to speak for themselves.

The art and politics of semiotic landscapes

We are reminded that the processes of semiotic inclusion/exclusion and translocation in our earlier discussion of Banksy's 'gentrification' cut both ways or, at least, follow more unpredictable pathways. In particular, we think here of writing and calligraphy which have always been such an important part of the visual arts, especially in the East Asian and Middle Eastern traditions, as well as in the West, especially under Modernity and Postmodernity (Clunas, 1997; Morley, 2003). For example, modern and contemporary artists in the West have either contributed to or borrowed heavily from the imagery of linguistic landscape around them. The late nineteenth century saw an explosion of 'billboard culture' in large cities of the industrialized 'West', in no small part shaped by the cultural and commercial poster designs by such artists as Jules

Chéret, Henri de Toulouse-Lautrec and Pierre Bonnard. Consequently, paintings of urban scenes by Edouard Manet, Gustave Caillebotte, Jean Béraud, Roal Dufy in Paris, or John Sloan in New York incorporated and documented various manifestations of these new, public literacy practices (Morley, 2003). Modernism was an urban art (Bradbury and McFarlane, 1976), both residing in cities, orienting to the urban experience as well as shaping and exploiting its aesthetic (Harvey, 1989; see above). Art, as well as broadcast and print media (Mitchell, this volume), and film (Bleichenbacher, 2008) draw on the imagery of linguistic landscapes and feed their representations back to audiences, creating their own scopic regimes and interpretations.

In the twentieth century, with art increasingly turning to the 'everyday' and 'mundane' for inspiration, writing gained in prominence as an artistic subject matter and medium – often indistinguishable. The affirmation of the ordinary and commonplace in the cubist art of Pablo Picasso and Georges Braque took the form of collages using cut-outs from newspapers, advertisements, sheet music, wine labels and so on. After World War II, many European artists associated with such movements as Art Brut and Arte Povera (e.g. Jean Dubuffet, Antoni Tàpies) drew on the imagery and connotative meaning of graffiti art as a reaction to the established artistic genres or as political acts of resistance. The European 'Nouveau Réalistes' active in the late 1950s and early 1960s (e.g. Raymond Hains and Mimo Rotella) made compositions from fragments of billboards and posters torn out from their original locations. In the 1960s, ordinary objects such as the Coca-Cola bottle, packaging for Brillo pads, Campbell soup cans, or Typhoo tea, all complete with their iconic shapes and logos, became the hallmarks of American and British pop-art. Jasper Johns' paintings of 'stencilled' alphabets and numbers became decontextualized, self-referential 'texts' with 'no meaning', and came to symbolize the depersonalized, industrial and militaristic aesthetic on the mid-twentieth century America. For Johns, such recontextualization of the anonymized yet familiar letters and numbers had subversive motivation and quality, because even though people may have known them, they had never seen them in the context of painting before (Morley, 2003).

In this way, artists bringing representations, recreations and reconfigurations of the urban (linguistic) landscape into art galleries – those typically decontextualized 'white cubes' – do not index any specific products, locations or communities. The Coca-Cola bottle and logo do not point to a place where Coca-Cola may be purchased or consumed; torn and reassembled, film posters do not advertise any particular cinema shows; 'graffiti' paintings do not unlawfully claim any specific walls; stencilled letters of the alphabet do not label any crates with military equipment. The viewers of these paintings and collages are not guided towards the consumption of the goods and services which used to be indexed by these texts before the act of recontextualization. Rather they become symbolic representations of the acts of consumption creating a particular vision of the world, iconizing and (de)legitimating contemporary consumer culture (see Machin and Jaworski, 2006: 363). By indexing specific *discourses* of industrialization, consumerism and globalization through recontextualized, self-referential posters, logos, letters, etc., the language in these 'text-paintings' becomes ideological in that it *connotes* the values of modernity and global capitalism rather than *denoting* particular objects, states or events. (Re)placing these mundane, profane texts in the frame of the sacred-like gallery space elevates them to the status of 'high art', while at the same time indexing the gallery space itself as a place of commerce, where symbols of consumerism become consumer objects commanding vast prices in their own right.

By the same token, and reversing yet again the direction of semiotic translocations, language-based art has also gone beyond galleries and into urban public spaces in the work of such artists as Jenny Holzer and Barbara Kruger, aiming to expand and reconfigure urban linguistic landscapes rather than 'simply' draw inspiration from them. For example, with their public displays of slogans, and agit-prop-style posters and billboards which appropriate the hegemonic discourses of state power, gender stereotyping and consumerism, Holzer and Kruger disrupt, fragment and confuse the spaces in which they occur, with the result of 'verbal anarchy in the street' (Foster, 1982: 88; quoted in Rose, 1995: 341). In this way, not unlike in the case of graffiti art, displayed language is deliberately used to create rupture and chaos, and to give new meaning to the space where it occurs.

Patrick Wright (1985: 237) notes that different worlds typically occupy the same localities, an observation echoed in Mac Giolla Chríost's (2007) discussion of urban 'proximity of difference': 'Cities are evocative places, places where people are drawn into all kinds of proximate relationships, often by chance, often fleetingly and often on an unequal basis' (Allen, 1999: 85, quoted by Mac Giolla Chríost's, 2007: 22). The act of creating place is in part a semiotic process which minimally requires a deictic, or other indexical expression to anchor it socially (Hanks, 2001). These acts of anchoring space may be more or less visible, legitimate or authentic (authenticating), thus creating spaces of different accessibility, marked by different degrees of power, development and injustice (e.g. Harvey, 1989, 1996, 2006). While post-War modernism brought to the (Western) city urban renewal and stark functionalism in the service of rapidly growing capitalism, the postmodern city with its urban regeneration, redevelopment and gentrification of post-industrial areas, acceleration of consumption and the shift away from the consumption of material goods to the consumption of services, brought about a mixture of urban styles, architectural spectacle and theatricality (Harvey, 1989). Commenting on the industrially advanced capitalist societies, Guy Debord (1995 [1967]: 120) notes that they '[eliminate] geographical distance only to reap distance internally in the form of spectacular separation'.

The city itself can be read as a text, as a festival of signs – an 'iconosphere' (Porębski, 1972; Chmielewska 2005, this volume; Gendelman and Aiello, this volume), in which the tensions between the globalizing and localizing displays of words and images manifest the aggressive ideology and dominance of global capitalism and often struggling, local identities of communities rooted in 'real' or 'imagined' places. As the competing voices of overlapping communities contend for visibility and for economic and political survival, the mosaic of different texts becomes commodified and objectified in creating a dazzling spectacle and an icon of the modern city scrutinized and consumed by the gaze of the international tourist. It is in this way that the topic of semiotic landscapes is not only timely but also politically relevant.

References

Adam, B. (1998), *Timescapes of Modernity: The Environment and Invisible Hazards.* London: Routledge.

Adams, K. L. and Winter, A. (1997), 'Gang graffiti as a discourse genre', *Journal of Sociolinguistics*, 1(3), 337–360.

Allen, J. (1999), 'Cities of power and influence: Settled formations', in J. Allen, D. Massey and M. Pyrke (eds), *Unsettling Cities: Movement/Settlement.* London: Routledge, pp. 181–227.

Andrews, M. (1999), *Landscape and Western Art.* Oxford: Oxford University Press.

Appadurai, A. (1990), 'Disjuncture and difference in the global cultural economy', *Theory, Culture and Society*, 7, 295–310.

—(1996), *Modernity at Large: Cultural Dimensions of Globalization.* Minneapolis, MN: University of Minnesota Press.

Backhaus, P. (2006), 'Multilingualism in Tokyo: A look into the linguistic landscape', *International Journal of Multilingualism*, 3(1), 52–66.

—(2007), *Linguistic Landscapes: A Comparative Analysis of Urban Multilingualism in Tokyo.* Clevedon: Multilingual Matters.

Banksy (2004), *Wall and Piece.* London: Arrow Books.

Banu, R. and Sussex, R. (2001), 'Code-switching in Bangladesh', *English Today*, 66, 51–61.

Barthes, R. (1994), 'Semiology of urbanism', in *The Semiotic Challenge.* Translated by Richard Howard. Oxford: Clarendon, pp. 191–201.

Barton, D. and Hamilton, M. (1998), *Local Literacies: Reading and Writing in One Community.* London: Routledge.

Bauman, R. (2004), *A World of Others' Words: Cross-cultural Perspectives on Intertextuality.* Oxford: Blackwell.

Bauman, Z. (1998), *Globalization: The Human Consequences.* Cambridge: Polity.

Bell, A. (1997), 'Style as audience design', in N. Coupland and A. Jaworski (eds), *Sociolinguistics: A Reader and Coursebook.* London: Macmillan, pp. 240–249.

Ben-Rafael, E., Shohamy, E., Amara, M. H. and Trumper-Hecht, N. (2004), *Linguistic Landscape and Multiculturalism: A Jewish–Arab Comparative Study.* Tel Aviv: Tami Steinmetz Center for Peace Research.

—(2006), 'Linguistic landscape as symbolic construction of the public space: The case of Israel', *International Journal of Multilingualism*, 3(1), 7–30.

Berger, J. (1972), *Ways of Seeing.* London: BBC and Penguin.

Bishop, H., Coupland, N. and Garrett, P. (2005), 'Globalisation, advertising and shifting values for Welsh and Welshness: The case of *Y Drych*', *Multilingua*, 24, 343–378.

Bissell, D. (2009), 'Visualising everyday geographies: Practices of vision through travel-time', *Transactions of the British Institute of British Geographers*, 34, 42–60.

Bleichenbacher, L. (2008), *Multilingualism in the Movies: Hollywood Characters and their Language Choices*. Tübingen: Narr Francke.

Blommaert, J. (ed.) (1999a), *Language Ideological Debates*. Berlin: Mouton de Gruyter.

—(1999b), 'The debate is open', in J. Blommaert (ed.), *Language Ideological Debates*. Berlin: Mouton de Gruyter, pp. 1–38.

—(2003), 'Globalisation and sociolinguistics', *Journal of Sociolinguistics*, 7, 607–623.

—(2005), *Discourse: A Critical Introduction*. Cambridge: Cambridge University Press.

Blume, R. (1985), 'Graffiti', in T. A. Van Dijk (ed.), *Discourse and Literature*, Vol. 3. Amsterdam/Philadelphia: John Benjamins, pp. 137–148.

Boudon, R. (1990), *La Place du desordre: Critique des Theories du Changement social*. Paris: Quadrige.

Bourdieu, P. (1983), *La Distinction: Critique Sociale du Jugement*. Paris: Les Editions de Minuit.

—(1993), *The Field of Cultural Production: Essays on Art and Literature*. New York: Columbia University Press.

Bradbury, M. and McFarlane, J. (1976), *Modernism, 1890–1930*. Harmondsworth: Penguin.

Butler, J. (1997), *Excitable Speech*. London: Routledge.

Calvet, L-J. (1990), 'Des mots sur les murs: Une comparaison entre Paris et Dakar', in R. Chaudenson (ed.), *Des Langues et des Villes (Actes du Colloque International à Dakar, du 15 au 17 décembre 1990)*. Paris: Agence de Coopération Culturelle et Technique, pp. 73–83.

—(1994), *Les Voix de la Ville: Introduction à la Sociolinguistique Urbaine*. Paris: Payot et Rivages.

Cameron, D. (2000), 'Styling the worker: Gender and the commodification of language in the globalized service economy', *Journal of Sociolinguistics*, 4, 323–347.

Cartier, C. and Lew, A. A. (eds) (2005), *Seductions of Place: Geographical Perspectives on Globalization and Touristed Landscape*. London: Routledge.

Cenoz, J. and Gorter, D. (2006), 'Linguistic landscape and minority languages', *International Journal of Multilingualism*, 3(1), 67–80.

Cheshire, J. and Moser, L-M. (1994), 'English as a cultural symbol: the case of advertisements in French-speaking Switzerland', *Journal of Multilingual and Multicultural Development*, 15(6), 451–469.

Chmielewska, E. (2005), 'Logos or the resonance of branding: A close reading of the iconosphere of Warsaw', *Space and Culture*, 8(4), 349–380.

Clunas, C. (1997), *Art in China*. Oxford: Oxford University Press.

Collins, J. and Slembrouck, S. (2004), 'Reading shop windows in globalized neighbourhoods: Multilingual literacy practices and indexicality', Working Papers on Language, Power and Identity No. 21. http://bank.rug.ac.be/lpi/LPI21.doc (accessed 27 August 2009).

Colls, R. (2002), *Identity of England*. Oxford: Oxford University Press.

Cosgrove, D. (1984), 'Prospect, perspective and the evolution of the landscape idea', *Transactions of the Institute of British Geographers*, 10, 45–62.

—(1998), *Social Formation and Symbolic Landscape*. Madison: University of Wisconsin Press.

—(2008 [1998]), 'Introduction to *Social Formation and Symbolic Landscape*', in R. Z. DeLue and J. Elkins (eds), *Landscape Theory*. New York: Routledge and Cork: University College Cork, pp. 17–42.

Cosgrove, D., Roscoe, B. and Rycroft, S. (1995), 'Landscape and identity at Ladybower Reservoir and Rutland Water', *Transactions of the Institute of British Geographers*, 21, 534–551.

Coupland, N. (2007), *Style: Language variation and Identity*. Cambridge: Cambridge University Press.

—(2008), 'Review of Backhaus (2007) and Gorter (2006c)', *Journal of Sociolinguistics*, 12, 250–254.

Coupland, N. and Jaworski, A. (2004), 'Sociolinguistic perspectives on metalanguage: Reflexivity, evaluation and ideology', in A. Jaworski, N. Coupland and D. Galasiński (eds), *Metalanguage: Social and Ideological Perspectives*. Berlin: Mouton de Gruyter, pp. 15–51.

Crang, M. and Thrift, N. (2000), 'Introduction', in M. Crang and N. Thrift (eds), *Thinking Space*. London: Routledge, pp. 1–30.

Crick, M. (1989), 'Representations of international tourism in the social sciences', *Annual Review of Anthropology*, 18, 307–344.

Crouch, D. (ed.) (1999), *Leisure/Tourism Geographies: Practices and Geographical Knowledge*. London: Routledge.

Culler, J. (1988), *Framing the Sign: Criticism and its Institutions*. Oxford: Blackwell.

Daniels, S. (1993), *Fields of Vision – Landscape Imagery and National Identity in England and the United States*. Cambridge: Polity Press.

Daniels, S. and Cosgrove, D. (1988), 'Introduction: Iconography and landscape', in D. Cosgrove and S. Daniels (eds), *The Iconography of Landscape*. Cambridge: Cambridge University Press, pp. 1–10.

—(1993), 'Spectacle and text: Landscape metaphors in cultural geography', in J. Duncan and D. Ley (eds), *Place/Culture/Representation*. London: Routledge, pp. 57–77.

Debord, G. (1995 [1967]), *The Society of the Spectacle*. Translated by Donald Nicholson-Smith. New York: Zone Books.

De Botton, A. (2003), *The Art of Travel*. London: Penguin Books.

De Certeau, M. (1984), *The Practice of Everyday Life*. Translated by Steven Rendall. Berkeley: University of California Press.

DeLue, R. Z. and Elkins, J. (2008), *Landscape Theory*. New York: Routledge and Cork: University College Cork.

Dray, S. (2004), '(W)rites of passage: Exploring nonstandard texts, writing practices and power in the context of Jamaica'. Unpublished PhD thesis. Lancaster University.

Duncan, J. and Ley, D. (1993), 'Introduction: Representing the place of culture', in J. Duncan and D. Ley (eds), *Place/Culture/Representation*. London: Routledge. pp. 1–21.

Eco, U. (2003 [1973]), 'Function and sign: The semiotics of architecture', in M. Gottdiener, K. Boklund-Lagopoulou and A. Ph. Lagopoulou (eds), *Semiotics.* London: Sage, pp. 241–290.
Edensor, T. and Millington, S. (2009), 'Illuminations, class identities and the contested landscapes of Christmas', *Sociology,* 43, 103–121.
Entrikin, J. N. (1991), *The Betweenness of Place: Towards a Geography of Modernity.* Baltimore: John Hopkins University Press.
Fairclough, N. (1999), 'Global capitalism and critical awareness of language', *Language Awareness,* 8, 71–83.
Featherstone, M. (1991), *Consumer Culture and Postmodernism.* London: Sage.
Ferrell, J. (1993), *Crimes of Style: Urban Graffiti and the Politics of Criminality.* New York: Garland Publishing.
Foster, H. (1982), 'Subversive signs', in *Art in America,* November, 88–92.
Friedman, J. (2002), 'Globalization and localization', in J. X. Inda and R. Rosaldo (eds), *The Anthropology of Globalization.* Oxford: Blackwell. pp. 233–246.
Friedrich, P. (2002), 'English in advertising and brand naming', *English Today,* 71, 21–28.
Garrett, P., Coupland, N. and Bishop, H. (2005), 'Globalization and the visualization of Wales and Welsh America: *Y Drych,* 1948–2001', *Ethnicites,* 5(4), 530–564.
Gastman, R., Neelson, C. and Smyrski, A. (2007), *Street World: Urban Culture from Five Continents.* London: Thames & Hudson.
Giddens, A. (1990), *The Consequences of Modernity.* Cambridge: Polity.
—(2000), *Runaway World: How Globalization is Reshaping our Lives.* London: Routledge.
Goffman, E. (1963), *Behavior in Public Places.* New York: Free Press.
—(1971), *Relations in Public.* New York: Harper & Row.
—(1974), *Frame Analysis: An Essay on the Organization of Experience.* New York: Harper & Row.
—(1981), *Forms of Talk.* Philadelphia: University of Pennsylvania Press.
Gombrich, E. H. (1999), 'Sculpture for outdoors', in E. H. Gombrich, *The Uses of Images: Studies in the Function of Art and Visual Communication.* London: Phaidon, pp. 136–161.
Gorter, D. (ed.) (2006a), 'Linguistic landscape: A new approach to multilingualism', Special issue of *International Journal of Multilingualism,* 3(1).
—(ed.) (2006b), *Linguistic Landscape: A New Approach to Multilingualism.* Clevedon: Multilingual Matters.
—(2006c), 'Introduction: The study of the linguistic landscape as a new approach to multilingualism', *International Journal of Multilingualism,* 3, 1–6.
Große, J. (2008), 'Urban Art Photography'. Berlin: urban-art.info (accessed 27 August 2009)
Haarman, H. (1989), *Symbolic Values of Foreign Language Use.* Berlin: Mouton de Gruyter.
Hall, E. T. (1966), *The Hidden Dimension.* Garden City, NY: Doubleday.
Halliday, M. A. K. (1982), 'The de-automatization of the grammar from Priestley's "An Inspector Calls"', in J. Anderson (ed.), *Language Form and Linguistic Variation: Papers Dedicated to Angus McIntosh.* Amsterdam: Benjamins, pp. 129–159.
Hanks, W. F. (2001), 'Indexicality', in A. Duranti (ed.), *Key Terms in Language and Culture.* Oxford: Blackwell Publishers, pp. 119–121.

Harvey, D. (1989), *The Condition of Postmodernity: An Enquiry into the Origins of Cultural Change.* Oxford : Blackwell.

—(1996), *Justice, Nature and the Geography of Difference.* Oxford: Blackwell.

—(2006), *Spaces of Global Capitalism: Towards a Theory of Uneven Geographical Development.* London: Verso.

Heath, S. B. (1989), 'Language ideology', in *International Encyclopedia of Communications,* Vol. 2. New York: Oxford University Press, pp. 393–395.

Hebdige, D. (1979), *Style: The Meaning of Subculture.* London: Methuen.

Huebner, T. (2006), 'Bangkok's linguistic landscapes: Environmental print, codemixing and language change', *International Journal of Multilingualism,* 3(1), 31–51.

—(2008), 'A framework for the linguistic analysis of linguistic landscapes', in E. Shohamy and D. Gorter (eds), *Linguistic Landscapes: Expanding the Scenery.* New York: Routledge, pp. 70–87.

Hunter, D. (2003), 'Cyberspace as place and the tragedy of the digital anticommons', *California Law Review,* 9(1/2), 439–519.

Hymes, D. (1972), 'Models of the interaction of language and social life', in J. J. Gumperz and D. Hymes (eds), *Directions in Sociolinguistics: The Ethnography of Communication.* New York: Holt, Rinehart and Winston, pp. 35–71.

Iedema, R. (2003), 'Multimodality, resemiotization: Extending the analysis of discourse as multi-semiotic practice', *Visual Communication,* 2(1), 29–57.

Irvine, J. T. (1989), 'When talk isn't cheap: Language and political economy', *American Ethnologist,* 16, 248–267.

Irvine, J. T. and Gal, S. (2000), 'Language ideology and linguistic differentiation', in P. V. Kroskrity (ed.), *Regimes of Language.* Santa Fe, NM: School of American Research Press, pp. 35–83.

Jackson, P. (1989), *Maps of Meaning: An Introduction to Cultural Geography.* London: Unwin Hyman.

Jaworski, A., Coupland, N. and Galasiński, D. (eds) (2004), *Metalanguage: Social and Ideological Perspectives.* Berlin: Mouton de Gruyter.

Jaworski, A., Thurlow, C., Lawson, S. and Ylänne-McEwen, V. (2003), 'The uses and representations of host languages in tourist destinations: A view from British TV holiday programmes', *Language Awareness,* 12(1), 5–29.

Jaworski, A. and Yeung, S. (2010, in press), 'Life in the Garden of Eden: The naming and imagery of residential Hong Kong', in E. Shohamy, E. Ben-Rafael and M. Barni (eds), *Linguistic Landscape and Transnationalism: Focus on the City.* Bristol: Multilingual Matters.

Jay, M. (1998), 'Scopic regimes of modernity', in H. Foster (ed.), *Vision and Visuality: Discussions in Contemporary Culture.* Dia Art Foundation No. 2 and Seattle: Bay Books, pp. 3–23.

Jewitt, C. and Triggs, T. (eds) (2006), *Screens and the Social Landscape.* Special issue of *Visual Communication,* 5(2).

Johnson, S. and Ensslin, A. (eds) (2007), *Language in the Media: Representations, Identities, Ideologies.* London: Continuum.

Johnstone, B. (2004), 'Place, globalization and linguistic variation', in C. Fought (ed.), *Sociolinguistic Variation: Critical Reflections.* New York: Oxford University Press, pp. 65–83.

Jones, R. H. (2005), 'Sites of engagement as sites of attention: Time, space and culture in electronic discourse', in S. Norris and R. H. Jones (eds), *Discourse in Action: Introducing Mediated Discourse Analysis*. London: Routledge, pp. 141–154.

Juffermans, K. C. P. (2008), 'Local emplacement and global identities in signboard and billboard literacies in urban Gambia', in A. Simo Bobda (ed.), *Explorations into Language Use in Africa*. Frankfurt am Main: Peter Lang, pp. 197–219.

Kahn, M. (2003), 'Tahiti: The ripples of a myth on the shores of the imagination', *History and Anthropology*, 14(4), 307–326.

Kallen, J. (2008), 'Tourism and representation in the Irish linguistic landscape', in E. Shohamy and D. Gorter (eds), *Linguistic Landscapes: Expanding the Scenery*. New York: Routledge, 270–283.

Kelly-Holmes, H. (2005), *Advertising as Multilingual Communication*. Basingstoke: Palgrave Macmillan.

Kress, G. and van Leeuwen, T. (2001), *Multimodal Discourse: The Modes and Media of Contemporary Communication*. London: Arnold.

Kumar, K. (2003), *The Making of English National Identity*. Cambridge: Cambridge University Press.

Landry, R. and Bourhis, R. Y. (1997), 'Linguistic landscape and ethnolinguistic vitality: An empirical study', *Journal of Language and Social Psychology*, 16, 23–49.

Lanza, E. and Woldemariam, H. (2008), 'Language ideology and linguistic landscape: Language policy and globalization in a regional capital in Ethiopia', in E. Shohamy and D. Gorter (eds), *Linguistic Landscapes: Expanding the Scenery*. New York: Routledge, pp. 189–205.

Lawson, B. (2001), *The Language of Space*. Oxford: Architectural Press.

Leclerc, J. (1989), *La Guerre des Langues dans l'Affichage*. Montréal: VLB éditeur.

Lefebvre, H. (1991), *The Production of Space*. Oxford: Blackwell.

Lewisohn, Cedar. (2008), *Street Art*. London: Tate Publishing.

Lynch, K. (1960), *The Image of the City*. Cambridge, MA: The MIT Press.

Lynn, N. and Lea, S. J. (2005), '"Racist" graffiti: Text, context and social comment', *Visual Communication*, 4(1), 39–63.

MacCannell, D. (1999 [1973]), *The Tourist: A New Theory of the Leisure Class*. Berkeley: University of California Press.

Mac Giolla Chríost, D. (2007), *Language and the City*. Basingstoke: Palgrave Macmillan.

MacGregor, L. (2003), 'The language of shop signs in Tokyo', *English Today*, 19(1), 18–23.

Machin, D. and Jaworski, A. (2006), 'Archive video footage in news: Creating a likeness and index of the phenomenal world', *Visual Communication*, 5(3), 345–366.

Malinowski, D. (2008), 'Authorship in the linguistic landscape: A multimodal–performance view', in E. Shohamy and D. Gorter (eds), *Linguistic Landscapes: Expanding the Scenery*. New York: Routledge, pp. 107–125.

Manco, Tristan. (2002), *Stencil Graffiti*. London: Thames & Hudson.

Markus, T. A. and Cameron, D. (2002), *The Words between the Spaces: Buildings and Language*. London: Routledge.

Marsh, P. and Collett, P. (1986), *Driving Passion*. London: Jonathan Cape.

Martínez, G. A. (2005), 'Globalization, urban space, and the linguistic landscape along the US–Mexico border', *Geolinguistic Inquiry*, 30, 103–115.
Massey, D. (1994), *Space, Place and Gender.* Cambridge: Polity.
—(2005), *For Space.* London: Sage.
Massey, D. and Jess, P. (eds) (1995), *A Place in the World: Places, Cultures and Globalization.* Oxford: Oxford University Press in association with The Open University.
Matless, D. (1998), *Landscape and Englishness.* London: Reaktion Books.
McArthur, T. (2000), 'Interanto: The global language of signs', *English Today*, 16(1), 33–43.
McCarthy, J. (2008), 'Rural geography: Globalizing the countryside', *Progress in Human Geography*, 32, 129–137.
McDonogh, G. W. (2003), 'Myth, space, and virtue: Bars, gender, and change in Barcelona's *Barrio Chino*', in S. M. Low and D. Lawrence-Zúñiga (eds), *The Anthropology of Space and Place.* Oxford: Blackwell, pp. 264–283.
Mills, C. (1993), 'Myths and meanings of gentrification', in J. Duncan and D. Ley (eds), *Place/Culture/Representation.* London: Routledge, pp. 149–170.
Modan, G. G. (2007), *Turf Wars: Discourse, Diversity, and the Politics of Place.* Malden, MA.: Blackwell Publishing.
Morley, S. (2003), *Writing on the Wall: Word and Image in Modern Art.* London: Thames and Hudson.
Norris, S. and Jones, R. H. (2005), *Discourse in Action: Introducing Mediated Discourse Analysis.* London: Routledge.
Olwig, K. R. (2008), 'The "actual landscape" or actual landscapes?' in R. Z. DeLue and J. Elkins. (eds), *Landscape Theory.* New York: Routledge and Cork: University College Cork, pp. 158–177.
Osborne, P. D. (2000), *Travelling Light: Photography, Travel and Visual Culture.* Manchester: Manchester University Press.
Panofsky, E. (1991 [1927]), *Perspective as Symbolic Form.* New York: Zone Books.
Pascoe, D. (2001), *Airspaces.* London: Reaktion Books.
Pennycook, A. (2007), *Global Englishes and Transcultural Flows.* London: Routledge.
—(2008), 'Linguistic landscape and the transgressive semiotics of graffiti', in E. Shohamy and D. Gorter (eds), *Linguistic Landscapes: Expanding the Scenery.* New York: Routledge, pp. 302–312.
Piller, I. (2001), 'Identity constructions in multilingual advertising', *Language in Society*, 30, 153–186.
Porębski, M. (1972), *Ikonosfera.* Warsaw: PWN.
Reh, M. (2004), 'Multilingual writing: A reader-oriented typology – With examples from Lira Municipality (Uganda)', *International Journal of the Sociology of Language*, 170, 1–41.
Rojek, C. and Urry, J. (eds) (1997), *Touring Cultures.* London: Routledge.
Rose, G. (1995), 'Making space for the female subject of feminism: The spatial subversion of Holzer, Kruger and Sherman', in S. Pile and N. Thrift (eds), *Mapping the Subject: Geographies of Cultural Transformation.* London: Routledge, pp. 332–354.
Rosenbaum, Y., Nadel, E., Cooper, R. L. and Fishman, J. A. (1977), 'English on Keren Kayemet Street', in J. A. Fishman, R. L. Cooper and A. W. Conrad (eds), *The Spread of English.* Rowley, Massachusetts: Newbury House Publishers, pp. 179–196.

Rumsey, A. (1990), 'Wording, meaning and linguistic ideology', *American Anthropologist*, 92, 346–361.
Rycroft, S. and Cosgrove, D. (1995), 'Mapping the modern nation: The National Land Use Survey 1932–34', *History Workshop Journal*, 40, 91–105.
Sahlins, M. (1976), *Culture and Practical Reason*. Chicago: University of Chicago Press.
Schivelbusch, W. (1986), *The Railway Journey: The Industrialization of Time and Space in the 19th Century*. Berkeley, CA: University of California Press.
Schlick, M. (2002), 'The English of shop signs in Europe', *English Today*, 19(1), 3–17.
Scollon, R. (2001), *Mediated Discourse: The Nexus of Practice*. London: Routledge.
Scollon, R. and Wong Scollon, S. (2003), *Discourse in Place: Language in the Material World*. London: Routledge.
Shaw, G. and Williams, A. M. (2004), *Tourism and Tourist Spaces*. London: Sage.
Shohamy, E. (2006), *Language Policy: Hidden Agendas and New Approaches*. London: Routledge.
Shohamy, E. and Gorter, D. (eds) (2008), *Linguistic Landscapes: Expanding the Scenry*. New York: Routledge.
Silverstein, M. (1979), 'Language structure and linguistic ideology', in P. R. Clyne, W. F. Hanks and C. L. Hofbauer (eds), *The Elements: A Parasession on Linguistic Units and Levels*. Chicago: Chicago Linguistic Society, pp. 193–247.
Silverstein, M. and Urban, G. (1996), 'The natural history of discourse', in M. Silverstein and G. Urban (eds), *Natural Histories of Discourse*. Chicago: University of Chicago Press, pp. 1–17.
Simmel, G. (1997), *Simmel on Culture: Selected Writings* (ed. by D. Frisby and M. Featherstone). London: Sage.
Sloboda, M. (2008), 'State ideology and linguistic landscape: A comparative analysis of (post)communist Belarus, Czech Republic and Slovakia', in E. Shohamy and D. Gorter (eds), *Linguistic Landscapes: Expanding the Scenery*. New York: Routledge. 173–188.
Smith, D. M. (2000), *Moral Geographies: Ethics in a World of Difference*. Edinburgh: Edinburgh University Press.
Sörlin, S. (1999), 'The articulation of territory: Landscape and the constitution of regional and national identity', *Norwegian Journal of Geography*, 53(2–3), 103–112.
Sperber, D. and Wilson, D. (1986), *Relevance: Communication and Cognition*. Oxford: Blackwell.
Spolsky, B. and Cooper, R. L. (1991), *The Languages of Jerusalem*. Oxford: Clarendon Press.
Thurlow, C. and Aiello, G. (2007), 'National pride, global capital: A social semiotic analysis of transnational visual branding in the airline industry', *Visual Communication*, 6, 305–344.
Thurlow, C. and Jaworski, A. (2003), 'Communicating a global reach: Inflight magazines as a globalizing genre in tourism', *Journal of Sociolinguistics*, 7, 579–606.
—(2006), 'The alchemy of the upwardly mobile: Symbolic capital and the stylization of elites in frequent-flyer programmes', *Discourse & Society*, 17, 131–167.
—(2010), *Tourism Discourse: Language and Global Mobility*. Basingstoke: Palgrave Macmillan.

Tuan, Y-F. (1989), *Morality and Imagination: Paradoxes of Progress*. Madison, WI: The University of Wisconsin Press.
—(1993), *Passing Strange and Wonderful: Aesthetics, Nature and Culture*. Washington DC: Island Press.
Urry, J. (1995), *Consuming Places*. London: Routledge.
—(2002), *The Tourist Gaze*. 2nd edition. London: Sage (1st edition, 1990).
—(2004), 'The "system" of automobility', *Theory, Culture & Society*, 21, 25–39.
—(2005) 'The "consuming" of place', in A. Jaworski and A. Pritchard (eds), *Discourse, Communication and Tourism*. Clevedon: Channel View, pp. 19–27.
—(2007), *Mobilities*. Cambridge: Polity.
Woolard, K. A. (1998), 'Introduction: Language ideology as a field of inquiry', in B. B. Schieffelin, K. A. Woolard and P. V. Kroskrity (eds), *Language Ideologies: Practice and Theory*. New York: Oxford University Press, pp. 3–47.
Wright, P. (1985), *On Living in an Old Country*. London: Verso.
Wylie, J. (2007), *Landscape*. London: Routledge.
Yurchak, A. (2000), 'Privatize your name: Symbolic work in a post-Soviet linguistic market', *Journal of Sociolinguistics*, 4(3), 406–434.

Chapter 1

Changing Landscapes: Language, Space and Policy in the Dublin Linguistic Landscape

Jeffrey L. Kallen

Introduction: Multilingualism and the multiple landscape

Spatial relations in the linguistic landscape

Studies of the linguistic landscape generally start from the assumption that signage is indexical of more than just the ostensive message of the sign. One of the first such studies, that of Rosenbaum et al. (1977), examined the relationship between Hebrew and English signage on Keren Kayemet Street in Jerusalem and the use of English in spoken interaction on the same street. Spolsky and Cooper (1991) not only dissected the multiple layers of historical reference in street signs in Jerusalem, but proposed more generally (pp. 81–84) that the act of sign creation in public spaces reflects discourse principles such as 'write signs in a language you know', 'prefer to write signs in the language or languages that intended readers are assumed to read', and 'prefer to write signs in your own language or in a language with which you wish to be identified'. According to Landry and Bourhis (1997: 25), 'the most basic informational function of the linguistic landscape is that it serves as a distinctive marker of the geographical territory inhabited by a given language community'. They further argue (p. 25) that the linguistic landscape informs 'in-group and out-group members of the linguistic characteristics, territorial limits, and language boundaries of the region they have entered'. Cenoz and Gorter (2006) describe linguistic landscape as both a reflection of and a formative influence on language as it operates in the social world. For them, the linguistic landscape 'reflects the relative power and status of the different languages in a specific sociolinguistic context', while it also 'contributes to the construction of the sociolinguistic context', given that speakers process the visual information made available to them in such a way that 'the language in which signs are written can certainly influence their perception of the status of the different languages and even affect their own linguistic behaviour' (pp. 67–68).

In these and similar approaches, the spatial notion of what constitutes the landscape appears to be relatively unproblematical. There is an implicit general view in most linguistic landscape research that only one linguistic landscape occupies a given physical space at a particular time. We can see this assumption most clearly in the territorial approach of Landry and Bourhis (1997): if, as they state, signage marks territory and boundaries, then competing languages are engaged in a zero-sum competition for dominance in a given terrain. It is this competition that is reflected in the linguistic landscape.

Some indication of heterogeneity in the definition of the linguistic landscape can be seen in the comments of, especially, Spolsky and Cooper (1991), Inoue (2005), and Backhaus (2005, 2007) in addressing the temporally-based variation that arises when landscapes retain the different signage practices of various times. In accounting for this kind of diversity, Backhaus (2005, 2007) develops an analogy with historical linguistics, suggesting that the landscape reflects what he terms 'layering', i.e. 'the coexistence of older and newer versions of given type of sign' (2007: 130). Yet even the recognition that 'layering lays bare different linguistic states in the history of the city' (Backhaus, 2005: 107) assumes that there is one landscape in a given area, albeit one which contains within it remnants of different stages in its development.

Drawing a distinction between 'top-down' official signage and private 'bottom-up' signage (e.g. Ben-Rafael et al., 2006) also implies that the linguistic landscape is not a homogeneous territory. This spatial metaphor ascribes position within a social hierarchy to the originators of signs, and focuses on the landscape as a reflex of social and linguistic hierarchies. I suggest that the contrast between 'top down' and 'bottom up' signage works best on the assumption that these different types of signage are in opposition within the same system, representing different interlocutors vying for the same structural position in the landscape. This assumption, though, is contrary to a great deal of everyday experience: the state is not in the business of opening hairdressers or small shops, and small shop owners do not usually take to relabelling streets.[1] This complementarity of domains suggests that the street name sign and the small shop sign are not directly competing for the same territory, nor do they simply represent different sources of comparable expressions. They live, in a very real sense, in different, if parallel, universes.

Rather than viewing the linguistic landscape as a single system, then, I propose to analyse it as a confluence of systems, observable within a single visual field but operating with a certain degree of independence between elements. What gives the landscape its discursive, and even at times chaotic, appearance is that these systems are not hierarchically nested within each other. Some are parasitic on others (e.g. certain types of graffiti or stickers placed on other signs), and some (e.g. litter, whose significance I discuss below) involve little conscious planning and considerable spatial independence. Each system can be seen as a separate answer to the fundamental question that Goffman (1974) poses in defining discourse frames: 'What is it that's going on here?' (p. 25).

The frameworks in the landscape can be defined by the functions of discourse entered into by interlocutors and by the language choices and forms of expression available to these interlocutors. I suggest that it is necessary to see the visual field in terms of separate visual discourse frameworks in order to understand how sign users answer the questions put by Scollon and Wong Scollon (2003):

> We need to ask of the stop sign the same four questions we would ask of a person: Who has 'uttered' this (that is, is it a legitimate stop sign of the municipal authority)? Who is the viewer (it means one thing for a pedestrian and another for the driver of a car)? What is the social situation (is the sign 'in place' or being installed or worked on)? Is that part of the material world relevant to such a sign (for example, is it a corner of the intersection of roads)? (p. 3)

In the discussion which follows, then, I will focus on five spatial frameworks within the linguistic landscape as I have encountered it in Dublin. These categories, discussed in further detail below, are labelled as follows: (1) the *civic frame,* in which the organs of the state typically have primacy in labelling and delimiting territory and in regulating behaviour; (2) the *marketplace,* in which the world of commerce, business, publication, public and private services, and other related activities provide the opportunity for everyday competition in the linguistic landscape; (3) *portals,* including physical (e.g. airports and train stations), capital (banks, currency exchanges and the like), and electronic (internet cafes, mobile phone providers, etc.) points that provide exits and entrances from the immediate linguistic and physical environment to environments elsewhere; (4) the *wall,* where graffiti and the use of temporary posters or stickers is the prime mode of expression; and (5) the *detritus zone,* where the transient effects of consumption and the discarding of language-labelled commercial goods contribute to the overall effect of language use in the environment. This list is neither exhaustive nor universal. We could easily suggest further categories such as (6) the *community,* which is concerned with the building or maintenance of non-commercial communities of practice as seen typically in social clubs, sports groups and local religious units, or (7) the *school,* i.e. education at all levels, whether public or private. Different cultures will of course have different categories or definitions of these categories. In all these subdivisions, though, different expectations as to discourse function and linguistic form are at work – different answers, in other words, to the question of 'what is going on' with signage.

Change in the Irish language environment

Until recently, the linguistic landscape in Dublin was very much a two-language affair. In private signage domains of all types, English has been predominant, and a great deal of public signage is also in English. In public domains, however, the constitutional designation of Irish as the first official language of the state (see Bunreacht, 2003) has ensured it a role in state-related functions such as street and place name labelling, traffic regulation, and the identification of public buildings of various kinds. The linguistic vitality of Irish as a community language is also seen in private signage: pubs, hairdressers, restaurants, shops and community groups in Dublin can all be cited which show Irish-language signage, though not in the proportions that can be found in parts of the country where Irish is used more intensively in the community (cf. Kallen, 2008). The use of languages other than English and Irish, as in the use of Chinese in the shopfronts of Chinese restaurants or the occasional use of continental European languages, has in the past been mostly peripheral. The overall dominance of English and the use of Irish in specific domains, together with the very limited use of other languages, could be seen to follow naturally from the general linguistic makeup of the city.

Recent times, however, have seen a dramatic change in the Dublin linguistic landscape. Three inter-related developments have helped to determine these changes: (1) diversification in international tourism, (2) the establishment of international retail businesses with a visible public presence, and (3) inward migration from a wide range of countries. In Kallen (2008), I suggest that tourists have a special role in shaping the Irish linguistic landscape, (a) by prompting signage that uses the anticipated languages of tourists in order to invite the tourist's attention or give information, and (b) by encouraging signage in which aspects of the Irish language and visually Gaelicized English (via special fonts and presentation) are presented in order to offer the promise of an authentic Irish experience to the tourist. The role of international commerce shows its own complexities, in which, on the one hand, an international company may use its 'home' language in overseas shopfronts and in-store advertising, and, on the other hand, a language that is perceived as 'foreign' may be used with an indexical function even though there is no intrinsic link between the economic home of the company and the language used in shop fronts (e.g. the shoe chain *Schuh*, which uses the German word for 'shoe' in its shop name and advertising but which started in Edinburgh and markets exclusively in the UK and Ireland). Though these topics are worthy of detailed study, this paper focuses on immigration and its possible role in the development of the Dublin linguistic landscape.

The linguistic impact of recent inward migration is difficult to assess. While details are hard to ascertain, Gallagher (2007) estimates that over 200 languages are spoken in Ireland today. Census data could be used to provide demographic evidence, but the language questions on the Irish census relate only to the use of Irish, and the birthplace data which are available provide only indirect evidence. Even this evidence, however, shows a striking growth in the number of Irish residents who were born outside of Ireland. Table 1.1 shows birthplace figures for the population in Leinster (the province that includes Dublin as its

Table 1.1 Population (Leinster and Republic of Ireland) by birthplace: 1986, 2006

	1986 Census		2006 Census	
	Leinster	**Republic of Ireland total**	**Leinster**	**Republic of Ireland total**
Total population	1,852,649	3,540,643	2,208,539	4,067,755
Place of birth:				
Republic of Ireland	1,735,776	3,316,643	1,873,210	3,466,023
Northern Ireland	21,867	36,538	25,112	49,171
England, Wales, Scotland	69,222	141,254	97,018	216,976
Poland	—	—	35,143	62,495
Lithuania	—	—	15,194	24,611
Latvia	—	—	8,479	13,854
Germany	1,915	3,853	6,168	11,544
Other European[a]	4,441	7,916	53,458	79,462
Nigeria	—	—	12,417	16,327
Other African[b]	—	—	17,360	25,484
Hong Kong	—	—	8,707	12,224
China	—	—	9,172	11,022
Other Asia[c]	—	—	29,690	41,864
United States	6,285	15,350	11,513	24,643
Other countries[d]	12,933	19,089	13,456	22,577

[a] includes 9 countries in 1986; Census (2008: 8) lists over 35 other European countries
[b] no African countries listed in 1986; Census (2008: 8) lists over 40 other African countries
[c] no Asian countries listed in 1986; Census (2008: 8) lists over 45 other Asian countries
[d] includes all other countries in 1986; Census (2008: 8) lists over 50 other countries

dominant constituent) and the Republic of Ireland as a whole (Central Statistics Office, 1993: 133; 2008: 8; 2007: 110). These figures are only a rough indication of possible language communities in the Dublin region: they are not broken down exhaustively by country; they rely on national, as opposed to language, categories; and they do not show the number of children born to immigrants (since these children are born in Ireland). In order to focus on relatively large national groupings, Table 1.1 lists only those birthplace countries for which more than 10,000 people are enumerated in the census for Ireland as a whole. Even with this simplification, the figures provide clear evidence of major demographic changes in the composition of the population over the last 20 years.

Figures such as those in Table 1.1, of course, provide just one way of looking at the underlying population characteristics which may influence the linguistic landscape. Other perspectives are available from figures on the number of immigrants obtaining documentation to work in Ireland (see Immigrant Council of Ireland, 2005: 4) and from evidence provided by the Department of Education of a modest but important expansion in the number of languages which are presented by students taking the Leaving Certificate examination at the end of second-level education (see Department of Education, 1989; State Examination Commission, 2007; State Examination Commission, n.d.). Information of this kind, which cannot be analysed in detail here, suggests that changes we may see in the Dublin linguistic landscape reflect both real demographic change and the differential effects of policy towards different languages.

Policy and diversity in the Dublin linguistic landscape

Looking at the landscape

Following from the above proposal to understand the linguistic landscape as an ensemble of multiple systems within the same visual field and not as a single system, we turn to an examination of signage in Dublin. This examination does not aim to be geographically comprehensive, nor does it use quantitative methods (cf. Huebner, 2006; Backhaus, 2007). The view of multiplicity in the linguistic landscape which I propose here does not encourage a simple quantitative approach. It would not be comparing like with like, for example, to contrast the number of bilingual street name signs (close to 100% in Dublin) with restaurant signs showing bilingualism in Irish English (such signs being extremely rare). Belonging, respectively, to the domains of the *civic frame* and the *marketplace* within the visual field, the street name signs and the restaurant signs would need to be analysed separately if quantification were to be meaningful. Rather than attempt such an analysis, the discussion which follows relies more simply on a search within a well-defined geographical area for evidence of bilingualism within the different signage domains of the visual field. The main area in this study covers a walk of roughly five kilometres, starting with Malahide Road on the north side of the city and including major streets in the city centre. Samples along this route were taken in March 2006 and March 2008, allowing for a small amount of change over time to be observed. This 'sample route' is supplemented by other data as appropriate. The overall picture of linguistic balance in Dublin is still that official signage tends to be bilingual in Irish and English, and most of the rest of the landscape is dominated by English: it is the newly-emerging picture of other languages finding a niche that concerns us here.

The civic frame

Unification of diverse types of signage into what I have termed *the civic frame* is based on a recognition of functional and formal similarities that define a discourse frame devoted to the activities of the state. The state has a virtual monopoly in using signage to regulate traffic, control litter, label public streets, encourage or prohibit various kinds of public behaviour, label government offices, mark jurisdictional boundaries and perform other such functions (discounting ad hoc supplements such as home-made 'No Parking' signs). In order for the state's use of signage to be recognized as valid, it must comply with

FIGURE 1.1 Irish and English, North Strand Road

certain formal characteristics: an official sign is usually of a prescribed type (e.g. the colour and shape of a STOP sign) and often bears the insignia or other identifying mark of the state. In semiotic terms, signage of this kind not only has a communicative function, but is indexical of state authority itself. In this section, I consider several types of government-based signage which together help to define a discourse frame in which the state addresses the general public.

In keeping with Irish language policy, street signs in Dublin are regularly presented in Irish and English. Bilingualism here is not dependent on linguistic vitality in the sense of everyday language use, nor is it in competition with languages such as Polish and Chinese which lack state recognition. The sign in Figure 1.1 displays an older orthographic system than that used in current signage design, leading to diachronic layering in the sense defined by Backhaus (2005, 2007). Despite this variation, the sign – by virtue of placement features (on a wall on the road indicated by the sign) and design features (meeting conventions as to size, shape and linguistic choice) – is recognizably a genuine act of signage that belongs within the civic frame. The specifics of placement features mean that this sign is a unique act of communication, fixed to a particular spot, but the conventions of signage mean that it is also indexical of a nearly infinite number of other such signs, which point to unique places but exercise the single function of communicating from the state to the public about space and territory.

Civic functions of a different kind are seen in bilingual regulatory signs as in Figure 1.2. State authority is indexed by the bilingual reference to Dublin Corporation in the top right hand corner and in the name given at the bottom of the sign.

In another image from the sample route (large temporary flags beside the River Liffey, not reproduced here), bilingual reference is also made to Dublin Corporation as the instigator of the message. These flags, however, refer monolingually to Dublin as *An Cathair le Gaeilge* ('the city with Irish') and thus function indirectly to encourage the use of Irish in addition to the presupposed use of English.

Figure 1.3 illustrates a state agency venturing outside the realm of official languages, featuring information in Portuguese and Arabic about road traffic

FIGURE 1.2 Keep Dublin Clean / Coinnigh BÁC Glan

FIGURE 1.3 Road safety regulations in Portuguese and Arabic, Marino Mart

regulations and safety. The picture shows a member of the *Garda Síochána*, the Irish police force, using a speed camera. This sign appeared in a shop window in March 2006, but was taken down shortly thereafter. The current website for the National Safety Council (www.nsc.ie) does not offer information in Portuguese or Arabic; the 'Rules of the Road', however, are available from this website in English, Irish, Polish, Russian and Mandarin Chinese. Figure 1.3 thus demonstrates that public safety concerns may become a point of entry in the official domain for languages that lack official status, even where there appears to be inconsistency as to which languages should receive this recognition.

The marketplace

We can define *the marketplace* as a discourse frame within the visual field that is concerned with the buying and selling of commercial goods and services. Whereas the civic frame relies on officially-defined formats (choice of language, use of government insignia, etc.) to demonstrate both civil authority and the functions that go with it, the marketplace speaks with many divergent, often competing, voices which, taken together, define the world of everyday local business. Figure 1.4 shows a linguistic vista of the type familiar in many multilingual cities. In this case, a banner advertising medical services, aimed at a Polish-speaking audience, is placed over a supermarket front with advertising in Chinese and English. This ensemble is quietly framed by the road traffic sign from the civic frame in Irish and English to the left.

FIGURE 1.4 Advertising in Polish, Chinese and English, Parnell Street

FIGURE 1.5 Hairdresser in English, Irish and Polish, Rathmines (see colour plate section)

Figure 1.5, from March 2008, demonstrates a complex system of what Reh (2004: 12) terms 'overlapping multilingual writing' (cf. Backhaus, 2007: 90–91). Red lettering in English denotes a proper name for the business and advertises particular services: the black and white lettering in English also shows specialist advertising. Green lettering in Irish (using colour indexically to indicate Ireland) overlaps only in part with the English message: it announces that the establishment is a men's hairdresser but makes no further advertising claims, instead welcoming customers with *Fáilte Isteach Roimh Cách*, 'Welcome in to all'.[2] The single Polish word in blue, *Zapraszamy*, 'welcome', does not give a monolingual speaker of Polish any knowledge of the business involved, but the barber's poles and a further sign in the window, which reads *TUTAJ PRACUJE FRYZJER Z POLSKI*, 'a barber from Poland works here', provide enough information to reach out to a Polish audience. It is important typologically to note that no one language contains all elements of the sign as a whole, viz. the name of the business, the products and services which it offers, and the act of welcoming intended customers.

Signage in the marketplace represents a study in its own right, and this overview cannot do justice to the entire field. From even this sample, though, it becomes evident that the distribution of languages in the private multilingual signage of Dublin is constrained by the nature of business and by conscious decisions on language display. Small shops, restaurants and hairdressers figure most prominently in the plurilingual signage of the sample area – Polish and Chinese are the most frequently used languages apart from English. Neither similarity of function nor size of the language community, however, guarantee similarity of language visibility. Census figures (Central Statistics Office, 2007), for example, show the Lithuanian population in Leinster to be nearly half the size of the Polish population, and roughly equal to that from China and Hong Kong, yet signage in Lithuanian is nowhere near as common as in Polish or Chinese. Whereas Polish shops regularly include displays in Polish, the main Lithuanian food shop in the sample displays the name LITUANICA surrounded on both sides by the monolingual slogan in English 'THE FINEST FOOD STORE', and the sign 'WELCOME': only a photograph of foods in the window hints at the Lithuanian produce within. Even restaurant choices are not predictable: though Chinese and Korean restaurants in the sample area commonly use these languages, the Japanese restaurant uses Japanese much more sparingly, and the shopfront of the Mongolian Barbecue is entirely in English.

These variations within the marketplace suggest that the discourse principles enumerated by Spolsky and Cooper (1991) should be seen in the light of the language ideologies of particular groups. For some, the visible use of community languages will be a vital way of maintaining in-group communication. Other sign interlocutors (e.g. owners of Chinese restaurants) may additionally gain the perception of authenticity from those outside the language group. It appears, though, that for still others, there are neither strong internal nor external motivations to use community languages in the linguistic landscape of the marketplace. For languages which are not independently visible in the civic frame, we may hypothesize that non-participation in the marketplace may presage eventual language loss.

Portals

No-one who observes the linguistic landscape in an area where recent immigration, population mobility, international retail banking and telephone and internet communication feature prominently can help noticing that sites associated with these functions are often rich in multilingual signage. Suggesting that there is a functional unity in this part of the linguistic landscape, I consider the discourse frame of *portals* to be one in which the focus is on entrances and exits, i.e. the movement of people or personal goods, either physically or virtually (as with the electronic transfer of funds).

The use of English, Irish and French in another sign on the Dublin–Belfast Enterprise train represents policy-related multilingual signage of an older type. The sign reads as follows:

IN AN EMERGENCY, BREAK THE
GLASS AND PUSH THE BUTTON.

> WHEN THE TRAIN HAS STOPPED
> PUSH DOOR AND SLIDE OPEN
>
> In am práinne, bris an ghloine
> agus brúigh an cnaipe.
>
> Nuair nach bhfuil an traein ag
> gluaiseacht, brúigh amach an doras
> agus sleamhnaigh
>
> En case d'urgence, cassez la vitre
> et appuyez sur le bouton
>
> Quand le train s'arrête
> poussez puis coulissez la porte d'accès.

Trilingual signage here predates recent immigration to Ireland, and Census data (Central Statistics Office, 1993; 2007) do not suggest that the use of French as the third language reflects demographic considerations. It is, instead, a way of adopting an international language on a train service that crosses an international border and was partly funded by the European Union. The sign is thus indexical of both the local language environment (using English and Irish) and a generalized sense of European international travel.

Figure 1.6 shows a recognition of recent trends in population movement, seen in the facility for car parking fees at Dublin Airport to be paid following instructions in Polish (shown here), English, French or Italian. Though Irish is found in various signs elsewhere in the airport, it is significant by its absence from this location. Since language choice in this case does not reflect state language policy, we can only speculate as to why these languages have been

Figure 1.6 Paying for car parking, Dublin Airport

chosen. The volume of traffic coming from particular countries may be influential, but since more passengers arrive annually from Germany and Spain than Italy or Poland (Central Statistics Office, n.d.), it may be suggested that other factors (e.g. the estimated likelihood that particular language groups will use airport parking facilities) have entered into consideration.

The technological portal is illustrated by another sign of a common type (found in Parnell Street in the sample area, but not reproduced here), which uses English, Chinese and Polish to advertise a mobile phone unlocking service. Since mobile phone unlocking is especially useful for people who have recently arrived in a new country and are planning to stay for longer than a conventional tourist's visit, the multilingualism of the sign is not merely business-related, but indexical of the relationship between personal mobility and international communications technology. This added level of indexicality, I suggest, places this kind of sign within the framework of *portals* rather than simple marketplace discourse.

The wall

Linguistic landscapes are not only associated with buildings and official signage. Though Backhaus (2007) favours the analysis of fixed signage only, the landscape as a visual entity undeniably contains transient signage as found in graffiti, temporary posters, labels, stickers, notes and various ephemeral forms of expression. Shops associated with specific language communities often include notice boards or other sites at which temporary, handwritten notes may be attached in the search for living quarters, employment, employees or goods and services. Temporary posters also serve to build the language community, by advertising events of interest to those who share the language. Such a poster is seen in Figure 1.7, from March 2006. Though the Polish in this poster is somewhat anomalous (viz. number and gender agreement between the adjectival modifier POLSKI 'Polish' and the head noun IMPREZKI 'entertainment' is violated, perhaps in an effort to achieve visual rhyme between the two words), the use of the linguistic code (note also the recent borrowing *shoty* 'shots') alongside the colours and graphics is certainly aimed at members of the Polish community. The legend 'Every Sunday night in Redz', however, may give evidence of additional interaction with a non-Polish speaking audience.

The detritus zone

The ultimate illustration of the ephemeral within the linguistic landscape lies in what we may call the *detritus zone* (see also Kallen, 2008). Litter, domestic and commercial waste, and other discarded goods hardly signal a linguistic intention on the part of those who contribute to the areas in which rubbish accumulates. Yet much of this material is indexical of population movement.

FIGURE 1.7 Polski Imprezki, near O'Connell Street (see colour plate section)

Picture a ticket from the Paris Métro lying on the ground in the London Underground. Though this ticket is presented anonymously and we have no idea how it got there, the traveller who has discarded the ticket may well have come to London directly from Paris via the Channel Tunnel – at least we are entitled to draw this conclusion. This movement is itself indexical of a technological advance within an integrated Europe that would have been impossible in the not very distant past. Figure 1.8 illustrates a type of cigarette packet which is familiar throughout the world, showing an international brand of cigarettes and a label that includes a stern health warning.

For our purposes, the significance of the discarded item in Figure 1.8 is that the health warning is in Romanian. The person who has discarded the cigarette packet may not have intended to contribute to the linguistic landscape, but the appearance of this packet in this location becomes indexical of the enhanced flow of traffic between Ireland and Romania. (I have noted similar packets in Spanish, Polish, Greek and Chinese on the sample route; a bilingual warning in

FIGURE 1.8 Cigarette health warning in Romanian, Malahide Road

Irish and English has also made a recent appearance.) Here we may refer to Conley (2003), who makes the point that the surrealist concept of the 'sculpture involontaire' sought to 'blur the distinction between ethnography as science and as aesthetic by examining familiar European objects with the same scientific detail as unfamiliar tribal objects' (p. 130). In this vein, I suggest that it is not only carefully considered signage that signifies in the linguistic landscape. Concern for the ethnography of the familiar also implies that keeping an eye on the ground for the most mundane discarded objects reveals a frame of unintentional discourse that nevertheless has indexical importance and has an impact on the linguistic landscape at any given moment.

Conclusion

The linguistic landscape in Dublin is undergoing a profound change, but this change is not distributed evenly throughout the landscape. So uneven is this distribution that I suggest dividing the landscape into different frameworks, each of which has its own set of discourse expectations. At the level of language policy and policy-driven signage – the civic frame – we can see that practice in Ireland still strongly favours the two official languages, although there is inconsistent evidence that other languages may be used for specific instrumental purposes. Signage in the marketplace ranges from the purely community-based monolingual sign through various mixed types, which may include Irish, English and the languages of immigrant communities. In areas of the landscape such as portals, where mobility and technology are to the fore, it may be argued that internationally-defined multilingualism is the default case, rather than policy-based bilingualism or the favouring of English that follows from the general dominance of English as a spoken language. If we were to analyse the Dublin linguistic landscape as a single unit, we would miss the separate expectations operating in different frameworks and see conflicting choices in operation where real choice does not exist. As our databases for the study of linguistic landscape expand, and as linguistic landscape studies take on increasingly complex social issues of community, society and globalization, I suggest that treating the landscape as a complex of inter-related discourse frames, each with its own principles of indexicality, will help us to understand, in Goffman's (1974: 25) phrase, 'what is it that's going on' in linguistic landscapes wherever we analyse them.

Acknowledgements

My sincere thanks to Adam Jaworski, James Lantolf and Esther Kallen for the valuable discussions I have had with them on earlier versions of this paper.

Notes

[1] Acts of transgression, where private individuals do impose their own choice of names in opposition to official signs, represent a special case, not a conventional choice.

[2] The Irish in this sign is not entirely standard: *gruagaire* is the standard spelling for the Irish word meaning 'hairdresser', and the words spelled <*Failte*> and <*Cach*> in the sign should be *Fáilte* and *Cách*.

References

Backhaus, P. (2005), 'Signs of multilingualism in Tokyo – a diachronic look at the linguistic landscape', *International Journal of the Sociology of Language*, 175/176, 103–121.

—(2007), *Linguistic Landscapes: A Comparative Study of Urban Multilingualism in Tokyo*. Clevedon: Multilingual Matters.

Ben-Rafael, E., Shohamy, E., Amara, M. H. and Trumper-Hecht, N. (2006), 'Linguistic landscape as symbolic construction of the public space: The case of Israel', in

D. Gorter (ed.), *Linguistic Landscape: A New Approach to Multilingualism.* Clevedon: Multilingual Matters, pp. 7–30.
Bunreacht (2003), *Bunreacht na nÉireann: Constitution of Ireland.* Dublin: Stationery Office.
Cenoz, J. and Gorter, D. (2006), 'Linguistic landscape and minority languages', in D. Gorter (ed.), *Linguistic Landscape: A New Approach to Multilingualism.* Clevedon: Multilingual Matters, pp. 67–80.
Central Statistics Office (1993), *Census 86. Volume 8: Usual Residence and Migration/ Birthplaces.* Dublin: Stationery Office.
—(2007), *Census 2006. Volume 4: Usual Residence, Birthplaces and Nationalities.* Dublin: Stationery Office.
—(2008), *Census 2006. Non-Irish Nationals Living in Ireland.* Dublin: Stationery Office.
—(n.d.), 'Air passenger movement (number) by Irish airport, foreign airport, direction and month', http://www.cso.ie (accessed 27 August 2009).
Conley, K. (2003), 'Modernist primitivism in 1933: Brassaï's "involuntary sculptures" in Minotaure', *Modernism/Modernity,* 10(1), 127–140.
Department of Education (1989), *Tuarascáil Staitistiúil/Statistical Report 1986–87.* Dublin: Stationery Office.
Gallagher, A. (2007), '"We see everyone on every side, but no one sees us": Ireland's changing linguistic profile', Paper presented at the Trinity Immigration Initiative Research Fair. Dublin, Ireland. http://www.tcd.ie/immigration/migrationfair2007.php (accessed 27 August 2008).
Goffman, E. (1974), *Frame Analysis: An Essay on the Organization of Experience.* New York: Harper & Row.
Huebner, T. (2006), 'Bangkok's linguistic landscapes: Environmental print, codemixing and language change', in D. Gorter (ed.), *Linguistic Landscape: A New Approach to Multilingualism.* Clevedon: Multilingual Matters, pp. 31–51.
Immigrant Council of Ireland (2005), *Background Information and Statistics on Immigration to Ireland.* http://www.immigrantcouncil.ie/ (accessed 27 August 2008).
Inoue, F. (2005), 'Econolinguistic aspects of multilingual signs in Japan', *International Journal of the Sociology of Language,* 175/176, 157–177.
Kallen, J. L. (2008), 'Tourism and representation in the Irish linguistic landscape', in E. Shohamy and D. Gorter (eds), *Linguistic Landscape: Expanding the Scenery.* London: Routledge, pp. 270–283.
Landry, R. and Bourhis, R. Y. (1997), 'Linguistic landscape and ethnolinguistic vitality: An empirical study', *Journal of Language and Social Psychology,* 16(1), 23–49.
Reh, M. (2004), 'Multilingual writing: a reader-oriented typology – with examples from Lira Municipality (Uganda)', *International Journal of the Sociology of Language,* 170, 1–41.
Rosenbaum, Y., Nadel, E., Cooper, R. L. and Fishman, J. A. (1977), English on Keren Kayemet Street', in J. A. Fishman, R. L. Cooper and A. W. Conrad (eds), *The Spread of English: The Sociology of English as an Additional Language.* Rowley, MA: Newbury House, pp. 179–194.
Scollon, R. and Wong Scollon, S. (2003), *Discourses in Place: Language in the Material World.* London: Routledge.

Spolsky, B. and Cooper, R. L. (1991), *The Languages of Jerusalem.* Oxford: Oxford University Press.

State Examination Commission (n.d.), '2007 Leaving Certificate statistics: Higher level both school and E10 candidates', http://www.examinations.ie (accessed 27 August 2008).

—(2007), '2007 Examination information: Non-curricular EU language subjects', http://www.examinations.ie (accessed 27 August 2008).

Chapter 2

Discourses in Transit

Mark Sebba

Recently, a number of frameworks have been put forward which provide approaches to the interpretation of bilingual and multilingual public texts such as street signs. In particular, the notion of 'linguistic landscapes' (Bourhis and Landry, 1997; Gorter, 2006) provides a way of thinking about multilingual public texts as reflections of the multilingual composition of an urban area, while Scollon and Wong Scollon (2003) analyse signs, including bilingual signage, in terms of the 'semiotics of place', using a framework which includes visual and textual components of signs as well as their geographical location.

In this chapter I will argue that fixed signs may indeed be valuable indicators of such things as multilingual composition of a community, public debates about language, public policy goals and power relations between languages, but they should not be seen in isolation from other types of public texts which are not fixed in space. 'Unfixed' or 'mobile' public texts, for example in the form of product labels, pamphlets, banknotes, stamps, tickets, handbills, flyers and general 'ephemera', are pervasive in contemporary society. Some of these connect to fixed texts (like street signs and billboards) via logos, colour schemes, layout and content. They are amenable to similar kinds of analysis in terms of their structure, layout and visual imagery. What is more, mobile texts require 'reading' in the same kind of way as fixed texts – for example, authority and authenticity are indexed in the same (or similar) ways. Both fixed and mobile texts may be involved in more than one discourse, for example a bus timetable may tell you about bus times but also about the importance of different places along the route and the kind of people who might be expected to use the bus services; these messages are likely to be reinforced (or occasionally contradicted) in various ways by the fixed signage of bus shelters, road markings etc., and are accessible to readers, although they are not part of the overt message. Thus while fixed signage is undoubtedly of great interest in its own right, it needs to be seen and analysed as a subset or 'special case' of the set of all public texts, which also includes mobile or 'non-fixed' public texts.

This chapter will focus on multilingual public texts, both fixed and mobile. As pointed out above, public texts may have an overt purpose (for example, to inform) but may participate in other discourses as well. In the case of multilingual texts, this may be a discourse about the relative value and status of the languages used in the text. I am not trying to suggest that multilingualism creates some kind of special bond between the fixed and the mobile public texts. Similar relationships can of course be found between fixed and mobile texts in monolingual (or predominantly monolingual) contexts as well. However, bilingual contexts provide particularly good illustrations because the discourses about languages and language values which texts in these situations represent are never, or very rarely, the *main* or overt message of the text.

'Signs', 'public texts' and the semiotic landscape

Within the developing literature on the semiotic landscape, there has been a great deal of interest in signs. Yet exactly what is meant by 'sign' seems not yet completely settled. As Backhaus (2007) points out, 'sign' has two potentially relevant meanings within this field (pp. 4–5). First, it is 'a key term in semiotics . . . any meaningful unit interpreted as standing for something other than itself'. Secondly, it is 'an inscribed surface displayed in a public space to convey a message'. 'Signs' in this second sense are also signs in the first sense, as 'they too stand for something other than themselves' (2007: 5). This ambiguity is potentially useful, but also potentially limiting, since 'signs' in the second sense are such a small subset of 'signs' in the first. Scollon and Wong Scollon (2003), for example, at times seem to take a very broad view of their subject matter:

> Geosemiotics is the study of the meaning systems by which language is located in the material world. This includes not just the location of the words on the page you are reading now but also the location of the book in your hands and your location as you stand or sit reading this. (p. x)

Yet at other times they seem to be concerned only with signs as physical objects:

> [S]igns are designed by sign-makers, they are made in the shops and workplaces of sign-makers, they are taken out to the relevant site, and finally, some worker puts them up and they become 'signs in place'. (p. 1)

This more restrictive interpretation of 'sign' seems to fit with the view of Landry and Bourhis (1997), who regard the linguistic landscape as consisting of 'the language of public road signs, advertising billboards, street names, place names, commercial shop signs, and public signs on government buildings' (p. 25). Other researchers in this area have observed that fixed signs are by no means the only candidates for elements of the linguistic landscape, but have taken a pragmatic position – as does Gorter (2006: 3): 'It has to be determined what belongs to the linguistic landscape. For instance, are texts on moving objects such as buses or cars to be included? For convenience sake they are probably not'.

Seen in a wider context, the decision to exclude everything apart from fixed signage from the definition of 'linguistic landscape' could be regarded as arbitrary. Almost all humans today live in a textually mediated world, and the texts which mediate and impact on our lives are by no means all fixed in place. An alternative approach, disregarding issues of 'convenience', would be to look at the *totality* of public texts, fixed or circulating, within a specified location. For example, Mechthild Reh (2004) sets out to explore multilingual literacy practices through a detailed description of public writing on display in an urban environment in Uganda. For her, one of the parameters required for a useful analysis is what she calls 'spatial mobility'.

> The parameter of spatial mobility relates to the objects inscribed and describes to what extent these are physically fixed. Such inscribed objects may be stationary, as in the case of buildings or large signboards, or movable, as in the case of newspapers, T-shirts, or books, and transitional forms also exist. (p. 3)

Although Reh is concerned with observing and documenting literacy practices rather than 'semiotic landscapes' as such, her paper amounts to a detailed description of the multilingual landscape of a town. Many of her observations are similar to those made by researchers working within the linguistic landscapes tradition. However, Reh explicitly includes inscribed objects which are stationary, movable, or 'transitional' between those states in her analysis.

What exactly constitutes a 'mobile' public text is an interesting and important discussion in its own right, and one which we do not have time to discuss here in detail. For our purposes we will take it to be any text which is exposed to members of the public – thus including the 'newspapers, T-shirts, or books' mentioned by Reh but also other everyday 'texts' which are rarely thought of as texts, such as banknotes, stamps and bus tickets. These circulate in large volumes and hence are 'read' by many people on a daily basis even though their familiarity means that their users may give them little more than a glance.[1]

One of the founding claims of the Linguistic Landscapes approach, as articulated by Bourhis and Landry (1997) is that 'the presence or absence of the in-group language in the linguistic landscape is related to how much speakers use their in-group language with family members, friends, neighbors and store clerks; in social gatherings; in cultural activities; and as consumers of in-group language . . . media' (p. 45). In other words, the visibility of written languages in public spaces correlates with the ethnolinguistic vitality of their spoken equivalents. While it may well be true in selected contexts, as a general statement it can be shown to be untrue, for reasons which Bourhis and Landry themselves allude to: 'the linguistic landscape may serve important informational and symbolic functions as a marker of the relative power and status of the linguistic communities inhabiting the territory' (Bourhis and Landry (1997: 23).

FIGURE 2.1 Cape Provincial Administration harbour sign (1997)

Thus rather than reflect the vitality of their respective language communities and the extent of language use, the publicly displayed texts which make up the linguistic landscape may provide evidence – to be understood only in context – of power relationships between languages (or rather, the groups who 'own' those languages) and policies designed to manage and control just those relationships.

As an example of this, we can take the linguistic landscape of South Africa during the period 1925–1994. During this period, there were two official languages, English and Afrikaans. The sign in Figure 2.1, photographed in 1997 just after the end of the era in question but which was certainly not new, typifies the public signage of its day. There are only two languages used in the text, English and Afrikaans. These are arranged in a strictly symmetrical way. For example, the initials of the relevant authority (Cape Provincial Administration – CPA or KPA) occupy symmetrical positions in the upper corners, while the words BY ORDER and OP LAS do the same in the lower corners. Only two font sizes and one type face have been used, but the same size is used for the same function in each language. The effect is to give the two languages equal prominence – in effect, to construct them as visibly equal – and at the same time to exclude any other language.

Bilingual fixed signs of this type were ubiquitous in South Africa during this period, but they did not exist in isolation from other bilingual texts. In fact, public texts of all genres, whether from the public sector (like bus tickets or examination papers) or from the commercial sector (like product labels and advertising leaflets), displayed this kind of symmetrical bilingualism with great predictability. This can be seen in the banknote (Figure 2.2), where geometrical

FIGURE 2.2 South African ten rand banknote, *ca.* 1980

symmetry and identity of type faces and fonts are used to construct the languages as equal, even down to small details.

Following Bourhis and Landry literally, one might conclude from this that most South Africans during this period spoke either English or Afrikaans. This is far from the truth. In public texts of the type under discussion, the ten or so other major languages of South Africa, at least five of which have numbers of speakers comparable to or greater than English and Afrikaans, do not feature at all. They are not part of the linguistic landscape: they have been 'erased' (Irvine and Gal, 2000).

These facts can be explained relatively straightforwardly by examining the hegemonic relationships between the speakers of the different languages, the language politics of the politically dominant group, and the language policies in force. Briefly: all political power during this period was held by white speakers of English or Afrikaans. A recent history of conflict between the speakers of these languages manifested itself as a demand for 'equality' between their languages, and this imperative was codified in the 1910 constitution, which established the Union of South Africa as a political entity. The constitution was very explicit in requiring equality of the two official languages. It declared that they

> shall be treated on a footing of equality, and possess and enjoy equal freedom, rights, and privileges; all records, journals, and proceedings of Parliament shall be kept in both languages, and all Bills, Acts, and notices of general public importance or interest issued by the Government of the Union shall be in both languages.[2]

Thus the politically dominant white population erased from public texts all but their own native languages, at the same time establishing an order in which those two languages should be constructed as equal to each other at all times. This construction of equality was reproduced throughout all public texts, fixed and mobile, both within the public sector (where it was a constitutional requirement) and the private sector (where speakers of English and Afrikaans provided the majority of the consumers of most packaged products).[3] This explains the distinctive appearance of the South African 'linguistic landscape', which by itself reflects little of the actual diversity of languages on the ground, while it also tells us nothing of the complex relationship between the two languages which do feature there (for example, the varying dominance ofEnglish over Afrikaans or vice versa through time, in urban vs rural contexts, in different domains, etc.). We can reasonably conclude that the South African linguistic landscape of this period was the result of an ideological project, which had the aim of constructing English and Afrikaans as official languages with equal prominence, and causing all other languages to disappear from public view.

My conclusion is that while the linguistic landscape (consisting of both fixed and mobile texts) is well worth studying, it must be studied in its sociohistorical context in order to be interpretable. I will now turn to a case study of a very different linguistic landscape.

Case study: English and Manx in the Isle of Man

The Isle of Man is an 'internally self-governing dependent territory of the Crown which is not part of the United Kingdom' with a population of about 80,000 and a land area of 572 sq. km.[4] The Manx language (*Yn Ghaelg Vanninagh*) is a member of the Celtic family, closest to Scottish Gaelic and Irish.

Manx has often been cited as a dead language: its 'last native speaker' died in 1974. However, there are still speakers of Manx alive who learnt the language as children from native speakers. A number of cultural and research organizations exist to document and promote Manx, and the number of speakers of Manx has steadily increased since 1971. Even so, according to the Manx national census of 2001, only 1,689 respondents (all of whom also speak English) declared that they could speak, read or write Manx Gaelic (with no definition of those terms being provided). This is only 2 per cent of the population, but as 47 per cent of the speakers of Manx were under 20, there were modest grounds for optimism that the language would survive and even prosper.

While for many years official policy was to devalue or disregard Manx, attitudes have changed, and the Isle of Man government has invested in the project of Manx revival since 1985. A Manx nursery school movement *Mooinjer Veggey* was established in 1996 (McArdle, 2005) and a state-run Manx-medium primary school (*Bunscoill Gaelgagh*) opened in 2001. Manx has now been accepted as having a role in business in helping to create a national identity, and specifically, in creating an identity separate from that of Great Britain/the United Kingdom/England, with all of which the Isle of Man risks being conflated. The Isle of Man Government's Business Plan for 2005–2008 'identifies a sense of "National Identity" as one of six overall aims' (McArdle, 2005); furthermore, this aim is linked with commercial development and marketing the island as a distinct (and distinctive) entity. A recent publication of the Manx Heritage Foundation, *A Guide to the Business Use of Manx* gives the following as some of the answers to the question 'Why use Manx'?

Extract 1

- It shows your commitment to the island and its cultural heritage;
- it contributes to the current debate about branding and marketing the island;
- a few words spoken at a conference can help distinguish the island from the UK and other jurisdictions.

Although finance is currently a major local industry, tourism has been well-established in the island since the nineteenth century and is a major contributor to the economy. During 2006 there were 306,000 visitors to the island, i.e. almost four times its number of permanent residents.[5] It is reasonable to conclude that the linguistic landscape of the island is configured with not only its permanent population, but also visitors, in mind.

In 1995 on my first visit to the Isle of Man (as a tourist), I was surprised to see the allegedly 'extinct' Manx prominently displayed in some public places – for example, on fire service and post office vehicles (Figure 2.3), street names (Figure 2.4) and some public buildings. It was also possible to select Manx as the language for instructions for using payphones (along with English and several other European languages). By my third visit in 2005, the amount of Manx visible in public had increased substantially. Most of the Manx which is visible in public takes the form of fixed signs – nearly all bilingual in Manx and English rather than exclusively in Manx. However, Manx texts are not confined

Figure 2.3 Isle of Man Fire and Rescue Service vehicle (2006) (see colour plate section)

FIGURE 2.4 Bilingual street name plate, Douglas, Isle of Man (1998)

to signage – they can be found in other places, even by visitors to the island, for example in bus and train timetables and leaflets from public bodies and services.

In the remainder of this section, I will look in more detail at the public texts which one might encounter on a visit to the Isle of Man, with a view to examining the relationship between English and Manx as represented in the linguistic landscape.

In official signage such as on public buildings and street name signs, Manx is almost always present, but appears with varying degrees of salience or prominence. Sometimes it has prominence equal or near-equal to English. So, for example, building namesigns on government buildings typically contain Manx and English in equal proportions and with approximately equal prominence (though this will be examined in more detail later). Elsewhere, for example on the fire engine in Figure 2.3, Manx and English have equal prominence but are displayed in parallel – in this case, one language on each side of the vehicle.

This small sample might make it appear that Manx and English, like English and Afrikaans in the South African case, are symbolically constructed as equal in public texts. The situation is actually very different. This becomes apparent immediately if we move beyond fixed signage to look at mobile public texts. Although Manx is *visible* in many such texts, when it occurs it is always to a very restricted extent.

For example, Figure 2.5 shows an information leaflet issued by the Department of Health. Manx is present in this text, but occupies exclusively *symbolic* spaces, which it shares (not always equally) with English. Manx occurs in this leaflet in exactly four places:

1. At the top of the page below the Department of Health logo and the English heading 'Health Services'.
2. Below the main heading, in a green band following the motto 'for the health of the nation'.
3. Underneath the Isle of Man Government logo (Figure 2.8). Here the Manx expression for 'Isle of Man government' is found immediately below the

HEALTH SERVICES

Shirveishyn Slaynt

Public Notice

Emergency Doctor Service

The present emergency GP service will change in two respects from 1st April 2003.

First, the present service, which applies to the patients of all GPs except patients registered with the Ramsey, Laxey and Port Erin group practices, will be extended to include those patients and thus become an all-Island service.

Second, responsibility for operating the service passes from MannDoc (a GP run co-operative) to the Primary Health Care Division of the Department of Health and Social Security.

The emergency GP service operates when your GP surgery is closed. If you have a medical condition that isn't life-threatening but cannot wait until the surgery opens, you should telephone your usual doctor's surgery and a recorded message will inform you of the number to call to speak to the doctor on duty.

The duty doctor will offer you medical advice over the telephone or advise you to attend a consultation at the out-of-hours surgery. In exceptional circumstances, the doctor may arrange a home visit. The out-of-hours doctor's surgery, based at Noble's Hospital is not a drop-in service and patients should note that they **will not** be seen by the duty doctor without an appointment.

The service is available from 6pm to 8am Monday to Friday, with 24-hour cover over weekends and bank holidays.

If you have chest pain or a life-threatening emergency you should always call 999.

DEPARTMENT OF HEALTH AND SOCIAL SECURITY

Rheynn Slaynt as Shickyrys Y Theay

Figure 2.5 Manx Department of Health leaflet (2005) (see colour plate section)

English, but is arguably too small to read (the actual height of the letters in the leaflet is less than 1 mm!).

4. On the bottom line, within a green band, giving the name of the issuing authority ('Department of Health and Social Security') which is also given in English above.

We may note that only in (4) could it be argued that Manx has more prominence than the English equivalent, being highlighted in green, in somewhat larger letters, and occupying the last position on the page. By contrast in (2) it has equal prominence with English and in (1) it is arguably less prominent by virtue of being in smaller characters, italicized, and in mixed upper and lower case where the English is entirely in capitals. In (3) it is so small that many people may not even be aware of it.

Thus where it does occur in this document, Manx could be said to be clearly positioned as of secondary importance to English. Equally significant is where Manx does *not* occur: it does not appear in the title of the document ('Public Notice: Emergency Doctor Service') nor anywhere in the informational text. The leaflet could reasonably be described as an English leaflet which also contains Manx in certain symbolically significant positions, in particular those which index the authority of the Government and its departments.

In fact this leaflet is typical of public texts which include Manx. Where there is any extensive amount of text, it is nearly always all in English, even where the title and other header material are in English and Manx. The Manx Telecom telephone directory – a book which is found in virtually every home and in public places as well – is another example that follows exactly this pattern: the information pages at the beginning of the directory each carry a header in English (for example: 'Investing in the Island') which is preceded by the Manx equivalent, on the same line, but in a smaller font. The rest of the text on each page is exclusively in English. Once again, Manx occupies a symbolically prominent position in the header, but is otherwise absent. Furthermore, it is constructed as secondary to English by being printed in a smaller typeface.

From these examples it can already be seen that while some public signage on signposts and buildings may be constructing Manx as equal to English, other public texts, at the same time as making Manx visible, are constructing it as *unequal* to English by various means. If we revisit the fixed public signage where Manx features prominently, we can see that there too Manx is arguably being constructed as secondary to English at least in some cases. For example, in the street name (Figure 2.4 above) the Manx version is in a slightly smaller font, occupies less space and is in mixed upper and lower case while the English is in capitals. In the bus stop sign (Figure 2.6), although the key words 'bus stop' and 'information' are given equal prominence in Manx and English in terms of size and position, the Manx is marked as 'other' by use of a traditional Celtic font. A Celtic font is also used for the Manx words in Figure 2.3. Exactly what the Celtic font is meant to index is not clear (it may or may not be historically appropriate) but in this context, it arguably constructs the text as 'ornamental' or 'decorative' rather than authoritative.

The same government agency, Isle of Man Transport, is responsible for the bus stop sign and many mobile public texts which provide information about services. Both their signage and literature are widespread in the island and likely to be seen by visitors as well as local residents. In many of these texts Manx

FIGURE 2.6 Isle of Man Transport bus stop sign (2005)

is present, but is constructed as secondary to English. For example, in a pocket rail timetable (not reproduced here), the Manx is marked out by use of a small narrow font, which takes up much less space than the English 'Railway Timetable' although the Manx equivalent 'eearroo traa ny raaidyn-yiarn') actually contains more characters. In Figure 2.7, a full-page advert for transport services, the Manx text is in a font size similar to the English, but is represented as 'other' than English by being printed in italics immediately below the English.

The bus timetable (Figure 2.8) is interesting in this respect. The timetable is part of a booklet, on whose cover Manx and English are both prominently displayed. Immediately inside, a page of notes and instructions for use are in English only. The timetables themselves, however, have a complex combination of Manx and English.

In the page illustrated, we can see that the route is shown prominently at the top of the page using the English place names.[6] Below this is a bold horizontal line and just below this we find the route given in Manx, in a smaller font which

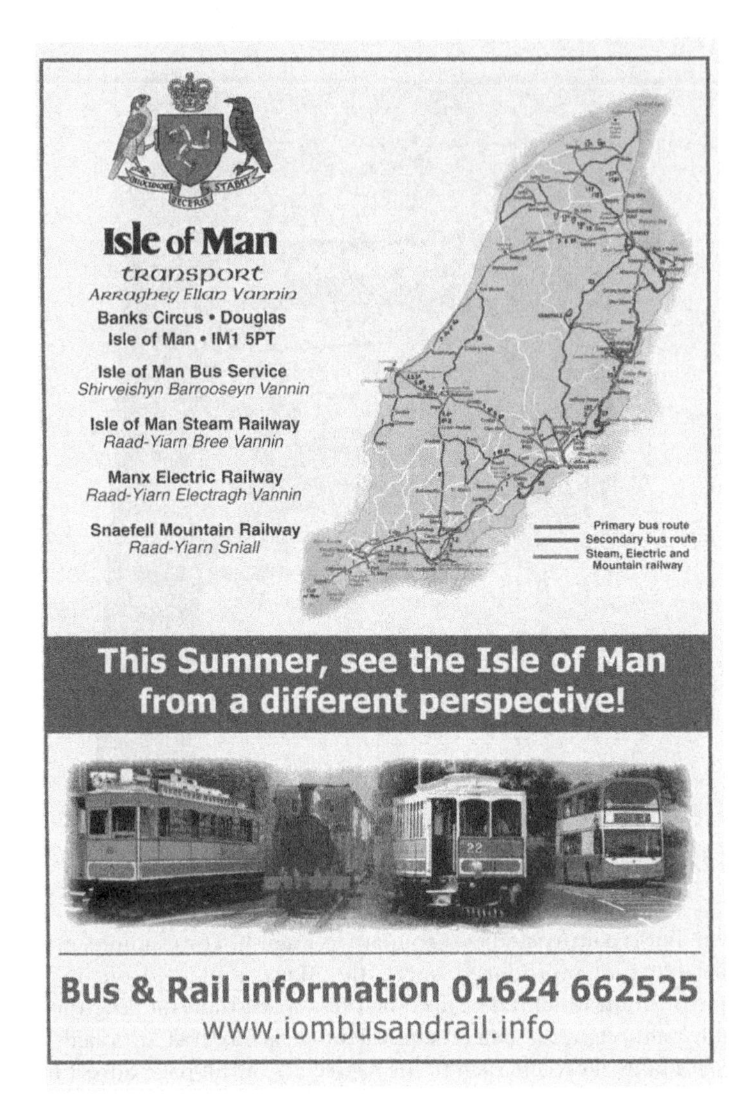

FIGURE 2.7 Transport services advertisement (2005)

uses both capital and lower case letters. This is flanked by boxes with the text 'Mondays to Saturdays' and the Manx translation. Below this is the timetable itself, which is entirely in English, including the footnotes. Next to the notes we find two 'black boxes', one in English and one in Manx, containing the text 'Sorry – No Sunday service' and the Manx equivalent in similar fonts. Below this is a box, marked as different by having curved rather than rectangular corners, containing information about the Snaefell Mountain Railway. This is entirely in English and there is no Manx translation on this page or elsewhere.

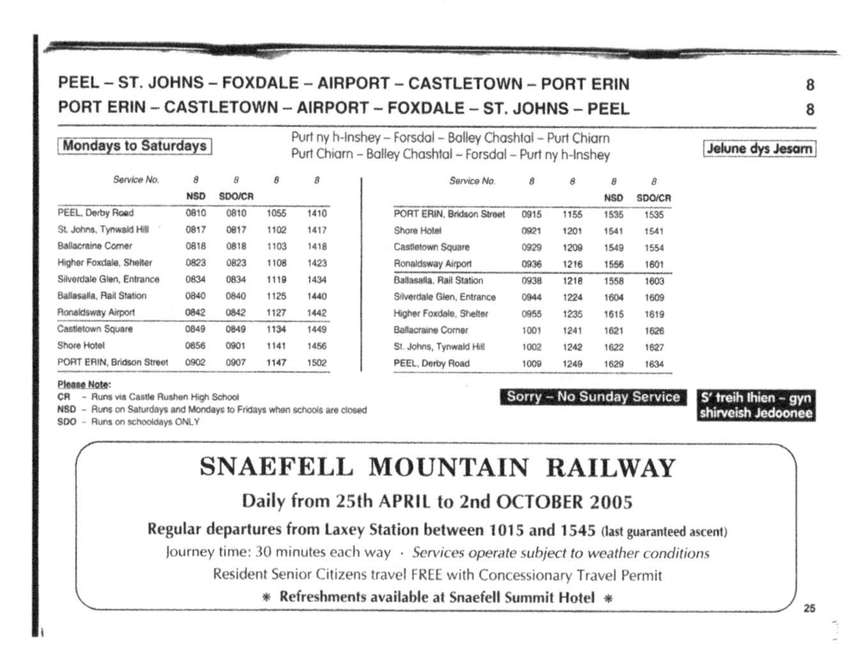

PEEL – ST. JOHNS – FOXDALE – AIRPORT – CASTLETOWN – PORT ERIN 8
PORT ERIN – CASTLETOWN – AIRPORT – FOXDALE – ST. JOHNS – PEEL 8

Mondays to Saturdays

Purt ny h-Inshey – Forsdal – Balley Chashtal – Purt Chiarn
Purt Chiarn – Balley Chashtal – Forsdal – Purt ny h-Inshey

Jelune dys Jesarn

Service No.	8	8	8	8
	NSD	SDO/CR		
PEEL, Derby Road	0810	0810	1055	1410
St. Johns, Tynwald Hill	0817	0817	1102	1417
Ballacraine Corner	0818	0818	1103	1418
Higher Foxdale, Shelter	0823	0823	1108	1423
Silverdale Glen, Entrance	0834	0834	1119	1434
Ballasalla, Rail Station	0840	0840	1125	1440
Ronaldsway Airport	0842	0842	1127	1442
Castletown Square	0849	0849	1134	1449
Shore Hotel	0856	0901	1141	1456
PORT ERIN, Bridson Street	0902	0907	1147	1502

Service No.	8	8	8	8
			NSD	SDO/CR
PORT ERIN, Bridson Street	0915	1155	1535	1535
Shore Hotel	0921	1201	1541	1541
Castletown Square	0929	1209	1549	1554
Ronaldsway Airport	0936	1216	1556	1601
Ballasalla, Rail Station	0938	1218	1558	1603
Silverdale Glen, Entrance	0944	1224	1604	1609
Higher Foxdale, Shelter	0955	1235	1615	1619
Ballacraine Corner	1001	1241	1621	1626
St. Johns, Tynwald Hill	1002	1242	1622	1627
PEEL, Derby Road	1009	1249	1629	1634

Please Note:
CR – Runs via Castle Rushen High School
NSD – Runs on Saturdays and Mondays to Fridays when schools are closed
SDO – Runs on schooldays ONLY

Sorry – No Sunday Service

S' treih lhien – gyn shirveish Jedoonee

SNAEFELL MOUNTAIN RAILWAY
Daily from 25th APRIL to 2nd OCTOBER 2005
Regular departures from Laxey Station between 1015 and 1545 (last guaranteed ascent)
Journey time: 30 minutes each way · *Services operate subject to weather conditions*
Resident Senior Citizens travel FREE with Concessionary Travel Permit
* Refreshments available at Snaefell Summit Hotel *

25

FIGURE 2.8 Isle of Man Transport bus timetable (2006)

How can we 'read' the relationship between Manx and English in this bus timetable? In a text addressed to both visitors and residents, different parts may be directed at different readers. Thus, the Snaefell Mountain Railway is mainly of interest to tourists, which could account for the text being in English only. Elsewhere on the page, Manx has a presence. Some of the information (for example, in the 'black boxes') is presented with equal prominence in both languages. However, Manx is also being shown as 'somewhat less important' than English. The Manx place names are lower in the page, and in a smaller font. The list of places and times itself, which occupies the central area of the page and is arguably the most important element for users of the timetable, is English-only; the words 'services' and the place names are not in Manx. The end notes which give additional important information about some services, are in English only. Thus the impression is produced, subtly but unambiguously, that while Manx is certainly a part of this document, it is secondary to English.

Bourhis and Landry (1997) point out that in some cases 'the language profile of private signs and government signs may be quite similar' while in other cases the two may be discordant (p. 27). For example, Reh (2004) found that in Lira, monolingual English public texts predominated in government and administration, as well as some parts of the private sector, while other parts of the private sector were more disposed to bilingualism. In the case of Manx, there are very

FIGURE 2.9 Label from Isle of Man Creameries milk

few public texts within the private sector which contain any Manx at all. The few that there are can be striking; for example, in one beachside café all items on the extensive cafe menu have been translated into Manx. This is very exceptional, however. In shops, a small number of local products are on sale, some of which have small symbolic insertions of Manx, for example on the labels of milk and in the masthead of the weekly newspaper, the *Manx Independent*. Though these public uses of Manx raise it to a level of visibility, it could be argued that they position it very clearly as of lesser importance than English: on the milk container (Figure 2.9), the only Manx words are the description of the product: 'bainney lieh-scarrit'. These occupy a position of relative prominence (at the top centre) and furthermore acquire some salience by virtue of being immediately below the English words 'semi-skimmed milk', which are by far the most prominent words on the label. However, the Manx is in letters much smaller than the English, is in black rather than green, and takes up much less space than the English both vertically and horizontally. All of this serves to position it as less important than English. Similar arguments apply to the newspaper masthead of a weekly paper, the *Manx Independent*, which contains information of interest to both locals and visitors. In this case, Manx is displayed in a prominent position (the masthead, at the top centre of the front page) but the Manx version of the title, 'Manninagh seyr' appears below the English and in a markedly smaller font, reducing its salience substantially and positioning it as secondary to the English.[7]

From these examples we can see that although the inclusion of Manx in these public texts has the effect of bringing it into the public gaze, it does *not* have the effect of making it appear equal to English. In fact Manx is confined, quite literally, to the 'margins' – to the header and footer areas of texts in many cases. Though it could be argued these parts of texts are salient and important in various ways, the fact remains that Manx is repeatedly positioned as secondary, both by being 'swamped' by the quantity of information in English and by subtle and not-so-subtle visual and graphical means.

Conclusion

So what can looking at this textual landscape tell us about the languages and the society that uses them? One thing we can see is that there is the potential for drawing different conclusions depending where we draw the boundaries of the linguistic landscape.

In the Isle of Man, for example, if we were to confine ourselves to looking at fixed public signage on official buildings, we would get an overall impression of equality of status for Manx and English. Other fixed signage, as we saw, gives a more ambiguous impression; in some ways Manx and English are constructed as 'equal' but in other ways Manx is constructed as 'other' and subordinate. Taking into account other public texts, including mobile ones, provides a different view, one which more realistically reflects the *de facto* status and relative number of speakers of each language. In such texts, Manx is largely 'marginal', confined to the symbolic spaces such as headers. In terms of quantity it is present much less than English and where it appears, it is often positioned as secondary to English.

Even where there is consistency between fixed and mobile texts in the linguistic landscape, however, it is a mistake to assume that they accurately reflect the power relations and vitality of languages on the ground. In pre-1994 South Africa, we find a very consistent pattern; equality of the two official languages, to the exclusion of all others, is constructed across a wide range of public texts, fixed and mobile, official and commercial. Banknotes, packaging and street signs were all 'singing from the same songsheet', but the message was one prescribed by public policy rather than a representation of the actual diversity of languages, their numbers of speakers and their relative status.

We can conclude that public texts, whether fixed or mobile, have to be read in the context of all other public texts which participate in the same discourse(s) and which impinge or may impinge on the consciousness of readers. I use 'discourses' here to mean both the main or overt discourse of the text (for example, healthcare discourse or transport discourse) as well as others (such as the discourse of language difference, the discourse of power relations between languages and their speech communities, and many other possible discourses). Furthermore, we must have knowledge of the wider social, historical and political context which has led to the current configuration of the linguistic landscape.

This conclusion raises a number of methodological and theoretical issues. First of all, how do we survey a landscape containing texts which are not fixed in space? As Gorter suggests (2006), texts on moving objects such as buses or cars are not very 'convenient' to take into account (p. 3). Still worse will be all those bits of paper – tickets, brochures, leaflets, packages and banknotes which clutter our lives. When are they part of the landscape and when not? At least fixed signs are to be read as 'discourses in place' only when they are in their proper place, or at least *some* fixed place: as Scollon and Wong Scollon (2003) put it, the sign has no binding meaning while it is in the back of the truck taking it to where it will be put up for the public to read (pp. 1–2). How then shall we deal with 'discourses in transit' like timetables, which may lie somewhere on a shelf for a while, then go for a long journey in someone's pocket, and eventually be thrown in a bin and taken to a landfill?

I suggest that we should think of public texts as having typical trajectories. We can agree with Scollon and Wong Scollon, for example, that the sign prohibiting nude bathing which they describe on page 1 of *Discourses in Place* began its existence somewhere in a sign-making shop, and was then taken in a vehicle to a spot where it was set up. Up to this point it had none of the 'in place' meaning that the authors attribute to it in its fixed site, though it still may have had meaning for its relatively few readers among the people who made and transported it ('they're getting tough on nude bathing again'). In a similar way, a mobile text like a bus timetable may begin its existence at a printing shop, and then find its way to a place where it is displayed, along with many others like it, for members of the public to take away. Eventually it will be picked up by someone and be used for a while as a source of information about bus times. During this phase it may spend time in someone's pocket or handbag, or on a home noticeboard or fridge door. At some stage, perhaps much later, it will be discarded and shredded, pulped or dumped in landfill. Like the fixed sign, it has periods when it is serving its main or overt purpose, and other periods when it is not (though it may have other uses, for example as a place to put a cup of coffee). However, as long as someone is reading it, even while it is underneath a coffee cup, it still has the potential to be participating in one or more discourses: for example, it may still be telling me that one language is preferred over another, even if it is not telling me the correct times of the buses.

Furthermore, non-fixed texts may be differentiated in terms of how prototypically 'public' they are (or are perceived to be) at different points in their trajectory. Some mobile texts are comparable to fixed signs in terms of exposure to the public (advertising on a bus, for example, or leaflets handed out to passers-by on a very large scale), while others, like bus timetables, are available to the public – and often on display for a time – but are more likely to be consumed in private before being discarded. Banknotes, meanwhile, probably have low salience in terms of their text (most 'readers' need to know only the denomination, which is often given by the colour or other non-textual means) but may have impact through their sheer numbers and the frequency and regularity with which they are encountered.

What exactly is the 'typical' trajectory of a particular type of public text is something we can determine by ethnographic research. In every culture where public texts exist, there will be practices surrounding them which we can observe and document. Some trajectories will be institutionalized and relatively predictable, others probably not. Furthermore, at different points in the trajectory different meanings of the text will be made or will take priority over others. We cannot predict, of course, that any specific text will follow the typical trajectory.

There remains the question of what looking at the multilingual textual landscape can tell us about the languages within the society we are studying. Surely the texts reflect something about that society, but what exactly is it? The case studies show that we need to be cautious about what inferences can be made by studying the textual landscape alone. We need ethnographic observation to set it in context: to tell us, for example, that English and Afrikaans are by no means the only languages in South Africa – even though they accounted for the great majority of public texts – nor did they have equal numbers of speakers or *de facto* equal status in all domains, despite the public texts being carefully engineered to show them as being 'on a footing of equality'. Likewise even the limited visibility of Manx in public texts overstates its significance in terms of numbers of speakers and as a means of communication in the Island. To understand this, it must be set in its context where Manx is a language with symbolic importance for the island (even for non-speakers of the language), which is also undergoing revival with official support.

In conclusion: in our textually mediated world we cannot open our eyes without being confronted by texts, fixed or mobile. This is our 'linguistic landscape' in which we live day to day. Within it, fixed signs are a special kind of public text which participate in discourses 'in place', but other public texts are no less involved in discourses, albeit 'discourses in transit'. To understand these texts fully, we need to see them as 'discourses in context': they cannot be interpreted without knowing more about the languages inscribed in them, their speakers, readers and writers, and the policies and power relationships which characterize the societies in which the texts are found.

Acknowledgements

I am grateful to the editors for valuable comments on an earlier version of this chapter, as well as to Susan Dray for comments on the first draft. Any errors are of course my own.

Notes

[1] The same could be said of many fixed signs, of course.

[2] South Africa Act, Section 137 – 'Equality of English and Dutch languages' (Dutch was later replaced by Afrikaans).

[3] The Constitution actually mentions only 'mobile' texts rather than fixed signage.

[4] Source: http://www.gov.im/isleofman/facts.xml (accessed 27 August 2009).

[5] Source: http://www.gov.im/tourism/trade/market.xml (accessed 27 August 2009).

[6] Most places in the Isle of Man have an English name and a Manx name, and these may be very different, e.g. Peel (English name) = Purt ny h-Inshey ('Town of the Island').

[7] To be precise, the capital I of Independent is 11 times taller than the I in the Manx version of the title.

References

Backhaus, P. (2007), *Linguistic Landscapes: A Comparative Study of Urban Multilingualism in Tokyo*. Clevedon: Multilingual Matters.

Bourhis, R. Y. and Landry, R. (1997), 'Linguistic landscape and ethnolinguistic vitality: An empirical study', *Journal of Language and Social Psychology*, 16, 23–49.

Gorter, D. (2006), 'Introduction: The study of the linguistic landscape as a new approach to multilingualism', *International Journal of Multilingualism*, 3(1), 1–6.

Irvine, J. T. and Gal, S. (2000), 'Language ideology and linguistic differentiation', in P. V. Kroskrity (ed.), *Regimes of Language*. Santa Fe, NM: School of American Research Press, pp. 35–83.

McArdle, F. (2005), *Manx Gaelic in Education in the Isle of Man*. http://www.gaelg.iofm.net/INFO/gaelg.htm (accessed 20 November 2007).

Reh, M. (2004), 'Multilingual writing: A reader-orientated typology – With examples from Lira Municipality (Uganda)'. *International Journal of the Sociology of Language*, 170, 1–41.

Scollon, R. and Wong Scollon, S. (2003), *Discourses in Place: Language in the Material World*. London: Routledge.

Chapter 3

Welsh Linguistic Landscapes 'From Above' and 'From Below'

Nikolas Coupland

Linguistic landscape is a metaphorical concept, extrapolated from the concept of natural landscape. Unravelling the notion of natural landscape poses its own challenges, not least because, unable to see the wood for the trees, we might conclude that we are no longer able to view what we call the natural world uncontaminated by human activity. Immediately setting aside that important issue, it might still be useful as a preliminary to consider the relationship between linguistic and natural landscapes. Here are Barbara Adam's (1998) illustrations of landscaped nature:

> animals grazing peacefully on a hillside, waves lapping gently up the pebble beach, a pine forest whistling in a storm, a river bursting its banks, a hurricane tossing houses and cars in the air like play-things, a bush fire raging out of control. (pp. 26–27)

These are very conventional instances, conforming to and limited by our cultural and mainly urbanized understandings of what 'real nature' is, and that is Adam's point. In fact these are not instances of nature itself. They are mediated *visualizations* of nature, and Durk Gorter (2006) reminds us that the term landscape conventionally refers either to an assemblage of natural features or to a pictorial representation of them (p. 82). Similarly, Hirsch (1995) notes 'the painterly origin of the landscape concept', which implies that there are different traditions and values operating behind particular artistic representations of landscapes (p. 2).

So we already have reason to think that we ought to be sensitive to the visualizations – the ways of seeing – that *linguistic* landscapes also entail in both their production and their consumption, as well as to any objective characteristics of their forms and distributions. Linguistic landscapes are visualizations of (mainly urban) modernity, and they can bring very different qualities of the contemporary urban experience into focus. As happy consumers, we might value linguistic landscapes as part of a bold, modern urban aesthetic (Judd and Fainstein, 1999). Alternatively, we might decry the denaturing of human environments (McNaughten and Urry, 1998). If we take this second stance, linguistic landscape starts to seem like an ironic concept. It refers to human agencies that have displaced natural landscapes and fashioned others in concrete and tarmac – paving paradise. Then they have overlaid language texts of various sorts on top of the built environment, sometimes creating images that are equivalent in scale and impact to natural landscapes. However we judge it, the visible languageing of towns and cities is a thoroughly contemporary global trend. It embodies contemporary ways of seeing urban spaces, not least for their commercial opportunity values, in branding and promotion and in asserting difference.

The most sustained analyses of linguistic landscapes so far have been mainly descriptive, interested in the distribution of linguistic text-types and forms in different cities (see Coupland, 2008 for a review). They have analysed the distribution of languages in bi- or multi-lingual contexts, and that is my own starting point here too. Bilingual Wales is an interesting setting for linguistic landscape research because of its rapidly changing political and sociolinguistic profiles. As I explain below, ideologies linked to language planning and policy are leaving their imprint on the visible environment in Wales, and the chapter is mainly an attempt to understand some of the 'ways of seeing Wales' that are inscribed in Welsh linguistic landscapes. Barbara Adam (1998) observes that, in the natural world, a landscape will sometimes function as a historical record of activity, human or non-human. She gives the example of lopsided, canted-over trees showing the influence over time of a prevailing wind direction and intensity. A landscape provides, she says, 'a record of reality-generating activity'; the visible phenomena making up a landscape have 'invisible constitutive activities inescapably embedded within them' (p. 54). I borrow this insight as a potentially useful approach to linguistic landscaping in Wales. What forces and processes have conspired to give Welsh linguistic landscapes their particular contemporary characteristics? Whose designs and priorities do they respond to? Are there competing value systems at work? How might they matter? In general, how are ideologies entextualized as linguistic landscapes in Wales?

The character of bilingualism in Wales can to some extent be read in this way, although we then move well beyond the simple indexical relationships that were mentioned in the original account of why we should study linguistic landscapes (Landry and Bourhis, 1997). Landry and Bourhis argued that language use in public signage tends to index the distinctive spoken language environment. So in Wales, having Welsh and English co-present in the Welsh landscape marks the status of Wales as 'a bilingual country'. If people perceive Welsh to be substantially present in the landscape, this might index the current revitalization of the Welsh language. This is a reasonable claim, and we certainly need to explore the metacultural functioning of linguistic landscapes – how, as cultural texts, they articulate the cultures that generate them. But my argument will be that some dominant characteristics of the Welsh linguistic landscape in fact point to an *aspirational* political ideology of 'true bilingualism', rather than to any objective realities of bilingual usage in Wales. If linguistic landscaping is underpinned by ideological processes, then we need to develop a less direct account of its indexical function and a more rounded understanding of metacultural processes. These arguments are taken up at the end of the chapter.

Sociolinguistic literatures have of course recognized that political and institutional influences shape linguistic landscapes. Peter Backhaus (2007) uses a conceptual distinction between 'top-down' and 'bottom-up' processes of influence (see also Gorter, 2006: 84ff.), referring to whether particular bilingual texts are (on the one hand) officially/municipally sanctioned/required 'from above', or (on the other hand) non-official or commercial initiatives 'from below'. But this distinction is a broad and difficult one. Top-down influence is clearly in evidence in Wales, not only in the government's policy documents pushing for 'a truly bilingual Wales' but also in specific bureaucratic interventions about how to design bilingual texts (see below). A good deal of the current Welsh bilingual landscape is directly influenced 'from above' via these institutional processes. Yet what should count as linguistic landscaping 'from below' is less clear, partly because commercial initiatives (which Backhouse considers to be 'from below') have their own 'from above' qualities, at least in my own reading of this concept. Most linguistic landscape texts are deeply commodified and commodifying artefacts. As I suggested above, they are often promotional texts in one sense or another, produced through processes of commercial design and marketing, not unlike many government-sponsored texts. But it is certainly possible to identify linguistic landscape texts that work outside of the remit of governmental authority, in less controlled and more creative ways.

The chapter examines an eclectic range of text-types, intended to illustrate some different genres of linguistic landscaping, both core and peripheral. Place-names, road signs and public notices can be considered core texts because they fall within the remit of national or local government policies and design principles. As just mentioned, a great deal of linguistic landscaping is an overt, 'from above' instrument of language planning in Wales. The principles on which these texts are generally designed shows rigidity and prescriptivism, and in some ways a naivety about how relationships between languages in multilingual environments are typically structured. For contrast, I then consider some T-shirt texts – landscaping in the same general sense of putting language on display in public arenas – produced by a small private company in Wales. These are peripheral texts, produced outside of dominant ideologies of language planning but still ideologically engaged. I will try, however, to maintain a distinction between 'core/periphery' and 'from above/from below'.

Bilingualism in Wales

The revitalization of the Welsh language in Wales makes it a rare and celebrated exception to the general pattern of minority languages suffering language shift and decline in a globalizing world. The demographics of Welsh language use are complex, and census data (including data from the 2001 national census in Wales, analysed by Aitchison and Carter in 2004) are difficult to interpret (Coupland, 2006). But there is a consensus of opinion that the number of self-declaring speakers of Welsh has stabilized, after a long twentieth century of steady decline, and that the number has begun to increase – to around 23 per cent of the population, which is more than half a million speakers. There was no decline in numbers (around 19 per cent) between the 1981 and 1991 censuses, but there was a detectable rise in 2001, largely attributable to the impact of compulsory learning of Welsh in secondary schools to age 16. Many of the 'new Welsh speakers' are young people in the urbanized south-east of Wales, which marks a major shift away from the pattern of Welsh being mainly transmitted through families in the 'heartland' areas in the rural north-west and south-west of the country. (Stages in the revitalization process are described in detail by Colin Williams [2001]; John Davies [2007] provides an authoritative historical overview; for a recent collection of empirical studies on Welsh see Coupland [forthcoming]; [Coupland and Aldridge, 2009].)

These gains have been won through a mix of direct action campaigns and, more recently, concerted policy initiatives led by Bwrdd Yr Iaith (The Welsh Language Board), which is now closely aligned with the devolved Welsh Assembly Government (WAG).[1] In 2008, WAG was in its third electoral term, having been originally established following a referendum in 1997. Through the Board, WAG has specific and detailed language planning designs in place. Its most comprehensive planning document is titled *Iaith Pawb* ('Everyone's Language'): *A National Action Plan for a Bilingual Wales*, and I refer to some of its text below.[2]

A particular set of language rights is formalized in a 1993 Act of (the UK) Parliament, which places a duty on public sector organizations in Wales to treat Welsh and English on an equal basis, when they provide services to the public in Wales. Local government services, post offices, universities, for example, are required to develop and maintain 'language schemes', detailing how they will make provision for the use of Welsh. The Act also gives Welsh speakers a right to speak Welsh in court, and places obligations on the Welsh Language Board to promote and monitor the use of Welsh. Because private sector organizations are not currently covered by the legislation, there is pressure from language activists and from some formal political quarters to draft a new Welsh language act, to widen the legislative remit of the existing Act and to strengthen the obligations it imposes. Other voices oppose such a move, usually mentioning the costs involved and the risks to economic competitiveness (cf. Ridler and Pons-Ridler, 1984).

In general, there are conflicting stances on how far and how fast Wales should travel towards a more consolidated bilingualism. It is commonly said that there is considerable 'good will towards Welsh' from most segments of Welsh society, including most monolingual English speakers, and this view is supported by research I have done with colleagues on attitudes to Welsh, both inside and outside Wales (Coupland, Bishop and Garrett, 2006; Coupland, Bishop, Evans and Garrett, 2006). The revitalization project is widely valued, although it is also felt to be inadequate by nationalist pressure groups such as Cymuned ('Community'), who are campaigning strongly against what they see as 'colonial' pressure being brought on Welsh-language 'heartlands', especially by 'English incomers' (Coupland and Bishop, 2006).[3]

The seeds to Welsh language revitalization were sown in the 1960s and 1970s in a period of wider ethno-political and nationalist awakening. A Welsh Secretary cabinet post in the Westminster government was created in 1964, which amounted to the first formal recognition that Wales deserved some distinctive political focus, however muted and inadequate it proved to be. This was also a period when the often bitter nationalist poetry of Saunders Lewis came to prominence, helping to galvanize what was a relatively ineffectual Welsh Nationalist Party, Plaid Cymru. Gwynfor Evans became Plaid's first elected MP in the 1966 Carmarthen by-election. Byddin Rhyddid Cymru ('the Free Wales Army'), a paramilitary group with tenuous links to the Irish Republican Army interested in burning second-homes in Wales and blowing up dams in Wales that provided water for English cities, was formed in Lampeter in 1963. After these haphazard but influential events, the institutionalization of a pro-Wales political consensus was in fact mainly carried forward by the Labour Party in Wales, whose members eventually campaigned successfully for a devolved Welsh Assembly.

Place-names in the Welsh landscape

Through the 1970s and progressively since then, Welsh linguistic landscapes have taken on new forms, and one key genre is the naming of places. Place-names are a significant focus for ideological work because they are very obviously metacultural resources. If a town has a 'Welsh' rather than an 'English' name, we might say it 'paints the town red' (red being the symbolic colour of Wales, as in the red dragon, the emblem on the national flag). Place-names have official status, appearing in authorized maps, guides and directories, and of course on road signs and on many commercial and public buildings. They are a key part of the visible cultural infrastructure. In spoken usage, they also have the quality of not being bound by the usual co-occurrence rules of language code use. That is, if a particular 'Welsh' place-name is the only version of that place's name, it must be used even if the matrix language is English. Welsh is thereby made more prominent even in an English-dominated sociolinguistic ecology, which is what we find in most of Wales.

I have scare-quoted 'Welsh' and 'English' because individual place-names cannot always be unambiguously assigned to either type. Town names in Wales fall into three broad types, related to historical patterns of Anglicization. One type, found mainly in South and Mid Wales, shows no influence from the Welsh language, as in Port Talbot, Swansea and Bridgend. Another type of name has been historically and continuously Welsh, mainly in the North and West of Wales, such as Llangollen, Caernarfon and Aberystwyth. A third type consists of Welsh-origin names that came to have conventional Anglicized forms, such as Carmarthen, Llanelly in its older spelling, Neath and Tenby. Several towns have had equivalent 'Welsh' and 'English' versions for some time, although using Anglicized or 'English' place-names, sometimes even in Welsh-language discourse, was common in earlier decades. In the selective list of geminated place-names, below, the 'English' forms in the first column have been the dominant forms of reference for Welsh people overall, although in some cases the between-language differences are minor, reflecting differences of grammaticalization (e.g. use of the definite article 'y') or spelling:

Abergavenny	Y Fenni
Barry	Y Barri
Brecon	Aberhonddu
Bridgend	Penybont
Ca(e)rnarvon	Caernarfon
Cardiff	Caerdydd
Cardigan	Aberteifi
Cardiganshire	Ceredigion
Fishguard	Abergwaun
Gower	Gwyr
Holyhead	Caergybi
Kidwelly	Cydweli
Lampeter	Llanbedr Pont-Steffan
Llandovery	Llanymddyfri
Milford Haven	Aberdaugleddau
Montgomery	Trefaldwyn
Newport	Casenewydd
Pembroke	Penfro
Port Talbot	Aberafan
Presteign	Llanandras
St Asaph	Llanelwy
St David's	Tyddewi
Snowdonia	Eryri
Swansea	Abertawe

Moves have been made since around 1970, and with particular vigour now, to assert and disseminate place-names of the sort listed in the second column above. This is a matter of promoting existing 'Welsh' versions, or (less frequently) of coining such versions when they have not existed, or of 'correcting' existing 'Welsh' versions that are considered to be inauthentic. One of the earliest linguistic manifestations of ethnolinguistic revitalization in Wales was the simple shift from the spelling of the place-name 'Llanelly' (a town in South-West Wales) to the spelling 'Llanelli'. The change respected the fact that word-final written *–y*, corresponding to the sound [i], is commonplace in English but not available in Welsh, where the letter *y* has different phonetic values. But a thorough programme of much more radical (re)Cymrification of Welsh place names began, and it was in full swing in 2008, supported by a complex institutional infrastructure run by Bwrdd Yr Iaith.

Sometimes Cymrification brings cultural references closer to the surface of place-names, for example when the name Caerfyrddin – a form that had currency among rural Welsh speakers in earlier decades – is given greater prominence alongside the previously dominant form Carmarthen (another South-West town). Caerfyrddin, analysable as 'caer' ('the fort') [of] 'Myrddin' ('Merlin') feeds off and into the Celtic mythology of Merlin the magician, and a Merlin festival for the region has been mooted. Road signs referring to the town of Neath acquired the parallel Welsh form Castell Nedd (implying 'the castle on the river Nedd'), which had been much less common in earlier Welsh usage. Bridgend had the equivalent Penybont ('the head of the bridge') and Tenby had Dinbych Y Pysgod ('Denbigh [or 'little town'] of the fish'). The result today is a rebranding of these and many other towns as 'more Welsh' or 'more bilingual' spaces.

Bwrdd Yr Iaith is currently driving forward a programme of place-name 'standardisation', via an established Standardisation Team working with regional Language Officers around Wales. The Team follows a set of *Guidelines for Standardising Place-names* which are available online.[4] Bwrdd Yr Iaith is not insensitive to the disruptive effects of neologisms or back-formations. Professor Hywel Wyn Owen of the Place-name Research Centre at Bangor University, speaking in an advisory capacity to the Association of Welsh Translators and Interpreters in 2002, mentioned the need to respect local uses of place-names, where possible.[5] He also commented that, in the designing of new Welsh place-name forms, 'laissez-faire won't do and neither will enforcement'. The Team's role is advisory only and their recommendations have to be decided on by local authorities. Owen also said that 'pedantic forms or antiquarian revivals should be rejected unless there is evidence that the revival has been accepted locally'.

Yet there is an over-riding ambition to 'correct' established anglicized spellings and lexicalizations, such as the name of Criccieth, a small town in North Wales, where standard Welsh orthography would specify the use of only one *c* in the middle of the word. Similarly with Cemmaes, to include only one *m*, but in this case also to replace *ae* with *ai*. Another example is pressure to replace the form Cader in the name of the mountain, Cader Idris, with Cadair, a familiar Welsh word meaning 'chair', the name then becoming more readily translatable as 'Idris's chair'. The earlier (and in fact still dominant) forms in the above examples are all long-standing usages that are nowadays subject to modification 'from above'. The Standardisation Team shows enthusiasm to 'rationalize' (it says) variation between older Anglicized place-names and to replace them with standardized Welsh forms, particularly where the linguistic differences involved are small. So, as happened earlier with the spelling of Llanelly/Llanelli, there is pressure to sustain only the 'properly Welsh' ways of referring to places such as Conwy (on the North Wales coast), although Conway has been and still is the heavily dominant spoken and written version. Similarly with Aberdyfi (over Aberdovey) and, in a current effort, Caerffili (over Caerphilly). It is likely that geminated names will persist for some time, however, in instances where there is greater interlingual distance, such as with Carmarthen/Caerfyrddin, Cardiff/Caerdydd (the national capital city) and Neath/Castell Nedd. In instances like these, the large majority of English-only speakers in Wales will probably continue to favour using the 'English' forms.

Overall, in the managed domain of place-names, there is concerted pressure to construct a 'more Welsh' linguistic landscape, either by supplanting Anglicized forms or by (re)imposing Welsh names alongside English ones. In fact this initiative is not limited to place-names inside Wales. It includes many place-names *outside* Wales, which the Team also seeks to standardize. So we see (e.g. in contemporary Welsh-language sports reporting on television) and hear (e.g. in train destination announcements) names like Caerfaddon for Bath, Briste for Bristol and Caeredin for Edinburgh.[6] If we look beyond the Welsh case for a moment, this pattern of naming of non-Wales places is not uncommon. In fact it is a rich field for studying sociolinguistic diversity, for example where English has invented and naturalized the use of distinctively Anglicized place-names like Gothenburg, Prague, The Hague and so on. But the ideological commitment in Wales to promote Welsh naming conventions within Welsh territory is not matched by a similar concern to preserve, for example, English conventions in the naming of English places. Here we see glimpses of the ideological contests that have been characteristic of Wales–England relations for centuries (R. Williams, 2003), resurfacing as struggles over linguistic landscape.

A specific ideology of bilingualism

The Welsh Assembly Government and Bwrdd Yr Iaith's main policy thrusts are (1) *material/technical* – to provide resources and help, e.g. for businesses and private sector institutions, towards bilingual provision and practice; (2) *educational* – to promote competence in Welsh through a comprehensive programme of teaching and learning at all levels of the education system; and (3) *language-ideological* – to engineer a positive public orientation through persuasion and argumentation in favour of bilingualism, so that 'right choices' will be made. But the question remains of what particular quality of bilingualism is being aspired to.

Bilingualism is realized in different societies in very different ways. Two (or more) languages can exist in conditions where most members of the community are competent speakers of both languages, or where very few of them are.

Status can be distributed evenly or entirely unevenly between languages and language groups, as in diglossic communities, as they were originally characterized by Charles Ferguson (1996). Wales was diglossic in the period when English was the 'high' variety, functionally specified as the language used in formal education and in business, with Welsh tending to be relegated to 'low' functions including use in family (but also religious) domains, and so on. Sociolinguistic accounts of bilingual situations inevitably document functional non-equivalences between languages – where particular languages fit into particular societal niches. Against this backdrop it is striking to find bilingualism being ideologized and aspired to as a sociolinguistic arrangement involving full equivalence between languages, and this is what we find in the Welsh Assembly Government's policy documents.

A principle of sociolinguistic equivalence was written into the 1993 Welsh Language Act. As we saw earlier, the Act placed a duty on the public sector to treat Welsh and English 'on an equal basis'. The ideology of equivalence reaches deep into planners' basic understanding of bilingualism, and into their specification of targeted outcomes. This is a laudable aim, even though sociolinguistic research suggests it is quite unlikely to be unattainable. Ironically enough, Iaith Pawb, the key policy document of the Welsh Assembly Government, has the Welsh title on the English version of the document without translation. But it is adamant about the importance of linguistic equivalence, as the following extracts show. I have added boldface for emphasis.

Extract 1: *Iaith Pawb*, Introduction: *Our Vision*

Our vision is a bold one and was set out in our policy statement on the Welsh language, *Dyfodol Dwyieithog: A Bilingual Future* published in July 2002. Our aspiration is expressed in the title of that document – **a truly bilingual Wales**, by which we mean a country where people can **choose** to live their lives through the medium of **either or both Welsh or English** and **where the presence of the two languages** is a source of pride and strength to us all. *Dyfodol Dwyieithog: A Bilingual Future* committed the Assembly Government to prepare and publish before the end of 2002 a national action plan which would set out in the clearest terms the strategy and the commitment of resources by which the goal of a bilingual Wales would be achieved. This document is that action plan.

Extract 2: *Iaith Pawb*, Section 2.15

But we want to look beyond mere numbers of people who can speak Welsh. We want Wales to be **a truly bilingual nation**, by which we mean a country where people can **choose** to live their lives through the medium of **either Welsh or English** and where **the presence of the two languages** is a **visible and audible** source of pride and strength to us all.

Extract 3: *Iaith Pawb*, Section 4.2

Iaith Pawb is the strategic framework which the Assembly Government will be implementing with local government, the Welsh Language Board and others. It focuses on:

- encouraging individuals to learn and use the Welsh language;
- extending access to Welsh medium education with initial emphasis on early years and post-16 sectors;
- empowering individuals **to make a genuine choice as to the language, or languages, through which they wish to live their lives**;
- an entitlement for all young people to a range of support services in **the language of their choice**;
- actively promoting the benefits of bilingualism.

These ambitious and in many ways impressive commitments foresee a bilingual community where Welsh and English are co-present and co-available in social life in Wales. 'A truly bilingual Wales' is the key phrase throughout the document. 'True bilingualism' is repeatedly defined in relation to 'choice' of Welsh or English. Iaith Pawb posits a citizenry empowered to make choices – indeed 'genuine choices' (Extract 3) – about code use, either overall or in specific social domains. 'Choice' is a keyword because, ideologically, it appears to redress the interventionist and authoritarian dimensions of policies shaping the bilingual sphere. 'Promoting' and 'encouraging' are also explicit formulations in Iaith Pawb (as in the above quotes), as they need to be; no-one thinks that choice alone is sufficient. But choice appears to open up a decision node between two parallel options – using Welsh or using English in free distribution.

These planning objectives of course go well beyond linguistic landscaping. But if 'the presence of the two languages' will be 'a source of pride and strength to us all' (Extract 1), and if 'the presence of the two languages' will be 'a visible and audible source of pride and strength to us all' (Extract 2), then there is a clear commitment to bilingual landscaping in one sense or another. Placenames, as we have seen, are emerging to be one important domain of ideological work, and one where issues of Welsh/English equivalencing can be directly relevant. But there are many others, including other sorts of public signage across Wales, bureaucratic materials (tax returns, vehicle licensing and electoral documents, etc.), education institutions' publicity, and so on. If we include the audible linguistic landscape (or soundscape), there may also be opportunities to construct 'truly bilingual' environments in public announcements, voicemail messages, automated queuing systems, and so on.

Parallel text bilingualism

Presenting both English and Welsh in parallel in landscape texts in Wales has already become firmly embedded as an ideological practice. Parallel text bilingualism is not only a textual design option; it is a fundamental aspiration of language planning in contemporary Wales. It is possible to format bilingual text, stylistically, following principles of parallelism in several different ways (see below), although some key principles underpin these designs. The main one is *equality*: Welsh and English must be given equal weighting and prominence, so that the same access is afforded to each language. *Equivalence* is interpreted in the specific sense that the textual content of Welsh and English must be identical; then once again *choice*, in the assumption that bilingual speakers/readers will be able to choose whether to access the content of a text either in Welsh or in English. A further principle is *code integrity*, requiring that Welsh and English text-elements must be presented as fully formed and separate from each other. Appeals to code integrity are what we saw being made in relation to place-name planning, where authentic Welsh lexis and 'correct' orthography is being imposed.

The ideology of parallel text bilingualism is in fact a very clear manifestation of standard language ideology (Milroy and Milroy, 1985; Lippi-Green, 1993), applied bilingually. It seeks to suppress variation within a code – various types of 'error' and unauthorized usage, in this case especially in relation to Welsh. But it also seeks to suppress variation in meaning between two codes in the same text, and variation in how linguistic meanings are accessed by users. Standard language ideology works through authentication and deauthentication – positing that only standard varieties are 'real' and have established historical validity, while claiming that non-standard varieties and blends are 'suspect' and 'ad hoc'. Standard language ideology surfaces in prescriptive (authenticating) documents and edicts. In May 2001, Bwrdd Yr Iaith published *A Guide to Bilingual Design*, and it runs an annual Bilingual Design Awards competition.[7] The Guide gives advice on typography and typefaces, for example how best to align Welsh and English text spatially, to cope with the two languages' different character sets. It offers seven different formats, which it refers to as 'standard layouts' for bilingual text. They are: 'parallel columns', 'parallel pages', 'block by block', 'top and bottom', 'back to back', 'tilt and turn' and 'consecutive'.

The *Guide to Bilingual Design* has a section on 'Language separation' (e.g. by colour or typeface), whose importance is explained in the following terms:

Extract 4: *Guide to Bilingual Design*, Section on *Language Separation*

> Ensuring that both languages are separated and easily identified is more critical if certain formats are chosen: block by block, parallel columns, or top and bottom. In these cases it is important that the two languages are not mixed in an inconsistent or haphazard way. Separation can be achieved in several ways – by using different colours, fonts or typefaces, or a combination of these.

This extract invokes, as standard language ideology always does, problems in understanding that it claims will arise from a 'mixing' of forms, a problem which standardization overcomes. Separate languages will be 'easier to identify', and so on. But there is also an implied dignifying and respectifying of language codes in this appeal to separateness. And because Welsh has, for centuries, been the stigmatized code in Wales, the appeal to parallelism is more particularly a move to validate *that* code. Here is the manual's introductory account of the advantages of parallel bilingual text.

Extract 5: *Guide to Bilingual Design*, Introduction

In the private and voluntary sectors, the choice of a bilingual approach will be made as a policy decision. Usually it will be based on perceived or proven advantages to the organisation. Here are some good reasons for making the choice:

- to emphasise the distinctive Welsh nature of an organisation or its products;
- to satisfy customer and client demand;
- to enhance customer service and care;
- to extend customer choice;
- to gain a PR or marketing edge;
- to enhance PR and harness goodwill at little extra cost.

These can all potentially lead to more business and goodwill.

Cost is often cited as a reason for not making more use of Welsh. However, through careful planning and by following the advice contained in this guide, additional direct costs can be kept to a minimum. Also the benefits, both financial and otherwise, of using Welsh should outweigh the additional expenditure.

These are promotional, commercial objectives. They identify one of the two main ideological domains in which parallel text bilingualism operates in Wales. Extending 'choice' in this context is a market-driven initiative. If consumers can be encouraged to make the right choices (which are choices of products and services, not of languages), organizations can 'gain a marketing edge'. What the *Guide to Bilingual Design* characterizes as 'good practice' is a set of design suggestions 'sponsored by Barclays' [Bank], with the English text set against a background of turquoise and the Welsh parallel text set against green. Turquoise is a principal global brand signifier of Barclays Bank; green is second only to red as the Welsh symbolic colour, and the colour 'field' in which the red dragon always figures. The other main ideological domain is bureaucratic prescription, where parallel texting is a requirement of government, filtered through public sector agencies. This is how we arrive at the bilingual designs of public signs that we shall look at shortly.

The 'equality' and so the 'parallelism' of some sorts of bilingual landscaping is subject to *policing* by Bwrdd Yr Iaith. Its panopticon includes the use of 'mystery customers' who (in 2002 at least) visited tourist attractions across Wales to assess 'the quality of bilingual service' in the sector. Similarly in 2003, the Board conducted a snapshot survey of bilingual websites. Its web-published results included a commentary on the inadequacies of South Wales Police's web presence – the police being policed, interestingly enough, for their use of language. Their site was found to lack addresses in Welsh, it had a less than 'fully bilingual' home page, and it failed to allow Welsh to 'penetrate into many of the site's levels'. The Welsh used was said to be 'a little stilted at times', and to show 'a lack of proofreading'.[8]

Parallel text public signage

Despite an insistence on equivalence, there are ideological cryptotypes – hidden, meaningful patterns – to be identified in parallel texts in Wales. Ron Scollon and Suzie Wong Scollon (2003), like Theo van Leeuwen (2005), draw attention to how textual placement can imply specific relationships between text elements, or in this case languages. So Welsh to the left of English might imply that Welsh is the given or already-familiar element, and in that sense favoured or at least more 'natural' – 'something already known to the receiver of the message and hence not in question' (Van Leeuwen, 2005: 204). Welsh above English, in Van Leeuwen's account of the semiotics of verticality, gives it the status of being an 'ideal' or 'idealized' element of the message. These claims deserve detailed empirical attention. But we can safely say that, whether or not left and top actually signify priority, and whether or not users interpret texts this way, there is ample evidence in Wales landscape data that designers *believe* that this sort of prioritization effects exist. They implement design principles of exactly this sort.

Going back to the *Guide to Bilingual Design* (2001), it is interesting that the manual regularly prioritizes Welsh over English, spatially, even though it is silent about this as a design principle. I presume this is because to prioritize one language over another undermines the espoused principle of equality. But Welsh and English quite commonly enter into planned priority relationships in Wales' landscapes. For example, English-first patterns dominate in Cardiff, and this relates to the character of bilingualism in the Welsh capital. Cardiff has historically been heavily Anglicized and is massively English-dominant in its demographics, and very largely remains so despite significant new advances of the sort I mentioned earlier.[9] In fact we can identify some intriguing new landscape isoglosses in bilingual signage in Wales. For example, travelling along the M4 motorway in South Wales, to the west of Swansea (in much of South-West Wales, then, although not in the extreme West) we find a regular pattern of displaying Welsh-first road-signs, with Caerfyrddin above Carmarthen and so on. On the other hand in South-East Wales, along the same motorway, the pattern shifts to English-first, into and past Cardiff.

Figures 3.1, 3.2 and 3.3 capture the flavour of other sorts of bilingual public signs and notices in Wales. Figure 3.1 shows (vertically) English-first bilingual signs directing pedestrians in Cardiff. Figure 3.2 is another multi-item sign, above the exit from Cardiff railway station, but this time giving Welsh priority

FIGURE 3.1 Pedestrian direction signs in Cardiff

FIGURE 3.2 Railway station exit sign in Cardiff

FIGURE 3.3 Stamp machine in a Carmarthen shopping street

(horizontally), which is unusual in the capital city. Figure 3.3, from Carmarthen/ Caerfyrddin, shows parallel use of Welsh and English on a stamp machine in a main shopping street. All its permanent text elements are repeated bilingually, with priority given this time to Welsh, which is consistent with the 'heartland' location (in a part of Wales where there is a denser proportion of Welsh speakers and arguably stronger ethnolinguistic identification).[10] Signs in Figures 3.1 to 3.3 fall within the responsibility of public sector or quasi public sector institutions – Cardiff City Council, National Rail and the Royal Mail. So we should expect to see bilingual landscapes that articulate the priorities of the 1993 Act, the WAG and Brwdd Yr Iaith, and 'equivalence' between languages in particular. What we in fact find is that the principle of equivalence is to some extent undermined by the text design – crytotypically giving priority to one language or another through the sequencing of languages.

The issue here is not purely the ideological prioritization of languages. Many paired words and phrases in the parallel languages in Figures 3.1 to 3.3 have very small interlingual distance between them, and in these cases parallel texting invites inferencing about its ideological underpinnings. Syntax apart, Stadiwm y Mileniwn and Millennium Stadium are very close in their authorized orthographic and phonological forms, Welsh and English. One needs to appreciate the value and legitimacy of independent linguistic systems in order to avoid the reaction that the formal duality is redundant or 'pedantic' (see the quotation from Hywel Wyn Owen, above). In fact, the taxi/tacsi instance was pilloried by the reactionary novelist Kingsley Amis (1986), in his book *The Old*

Devils, betraying a decided lack of sociolinguistic empathy and awareness. He quipped that taxi/tacsi was 'for the benefit of Welsh people who had never seen a letter x before', a comment based in a crass, exclusionary ideology of monolingualism. It entirely misses the meanings of egalitarianism and linguistic entitlement that bilingual landscapes can symbolize. Even so, Amis-like interpretations, or the less derisory view that parallel text bilingualism is 'just for show', remain an unfortunate potential consequence of a strict standard language ideology and a narrow and formalist interpretation of linguistic equivalence.

To look at this issue more constructively, we can say that the value of a bilingual landscape increases in proportion to the *diversity* of cultural meanings that are articulated from the different resources of the languages in question. Form-focussed bilingualism, when it is over-played, risks trivializing the value of bilingualism itself. With that positive criterion in mind, we would look for aspects of bilingual landscape texts that make creative use of the grammatical, semantic and cultural resources of both Welsh and English.

A very simple instance of creative bilingual entextualization is the image in Figure 3.4, which exploits the language-typological differences of Welsh – an OV (object-verb) language – and English – a VO language. It is characteristic of OV languages to place classifier nouns before head nouns, and this allows a head noun that can be interpreted as such in both languages to be preceded by a Welsh classifier and to be followed by an English classifier, in a three-part structure. 'BIZZ' is an informal neologism, a short-form for 'business', that isn't a standard word in either language, but it seems to capture the informal atmosphere of the social club that it brands. Although 'CLWB' and 'CLUB' are very

FIGURE 3.4 Clwb Bizz in Carmarthen

FIGURE 3.5 Subway sign at Cardif railway station

close standard forms in the respective languages, the text avoids the dullness of standard language equivalencing. The three-part syntactic device exploits the physical design of this particular window frame, although it is quite commonly seen in other contexts.

Another interesting example of a blending of Welsh and English is a large sign that for many years has graced the subway at Cardiff railway station (Figure 3.5), directing travellers to the platform areas. I don't know whether its origin was as a typographical error or not, but it manages to present itself as some sort of creative bilingual blend. It avoids subordinating itself either to standard English (by using the two 'f's in 'platfforms', which are used in standard Welsh to write the 'f' sound) or to standard Welsh (the 's' plural on 'platfforms' is an English morpheme, not a Welsh one).[11]

Cowbois.com

The 'Platfforms' text is particularly striking because, like the texts in Figures 3.1, 3.2 and 3.3, it falls within the institutional remit of a quasi public sector institution. As a private members' club, not subject to the prescriptions of Bwrdd Yr Iaith, BIZZ (in Figure 3.4) is freer to innovate. But there are business opportunities specifically in exploiting bilingual creativity itself. Semiosis can be marketed, and one way of selling in Wales is to develop and market bits of linguistic landscape that hint at and play with the bilingual environment in Wales and the cultural history that has created it. That is, Barbara Adam's (1998: 54) idea, that landscapes can have 'invisible constitutive activities inescapably embedded within them', might be used to trigger metacultural awareness and, incidentally, turn a profit.

An example is the small company Cowbois, based in Y Bala (Bala, in English) in North Wales, that sells Wales-themed T-shirts by mail order via the web. Figures 3.6 to 3.8 are examples of their products.[12]

One of Cowbois' texts is Merched Beca ('Beca's girls' or 'daughters'), although it is sometimes printed in script that obscures and challenges this 'standard Welsh' representation. The version in Figure 3.6 omits an E, has

FIGURE 3.6 Merched Beca T-shirt (Cowbois)

FIGURE 3.7 Bachwr T-shirt on a female (Cowbois)

FIGURE 3.8 República de Gales T-shirt (Cowbois)

uneven spacing and uses 8, 4 and a reversed 3 in place of alphabetic letters.[13] The text is playfully mystificatory. It throws out a linguistic and metacultural challenge. Can you read the text and do you have any idea what it refers to, historically and culturally? This is, then, a portable and talkable bit of linguistic landscape. It is textually monolingual (Welsh), but far from standardly so. It includes no English text, but it refers obliquely to historical English–Welsh antagonisms. Beca (Rebecca) is the key figurehead in the historical context of the Rebecca Riots of 1839–1843, when men, tenant farmers, dressed as women to attack the tollgates where tolls were charged to use roads in Wales. The Rebecca Riots were a moment of opposition to authority enshrined in English law, when tolls were probably paid to English-speaking landowners. Rebecca is a moral cause more than an actual person, said to have derived from a passage in the Bible where Rebecca talks of the need to 'possess the gates of those who hate them' (Genesis 24:60).

'Bachwr' (Figure 3.7) is a Welsh word linked to the verb *bachu*, sometimes meaning 'to grapple'; the *-wr* suffix is a personalizer, hence it means 'one who grapples'. The meaning was extrapolated relatively recently to refer to the person playing in the middle of the front row in rugby. The number 2 on the T-shirt in Figure 3.7, above BACHWR, is the shirt-number always worn by the person playing in the middle of the front row. The first level of metacultural mystification here is to invoke the world of rugby, an iconic Welsh practice, through an image of someone wearing a T-shirt that is clearly not a rugby shirt. This raises potentially interesting dissonances between the physique of a male shirt wearer and that of a stereotypical front row rugby forward, who would be heavily-built and look combative. The semiosis is deeper and much more ironic, however, when a Bachwr shirt is worn by a female (as in Figure 3.7). The recoverable meanings now require a further layer of interpretation. If we get the rugby reference, we probably get to the English word 'hooker', the name of the person who packs down in the middle of the front row, who 'hooks' the ball back when it is fed into the scrum. Then we find another possible referent for the form 'hooker' – a woman ironically labelling herself as a sex worker. The bachwr shirt therefore manages to refer to Welsh cultural sporting mythologies of sport, then to overlay issues of gender and sexuality on top of them, and bring all this up for fleeting metacultural reassessment. Having said that, such inferential chains will probably be followed in different ways by different users and viewers.

Cowbois also make use of Spanish texts, but still in reference to cultural values in Wales. *República de Gales* (Figure 3.8) is a dense reference to a republican political quest – for Wales to become an independent democratic state in Europe, perhaps. It also possibly refers to the struggle for republicanism in Spain through the Spanish Civil War, 1936–1939s, and to the involvement of many Welsh republican sympathizers who fought against the Franco regime. The use of Spanish raises several inferences. By avoiding both Welsh and English text, it presents the hypothesis of a Welsh state from a Spanish or mainland-European perspective. If we read the text as a spatially-defining label (in the way that place-name signs announce the actuality and location of towns or cities), it functions as an announcement that a Welsh state has already been achieved, and the cultural 'feel' in North-West Wales (where Cowbois is based) might be consistent with this announcement. So by an indirect route, *República de Gales* brings us back to the familiar historical antagonisms that we referred to above in connection with Beca.

'From above' and 'from below'

The Cowbois T-shirts and the selective instances of public signage in Wales that we have looked at are landscape texts that feature in very different contexts of production and reception. They carry their meanings to different groups of users, from different sources, for different purposes. Cowbois.com is a commercial venture that trades off ironic, creative and deeply coded textual representations of cultural values and antagonisms. Public sector signage is an institutional articulation of an explicit and prescribed set of legislative and language planning principles. Looking at these text-types in the same analysis, I am in danger of being criticized for trying to compare apples and oranges, although (as with apples and oranges) we could argue about whether there are more similarities than differences involved. All the texts we have considered find their cultural values in the complex language-ideological mix of contemporary Wales. But in the contrasts between the different genres we get, I hope, some insight into the different ways of seeing, and the different reality-generating activities, that make linguistic landscapes function the way they do. In particular, the contrast might press us to reconsider the 'from above/from below' distinction which strikes me as a fundamental question behind the concept of a linguistic landscape.

We need to see *all* linguistic landscaping as generated 'from above', if, as I propose, this means that it is conditioned by language-ideological forces and strategies that find value in putting linguistic text into the visible environment for some particular purpose. Place-name planning and what I have been calling parallel text bilingualism are clear and specific official/municipal responses to a set of ideological assumptions about what a 'truly bilingual Wales' is and should be, imposed from above through the core institutional activity of language planning. We were able to read off these ideological principles quite directly from Iaith Pawb and from other key documents that influence the designing of road-signs and public notices in contemporary Wales. Parallel texting is intended to fulfil an ideological commitment to linguistic equality, equivalence, code integrity and, above all, offering an apparently straightforward choice between the use of Welsh and English.

I made the point that, overall, this is a standard language ideology, applied bilingually, and it is to be expected that an ideology of standardization will constrain public displays of written language. But the pressure to set texts using both languages in close (and sometimes covertly prioritized) relationships to each other introduces its own risks. Standard language ideology is often claustrophobic, and paralleling dulls the creative edge of bilingualism. The way standard language ideology suppresses variation sometimes lays it open to the change of being pedantic and overly institutionalized. To my mind these are rather general risks to the revitalization of Welsh, beyond the issue of landscape itself. The sometimes exclusionary attitudes of first-language speakers to Welsh learners' 'inauthentic' Welsh speech (Robert, 2009) and over-exuberant 'anti-colonial' attitudes to 'English incomers' and their linguistic non-conformity to idealized Welsh norms (Cymuned.net) pattern this way too.

Government-led ideologies of language in Wales are also highly marketized. We saw that Iaith Pawb envisions a truly bilingual Wales coming about through the exercise of 'genuine choice' between languages in all segments of society, much as consumers exercise choice between products in competitive markets, supposedly leading to economic growth. This would appear to be more than a superficial aspect of how planning texts are written, in that many other trappings of 'free market capitalism' and neo-liberal discourse feature in promotional initiatives in Wales. We have language mentoring, targets, promotional campaigns and attainment monitoring, and of course there is real economic payoff for Welsh speakers in many workplace domains. But neo-liberal and globalist discourse and its rhetoric of choice and competition hide the fact that there are winners and losers in competitive markets (Fairclough, 2006: 60), and I have already suggested that 'choice' between languages is in any case a sociolinguistically compromised concept. It is not without precedent for well-meaning and dynamic language planning initiatives to give rise to unforeseen inequalities (Tollefson, 1991).

Taken together, a marketized model of planning and the aspiration to a form-focused, parallel text bilingualism may well prove to be too restrictive in Wales. Reinvigorating Wales and the Welsh language is more than a matter of putting more (and more standardized) Welsh into the landscape alongside English and equivalencing up to English. Complementing rather than paralleling, maximizing the different cultural resources of both Welsh and English, and finding cultural value in the interplay between languages, are likely to be more productive. Planning for diversity requires an open ideological stance that is not yet in evidence, and it will also mean taking the debate beyond the linguistic and social categories of Welsh and English themselves (Williams, Evans and O'Leary, 2003).

Metacultural vitality is certainly what we see in the Cowbois texts. Cowbois recycle language ideologies too, although in the examples we have considered they steer well clear of authorized forms and planned equivalences. The appeal of their texts is that you have to work at unravelling their ideological sources and trajectories. They are intriguingly dense metacultural projections. Some of their political orientations are actually not that different from Bwrdd Yr Iaith's: they are strongly pro-Wales and pro-Welsh and in their own ways they take a stand against English hegemony. But they expose historical and contemporary *non*-equivalences between Welsh and English, rather than relying on a textual metaphor of free-choice bilingualism. They engage, ironically and obliquely, in the ideological contest that has defined Wales, rather than merely flooding the linguistic landscape of Wales with formalist parallelisms. They *don't* assume that linguistic text has direct indexicality.

In their small-scale commercial field, Cowbois generate their texts 'downwards' too, in the service of ideological stances, through self-conscious design, but most definitely outside the confines of government prescriptions. It is interesting to speculate about what the market appeal of parallel text representations of Welsh and English, on T-shirts or elsewhere, could possibly be, and there probably isn't any. The perceived value of much parallel texting in Wales seems to be vicarious – simply that it signals conformity to an established core governmental approach, taken on trust. This may be why several banks and other private sector organizations (which are not currently under a legal obligation to deal with clients bilingually) are going that way in their public signage. In the much less strongly institutionalized periphery, where Cowbois operate, conformity can give way to creativity and indirect indexicality.

As I noted above, this leaves me in the position of being unable to identify any forms of linguistic landscaping that do *not* have a 'downward' direction of reality generation – department store notices, magazine covers, bumper stickers and so on. The most vernacular landscape text-types, which might include bodily tattoos, hand-written small-ad notes in corner shop windows or the cries of street vendors, will typically lack authority to impose themselves and institutional weight. We might refer to these as 'grassroots' landscape initiatives, but even these instances, which certainly merit investigation, are likely to show the defining characteristic of linguistic landscaping: it services an ambition to make a planned impact on others by designing language texts 'downwards' into public spaces.

In Wales we have the luxury of being able to sustain a critical debate about the merits and demerits of minority language planning ideologies, against a backdrop of what seems to be a fairly buoyant revitalization of the Welsh language. It remains to be seen how much more deeply the government's ideology of 'true bilingualism' will penetrate into Welsh cultural life. I have been pointing to its limitations mainly on aesthetic grounds – that it is a rather dull and unattractive model of how languages should inter-relate in a bi- or multilingual country. But a more serious objection might become relevant. It is that, for all the current rhetoric of 'one Wales', Wales might move towards being a non-community where Welsh people, confronted with the 'choice' of leading their lives through Welsh or English, align themselves with different, parallel conceptions of being Welsh.

Acknowledgements

I am grateful to Adam Jaworski and Crispin Thurlow for their extremely helpful critical input into an earlier draft. A version of this chapter was presented at Sociolinguistics Symposium 16 in Limerick, July 2006.

Notes

1 See http://www.bwrdd-yr-iaith.org.uk/ (accessed 27 August 2009).
2 See http://www.bwrdd-yr-iaith.org.uk/cynnwys.php?pID=109&langID=2&nID=96 (accessed 27 August 2009).
3 See http://cymuned.net/blogsaesneg/?page_id=21 (accessed 27 August 2009).
4 See http://www.bwrdd-yr-iaith.org.uk/cynnwys.php?pID=109&nID=2461&langID=2 (accessed 27 August 2009).
5 The text of Owen's lecture is available at http://www.bwrdd-yr-iaith.org.uk/cynnwys.php?pID=109&nID=2272&langID=2 (accessed 27 August 2009).
6 The Standardisation Team's guidelines for selecting the names of capital cities/cities outside Wales is available at http://www.bwrdd-yr-iaith.org.uk/cynnwys.php?pID=109&nID=2439&langID=2 (accessed 27 August 2009).
7 Details of the scheme and its underlying principles are available at http://www.bwrdd-yr-iaith.org.uk/cynnwys.php?pID=109&nID=2588&langID=2. The Guide itself is available at http://www.industry.visitwales.co.uk/upload/pdf/a_guide_to_bilingual_design.pdf (accessed 27 August 2009).
8 http://www.bwrdd-yr-iaith.org.uk/cynnwys.php?pID=109&nID=215&langID=2 (accessed 27 August 2009).

[9] I am aware of using the English version of this place-name, which is majority usage, though of course not uncontentious.

[10] The unplanned presence of the Coke cup in this photo is deeply ironic. It perhaps suggests that even the most assiduous language-ideological plans cannot counter the onward march of globalized English among language users, assuming for the moment that 'Coke' is an English word.

[11] Perhaps the best example of creative non-parallelism in recent years is the celebrated bilingual inscription in large letters on the Wales Millennium Centre:

CREU GWIR ('Creating truth') IN THESE STONES
FEL GWYDR ('like glass') HORIZONS
O FFWRNAIS AWEN ('from the furnace of inspiration') SING

People sometimes fail to identify the precise boundaries between Welsh and English and regularly assume that Welsh and English elements 'mean the same'. In fact it is the suggestive interplay between juxtaposed Welsh and English elements that gives the text its creative power.

[12] I am very grateful to Wyn ap Gwilym and to Cowbois, Gweithdai Penllyn, Stryd Y Plase, Y Bala, Gwynedd LL23 7SW, for supplying these images and for giving permission for them to be reproduced here.

[13] In a personal note, Adam Jaworski suggests that the styling of Merched Beca, with the omitted 'E', self-consciously deviant spacing, and the use of 'wrong' letters/combining of letters and numbers, seems to appropriate features of grass-roots literacy and new media spelling, as in text messaging. Also that this simultaneously creates an archaic and contemporary/sophisticated feel. I very much agree with this stylistic analysis, but have reservations about the 'grassroots' status of these commercial entextualizations, which might be better described as stylized appropriations of grassroots design.

References

Adam, B. (1998), *Timescapes of Modernity: The Environment and Invisible Hazards.* London: Routledge.

Aitchison, J. and Carter, H. (2004), *Spreading the Word: The Welsh Language 2001.* Talybont: Y Lolfa.

Amis, K. (1986), *The Old Devils.* London: Hutchinson.

Bakhaus, P. (2007), *Linguistic Landscapes: A Comparative Analysis of Urban Multilingualism in Tokyo.* Clevedon: Multilingual Matters.

Coupland, N. (2006), Review of John Aitchison and Harold Carter (eds) (2004), 'Spreading the Word: The Welsh Language 2001'. Talybont, Ceredigion: Y Lolfa Cyf. *Language in Society,* 35(3), 449–453.

—(2008), Review of P. Bakhaus (2007), *Linguistic Landscapes: A Comparative Analysis of Urban Multilingualism in Tokyo* and D. Gorter (ed.) (2006), *Linguistic Landscape: A New Approach to Multilingualism. Journal of Sociolinguistics,* 12(2), 250–254.

—(forthcoming), *Language, Identity and Performance: Sociolinguistic Perspectives on Wales.* Cardiff: University of Wales Press.

Coupland, N. and Aldridge, M. (eds). (2009), 'Sociolinguistic and subjective aspects of Welsh in Wales and its diaspora', Thematic issue of *International Journal of the Sociology of Language*, 195.

Coupland, N. and Bishop, H. (2006), 'Ideologising language and community in post-devolution Wales', in J. Wilson and K. Stapleton (eds), *Devolution and Identity*. Burlington, VT: Ashgate, pp. 33–50.

Coupland, N., Bishop, H. and Garrett, P. (2006), 'One Wales? Reassessing diversity in Welsh ethnolinguistic identification', *Contemporary Wales*, 18, 1–27.

Coupland, N., Bishop, H., Evans, B. and Garrett, P. (2006), 'Imagining Wales and the Welsh language: Ethnolinguistic subjectivities and demographic flow', *Journal of Language and Social Psychology*, 25(4), 351–376.

Davies, J. (2007), *A History of Wales*. Harmondsworth: Penguin.

Fairclough, N. (2006), *Language and Globalization*. London: Routledge.

Ferguson, C. (1996), *Sociolinguistic Perspectives: Papers on Language in Society, 1959–1994* (T. Huebner, ed.). New York: Oxford University Press.

Gorter, D. (ed.) (2006), *Linguistic Landscape: A New Approach to Multilingualism*. Clevedon: Multilingual Matters.

Hirsch, E. (1995), 'Landscape: Between space and place', In E. Hirsch and M. O'Hanlon (eds), *The Anthropology of Landscape: Perspectives on Place and Space*. Oxford: Oxford University Press, pp. 1–30.

Judd, D. R. and Fainstein, S. S. (eds) (1999), *The Tourist City*. New Haven, CT: Yale University Press.

Landry, R. and Bourhis, R. (1997), 'Linguistic landscape and ethnolinguistic vitality: an empirical study', *Journal of Language and Social Psychology*, 16, 23–49.

Lippi-Green, R. (1993), *English with an Accent: Language, Ideology and Discrimination in the United States*. London: Routledge.

McNaughten, P. and Urry, J. (1998), *Contested Natures*. London: Sage.

Milroy, J. and Milroy, L. (1985), *Authority in Language: Investigating Language Prescription and Standardisation*. London: Routledge.

Ridler, N. B. and Pons-Ridler, S. (1984), 'Language economics: A case study of French', *Journal of Multilingual and Multicultural Development*, 5(1), 57–63.

Robert, E. (2009), 'Accommodating "new" speakers? An attitudinal investigation of L2 speakers of Welsh in south-east Wales', *International Journal of the Sociology of Language*, 195, 93–115.

Scollon, R. and Wong Scollon, S. (2003), *Discourse in Place: Language in the Material World*. London: Routledge.

Tollefson, J. (1991), *Planning Language, Planning Inequality*. New York: Longman.

Van Leeuwen, T. (2005), *Introducing Social Semiotics*. London: Routledge.

Williams, C. (2001), *Language Revitalization: Policy and Planning in Wales*. Cardiff: University of Wales Press.

Williams, C., Evans, N. and O'Leary, P. (eds) (2003), *A Tolerant Nation: Exploring Ethnic Diversity in Wales*. Cardiff: University of Wales Press.

Williams, R. (2003), *Who Speaks for Wales?* Cardiff: University of Wales Press.

Chapter 4

Ideological Struggles on Signage in Jamaica

Susan Dray

Roadside signs are typically short on linguistic content. This is not surprising given the limited amount of time that motorists or pedestrians can be expected to spend reading them. Producers of signs capitalize on local systems of meaning-making that go beyond the linguistic inscription in order to communicate effectively with the target audience in the time and space limitations of this public landscape. Socio-cultural systems of meaning convey values and beliefs through the materials and technologies of inscription as well through a sign's physical location and its social functions.

Work on multimodal communication (Kress and van Leeuwen, 1996), and on signage (Backhaus, 2007; Scollon and Wong Scollon, 2003) has tended to examine systems of meaning in the visual landscapes of what Milroy (2001) calls 'standard language cultures', where there is a consensus within the monolingual or multilingual society about the functions and form of the local standard language(s). This chapter explores the relationship between the visual language of signage and other systems of meaning-making in Jamaica – a society with a very different language situation. Frequently defined as diglossic (Ferguson, 1964), Jamaicans live with two language varieties which are perceived to be socially differentiated forms of the same language. The 'high' or standard language is associated with formal and high status functions such as governance and education and the associated written forms. The 'low' or vernacular variety is associated with conversational and everyday functions. Non-formal, 'everyday' writing is not recognized within this ideological frame and consequently the functional boundary between the high and low language forms is clear: the vernacular is considered to be 'unwritable'.

The diglossic model falls into the same ideological trap as the speakers it describes, who recognize as 'writing' only those texts that conform to the standard. The model presents the functions and uses of low and high language forms as a dichotomy and conflates speakers' perceptions with its own taxonomy, failing to recognize the existence of written forms of the non-standard vernacular as 'writing'. This effectively delegitimizes these signs and closes off the possibility of investigating the spaces in the society where they may have legitimacy (Dray, 2004). This is part of the hegemonic project at work in a society, and although recent work on non-standard written language has begun to expose the spaces where it is a powerful (although usually playful) visual medium for asserting social identities (Androutsopoulos, 2000; Jaffe, 2000; Thurlow, 2003), the focus has so far been on marginalized groups – especially young people and linguistic minorities – in standard language cultures. This chapter explores further the functions of non-standard language in Jamaican society where speakers of the local creole vernacular are in the majority and although linguistically 'marginalized' perhaps from a global perspective, have access to the semiotic resources available along the roadside that enables island-wide influence on the national landscape.

Jamaica is usually described as an English-speaking island, although the majority of the population speaks a non-standard Creole as a first language, known locally as Patois. Jamaican Creole is grammatically distinct from its lexifier language, English, but hegemonic discourses, both within Jamaica as well as extra-nationally, perpetuate the notion that it is a dialect of English and it is commonly viewed as 'bad' English. In this chapter I use the term 'standard language' to refer to the largely invariant, codified orthography of Standard English.[1] Any spelling that falls outside of this code has been classed as non-standard. This method for identifying non-standard vernacular written forms on signage is not necessarily aligned with the local Jamaican view of what constitutes Standard English. For example, the government sign in Figure 4.1 contains the vernacular element *walk good* as an integral and equal element of the main message of the sign. 'Walk good' is a Creole phrase meaning 'safe journey'. It has become reappropriated in the speech of Jamaican English speakers and is no longer stigmatized in the same way as other phrases still associated with the vernacular. The civil servant who designed this sign considered this phrase to be English, not Creole (Dray, 2004), as did the majority of Jamaican linguistics students I consulted.

There is a common perception in Jamaica that all signage is written in English. Jamaican English speakers and Creole speakers alike informed me that I would not be able to find any signs written in Creole, as a result of a belief that Creole

FIGURE 4.1 Government road sign (metal, seen on all main roads)

should not, or could not, be written. Such local interpretations highlight the difficulties with assigning semiotic frameworks across cultures and speech communities and reinforce the significance of recognizing local reappropriations of linguistic forms and the ways in which values associated with these forms may also change.

Local systems of meaning: Inscription and place

Systems of meaning on signage are achieved through the interplay between the visual arrangement of marks or inscriptions (Kress and van Leeuwen, 1998), and the materials and technologies used to produce these inscriptions and their emplacement in the physical world (Scollon and Wong Scollon, 2003). Building on this, in Dray (2004) I argue that the choice of inscription materials and technologies and the arrangement of marks inscribed on a surface depend in part on the location of the communicative exchange being performed by the sign in a particular social activity and the nature of the relationship between the producer and receiver of the sign.

To illustrate how this works consider, for example, a situation in which I was involved where a public bar was the venue for a private party. The bar had a dress code forbidding bare torsos and untidiness, which was usually communicated to customers through a sign at the entrance to the establishment saying 'No shirt, no service'. For the party, this information needed to be communicated to the invitees before they arrived at the bar to ensure their attendance. The difficulty was that while there was an established phrase in English, typically associated with the discourse of written invitations – 'Dress code applies' – this was not suitable for the cultural context in which this party was taking place – in rural Jamaica where the local 'dress code' was not only much less formal than that implied by the English phrase, but may also have been an unfamiliar phrase to some invitees. The nearest local equivalent phrase, 'No shirt, no service', was not suitable because of the need to shift the site of communicative exchange from the bar to the homes of the invitees and also because of the illocutionary force of the message. The nature of the relationship between the party's host, who wanted people to attend, the bar owner, who wanted people to buy drinks, and the invitees, who had the choice to stay at home, meant that the directive needed to be mitigated. To avoid misunderstandings and causing offence a vernacular phrase – 'Pretty up yuself or yuh nah get in' (Pretty yourself up or you won't get in) was chosen. This phrase playfully draws on the vernacular language of everyday life in order to negotiate the need to express regulations without appearing authoritative. This discoursal strategy is recognized by Fairclough (1994), referring to institutional language, as 'conversationalization'. It is the systematic manipulation of informal and familiar ways of speaking or writing, that is typical of everyday conversation, and employed to achieve a strategic aim.

In this invitation the only conversationalized element of the text was the phrase referring to the dresscode. The non-standard orthography of this phrase intentionally distanced it from the rest of the standard text and the intention was further emphasized by the fact that the invitations were word-processed. This technology is associated with standard language practices and the clear demarcation at phrase level between the standard and the vernacular served to present the message as light-hearted, which potentially compromised the importance of the message, but nevertheless sustained good relations.

In standard language cultures it would not be unreasonable to expect that the majority of roadside signage drawing on a local non-standard vernacular would be undertaking a strategic mission through the process of conversationalization. Typical examples would be slogans on advertisements. On Jamaican signs it is possible to identify other approaches to using the vernacular and these are outlined below. Figure 4.2 provides an example of a sign in which Creole elements conversationalize the sign but not in an attempt to conceal the strategic intentions of selling produce and controlling the financial behaviour of the customer, but rather as a means by which to overtly convey these to a local audience.

Throughout this sign non-standard combinations of upper and lower case letters, the variable spacing between words and lines and the unlevel lines of text visually signal a non-standard orthography. The sign is peppered with

FIGURE 4.2 Sign nailed to a roadside fruit and vegetable stall (see colour plate section)

vernacular forms and other than the standard plural inflection *-s* on fruits and vegetables, the first half of the text represents the local vernacular (which does not mark possessives or plurals), with Standard English writing conventions. The second half of the sign draws on the standard written phrase, typically associated with public signage 'strictly no . . .'. This conversationalizes the message through the phonetically motivated representation of the vernacular pronunciation of strictly (STRiCLY). Additional non-linguistic triggers reinforce the message. The 'O' in 'NO' which is humorously drawn as a shouting face, emphasizes the categorical stance with which the use of cash is insisted. In addition, the black border around the larger letters informing of no credit draws reader's attention to this part of the sign.

However, it may be the case that the primary benefit of this sign to the stall holder is in the material existence of the sign itself, rather than in the visual content: The old piece of board, probably an off-cut from a large sheet typically used for flooring and the lack of colour in the hand-painted inscription might be interpreted as not contributing much to the reputation of the business, but in fact this might not be an accurate local reading. The linguistic resources used in this sign are fully adequate to communicate effectively in the local culture in which the sign was produced, and although it is 'non-standard' in several dimensions (material, spelling, punctuation, layout) it may not necessarily lose authority as a result. Blommaert (2005) terms such localized practices of representing linguistic resources visually as 'grassroots literacy', noting that the artefacts produced do not necessarily translate well across cultures or scales, where the values attributed to the written artefact, and more specifically, its content and function, become evaluated with an external set of criteria. Some stall holders I spoke with viewed their vernacular-influenced signs as English, stating that the sign was necessary because its existence showed that the stall was a serious business, even though the message inscribed on the sign did not appear to be necessary. In some cases it was the material existence of the sign, rather than its communicative content, which was deemed more beneficial for trade because it indexed a genuine commercial activity.

The material presentation of a sign is, as Kress and van Leeuwen (1996) indicate, 'a separately variable semiotic feature' (p. 231), which irrespective of the linguistic content can affect how a sign is interpreted and its legitimacy for the target audience. Kress and van Leeuwen observe that the local values attached to different materials and technologies of sign production are determined according to the availability of resources and regulatory structures which control the visual landscape. For example, in some public spaces in some societies fly-posters may be prohibited. In Jamaica unlicensed 'permanent' and ephemeral signage is deemed illegal and is periodically removed by the government, but the regulation of signage on the Jamaican roadside nevertheless proves very difficult to sustain.[2] A common strategy which successfully negotiates the government's removal procedures is to inscribe signs on surfaces which are already part of the physical landscape. Examples include walls, tree trunks, large rocks and the sides of buildings (Figures 4.3 and 4.4).

FIGURE 4.3 Hand-painted sign on corrugated zinc fence

FIGURE 4.4 Hand-painted sign on external wall of a restaurant (see colour plate section)

Locating the sign in social activity: (Dis)embedding

Like the party invitation discussed above, roadside signs may contribute to social activities which are not taking place in the same place as the sign.

Signage containing non-standard language forms informed this analysis and contributed to four social activities: selling goods or services, controlling social behaviour, providing public information and advocating social identities and

Table 4.1 Distribution of signs across the social activities in which they participate

Type of communicative exchange	Social activity	Frequency of signs (n)
Activity Exchange	Selling	161
	Controlling	28
Knowledge Exchange	Informing	17
	Advocating	106
Total number of signs		**312**

actions.[3] The focus of the first two of these activities is on getting the audience to do things. The focus of the latter two activities is on exchanging information. Following Fairclough (2003), I refer to these as 'activity' and 'knowledge' exchanges respectively (Table 4.1).

I have categorized signs which perform a communicative exchange as an integrated part of the social activity as *embedded* in that activity. In such cases the sign is situated within a social activity that is physically co-occurring and so contextualizes the sign. For example, the sign on the zinc fence in Figure 4.3 is embedded at the site where it is attempting to regulate public behaviour by appealing to social attitudes towards urinating ('nasty') and the practicalities of smoking cannabis ('danger'). This sign contributes to more than one activity and has been included in the frequency counts only once and categorized according to the sign's primary activity. The primary activity was determined by the amount of space afforded to each activity on the sign – either in terms of font size or amount of inscription. Several activities may be achieved with a single phrase (see for example Figures 4.9 and 4.10 which attempt to sell and advocate simultaneously). In cases such as these where the visual element of the sign provides no clue to the primary activity, consideration is given to the proximity of the sign to the social activities that it contributes to in order to determine the principle motivation for the sign's existence.

For example, in Figure 4.4 the activity exchange of buying and selling food at King Dango Man's restaurant does not explicitly specify the type of food on offer but achieves this implicitly through its lexical, code and graphic choices indexing the identity of the restaurant as rastafarian. The reference to the rastafarian reggae artist Bob Marley, the respectful use of 'king' and its rastafarian equivalent 'ras', the English/Creole playful phrase 'NUFF RASPECT TO!', and the symbolic image of a crown, allow all who possess the relevant socio-cultural knowledge to infer that the food will comply with rastafarian dietary requirements. The sign appears to be advocating the rastafarian religion but in fact it is a vehicle for advertising a particular type of product (Rastafarian food), which makes it a commercial sign oriented primarily to the activity of selling.

Other commercially-oriented signs make similar claims to local identity even when the service/goods provider is a global brand. For example, the text in Figure 4.5 combines the logo of a fast food chain with a tag line typical of the

FIGURE 4.5 Metal sign on a traffic island in a busy urban road at the entrance to KFC

voluntary sector – *This median is proudly maintained by KFC.* This is not an atypical strategy found in much contemporary, corporate advertising, whereby the key 'selling point' of the company is construed through maintaining its image as 'caring', possibly motivated – as in this case – by the international criticism of the socially irresponsible behaviour of global fast food chains. Here, a franchise for KFC positions itself as caring for a local community, however it does not simply resort to a bold, matter-of-fact statement to this effect written in block capitals combined with the company's logo. It appropriates the voice and identity of the local community through the use of a slogan in the vernacular 'Nice Up Your City // Nice Up Yourself', and *styling* it on the grassroots literacy signs of the type discussed above: using 'hand-written' (but neat) typography, no punctuation, non-standard capitalization, accompanied by a child-like drawing of a flower, all of which conversationalizes and personalizes the sign disguising its economic motivation.

Not all signs are co-located with the social activity in which they participate. Signs are *disembedded* if they perform exchanges that take place at a different time and place from the activity and so communicate without the benefit of the context supplied by the activity. In Figure 4.6, the billboard located on a main road is participating in the activity of selling airline tickets of the national airline at a distance.

Tables 4.2a and 4.2b show the distribution of the signs in the corpus across the four social activities identified above. Each activity tends to be dominated by signs produced with a particular production technology depending on whether the signs are embedded or disembedded. Embedded signs are more likely to be written by hand in all the activities, while disembedded signs are more likely to be printed, with the exception of signs that do advocacy work, such as graffiti.

FIGURE 4.6 Large billboard poster for Air Jamaica (on a main highway) (see colour plate section)

This complementary distribution of the use of technologies can be partially explained by their different affordances: Since embedded texts tend to be written for individual, locally situated activities they are more likely to only be produced once – usually by hand. They are often painted directly onto an appropriately situated surface, such as the side of a handcart, a cool box or a wall (e.g. Figure 4.3 and 4.4). This 'low' technology produces texts that are materially more permanent than those of printed texts. Printed texts are more likely to be mass-produced for wide distribution and, as has been noted, are more likely to be disembedded (e.g. Figure 4.6). The lifespan of these mass-produced texts – billboard posters, fly posters or campaign posters – tends to be short, as they are pasted over with new posters or left to deteriorate.

Overall, handwritten signs clearly outnumber printed signs for both embedded (113 out of 144) and disembedded (118 out of 171) signs. Thus less expensive materials and low technology involving handwriting are the most likely resources for inscription for producers of signs that contain non-standard language forms. This overall distribution is not representative across all activities, however, with the most notable difference being in disembedded signs participating in selling activities where print technology dominates. A closer examination of this category (Table 4.2c) reveals that over half (35 out of 66) of these signs are promoting entertainment events, specifically those of the Jamaican dancehall, and the distribution of this sub-category of selling is more evenly weighted across hand and print technologies, showing no clear preference for one technology over the other. (Promotional signs for Jamaican dancehall events are explored further below.)

Table 4.2a Distribution of signs which are *embedded* in a social activity

Type of communicative exchange	Social activity	Frequencies (n)		
		'Print' technology	'Hand' technology	Total
Activity Exchange	Selling	5	90	**95**
	Controlling	1	21	**22**
Knowledge Exchange	Informing	2	15	**17**
	Advocating	0	7	**7**
Total		**8**	**133**	**141**

Table 4.2b Distribution of signs which are dis*embedded* from a social activity

Type of communicative exchange	Social activity	Frequencies (n)		
		'Print' technology	'Hand' technology	Total
Activity Exchange	Selling	47	19	**66**
	Controlling	5	1	**6**
Knowledge Exchange	Informing	0	0	**0**
	Advocating	1	98	**99**
Total		**53**	**118**	**171**

Table 4.2c Distribution of disembedded signs attempting to sell goods or services, showing the proportion of signs advertising entertainment (dancehall) events

	Print technology	Hand technology	Totals
Signs for dancehall events	19	16	**35**
Signs for other products/services	28	3	**31**
Totals	**47**	**19**	**66**

Ideological approaches to linguistic inscription

Visual language on Jamaican signage combines standard and vernacular forms in three ways, each embodying different language ideologies and communicative strategies.

Visual language as monolingual

A monolingual approach makes no visual distinction between the vernacular and the standard at phrase level, and no attempt to present the vernacular as distinct from a standard written form either by presenting it as 'speech' or visually distancing it from the standard. Monolingual signs use the vernacular to communicate the main message rather than to mitigate a message and/or index a local identity. Figure 4.3 is typical of a number of signs that draw largely on the vernacular as a visual resource for achieving the maximum impact in sending home a very explicit directive. The inscribed surface – a corrugated zinc door – is already part of the urban landscape and the inscription is hand-painted. This resourcefulness is commonplace in Jamaica, and the low technology should not be read as an indication of a sign lacking authority. In fact, although line spacings are erratic and the letters are not professionally painted, the use of colour successfully emphasizes the links between the value judgments 'nasty' and 'danger' with the activities of 'pissing' and 'skinning up' (i.e. smoking) respectively, and the colourfulness and cleanliness of the sign enhances its visibility in run down surroundings, adding to its visibility. The consistent use of uppercase letters emphasizes the authoritative stance of the message.

Visual language as diglossic

A diglossic approach segregates the vernacular and standard forms both visually and functionally. Most typically, this is achieved by relegating the former to the representation of speech with the use of quotation marks or with speech bubbles (Figure 4.8), or through anchoring the text with images of the implied speaker as in Figure 4.7, or any combination of these. For example, in Figure 4.8

FIGURE 4.7 Paper poster stuck to tree trunk in the car park of a bar

FIGURE 4.8 Large billboard poster on a main highway (see colour plate section)

a billboard advertisement perpetuates the diglossic view of Jamaica's language situation through the visual representation of English as the written medium in the standard phrase at the bottom of the sign 'There's a better way to get Fresh cows milk!', while Creole is used for the first part of the young girl's 'spoken' comment 'Mama I bring home de . . .'. The rest of the girl's utterance – '100% fresh cows milk' – is arguably uttered in 'standard' English (despite the 'missing' apostrophe in 'cows' and odd capitalization of 'Fresh'), which can be explained as a switch to a typical advertising slogan claiming excellence for the product – in this case purity ('100%') and freshness. The relative status imbalance between the spoken Creole and written Standard English is emphasized by the larger font size of the English text, matching that of the tagline at the bottom of the sign. Besides, Creole is also associated here with the rather silly behaviour of the girl (bringing a cow home to drink milk rather than buying milk in a shop), emphasized by the 'silly' look on her face. In this way, Creole is used to index a rural, Creole and somewhat backward if authentic identity, while English is used to promote a modern, 'quality' product.

Likewise, in Figure 4.7, the vernacular and the standard are visibly disconnected. Despite the 'spoken' vernacular text being larger than the English below, it uses a more, 'handwritten' typeface indexing a more personalized and informal voice in contrast to the official and authoritative Standard English orthography below. All these differences in the use and representation of the two codes reinforce the hegemony of English and the dominant view that Creole can only be spoken, not written (even when it's written!).

Visual language as bilingual

A bilingual approach represents the vernacular with standard and/or non-standard written forms, which do not explicitly represent speech, but index the vernacular through the use of idiomatic expressions or proverbs, typically associated with oral communication (although not visually marked as such), and separated from the standard at clause or sentence boundaries. This distance may be visually emphasized by positioning the vernacular apart from the standard text as in Figure 4.6, where the vernacular phrase 'big a yard' (big at home) is not only set apart from the Standard English phrase 'big abroad' but its use as a local marker of identity is corroborated through the background image of Jamaica's national flag. The combination of the vernacular phrase 'big a yard' and the standard phrase 'big abroad' achieves a rhyme in local pronunciation, but relies on local knowledge for effect, as the aural pun is not indexed visually.[4] The parallel representation of Standard English as a marker of the non-local ('abroad') and specifically as a marker of American identity through the inclusion of the USA's national flag is striking. It positions Jamaica's official language as extra-local, and this is further reinforced by its position on the right-hand side of the billboard, the side that Kress and van Leeuwen (1996) note is the place where Western cultures expect to find'new' information, since the 'old' or 'given' information tends to be found on the left.

Tables 4.3a and 4.3b show how these approaches are distributed across the signs according to the categories in Tables 4.2a and 4.2b.[5] (Promotional signs for dancehall events have been excluded from Tables 4.3a and 4.3b and are dealt with further below.)

Table 4.3a Distribution of ideologies of language on roadside signs embedded in a social activity (excludes dancehall signage)

Communicative exchange	Social activity	'Print' technology	'Hand' technology
Activity Exchange	Selling	*Bilingual*	*Bilingual* *Monolingual*
	Controlling		*Bilingual* *Monolingual*
Knowledge Exchange	Informing		*Bilingual* *Monolingual*
	Advocating		*Monolingual*

Table 4.3b Distribution of ideologies of language on roadside signs disembedded from a social activity (excludes dancehall signage)

Communicative exchange	Social activity	'Print' technology	'Hand' technology
Activity Exchange	Selling	*Bilingual* *Diglossic*	
	Controlling	*Diglossic*	
Knowledge Exchange	Informing		
	Advocating		*Monolingual*

Tables 4.3a and 4.3b indicate that hand-produced signs frequently construct a monolingual view of language across all activities, whereas printed signs do not. Printed signs are more likely to make a functional distinction between the standard and the vernacular, marking the vernacular as speech (diglossic) or visually distancing it from the standard (bilingual). A bilingual approach is evident in hand-produced signs across all activities except those that advocate. Signs that do advocacy work do not represent the vernacular and the standard as distinct varieties. The distribution of diglossic and monolingual approaches to visual language across the activities is complementary. The more expensive print technologies are unsurprisingly the domain of diglossic signs, which represent the linguistic, institutionalized hegemony and also tend to be confined to disembedded signs that attempt to instigate action at a distance.

Monolingual signs are always produced with hand-written, low technology. Monolingual printed signs are absent from the corpus (the striking exception is dancehall posters; see below) and a possible reason for this is that print technology enables institutional or DIY regulatory procedures such as copyediting or spellcheckers. 'Monolingual' texts combine standard and non-standard language forms without visually distinguishing between the two. The signs are usually individually handwritten or handcrafted and therefore less regulated than other signs, their production being potentially dependent on just one individual's handiwork. The unregulated potential of hand-produced signs has two effects: First, the signs commonly draw on vernacular and standard language forms in highly integrated yet variable ways as a consequence of the individual producer's linguistic repertoire. Secondly, the visual representation of language – the use of letters, punctuation, layout and other marks – is also highly variable. Nevertheless, there are some commonly occurring patterns that involve the mixing of standard and non-standard forms intrasententially at the level of grammar, often co-occurring with vernacularized stylistic devices. A common occurrence is an inconsistent mix of standard inflections, such as *-s* or *-ed* with equivalent uninflected vernacular forms. These are often accompanied by a visual representation that reinforces the non-standard look, for example, by alternating upper and lower case letters and the use of irregular spacing and letter sizes and creative use of alphabetic symbols (e.g. the 'face' in the 'O' of 'NO' in Figure 4.2) and punctuation (e.g. the exclamation mark in Figure 4.4).

Such texts, when viewed from the perspective of the bilingual or diglossic models of language use are often evaluated as 'incorrect'. But while 'correct' language may contribute to a sign's authority and status in one activity, it may not be a criterion for status in another. Indeed Blommaert (2005) notes that the meaning of a sign cannot be detached from the values that are attached to it locally because 'prestigious ways of using language in one community may be stigmatised in other communities and discourse forms may "lose function"' (p. 120).

In line with Blommaert's observation, but reversing it, this analysis has identified the signs for dancehall events as a site of ideological struggle where the Jamaican vernacular 'gains function' – where it is clearly appropriate and therefore authoritative in a written form. A further selling activity where non-standard language is the norm and signage is dominated by the monolingual ideology is that promoting public transport which is run privately by individuals, not the state. Both of these activities are undertaken in the main by individuals running businesses aimed at and valued by the Creole-speaking community and indicate a space in which the government's hegemonic project to write in Standard English only is contested. They are discussed below.

Signage on public transport

Public transport is the most common means of travel for the majority of Jamaicans. Many buses and taxis, particularly in rural areas, are run as private businesses by individuals and competition to attract passengers can be fierce. Passengers travelling the same route every day may have a preferred driver with whom they choose to travel (or a driver who they wish to avoid), and it is common practice for drivers to individualize their vehicles by customizing them with a 'tag'. This is often 'engraved' into the tinted plastic sunshield or 'sunstrip' on the front and rear windows of the vehicle. This is sometimes done by the driver or owner of the vehicle, but can also be done by more skilled craftsmen who may also include intricate designs in addition to, or instead of text. The sunstrip in Figure 4.9 has been crafted with more skill than the one in Figure 4.10, which is less uniform in terms of spacing and lettering. The more 'professionally' produced sunstrips nevertheless draw on the vernacular in similar ways to the 'DIY' sunstrips, indicating that the vernacular is an uncontested code for this kind of public signage. This self-identifying practice for drivers and their vehicles has a double function. Apart from serving as an individual badge or logo, they also attract customers by advocating and establishing shared

FIGURE 4.9 Text cut into plastic sun protection coating 'Mi A God Pickney' (back window of public bus)

FIGURE 4.10 Text cut into plastic sun protection coating 'Let Hi Goh Mek Hi Bun' (back window of public bus)

beliefs and identities, often by drawing on local discourses associated with the Jamaican dancehall or with religious practices. In Figure 4.10 the vernacular phrase 'let hi go, mek hi bun' has religious undertones, reminiscent of the biblical use of 'let'.[6] Religious discourse is commonly drawn on in the performed lyrics of the dancehall and the intertextual clue in this phrase is the word 'bun' ('burn', i.e. destroy/kill/hurt), a frequently used word in the dancehall and in everyday conversation.

The discourses of sunstrips are in many ways similar to those of graffiti, promoting identities and beliefs, albeit commercially rather than politically motivated (although these signs do also do advocacy work). The differences, however, are in the materiality of the signs and their functions. Graffiti may be present on a wall for a relatively long time, but its intended message may remain 'invisible' to many especially if it is perceived as defacement. Taxi and bus sunstrips on the other hand are visible to those members of the public in whose interest it is to get a ride. These signs are also durable and because they are mobile (some public vehicles cover large stretches of the island) they are potentially influential by promoting values over a large area. Thus, the sunstrip signs, although rather brief, are more likely than any other signs in my sample to index 'authentic' and 'legitimate' written Creole which is not subordinated to the 'standard'.

Dancehall signage

Jamaican dancehall music and culture is extremely highly valued by groups within Jamaican society. Successful singers and DJs are skilled lyricists, providing relevant social commentary as well as demonstrating considerable improvisational skills with rhythm and rhyme (Devonish, 1996; Stolzoff, 2000). The associated discourses and practices of the dancehall permeate many areas of everyday life and in the visual landscape traces are commonly found in the tags on public transport for example (see above).

Signs promoting live dancehall performances and mobile discos or 'sound-systems' playing recorded dancehall music are ubiquitous in the Jamaican landscape. The signs are produced using a wide range of technologies and materials which leads to variability in the use of images, typography and colours. Until a few year ago, posters advertising dancehall events were mostly handwritten and photocopied, but over the last decade printed posters have become more commonplace and it is now becoming increasingly common to see posters make use of computerized graphics and photographs. The types of production technology range from hand-painted or stencilled onto board or handwritten on paper and photocopied (Figure 4.11), to being printed on a home computer or printed professionally with sophisticated graphics.

Hand-produced dancehall signs tend to have a homemade appearance, which is a result of the production procedure, rather than a deliberate technique, and the intention is arguably to avoid this 'look' if the printing budget allows. The foundations of this particular cultural practice are rooted in a value system that prioritizes wealth and this is indexed through sleek, glossy, colourful signs. Hand-produced signs signal an inexpensive show with less well-known performers or DJs.

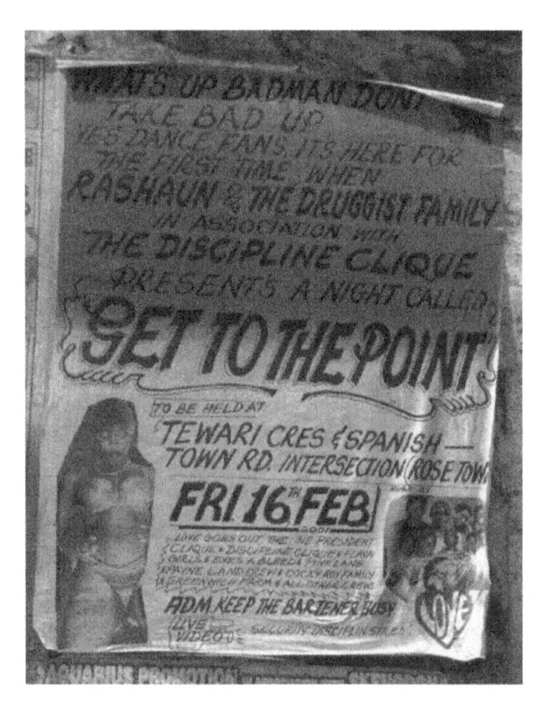

FIGURE 4.11 Handwritten sign with pasted-on images, printed on coloured paper

The affordances of print technology enable the inclusion of colourful photographs and digital imagery. Technologically sophisticated dancehall posters tend to afford more space to photographs and images than to text. Handwritten signs have traditionally filled the space with more text or larger fonts, although some find ways of including images (e.g. Figure 4.11). Despite this preference for image over text, and the reduction in visual language, it is possible to identify a common discoursal formula in dancehall posters. Typically the posters include a greeting or introduction, the theme or name of the event, names of the organizers and of the performers or soundsystems, details of the date and venue and the cost and instructions about behaviour. Much of this formula visually reproduces the oral delivery of the same information often announced over a loud-speaker promoting the event from a passing vehicle.

The theme of the event usually draws on vernacular phrases or expressions that have been popularized in the lyrics of dancehall performers. This reappropriation of an oral form of communication to a visual form is not always possible within the constraints of standard spelling conventions. Writing about dancehall posters in the early 1990s, Devonish (1996) observed that 'the spelling conventions used for Creole on normal Dance Hall posters are quite conservative . . .[the producers] retain English spellings even when the Creole equivalent is pronounced quite differently' (p. 108). The 35 texts promoting dancehall events in this sample were collected a decade later and no longer support this observation. Signs now draw on unconventional spellings to visibly represent the vernacular pronunciation, even though an equivalent standard form is available, e.g. *waan* (want); *si* (see); *truss* (trust); *true* (through) (see,for example, Figure 4.12). At the level of individual vernacular items, there is evidence of an informal consensus of representation for certain words. Two common examples are *kru* (crew/gang) and *wi* (we). With regard to non-standard spellings, there is no internal consistency within the different production technologies. Both printed and hand-produced texts may represent the vernacular with standard or non-standard forms.

Standard spellings tend to be more dominant if the technology is more sophisticated. This potential 'standardization' of the language on dancehall posters is a result of changing technological practices that are more highly

FIGURE 4.12 Visual representation of dancehall event theme

regulated. However, this only partially explains the variability in the language of dancehall posters. Different technologies require different financial resources and the amount of funding available to different promoters of dancehall events varies enormously (Stolzoff, 2000). Promoters with more funding available to them have the opportunity to use more sophisticated technology, which not only allows access to copyediting procedures, but also may need to attract a more global audience. Well-financed events are able to attract internationally recognized performers and the typical use of Standard English on these signs reflects the promoters' attempt to attract a less localized audience. Less well-financed events continue to emphasize the localness of these entertainment events, rooting the activity in the Creole-speaking community through the use of vernacular forms. Dancehall posters may manifest monolingual, bilingual or diglossic approaches to visual language and this instability is explained by the significance of this cultural practice across all groups in the society, who bring with them the full range of resources, linguistic and financial.

Conclusion

During the period in which the signs in this dataset were collected, the Jamaican Ministry of Education, Youth and Culture published Jamaica's first ever language education policy (MOEY&C, 2001) in which it explicitly afforded to the Creole vernacular the status of a language. This signalled a step-change in the government's rhetoric of the Jamaican language situation, however, as I have argued elsewhere (Dray, 2004), this policy change was introduced to maintain the *status quo* with regard to the current linguistic hegemony of English by recognizing Jamaican Creole only as fulfilling its 'low' functions. In principle, the government did not intend to alter the functional distribution of the two varieties recognizing English as the sole language of literacy. This chapter has gone some way to showing that in practice things are different.

At the level of language use, the linguistic hegemony may be shifting slowly in favour of the Creole. The roadside signs discussed in this chapter demonstrate that although both codes appear to have relatively distinct patterns of distribution and functions, and occupy competing ideological positions, the Creole vernacular is increasingly present in visual public communication. In the Jamaican context, sign production technologies, such as home computers and print shops, may bring with them regulatory practices, but these do not guarantee the production of standard language signage. There are times when the use of Creole is more appropriate than the standard for a local audience. On occasions even government and corporate signage bows to this pressure in order to demonstrate solidarity with the local audience – usually for strategic purposes.

Hand-produced signage provides a space for the vernacular, where institutional regulatory processes have little control. The strengths of these hand-produced signs are their ubiquity and longevity and the socio-cultural context where local 'grassroots literacy' embodies different values about signage. Some of these texts are more visible to the public than others but they all nevertheless contribute towards visual forms of communication that may evolve with time, through becoming absorbed and reappropriated in other discourses. This intertextuality is already evident in the highly technologized signage of institutional advertising, and institutional attempts at social control, which draw on forms of the spoken vernacular, albeit in principled and limited ways.

Notes

[1] The parameters used for defining Standard Jamaican English tend to be prescribed by British and American English grammar books and dictionaries. The Dictionary of Caribbean English Usage (Allsop, 1996) was developed to document and prescribe 'acceptable' forms of English in the Caribbean. To distinguish this variety from other varieties of internationally acceptable English, the codification had to include a number of Caribbean Creole features. (For a critical discussion of this dictionary project see Devonish, 2003).

[2] See for example: *'We have teeth and we're going to bite' – Mayor warns of offensive against illegal signs.* Jamaica Gleaner, 29 October 2007, http://www.jamaicagleaner.com/gleaner/20071029/lead/lead3.html (last accessed 20 July 2008).

[3] The corpus comprises 312 signs, collected between 1999 and 2003, which all include non-standard language forms. Some of these forms are recognizably part of the vernacular repertoire, while other forms are neither Standard English nor Creole forms, but display influences from both. These signs not only provide evidence of the written language forms of professional or trained writers working within institutional settings such as the advertising industry or the civil service, but they also document the everyday vernacular writing of individuals who write outside of the direct control and regulatory constraints of institutionally engineered written standards. Unsurprisingly, the majority of these non-standard signs are not produced by the government, but there are a few which have been produced by government institutions, indicating some slippage between the boundaries of Creole and English, even by the most rigorous advocates of Standard English.

[4] The term 'a yard' (*a ja:d*) in Jamaica is used in standard and vernacular discourse to mean ' to/at home' or 'to/in Jamaica'.

The vernacular equivalent of abroad (local pronunciation: [abra:d]) is *a forin.*

[5] Cells containing less than 5 signs in Tables 4.2a and 4.2b have been discounted in Tables 4.3a and 4.3b.

[6] In the Jamaican vernacular, 'mek' (make) can be translated as 'let'.

References

Allsopp, R. (1996), *Dictionary of Caribbean English Usage.* New York: Oxford University Press.

Androutsopoulos, J. K. (2000), 'Non-standard spellings in media texts: The case of German fanzines', *Journal of Sociolinguistics*, 4(4), 514–533.

Backhaus, P. (2007), *Linguistic Landscapes: A Comparative Study of Urban Multilingualism in Tokyo*. Clevedon: Multilingual Matters.

Blommaert, J. (2005), *Discourse: A Critical Introduction*. Cambridge: Cambridge University Press.

Devonish, H. (1996), 'Vernacular languages and writing technology transfer', in P. Christie (ed.), *Caribbean Language Issues: Old and New*. Kingston, Jamaica: University Press of the West Indies, pp. 101–111.

—(2003), 'Language advocacy and "conquest" diglossia in the "anglophone" Caribbean', *Cross Cultures*, 65, 157–178.

Dray, S. (2004), '(W)rites of passage: Exploring nonstandard texts, writing practices and power in the context of Jamaica', Unpublished doctoral dissertation, Lancaster University, 2004.

Fairclough, N. (1994), 'Conversationalisation of discourse and the authority of the consumer', in N. Abercrombie, R. Keat and N. Whiteley (eds), *The Authority of the Consumer*. London: Routledge, pp. 253–268.

—(2003), *Analysing Discourse: Textual Analysis for Social Research*. London: Routledge.

Ferguson, C. A. (1964), 'Diglossia', in D. Hymes (ed.), *Language in Culture and Society*. London: Harper & Row, pp. 429–439.

Jaffe, A. (2000), 'Non-standard orthography and non-standard speech', *Journal of Sociolinguistics*, 4(4), 497–513.

Kress, G. and van Leeuwen, T. (1996), *Reading Images: The Grammar of Visual Design*. London: Routledge.

—(1998), 'Front pages: (the critical) analysis of newspaper layout', in A. Bell and P. Garrett (eds), *Approaches to Media Discourse*. Oxford: Blackwell, pp. 186–219.

Milroy, J. (2001), 'Language ideologies and the consequences of standardization', *Journal of Sociolinguistics*, 5(4), 530–555.

Ministry of Education Youth and Culture (2001), *Language Education Policy*. Kingston, Jamaica.

Scollon R. and Wong Scollon S. (2003), *Discourses in Place: Language in the Material World*. London: Routledge.

Stolzoff, N. C. (2000), *Wake the Town and Tell the People: Dancehall Culture in Jamaica*. Durham and London: Duke University Press.

Thurlow, C. (2003), 'Generation txt? Exposing the sociolinguistics of young people's text-messaging', *Discourse Analysis Online*, 1(1), from http://faculty.washington.edu/thurlow/papers/Thurlow(2003)-DAOL.pdf (accesseed 20 July 2008).

Chapter 5

Sex in the City: On Making Space and Identity in Travel Spaces

Ingrid Piller

When I moved to the city of Basel in Switzerland from Australia in 2005, one of my first impressions was the high visibility of the sex industry. In Sydney, outside of the red-light district of Kings Cross, explicit signage to mark the presence of a nightclub, strip bar or adult video shop is muted, and I had gone about my daily life for years without being particularly aware of the presence of the sex industry in the city. In Basel, and other continental European cities, such ignorance is almost impossible to maintain. Beate Uhse, the German sex store chain, has shops marked in bright red signage at many petrol stations and convenience stops on the continent's highways. Shop windows with life-size dolls dressed in lingerie, pictures of women in sexual poses, and explicit language on shop signage seems to be distributed all over the city space. At one point, early during my stay in Basel, my partner and I were house-hunting in a middle-class neighbourhood and between viewing appointments had half an hour to spare for a coffee break. Not knowing the neighbourhood, we set out in search of a coffee shop: before we came upon one, we had come across two sex shops and a brothel – and had of course become doubtful about the suitability of the neighbourhood for a young family. Explicit displays can sometimes be unavoidable as I found when I took my then 3-year-old daughter along to the central offices of the road and traffic authority and the only way to get there from the tram stop was to walk past a huge kinky display window of a nightclub with space-themed dolls in bright colours.

Initially, it seemed to me that the sex industry was everywhere and this led me to wonder whether I had ended up in some particularly sex-obsessed place. Regular sex-related headlines in the free daily papers such as 'Germany: 500,000 are suffering from addiction to sex' (*20 min*, 5 July 2005: 11; my translation) and ads for nightclubs and brothels even on the front page did nothing to change that impression. However, as I got to understand the city space better, it became clear to me that the sexualization of public space is restricted to travel spaces, i.e. spaces where people circulate and where mostly non-local people go about their business. In this paper I will first describe the sexualization of public spaces and I will show that sexualization is one way to mark a space as travel-related. In a second step, I want to explore the relationship between the semiotics of the sex industry and the semiotics of Swiss tourism, particularly the ways in which multilingualism is associated with the sex industry. Overall, I will argue that high levels of mobility are connected to a high visibility of the sex industry and that signage for sexual services is a way to mark spaces as spaces of mobility. Furthermore, the ways in which Swiss travel spaces are sexualized is specific to the discursive construction of Swiss tourism and Swiss national identity as upper class, high quality and multilingual.

Sex tourism in Switzerland?

If asked for your associations with Switzerland as a tourism destination, it is unlikely that 'sex' would spring to mind. Although tourism is undoubtedly associated with love, romance and sex, Central and Northern European destinations are probably among the least sexy and erotic destinations internationally. Sex tourism can be defined as travel with the primary purpose of entering into 'some form of sexual–economic exchange with women, men or children resident in the host destination' (O'Connell Davidson, 2001: 7). Additionally, even if sex may not be the primary purpose of travel, holidays are often associated with 'sun, sand, sex' and tales of romance have become a separate genre of travel writing (Wylie, 1998) and 'flirt guides' have made their appearance in the guide book market (Einhart and Muschiol, 2005). During the world cup in Germany in 2006, Swiss Tourism ran a campaign aimed at women, in which Switzerland was presented as a romantic and erotic destination: Swiss men were described as less interested in football than in 'you girls' and Switzerland thus as a destination that women could escape to from their local men's negligence.[1] This attempt to use eroticism to market Switzerland as a tourism destination was tongue in cheek and exceptional. The more widely held stereotype about (the lack of) Swiss eroticism is probably best summed up by the joke making the rounds on the internet that says:

> Heaven is where the Police are British, the Chefs are French, the Mechanics are German, the Lovers Italian and it's all organized by the Swiss. Hell is where the Chefs are British, the mechanics are French, the lovers are Swiss, the Police are German and it's all organized by the Italians.

If sex and romance are used in general tourism marketing in the Swiss context, they are not usually associated with Switzerland as a destination but with other – Mediterranean or tropical – destinations. The chain travel agency l'tur, for instance, ran a billboard campaign in Switzerland in 2005, which depicted the torso of a woman with the contours of her large erect nipples visible through her jumper. The associated headline asked 'Frostbeulen?' 'Frostbeulen' are *chilblains* in English but the literal translation would be *chill bumps*. Metonymically, the word also refers to people who feel the cold easily. The message then goes on to advise that 'a beach holiday helps'.

While Switzerland is not a sex tourism destination per se or even a particularly erotic or romantic destination, Switzerland's sex industry is an ancillary business to other forms of travel, mostly conference travel. Basel, the city which is the focus of this paper, is a major regional exhibition centre and hosts a number of high profile trade fairs each year such as the international jewellery show *Basel World*, the art show *Art Basel*, or the building industry's trade exhibition *Swissbau*. The latter in particular is said to contribute to a significant expansion in commercial sex services each year, as explained by an advertising placement agent:

> 'During the Swissbau trade fair we've got a massive increase in sex ads' says Meral Metinoglu of Publicitas Basel. 'Pimps invest more money, commission designed ads and also advertise in papers they usually ignore. That is a trend that can be observed during every event that brings business people into the city.' (Loser, 2005; my translation)

It is not only the case that the sex industry follows exhibition and conference facilities. On the contrary, the sex industry is seen as enhancing a conference destination. In a published focus group interview with a range of actors in the Swiss sex industry, the owner of a brothel chain argues that the availability of commercial sex provides a competitive edge in the competition between different exhibition and conference destinations:

> Q: What's the authorities' position with regard to prostitution?
> A: They only act when there are excesses. Because an attractive prostitution sector is useful for the community; for instance, it increases congress tourism. The authorities know that from experience. Because in my brothels guests from the highest ranks meet, people whose faces are known from magazines. (Mingels and Gimes, 2006; my translation)

The overall size of the sex industry in Switzerland is staggering. The 2005 police report on national security provides the following numbers:

> Everywhere in Switzerland the number of prostitutes and relevant establishments increased in 2005. In Zurich, for example, the number of prostitutes has risen by almost 20% since 2003; in Basel a new brothel opened on average every two weeks in 2005. For the whole of Switzerland, the profits of the sex industry are estimated to be around CHF 3.2 billion per annum. (Bundesamt für Polizei, 2006; my translation)

Data

It is against this background that the sexualization of public space needs to be understood. In order to explore how travel spaces in Basel are sexualized and how the sex industry in Switzerland is semioticized, I collected data from four sources: (1) shop fronts; (2) advertising in local newspapers; (3) prostitutes', nightclubs' and escort agencies' websites; and (4) clients' blogs. All these data are in themselves evidence of the sexualization of public space. This is most obviously the case for shop fronts of adult entertainment stores and night clubs, which were collected on walks through the city. I took pictures of sex industry outlets and marked them on a map. Advertising in local newspapers also enjoys a high degree of public visibility, particularly front page ads in free newspapers such as *Baslerstab* and *20 min*, which can be picked up from distribution points located mostly at bus and tram stops. Sampling of ads for commercial sex, which in addition to ads for sex shops, nightclubs and brothels, includes ads by individual prostitutes, was done on an opportunistic basis. After an initial database of such ads was collected over one week in May 2005, additional ads were included over the next 18 months whenever I happened to come across a new one. Overall, ads changed very little during that period.

Websites and clients' blogs, which are usually read in private, may seem to be less relevant to an enquiry into the sexualization of public space. However, even in a context where the sex industry is relatively visible, such as the one described here, the very nature of the sex industry ensures that most of it 'goes on behind closed doors' so to speak and is not readily perceptible to a traveller, who may spend only a day or two in a city. Thus, prospective punters from out of town will need to draw on information sources beyond accidental encounters with shop fronts and newspaper ads in order to find venues where they can obtain commercial sex. This may be particularly true of time-poor conference travellers seeking high quality – and less visible – escort services. Drawing on Symanski (1981), Jackson (1989) explains the reduced visibility of 'high class' commercial sexual services with reference to the geography of prostitution and its internal hierarchies, which he relates to the class structure of the wider society:

> 'High-class' prostitutes (or 'call-girls') visit their clients' home, hotel, or party; 'lower-class' prostitutes (or 'street-walkers') work in more public places and take their clients to their own home, hotel, or rented room. (Jackson, 1989: 115)

The sociological literature on the sex industry is now in unison that the internet can no longer be ignored by any investigation into commercial sex (Davies and Evans, 2007). In May 2006, the data set was therefore expanded to include 120 websites of brothels, escort services, nightclubs, swinger clubs, massage parlours, and self-employed prostitutes operating in Switzerland.[2] These websites were used to collect descriptions of the location of the venue (Basel ones only) and all of them were analysed for their language use and any references to multilingualism. Additionally, I visited the World Sex Guide site at http://www.worldsexguide.com/guide/Europe/Switzerland/index.htm on 6 May 2006 and collected 15 narratives by English-speaking punters about their experiences using prostitution services in Switzerland. The World Sex Guide site – and many similar ones – are used by punters to rate and rank the service they have received in much the same way that other consumer sites are dedicated to sharing experiences with services and to recommend services or complain about them (Durkin and Bryant, 1995; Holt and Blevins, 2007).

The sexualization of public space

In order to explore the semioticization of Basel travel spaces as spaces of commercial sex, one needs to first take a closer look at the geography of Basel. Specifically, I will now explore how the spatial organization of Basel is related to the sexualization of its public spaces. The interrelationship between sexuality and space and the spatial organization of sexual practices has received increasing attention in the sociological literature in recent years (Betsky, 1995; Binnie and Valentine, 1999; Green et al., in press; Laumann et al., 2004; Stansell, 1986; Walkowitz, 1992). This work has increasingly moved away from a view of space as a physical container where sexual practices occur. Rather, space is increasingly seen as serving 'an active, productive and socializing function in sexual sociality' (Green et al., in press: 2). In order to understand how Basel as a travel space produces spaces for the sex industry, I take my cue for the description of Basel's geography from the city's tourism website.[3] The page about 'location and arrival' has five sections: 'situation', 'by air', 'by car', 'by rail' and 'public transport'. In terms of Basel's location the web page points out that 'Basel is situated in the heart of Europe, at the border triangle where Germany, France and Switzerland meet'. The fact that the border to France and Germany runs through the city – the French municipality of St Louis and the German municipality of Lörrach can both be considered part of the Basel conurbation – or in close proximity is a major factor in making car travel around Basel more marked as 'travel' than might otherwise be the case. As Switzerland is not a member of the European Union, the border checkpoints are still staffed and travellers can expect to have to show their passports when travelling in either direction. I will now explore the sexualization of each four means of arrival as identified by Basel Tourism separately.

Airport

The EuroAirport, which serves Basel, as well as the French city of Mulhouse and the German city of Freiburg, is located on French territory, about 10 km from the city centre of Basel. Maybe due to its location, the airport is the only arrival and departure point that does not feature actual sex industry outlets such as nightclubs or sex shops in its immediate environs. However, it features a significant amount of advertising in the form of billboards and fliers for such outlets in the city. These materials serve two explicit functions: to advertise for the availability of commercial sex services and to provide travellers with names, addresses and phone numbers so that they can actually find the venues where the services are available. As an example, I will describe a billboard not from the EuroAirport but from Zurich Airport, which is about a 100 km away and the main hub for long-haul travellers from and to Basel. In September 2006 I took a photo of the huge billboard ad for a gentlemen's club (see Figure 5.1). The billboard is striking for a number of reasons: to begin with, it is about 8 metres wide and 3 metres high and thus fills the entire view out of the exit door of the arrivals terminal opposite which it was displayed. This exit, which leads to a car park, taxi ranks and bus services, is located only a few metres after customs and so the billboard could well be described as the first sight of Switzerland a passenger might ever get. The billboard is almost entirely filled by the image of a lingerie-clad woman lying on a bed and staring straight at the viewer. Above her legs and buttocks, the slogan 'let's talk about . . .' is printed in a curved line. The billboard also contains the address and name of the nightclub. The size of the billboard and its prominent location combine to not only advertise for this particular nightclub but to give a high level of prominence – there is almost a sense of urgency about it – to commercial sex generally. Indeed, the level of advertising for the sex industry is so high, that sometimes the viewer needs to look a second time in order to establish whether a given billboard is an ad for the sex industry or some other product or service. In March 2006, for instance, a billboard very similar to the one in Figure 5.1 was on display in the departure

FIGURE 5.1 Billboard of a Zurich gentlemen's club at Zurich airport

hall of Basel Airport: the poster is dominated by the image of a lingerie-clad woman in a suggestive pose against the slogan 'Pour vous servir' '*To serve you*'. However, the ad is actually not for a nightclub but for the lingerie chain Lise Charmel.

Checkpoints

Arrival in or departure from Basel by car is punctuated by international border checkpoints. These border checkpoints are marked in a number of official ways, such as the presence of buildings to serve various custom purposes, uniformed personnel, marked police and border patrol vehicles, and official signage indicating entry into another national territory. In addition to these official markers, the border is also marked by the presence of sex shops and nightclubs in the immediate vicinity of the checkpoints on the German and, to a lesser degree, the French side of the border. The strong presence of the sex industry close to the border can be explained by the fact that goods and services are generally cheaper in France and Germany than in Switzerland. In the same way, that many Swiss residents choose to do their weekly grocery shopping in France or Germany, price-conscious punters obviously also choose to seek sexual services across the border. Checkpoints are not only sexualized by the presence of outlets of the sex industry in their environs but also by references to the checkpoints in ads for such services. An ad for a brothel that appeared two to three times per week during most of the 18 months of data collection provides its location in the following way: 'Weil a. Rhein/Zoll Otterbach', '*Weil a. Rhein/Checkpoint Otterbach*'.

Central Station

The Central Station and its surrounding area is another space that is highly sexualized through the fact that numerous sex shops and nightclubs with explicit displays and signage can be found there. Again, advertising frequently identifies the position of an outlet relative to the Central Station. The phrase 'wenige Gehminuten vom Bahnhof SBB', '*only a few minutes' walk from the Central Station*' can be found in numerous newspaper ads and on websites.

Public transport

Public transport cannot be conceived of as a fixed space in the same way that the airport, checkpoints and the central station are. Public transport takes passengers through the 'heartland' of the city and it is consequently sexualized differently. Trams and buses certainly take passengers past outlets of the sex industry and sometimes through streets where these are heavily concentrated – for instance, around the central station (see above) or the exhibition square (see below). However, largely confined to specific corridors cutting across and distinct from the public areas they intersect, the two main mediums through which public transport participates in the sexualization of public space are free newspapers and graffiti. Containers of free newspapers can be found at almost every tram and bus stop – for most of 2005 and 2006, there were two morning papers, *Baslerstab* and *20 min*, and in late 2006, a free evening paper, *heute*, became available, too. These papers are obviously financed through advertising and a significant portion of the ads are for the sex industry. These ads range from highly visible quarter-page front-page ads for major nightclubs to the classified ads where self-employed prostitutes offer their services. Uptake of these newspapers is high – at many stops none are left by 8 a.m. – and with them advertising for the sex industry keeps circulating.

Graffiti also contribute to the pervasive sexualization of public space: trams, busses and waiting areas are mostly clean and well-maintained by anyone's standards but even so no one seems to be able to keep up with the countless little engravings of 'sex' and the crude texta drawings of genitalia. Some of these graffiti seem to serve the purpose of establishing contact for a sexual encounter such as 'fuck me [phone number]' or 'I need sex I'm a bitch call now [phone number]', which I've both seen on the back of tram seats. However, scribbles of 'sex', 'fuck' or 'sex is geil' ('sex is horny') do not even serve the potential purpose of establishing contact. While they may serve some adolescent purpose of emotional release for the writer, the overall effect is their contribution to the wider sexualization of public space.

Travel spaces and tourist spaces

In this section, I have shown that the four travel spaces of Basel as identified by the Basel Tourism Board – airport, checkpoints, central station and public transport – are all highly sexualized spaces. However, travel spaces are not equal to tourism spaces. While all tourists obviously need to travel, i.e. make use of transport, travel spaces are not usually destinations per se. Rather, they are the non-spaces of globalization (Ritzer, 2007) that keep people circulating to and from their destinations. Tourists use these non-spaces to come to Basel mostly for two reasons, either for business or culture. Business travellers would typically attend trade fairs, conferences or exhibitions. Unsurprisingly, another Basel space where many of the sex industry outlets are clustered is around the Messeplatz ('exhibition square'), the site of Basel's trade fairs. Cultural tourists, on the other hand, are attracted to Basel because of its historical architecture, its museums and art galleries. In contrast to the exhibition square, key cultural tourism spaces such as the areas around the town hall or the cathedral are 'marked' by the absence of sex industry outlets.

Sexing multilingualism

The sexualization of non-spaces can be considered a generic phenomenon that can be observed in many spaces of high mobility that may be geographically, culturally, socially or historically very diverse. Ringdal (2004), for instance, speculates that prostitution historically first developed in ancient Mesopotamia and spread from there along the Silk Road and other trade routes. However, while the high visibility of the sex industry in travel spaces may be generic, its actual semiotics are always specific to a particular socio-historical context. I will therefore now move on to consider the ways in which the Swiss sex industry is eroticized and argue that it is consonant with the overall image of the country projected nationally and internationally. Red light districts and sites of commercial sexual activity are often seedy, shady and marked as lower class (as pointed out by Jackson [1989] in the quote above). However, this is not the way the sex industry is semioticized in Switzerland. Rather, advertising for sexual services focuses on quality and cleanliness, in a way that is very similar to the exploitation of these national stereotypes in tourism advertising more generally. Multilingualism is often presented as an aspect of quality, evidence of the industry's 'high standards'. The slogan of a Geneva brothel, for instance, says 'Quality for gentlemen since 1968'. If one didn't know that the slogan referred to a brothel, it could just as well refer to a Swiss watch (although one would expect a date a century or two before 1968). References to quality and cleanliness also abound in the punters' evaluations on the World Sex Guide site, with statements such as 'I found the standards of cleanliness and hospitality in the studios and brothels to be second to none', 'big swimming pool, saunas all with usual Swiss cleanliness and quality' or 'the most elegant Swiss clean establishment with big swimming pool Jacuzzi, sauna, steam baths, showers, bar and some 15–25 of the most gorgeous women 8–11 to please a man'.

Multilingual proficiency emerges as a key aspect of high quality. My data show that multilingual proficiency is eroticized, if not fetishized. Using English advertising and describing the sex workers' language skills in English, German and French is one way to associate the industry with 'quality'. Of the 120 sex service websites in my data set, 72 (60%) were monolingual and 47 (39%) bi- or multilingual (there was also one website that did not use any language at all and consisted purely of pictures). Figure 5.2 shows the languages and language combinations used.

In comparison to an analysis of the languages used on the websites of Swiss tourism boards (Piller, 2007), the high incidence of monolingual websites is striking, as is the more limited role of English. However, on closer inspection most of the German monolingual websites are websites of swinger clubs and self-employed prostitutes. One way for night clubs, brothels and escort services to signal their higher level of professionalism (for want of a better word) is the use of multilingualism on their websites.

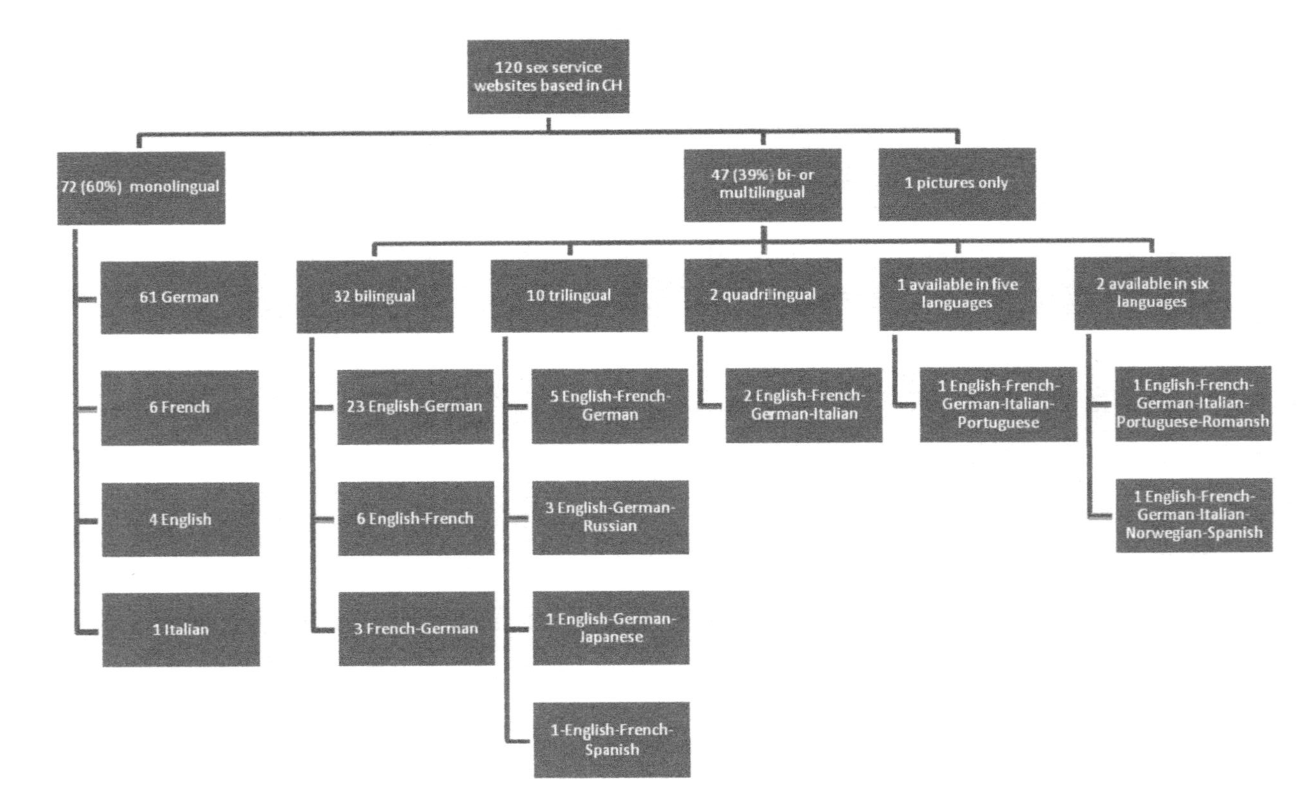

FIGURE 5.2 Language choice on websites of commercial sex providers in Switzerland

In addition to the languages in which the websites appear, there is frequent explicit mention of multilingualism. Many of these websites provide a profile of the sex workers employed there. Sometimes, this is a general profile of the type of woman employed, and these general profiles often feature references to the sex workers' language skills. The following is a good example of the ways in which multilingualism and quality can be linked in such profiles:

> Beautiful, sensual, well-groomed from top to toe, elegant and cultivated, mostly multilingual and of perfect education – their distinction and femininity means that they know how to make your encounters incredible moments of high-spiritedness, of happiness and of bliss. (French original; my translation)

These websites also frequently provide individual profiles through a link to 'our ladies' or 'our girls'. Mostly, these individual profiles consist of a first name and one or more pictures of a semi-naked woman in sexual poses. Sometimes, additional information is provided about the featured women, and if there is, it often lists their languages, as in these examples: 'Donna: Conversation: German, English, French, Spanish' or 'Hi, I'm Michelle! I am a young and charming Swiss lady. I speak 4 languages (German, English, French and Italian), so I'm sure we will not have communication problems!'

Multilingualism is not only valued on the websites of sex service providers but also by punters as the following quote from the World Sex Guide site demonstrates: '. . . fucked there a couple of girls, some of the near Eastern area like Victoria from Latvia and another girl (whose name I forgot) from Slowenia [*sic*], but the girls are classy, speak German and/or English and/or French'.

This association of sex work with multilingualism and quality occurs in a context where multilingualism is stereotyped as a central aspect of the national identity. It also needs to be placed in a context where the majority of sex workers are actually migrant women from Eastern Europe, Latin America and the Caribbean (Le Breton and Fiechter, 2005); as is apparent from the quote above and the way how origin from 'the near Eastern area' is set in opposition to class ('but'). Multilingualism – or rather proficiency in the Western languages German, English and French – is adduced as evidence of 'classiness'. Much of the advertising for the sex industry draws on sex workers' Otherness, i.e. their Russianness, Brazilian-ness or Asian-ness. Ethnicity is often used to promise extraordinary feminine beauty, hotness and – most frequently – 'tabooIessness'. At the same time, it almost seems that the Other's overwhelming sexuality is contained in institutions which semiotically align themselves with the national stereotypes of quality, cleanliness and multilingual proficiency in their advertising.

Conclusion

Internationally, a significant portion of tourism revenue is generated through sexual exploitation and the burgeoning sex industry has become a key emblem of globalization (Cohen and Kennedy, 2007). Travel creates the market in which the sex industry flourishes and the incidence of travel is directly linked to the availability of commercial sex (Seabrook, 2007). Unsurprisingly then, the non-spaces of mobility become semioticized as sexual spaces. In one sense, this sexualization of travel spaces is a response to the needs of travellers. 'Knowing where to go' is a recurring topic in the punters' narratives on the World Sex Guide site, as in this one, who writes: 'if you know where to go Zurich can be a paradise in Europe'. However, at the same time, the coincidence between travel spaces and sex industry outlets normalizes the sex industry. This normalization of the sex industry sexualizes the public space for everyone, irrespective of where you stand on the sex industry and commercial sex. The sexualization of public space occurs in a wider context where the representation of women as sex objects has become acceptable again as part of 'raunch culture' (Levy, 2005).

While I see the sexualization of travel spaces described in this chapter as a global phenomenon, it plays out in locally specific ways. Localization in the Swiss context occurs through the association of commercial sex with quality, cleanliness and with multilingualism as an aspect of quality. While it may be surprising to see this high level of visibility of the sex industry in Swiss travel spaces, their style nonetheless also fits in with the glamorous, high-end, international (business) travel image of the country, which – like many other tourism destinations and, indeed, products of all kinds – has long relied on the adage that 'sex sells' in their marketing:

> By 1900 the 'first posters selling goods began to appear, and their visual style was determined by the conventions of official art, including the affixing of meaning – any meaning – to a pretty girl – any pretty girl'. (Warner, 1985: 86)
>
> The message though was always the same: buy the product, get the girl; or buy the product to get to be like the girl so you get your man. (Wykes and Gunter, 2005: 41)

Also in the context of globalization, sex work has become yet another contemporary employment sector where language and communication skills are key employment skills (Cameron, 2000; Heller, 2003; Piller and Pavlenko, 2007). While prostitution used to be conducted in ways that limited any exchange between punter and sex worker to the sexual act, conversation has become part of the service, particularly at the upper end of the market. As punters are increasingly on the look-out for a 'girl-friend experience' when procuring sexual services (Bernstein, 2005), the ability to communicate is obviously central. Language work in the global sex industry centring around travel is thus another locus that contributes to the spread of English as a lingua franca. As the billboard in Figure 5.1 says: 'Let's talk'.

Acknowledgements

The data for the present paper come from a larger research project on 'Languages, identities and tourism: Towards an understanding of social and linguistic challenges in Switzerland in the context of globalization' funded by the Swiss National Fund (project number 108608) as part of a national research program on 'Language Diversity and Linguistic Competence in Switzerland' (http://www.nfp56.ch/ [accessed 27 August 2009]). I gratefully acknowledge the Swiss National Fund's financial support as well as the intellectual contribution of my co-investigator Alexandre Duchêne, who also provided helpful comments on an earlier draft of this chapter. Some of the data for this chapter were collected by Sixta Quassdorf, whose research assistance I also gratefully acknowledge. Thanks also go to Adam Jaworski and Crispin Thurlow for their insightful comments on an earlier version of this chapter.

Notes

[1] Webpage for the Swiss tourism authority: http://www.myswitzerland.com/en/movies/wm/ (accessed 10 May 2008).

[2] These websites were accessed through five portal sites, namely www.rotlicht.ch, sexnet.ch, www.amateurinnen.ch, www.honeybunny.ch and www.auktionsex.ch.

[3] http://www.basel.com/en.cfm/baselinfo/lageanreise/ (accessed 10 May 2008).

References

Bernstein, E. (2005), 'Desire, demand, and the commerce of sex', in E. Bernstein and L. Schaffner (eds), *Regulating Sex: The Politics of Intimacy and Identity*. London: Routledge, pp. 101–125.

Betsky, A. (1995), *Building Sex: Men, Women, Architecture, and the Construction of Sexuality*. New York: William Morrow.

Binnie, J. and Valentine, G. (1999), 'Geographies of sexuality: A review of progress', *Progress in Human Geography*, 23(2), 175–187.

Bundesamt für Polizei. (2006), *Bericht Innere Sicherheit der Schweiz 2005 [2005 Internal Security Report for Switzerland]*. Berne: Bundespublikationen. www.fedpol.admin.ch (accessed 27 August 2009).

Cameron, D. (2000), *Good to Talk? Living and Working in a Communication Culture*. London: Sage.

Cohen, R. and Kennedy, P. (2007), *Global Sociology* (2nd edn). Basingstoke: Palgrave Macmillan.

Davies, K. and Evans, L. (2007), 'A virtual view of managing violence among British escorts', *Deviant Behavior*, 28(6), 525–551.

Durkin, K. and Bryant, C. D. (1995), 'Log on to sex: Some notes on the carnal computer and erotic cyberspace as an emerging research frontier', *Deviant Behavior*, 16, 179–200.

Einhart, E. and Muschiol, C. (2005), 'Flirt guide', *Glamour*, 56–64.
Green, A. I. et al. (in press), 'Space, place and sexual sociality: Towards an "atmospheric analysis"', *Gender, Work & Organization.*
Heller, M. (2003), 'Globalization, the new economy, and the commodification of language and identity', *Journal of Sociolinguistics*, 7(4), 473–492.
Holt, T. J. and Blevins, K. R. (2007), 'Examining sex work from the client's perspective: Assessing johns using on-line data', *Deviant Behavior*, 28(4), 333–354.
Jackson, P. (1989), *Maps of Meaning: An Introduction to Cultural Geography.* London: Routledge.
Laumann, E. O. et al. (eds) (2004), *The Sexual Organisation of the City.* Chicago: Chicago University Press.
Le Breton, M. and Fiechter, U. (2005), *Verordnete Grenzen – verschobene Ordnungen: Eine Analyse zu Frauenhandel in der Schweiz [Ordered borders – shifted orders: An analysis of the trafficking of women in Switzerland].* Berne: eFeF.
Levy, A. (2005), *Female Chauvinist Pigs: Women and the Rise of Raunch Culture.* New York et al.: Free Press.
Loser, P. (2005, 28-01-2005), Wenn aus zwanzig Minuten zehn werden: Während der Swissbau floriert das Rotlichtmilieu [When twenty minutes turn into ten: Prostitution thrives during the Swissbau trade show]. *Basler Zeitung.*
Mingels, G. and Gimes, M. (2006, 11-03-2006), Milieu-Gipfel [Redlight summit]. *Das Magazin.*
O'Connell Davidson, J. (2001), 'The sex tourist, the expatriate, his ex-wife and her "other": The politics of loss, difference and desire', *Sexualities*, 4(1), 5–24.
Piller, I. (2007), 'English in Swiss tourism marketing', in C. Flores and O. Grossegesse (eds), *Wildern in luso-austro-deutschen Sprach- und Textgefilden: Festschrift zum 60. Geburtstag von Erwin Koller [Roughing it in the linguistic and textual wilds of Portuguese, Austrian and German: Festschrift for Erwin Koller on the occasion of his 60th birthday].* Braga, PT: Cehum – Centro de Estudos Humanísticos, pp. 57–73.
Piller, I. and Pavlenko, A. (2007), 'Globalization, gender, and multilingualism', in H. Decke-Cornill and L. Volkmann (eds), *Gender Studies and Foreign Language Teaching.* Tübingen: Narr, pp. 15–30.
Ringdal, N. J. (2004), *Love for Sale: A World History of Prostitution.* Translated by R. Daly. New York: Grove Press.
Ritzer, G. (2007), *The Globalization of Nothing.* London: Sage.
Seabrook, J. (2007), *Cities.* London: Pluto Press.
Stansell, C. (1986), *City of Women: Sex and Class in New York, 1789–1860.* Urbana, IL: University of Illinois Press.
Symanski, R. (1981), *The Immoral Landscape: Female Prostitution in Western Societies.* Toronto: Butterworths.
Walkowitz, J. (1992), *City of Dreadful Delight: Narratives of Sexual Danger in Late-Victorian London.* Chicago: University of Chicago Press.
Warner, M. (1985), *Monuments and Maidens: The Allegory of the Female Form.* London: Picador.
Wykes, M. and Gunter, B. (2005), *The Media and Body Image: If Looks Could Kill.* Los Angeles: Sage.
Wylie, J. B. (ed.) (1998), *Love & Romance: True Stories of Passion on the Road.* San Francisco, CA: Travelers' Tales.

Chapter 6

Spatial Narrations: Graffscapes and City Souls

Alastair Pennycook

For a small subcultural tourist group, graffiti have become an object of their travelling gaze. Jinman (2007), for example, reports that Melbourne's graffiti have achieved international renown to the extent that tourists head straight for some of the best-known alleys. One such is Hosier Lane, just off Federation Square in central Melbourne, where two young Korean women, having seen Melbourne street art on Korean television are now examining and photographing 'a dense, lurid collage that ranges from rudimentary signatures drawn in marker pen to giant dayglo paintings and intricate paper prints pasted on the wall. "Very good," says one, indicating a playful image of a moon-faced Asian child hugging a docile killer whale. "I like it very much"' (p. 11). Such graffiti tourism can be seen as part of the broader domain of hip-hop tourism (Xie, Osumare and Ibrahim, 2007), which in turn is related to music tourism more generally (Gibson and Connell, 2005). As Xie et al. (2007) explain, 'The ghetto or the hood, which were once a source of sublime terror and fear, have been transformed by Hip-Hop into an enticing landscape for tourism: an image, a sound, graffiti mural waiting at a distance for visual and sensory consumption by those who come from farther afield' (p. 456).

While such graffiti areas have become tacitly sanctioned (the tourist gaze, especially when supported by tourist dollars, plays a part in constructing the city), for many city officials, dwellers and visitors graffiti remain precisely that which should not be seen.[1] Graffiti beckon from our peripheral vision as we traverse urban landscapes in cars, trains, buses, rickshaws or on foot, yet for many they are little more than passing flashes of indecipherable colour, reminders of anti-social tendencies and the ubiquity of global subcultures. In this paper, however, I want to make a case for an understanding of graffiti as part of the urban landscape, as one of the ways in which cities are brought to life and space is narrated. Graffiti, as both products of artists moving through an urban landscape and as art viewed in motion, are part of the articulation of the cityscape. That graffiti are deemed a threat to property, propriety and pristine walls has to be seen in terms of struggles over the preferred semiotics of a city.

Insistently and colourfully reminded that graffiti will farewell and welcome them from city to city, the possible discomfort for global travellers needs to be understood in terms of the flattened class images of the global that tourism and travel produce. It is to an understanding of graffiti, its opponents and alternative urban semiotics that I now turn.

Graffiti as counter-literacies

My interest here is not centrally with the textual scribblings on toilet walls sometimes associated with the term, but rather the large hip-hop style pictures and texts (see Figure 6.1), or the more recent development of stencil art (Figure 6.2). Graffiti or 'writing' is seen as one of the four core elements of the broader hip-hop culture (rapping or MCing, scratching or DJing, and break-dancing being the others): A classic hip-hop crew might be made up of one representative of each of the four elements, though graffiti has also developed into a distinctive subculture of its own, with attendant terminology such as *tag* (the most basic form of graffiti, a writer's logo or stylized signature with marker or spray paint), *buff* (the removal or covering up of graffiti), *blockbuster* (big, square letters, often tilted back and forth, usually in two colours), *throwup* (variously used to mean a quickly painted piece with one layer of spray paint and an outline, or also bubble letters of any sort, not necessarily filled), *bomb* (to cover an area with tags, throwups, etc.).

Figure 6.1 Graffiti, Sydney (see colour plate section)

FIGURE 6.2 Stencil art, Melbourne (see colour plate section)

Doing graffiti, then, can be understood as part of a subcultural activity that is about participation in a hip-hop/graffiti crew: It may be the process of writing/drawing illicitly as much as the subsequent traces of that writing that matters. As Hansen (2005) shows, for a number of graffiti tourists to Melbourne (from Sweden, Germany and the US), the point is not to come and observe but to participate. Christen (2003) goes as far as to claim that graffiti crews 'resemble medieval guilds or trade unions, with apprentices assisting on works designed by masters, often painting backgrounds and filling in outlines in preparation for the finer detailed work' (p. 63). Rahn (2002) likewise suggests that graffiti writing 'provides a structure of traditional skills, mentors, and codes' (p. 191). While a case can therefore be made that participation in graffiti production may have important social, cultural and educational values, it is also its unsanctioned deployment in public space that is central. Although graffiti artists may do commissioned or legal work (rather than attempt to enforce 'zero tolerance' strategies [see below], some councils commission well-known artists to produce works on commonly-painted walls in order to discourage others, bringing both respect and suspicion from other street artists), graffiti largely depends on its confrontation with the lines of authority around public space.

A common argument among graffiti artists is that the legally sanctioned billboards and advertisements that adorn urban environments are a greater eyesore than graffiti, and it is only the fact that capitalist-influenced laws make one legal and the other not that turns their art into an underground activity. As Melbourne street artist Vexta puts it, 'I don't want to live in a city that's really bland and covered in grey and brown and advertising. I never said it was OK to put a billboard on the top of Brunswick Street [a well-known Melbourne street], so who's to say that I can't put up a small A4 size image in a back laneway' (cited in Coslovich, 2005; and see Hansen, 2005). Scollon and Wong Scollon (2003) argue that the occurrence of graffiti 'in places in which visual semiosis is forbidden' (p. 149) render them as *transgressive* since 'they are not authorized, and they may even be prohibited by some social or legal sanction' (p. 151). Rather than accepting this pre-definition of the authorized and the transgressive, however, with its unproblematized distinction between the permitted and the proscribed, it may be more useful to take up Conquergood's (1997) understanding of graffiti writing as a *counterliteracy* that challenges, mimics, and carnivalizes the relations between text, private ownership, and the control of public space:

> This outlawed literacy grotesquely mirrors and mocks the literate bureaucracy that administers licenses, receipts, badges, diplomas, ordinances, arrest warrants, green cards, and other deeds of power and possession. What distinguishes graffiti writing from other subaltern literacies is its criminalization: more than an illegitimate literacy, it is illegal. (pp. 354–355)[2]

Graffiti writing challenges assumptions about who has access to public literacy, who controls the space, who can sanction public images and lettering, who gets to decide on what a city looks like.

City souls and buffed landscapes

Cities are always being cleaned, scrubbed – *buffed* as the graffiti world calls it – to present an acceptable face to the world. This battle has a long history, as Castleman (2004) shows, since to be seen to be easy on graffiti may be seen as being light on crime. Indeed, it is not uncommon for cities to have specific 'graffiti management' plans. As the City of Melbourne explains (City of Melbourne, 2007), its 'whole-of-Council approach to graffiti management . . . is committed to providing a clean, vibrant, safe and welcoming atmosphere for all city residents, workers and visitors'. When Melbourne hosted the Commonwealth Games in 2006, the anti-graffiti campaign was intensified so that any graffiti in the inner city (suburbs, where visitors were less likely to wander, were of far less concern) would be removed within 24 hours.[3] As a media release (Minister for Police and Emergency Services, 2005) explained, 'a specialist anti-graffiti police taskforce' was to be set up 'to crack down on graffiti'. It would 'initially target inner Melbourne and Commonwealth Games venues and precincts'. As the Minister explained, 'Graffiti is an act of vandalism. Graffiti is not only ugly and unsightly, it is a serious criminal offence. . . . This blitz on graffiti will make sure Melbourne is looking its very best in the lead up to the Commonwealth Games'. As this 'blitz' was reported in the press, the 'rapid-response clean-up crew . . . as part of a round-the-clock attack on graffiti during the Commonwealth Games' aimed both to keep clean those parts of the city likely to be seen by visitors, as well as 'to catch vandals in the act and to remove graffiti' (Kelly, 2006).

The classification of graffiti as vandalism is an important discursive move. Although the City of Melbourne plan acknowledges that 'vandalism in the form of graffiti' may only be responsible for 'diminishing *perceptions* of the city's cleanliness and safety' (City of Melbourne, 2007; my emphasis) – thus suggesting that the problem may be that graffiti produce negative images of the city rather than being detrimental themselves, and thus perhaps invoking the 'broken window' theory of public space (like a broken window, graffiti will invite more vandalism) – this emphasis on vandalism, on graffiti as destruction, has to be seen in relation to a long history of discrimination along lines of class, race, gender and ethnicity that constructs the sullied other. As Metcalf (1995) makes clear, colonial discourse was insistent in its construction of native populations as dirty and disease-ridden. In her study of conflicting images ('turf wars') of a contemporary urban community, Modan (2007) points out that 'Much discrimination and persecution is partially accomplished by language of cleanliness and filth' (p. 141). And for those who do not know how to read the signs of the graffiti world, as Milon (2002) suggests, tags are often seen as 'incomprehensible hieroglyphic signatures that aggressively pollute the visual space of the inhabitant, a type of filth that damages the City's attractiveness. These marks are felt as dirty, exterior marks on the City' (p. 87). This struggle over urban space is as much about class as it is about crime.

From a graffiti artists' worldview, by contrast, this is not vandalism but public art; it is an issue of adorning rather than destroying public space. For the perpetrators, makers or writers of graffiti, their work is about style, space, identity, and reimagining the city. Melbourne, some suggested, was overlooking the tourist potential of its recently acclaimed status as 'the stencil capital of the world' (Smallman and Nyman, 2005). As reported in *The Age*, while 'more than four kilometres of graffiti has already been erased from venues and transport routes', for the artists, 'Melbourne's graffiti is itself a colourful tourist attraction and painting over it on rail corridors make a boring view for commuters and Games visitors' (Edwards, 2006a). As Jake Smallman (2005) suggests, Melbourne 'was known as one of the top 10 street art cities in the world and the clean-up was a shame' (cited in Edwards, 2006a).

There is more at stake here, then, than competing views of what constitutes art, or whose vision of the preferable look of a city should prevail. What *is* being buffed when the authorities wipe the city clean, and what might we be able to learn about urban semiotics if graffiti were more readily incorporated into a possible vision of a city for both internal and external consumption? In the next section, I argue that an understanding of *global graffscapes* in relationship to urban landscapes, space and movement, opens up alternative ways of thinking about how we interact with cities. As Coslovich (2005) asks, referring again to the 'gritty, glorious backdrop of street and stencil art' in Hosier Lane in Melbourne, 'Who needs the Harbour Bridge' (a reference to Sydney's famous tourist icon, and the long-term Sydney-Melbourne rivalry) 'when your city has soul?' It is to an understanding of graffscapes as city souls that I shall now turn.

Graffscapes, place, style and movement

While the texts on toilet walls may vary from the graphic (For good cock, call 8653002) to the cryptic (Back soon – Godot), hip-hop graffiti are not generally aimed at easy public consumption. Not intended to be interpretable by people outside the subculture of hip-hop/graff writers, graffiti are about style and identity: As van Treeck (2003) argues, the different graffiti styles – from tags to throwups, and from local city styles to where they are positioned (under bridges, on the sides of bridges, on trains, inside tunnels, on derelict buildings, high up, low down) – are an important part of identity formation. From risk taking, to opposition to bourgeois sensibilities, from mapping parts of the city, to developing a recognizable style, from placing pieces in juxtaposition to officially sanctioned signage (commercial advertising, road signs and so on), to locating oneself within a particular spatial, class and ethnic subculture of the city, graffiti are about establishing particular types of identity.

While much is often made of graffiti and turf wars, of the role graffiti play in urban territorial claims, it is important to understand that graffiti writing is equally about style, identity, and reinterpreting the public space. In the same way that *parkour* – the art of fluid, physical movement through urban landscapes developed in the suburbs of Paris and other French cities – reclaims the drab concrete environments designed for working class and predominantly immigrant communities by reinterpreting the cityscape through physical movement, so graffiti is not, as a bourgeois reading would have it, only about bespoiling the public space, but rather is about the semiotic reinterpretation of urban environments.[4] Graffiti and *parkour* transform cities into different kinds of places that carry not only the designs of urban planners but also the redesigns of urban dwellers.

Graffiti are thus in part a revisioning of urban landscapes. Landscapes may be seen as distinct from the land on which we dwell by dint of our investment in their appearance (Urry, 1995, 2002). Similarly, Cannadine (2000; and cf. Schama, 1995) points out that landscape is produced not only by planting, cutting, diverting and shaping (landscaping) but is also 'the process whereby those trees, rivers and flowers become invested with meanings and morals and myths, and that process is as much a matter of perception and politics, of language and rhetoric, of feeling and sentiment, as it is the result of the conscious acts of landscaping themselves' (p. 188). This helps us to move beyond the sociolinguistic trap whereby places and contexts are seen only as static backdrops against which language occurs, and instead to engage in 'progressively more acute analyses of the ways in which places in time and space come to have subjective meanings for the humans who live and act within them' (Scollon and Wong Scollon, 2003: 12).

Drawing distinctions between the urban landscape (*paysage*) and the urban face (*visage*), and between a view of graffiti as scars that 'pollute the visual space of the inhabitant', or as 'expressions that fully participate in the life of the City' (p. 87), Milon (2002) argues that graffiti can be seen as 'integral parts of the City; they contribute to the definition of its exterior aspect, its size, as well as to the definition of its interior design, its soul' (p. 87). From this perspective, these 'expressions that shape the City's landscape' (p. 88) can be seen, not as scribblings that cover up an urban backdrop whose interpretation is complete, but as part of the mobile expression of the changing metropolitan face, part of a city's soul. Landscapes are not static spaces: 'The language of landscape is . . . a language of mobility, of abstract characteristics, since landscape talk is itself an expression of the life-world of mobile groups' (Urry, 2005: 25). Space, as Soja (1989), drawing on Foucault, points out, has been treated as dead, fixed, immobile: Time moves, space stands still. Yet space needs to be seen in a much more dynamic sense, as much more than a backdrop since 'the organization and meaning of space is a product of social translation, transformation, and experience' (pp. 79–80). Space therefore needs to be understood as a 'social construct that anchors and fosters solidarity, oppression, liberation or disintegration' (Ma, 2002: 131).

The location of graffiti around transport (bridges, trains, railways), furthermore, suggests not only the availability of writable walls and the cult of daring that makes a virtue of tagging inaccessible public space, but also the importance of movement and visibility: Just as Tibetan buddhist prayer flags are strung across windy areas so that they can flutter in the breeze, and prayer wheels may be either turned by hand or even made to rotate by water (small shrines can be found in the mountains of Bhutan, their prayer wheels kept in constant motion by a passing stream), so graffiti are not only about placement but also movement. This is not merely a case of urban mobility, but rather the construction of meaning from movement. While graffiti may be oppositional, 'it is not formless or disorganized. Like other guerrilla formations, it has its own internal structure and highly efficient strategies for mobilizing meaning' (Conquergood, 1997: 358). Indeed meaning is mobilized in several senses.

De Certeau's (1990) well-known discussion of walking in the city 'as a space of enunciation' (p. 98) captures this dynamic well since in this view it is the act of walking that gives meaning to the urban system.[5] Pushing this insight further however, we might want to suggest that rather than walking in the city giving meaning to the prior system of urban meaning (the enunciation of *la langue*), it is rather movement through the city that performatively produces meaning (see Pennycook, 2007). Moving through the urban landscape does not so much bring meanings to life as it makes meanings possible: It is a spatial realization of place. Graffiti, as São Paulo graffiti artist Ninguém explains, 'is about conquering space. What I like is that I can draw or illustrate the places I move in and out of all the time – the trains, buses, etc. Better said, I can use these places to imagine. Imagination is key to graffiti and it is what attracted me' (cited in Pardue, 2004: 426). Graffiti is thus far more than a string of individual identity marks or tags but rather involves a process of narration and *imaginação* (imagination).

To talk of graffscapes, therefore, is to invoke several significant ways of thinking: By locating graffiti within an understanding of landscapes as constructed, interactive, expressive, semiotic resources, we can start to see such street art not as immobile text on static city walls but rather as part of the integrative life of the city that gives it meaning. The term graffscapes also draws on Appadurai's (1996) vision of global ethnoscapes, mediascapes, technoscapes, financescapes and ideoscapes, which in accord with the discussion of landscapes above, 'are not objectively given relations that look the same from every angle of vision but, rather, deeply perspectival constructs, inflected by the historical, linguistic, and political situatedness of different sorts of actors' (p. 33). Appadurai's (2001) understanding, furthermore, that we are living in 'a world of flows', that 'we are functioning in a world fundamentally characterized by objects in motion', which include 'ideas and ideologies, people and goods, images and messages, technologies and techniques' (p. 5) allows us to see that it is not only the city dwellers that are in motion but also the graffiti. Graffiti artists weave new imaginary relations across the urban landscape as they create intertextual city links; and graffiti are perceived by people in motion, as tourists, commuters, drivers, cyclists, walkers pass through these global graffscapes.

Graffiti move across a globalizing world, adorning walls from Reykjavik to Rio, greeting new arrivals in a city with a sense of urban familiarity.[6] In the same way that the *global semioscape* (Thurlow and Aiello, 2007) offers both commonality and difference across space, global graffscapes are intertextually linked across urban landscapes, moving the traveller across and within cities. Graffscapes are a reminder of both the locality of global style and the globality of local style. Graffiti are also, however, as Milon (2002) reminds us, 'the translation of social unrest' (p. 87), an image of the city that reflects not only the desired objects of the bourgeois gaze – history, tradition, architecture, investment – but also those more threatening urban stories of subcultural struggle, class and social disquiet. Graffscapes also remind us that in this battle over what texts are permissible in public space, there is a struggle over possible ways of making sense, not the urbanity of international multilingualism but the intertextual world or urban semiotic resources (Makoni and Pennycook, 2007).

Contested zones and stained glass windows

When the 'zero-tolerance' campaign got under way in Melbourne before the Commonwealth Games, artists responded in a number of ways. As reported in *The Age* (Edwards, 2006b), 'In the graffiti war, it seems you can fight city hall – as long as you keep moving'. As Melbourne City Council and police continued their widely publicized crackdown on graffiti in order to keep the city 'clean' during the Commonwealth Games, a group of artists developed a roaming graffiti wall (Figure 6.3), made up of five large panels of stencil art, carried through the central business district of the city, passing along laneways that had formerly carried extensive graffiti art. According to local artist Patrick Jones, 'We received a lot of support, especially from international visitors, with lots of people taking photographs and talking to us' (cited in Edwards, 2006b). Melbourne's graffiti art scene was widely respected, he explained, and visitors were often more interested in the immediacy of a moving graffiti wall than the bourgeois estrangements of art galleries.

A more challenging reaction came from the internet, however. Police found that not only did they have to follow a walking wall of graffiti around the city but the battle had also moved into a different space, or rather into the interactive space between the internet and city walls: 'Police are investigating one website running the "Melbourne Graffiti Games" and offering gold, silver and bronze medals. Categories include most daring placement, best caricature of the mayor or councillor, most seditious piece and largest graffiti piece' (Kelly, 2006). Soon the use of a modified version of the Games' logo – the two running and jumping

FIGURE 6.3 Roaming graffiti wall, Melbourne

figures in the original were now seen holding spray cans (see Figure 6.4) – was banned as the police put pressure on the site owners to stop their promotion and display of 'dozens of photos of illegal graffiti – some with vandals pictured in the act' (ibid.). While the Commonwealth Games continued, and while Indigenous Australians made their own protest under the banner of the 'Stolenwealth Games', graffiti artists waged a new battle for public space and imagery. Even if graffiti in the city would be buffed within hours, a digital image could be placed online, and people could vote according to the various categories (see Figure 6.5).

A rather different response from the zero tolerance campaign being fought out in Melbourne comes from Father Gwilym Henry-Edwards of St Luke's

FIGURE 6.4 Graffiti Games logo

FIGURE 6.5 Online graffiti competition

Anglican Church, Enmore, Sydney, which he describes as a 'traditional church, in that we acknowledge that God works in many different ways' (Cited in Compass, 2006). As he goes on, 'The stained glass windows that we have – some of them are very historic over a hundred years old – and that medium of stained glass spoke very clearly to the people of the past, and this' he continues, gesturing to the wall of graffiti behind him (see Figure 6.6), 'speaks to people of the present and the future'. He goes on to explain that this wall of graffiti painted by Sydney graff artist Mistery, has received:

> a lot of very positive comments. There's a lady in one of the houses just down the lane who sits up in her window and has been watching Mistery working on it, and saying how wonderful it is to see such artistry on the wall. Because this expresses something which is important to people, and important to Mistery. It expresses his faith, his beliefs and people can see that and they appreciate it. (Compass, 2006)

Like a number of more enlightened urban dwellers, Father Henry-Edwards can see the benefits of engaging with the stained glass windows of the twenty-first century, a contemporary semiotic resource that tells an alternative story of the world. This dissolution of the division between the sacred (stained glass) and the profane (graffiti) invites us to reflect on what texts are sanctioned, what urban literacies allowed, what voices heard, which windows broken, which souls saved (and which buffed).

FIGURE 6.6 And the Word Became Flesh (see colour plate section)

Graffiti writing, as Conquergood (1997) points out, 'performatively constitutes middle-class and public spaces into contested zones of contact, site-specific theaters of defiance where excluded others re-present themselves' (p. 358). To treat graffiti only in terms of dirt or vandalism, to present a 'buffed' cityscape, is to stamp middle-class sensibilities on the urban landscape, to create the *bourgeoiscape*. To present only the buffed *paysage* rather than the living *visage* of the city is to reduce the possibilities of urban meaning-making. To travel though cities with an eye only for sanctioned texts is to operate within a very particular position on class, culture and the city. To overlook global subcultural commonality is to turn one's back on global flows of meaning in favour of a sanitized, class-based image of the local. To ignore the local upswelling of urban unrest depicted through graffiti is also to ignore the local in favour of a flattened class image of the global. Fortunately, graffiti, like language, are hard to control: Just as Singlish in Singapore reclaims the buffed linguascapes imposed by the state's 'speak good English' campaigns, so graffiti artists reclaim the buffed cityscapes that cannot last. Graffiti highlight several ways in which the buffed cityscape and the overlooked graffscape unsettle global relations of space.

The understanding of graffiti that I have been trying to open up here suggests a need to include a dynamic account of space, text and interaction: Readers and writers are part of the fluid, urban semiotic space, and produce meaning as they move, write, read and travel. The styles and locations of graffiti are about identity; they are statements of place, belonging, group membership and style. Landscapes are not mere backdrops on which texts and images are drawn but are spaces that are imagined and invented. Urban graffscapes are animated by the movement and interactions of city dwellers. If, as has become common recently, we view language in terms of practices, as an activity, in terms of 'languaging' (e.g. Shohamy, 2006), so too is it useful to see graffscapes not only as systems of meaning but also in terms of the active process of *graffscaping*. These are not only intertextual urban spaces but also discursive productions of the landscape. Landscapes are not mere canvases or contexts but rather integrative and invented environments. The importance of movement, of interactive spaces, brings a focus on place as dynamic, on city landscapes as having been graffscaped. Graffiti, as the stained glass windows of the twenty-first century, give cities soul.

Notes

[1] Indeed the rise of British street artist Banksy has also greatly increased the value of some city walls.

[2] I am indebted to Crispin Thurlow's comments on an earlier draft of this chapter for pointing to the problems with too easy an acceptance of the notion of transgression. More generally, this chapter has been considerably improved as a result of suggestions by the editors, Adam Jaworski and Crispin Thurlow.

[3] Held every 4 years, the Commonwealth Games is an international Olympics-type sporting event for the 53 member nations of the Commonwealth of Nations (formerly the British Commonwealth). The Indigenous Australian protest – the Stolenwealth Games – pointed to the irony of this term.

[4] Also known as *Yamakasi*, the name of one well-known group of practitioners, *l'art du déplacement* (the art of displacement) or free running. See http://www.le-parkour.com/ (accessed 20 January 2009).

[5] It is a shame that the English translation elides the original – 'l'énonciation (le speech act)' – as only 'speech act'. While de Certeau's gloss of enunciation as a speech act is itself problematic, the English translation misses the significance of enunciation.

[6] See, for example, the global graffiti on sites such as graffiti.com. Although graffiti can also be found in rural settings, they remain a largely urban phenomenon.

References

Appadurai, A. (1996), *Modernity at Large: Cultural Dimensions of Globalization*. Minneapolis: University of Minnesota Press.

—(2001), 'Grassroots globalization and the research imagination', in A. Appadurai (ed.), *Globalization*. Durham: Duke University Press, pp. 1–21.

Cannadine, D. (2000), *Class in Britain*. London: Penguin.

Castleman, C. (2004), 'The politics of graffiti', in M. Forman and M. A. Neal (eds), *That's the Joint: The Hip-Hop Studies Reader*. New York: Routledge, pp. 21–29.

Christen, R. S. (2003), 'Hip hop learning: Graffiti as an educator of urban teenagers', *Educational Foundations*, 17(4), 57–82.

City of Melbourne (2007), *Graffiti Management*. http://www.melbourne.vic.gov.au/info.cfm?top=145&pg=1150 (accessed 5 October 2007).

Compass (Sunday, 6 August 2006). *The Mistery of Hip Hop*. Television broadcast. Australia: ABC.

Conquergood, D. (1997), 'Street literacy', in J. Floord, S. Brice Heath and D. Lapp (eds), *Handbook of Research on Teaching Literacy through the Communicative and Visual Arts*. New York: Simon & Schuster, pp. 354–375.

Coslovich, G. (2005, 4 December), 'Our colourful underbelly', *The Age*. (Melbourne).

de Certeau, M. (1984), *The Practice of Everyday Life*. Translated by S Randall. Berkeley: University of California Press. (*L'invention du quotidien, 1. Arts de faire*. Paris: Gallimard, 1980).

Edwards, L. (2006a, 2 March), 'Graffiti blitz gives city a quick facelift', *The Age*. Melbourne.

—(2006b, 16 March), 'Stencil art on the run thwarts graffiti crackdown', *The Age*. Melbourne.

Gibson, C. and Connell, J. (2005), *Music and Tourism: On the Road Again*. Clevedon, UK: Channel View Publications.

Hansen, N. (2005), *Rash* [DVD]. Melbourne: Mutiny Media.

Jinman, R. (2007, 9 April), 'Street art moves to a posh new hang-out'. *The Sydney Morning Herald*. Sydney, p. 11.

Kelly, J. (2006, March 15), '24-hour attack on graffiti'. *Herald Sun*. Sydney.

Ma, E. K. W. (2002), 'Translocal spatiality', *International Journal of Cultural Studies*, 5(2), 131–152.
Makoni, S. and Pennycook, A. (2007), 'Disinventing and reconstituting languages', in S. Makoni and A. Pennycook (eds), *Disinventing and Reconstituting Languages*. Clevedon: Multilingual Matters, pp. 1–41.
Metcalf, T. (1995), *Ideologies of the Raj*. Cambridge: Cambridge University Press.
Milon, A. (2002), 'Tags and murals in France: A city's face or a natural landscape?', in A-P. Durand (ed.), *Black, Blanc, Beur: Rap music and Hip-Hop Culture in the Francophone World*. Lanham, MD: The Scarecrow Press, pp. 87–98.
Minister for Police and Emergency Services (2005), Media Release. http://www.legislation.vic.gov.au/domino/Web_Notes/newmedia.nsf/b0222c68d27626e2ca256c8c001a3d2d/0e47076ab0768debca2570bf007f8989!OpenDocument (accessed 5 October 2007).
Modan, G. (2007), *Turf Wars: Discourse, Diversity and the Politics of Place*. Oxford: Blackwell.
Pardue, D. (2004), '"Writing in the margins": Brazilian hip-hop as an educational project'. *Anthropology and Education*, 35(4), 411–432.
Pennycook, A. (2007), *Global Englishes and Transcultural Flows*. London: Routledge.
Rahn, J. (2002), *Painting Without Permission: Hip-Hop Graffiti Subculture*. Westport, CO: Bergin and Garvey.
Schama, S. (1995), *Landscape and Memory*. New York: Alfred Knopf.
Scollon, R. and Wong Scollon, S. (2003), *Discourses in Place: Language in the Material World*. London: Routledge.
Shohamy, E. (2006), *Language Policy: Hidden Agendas and New Approaches*. London: Routledge.
Smallman, J. and Nyman, C. (2005), *Stencil Graffiti Capital: Melbourne*. New York: Mark Batty.
Soja, E. (1989), *Postmodern Geographies: The Reassertion of Space in Critical Social Theory*. London: Verso.
Thurlow, C. and Aiello, G. (2007), 'National pride, global capital: A social semiotic analysis of transnational visual branding in the airline industry', *Visual Communication*, 6(3), 305–344.
Urry, J. (1995), *Consuming Places*. London: Routledge
—(2002), *The Tourist Gaze* (2nd edn). London: Sage.
—(2005), 'The "consuming" of place', in A. Jaworski and A. Pritchard (eds), *Discourse, Communication and Tourism*. Clevedon: Channel View Publications, pp. 19–27.
van Treeck, B. (2003), 'Styles – Typografie als Mittel zur Identitätsbildung', in Androutsopoulos, J. (Hg/eds), *HipHop: Globale Kultur – Lokale Praktiken*. Bielefeld: Transcript Verlag, pp. 102–110.
Xie, P. F., Osumare, H. and Ibrahim, A. (2007), 'Gazing the hood: Hip-Hop as tourism attraction', *Tourism Management*, 28(2), pp. 452–460.

Chapter 7

Cyberspace and Physical Space: Attention Structures in Computer Mediated Communication

Rodney H. Jones

Mr. Lam is a secondary school English teacher in Hong Kong. His school, like nearly every school in the territory, is equipped with a 'Multimedia Learning Center' (MMLC), but Mr. Lam never uses it. 'When you take your class there,' he says, 'it's a constant battle for their attention. They go crazy in the MMLC.' Another teacher agrees. 'As soon as they come into contact with computers, the class is out of control.' For some teachers, the problem goes beyond controlling students in the MMLC. Computers, they insist, have even made it more difficult for them to manage their ordinary classrooms. 'It's the on-line games,' one insists. 'They can't pay attention to anything else. They fall asleep in class.'

Many popular and scholarly treatments of computer mediated communication in recent years have focused on how computers have 'despatialized' communication (Katriel, 1999), allowing us to communicate over vast distances and interact in virtual environments whose spatial characteristics differ considerably from the physical world, environments in which we can, for all intents and purposes, leave physical space and our physical bodies behind (Haraway, 1991; Turkle, 1995). What the quotations above illustrate, however, is that among the most profound effects of these technologies is the way they have altered spatial configurations and social relationships in the physical spaces – classrooms, living rooms and offices – where people use computers. One domain in which these changes have been most dramatic has been education, where the presence of computers has significantly changed the way teachers and students orient themselves towards the physical spaces of classrooms and lecture halls.

From the point of view of teachers like those quoted above, these changes have been less than successful. Central to their concerns is the effect they perceive the presence of computers has on students' ability to pay sufficient attention to what is going on in the physical world around them, a fear that is reflected in both popular and scholarly treatments of the computer use of young people (Hembrooke and Gay, 2003; Healy, 1998; Jensen et al., 1997). Similar concerns about attention have been raised regarding the effect of computers on the space of the home, where they are blamed for isolating children from their parents and the day-to-day activities of family life (DeGaetano, 2004;

Lau and Au, 2002; Winn, 2002). Many parents and teachers feel as if they are engaged, in the words of Mr. Lam, in a 'constant battle' for young people's attention, and their adversary in this battle is technology itself. These attitudes partly have their source in wider media and educational discourses about computer mediated communication linking it to a decline in literacy, cognitive ability and moral standards (Thurlow, 2006).

This paper examines the ways teenagers in Hong Kong use computers at home and in school and the effect it has on the ways they orient themselves towards these physical spaces and other people who are present in them. It takes as a central aspect of this phenomenon the very concern raised above – the impact of computers on students' ability to 'pay attention' – and in so doing, argues that the key to understanding the relationship between computers and the physical world is understanding the role of 'attention' in the social construction of space. The data for my discussion comes from a participatory ethnographic study of computers and youth literacy in Hong Kong, which involved tracing the in-school and out-of-school literacy practices of 50 secondary school students (aged 14–17) for 6 months.

The kinds of data collected include diaries, screen movies of participants' computer use, focus group discussions and in-depth interviews with students, teachers and parents, and onsite and video observations of teenagers using computers in various in-school and out-of-school settings. The methodological framework for the study comes from *mediated discourse analysis* (MDA) (Norris and Jones, 2005; Scollon, 2001; Scollon and Wong Scollon, 2004), an approach which examines the role of discourse and other mediational means (for example, computers, telephones, furniture and seating arrangements) in affecting the kinds of social actions that people can take, and thus the kinds of identities and social relationships they can construct.

The difference between a mediated discourse approach to computer use and other discursive work in computer mediated communication (see for example Danet and Herring , 2007; Herring , 1996) is that rather then focusing primarily on discourse, MDA begins by asking what actions are being taken by participants and how discourse is (or is not) being used to take them.

Space and attention structures

All actions take place in multiple and overlapping spaces, built spaces, geographical spaces, political spaces, personal spaces, spaces that extend inward to the innermost spaces of our bodies, and outward through rooms, buildings, cities, nations and beyond, spaces that extend across biological, physical and social processes (Scollon, 2005). This is not, however, the way we experience space. Through our actions, we make space *finite* by inscribing onto it a sphere or 'circumference' of operation with our attention. For Lefebvre (1991), this 'lived space' of activities occurs as an interaction of 'perceived space' (*l'espace perçu*), the material objects that exist in the world and their relationship with one another, and 'conceived space' (*l'espace conçu*), the mental conceptions and symbolic representations we have of space. But 'lived space', what Lefebvre calls 'third space', is more than just the overlay of mind onto matter. It is conceived in social actions and determinant of what kinds of social actions can be taken in it. It is not something we inhabit; it is something we 'do'.

And it is not, something that we do alone. Spaces are constructed not just through the objects and boundaries that surround us and the habitual ways we conceive of them, but also through interaction with others who are operating in the 'same' space. Scollon and Wong Scollon (2004) call these three elements of social space the *discourses in place* (the physical/semiotic setting), the *interaction order* (the social relationships among participants) and the *historical body* (the life experiences-memories, learning, skills and plans) of the individuals. Each of these elements helps to determine how we 'live' space by structuring our attention in particular ways that make some kinds of social actions possible and others impossible.

In an earlier paper (Jones, 2005), I argued that attention is a vital component in the way we experience and interact with space – both physical and virtual – and built upon Lanham's (1993) notion of 'attention structures' – socially and technologically mediated 'frames' or 'organizers' which result from the interaction of the *discourses in place*, the *interaction order*, and the *historical body*. 'Attention', I proposed not as a mere cognitive construct, but also a social one; all social interaction has its basis in conventions for giving, getting and displaying attention. 'Attention structures', then, consist of both cognitive frameworks and social frameworks for distributing and attracting attention.

Discourses in place or the physical environments in which we take actions channel, block or amplify our attention with walls, windows, doors and furniture as well as with written or spoken texts, images, sounds and the technologies through which they are delivered. *Interaction orders* channel our attention through socially developed ways of 'paying attention' to different kinds of people and in different sorts of social situations. Finally, the experiences stored within our *historical bodies* help us to determine which facets of different situations require focal attention and which facets can be backgrounded. Through learning, our historical bodies also allow us to *not* pay attention to particular aspects of a social action in order to be able to distribute our attention more efficiently (Schmidt, 2001).

The ways each of these elements channels our attention and allows us to undertake particular social actions are dynamically determined by the way they interact with the other elements. The habits of 'paying attention' in an individual's *historical body* are built up through contact with various *discourses in place* and various *interaction orders*. The ways we manage attention in *interaction* depends on the *history* of interactions between individuals and within particular *places*. And *physical environments* are often designed to accommodate or enforce particular *interaction orders* or the plans schemes or habits of particular *historical bodies*. At the same time, attention structures within these three elements can also work at cross-purposes. You may, for example, have developed within your historical body an attention structure for crossing the street in one country which you find slightly out of synch with the attention structure embodied in the environment and social conventions of another place, or the attention structure embodied in your relationship with the person with whom you are crossing the street might cause you to disregard or even behave at odds with the discourses in place or your own inclinations. In other words, the attention structures embodied in these three elements of a mediated action can be, to a certain degree, either in or out of 'synch' with one another.

The process of understanding how computers change the ways physical spaces are experienced, then, involves understanding something about the physical spaces themselves and the objects in them, the interactions that occur in these spaces, and at the habitual ways the individuals involved conceive of space. Hollaway and Valentine (2003) theorize that young people build their identities by travelling across three main social spaces: home, school and cyberspace, and that children's online actions are invariably affected by the discourses and interactions in these other spaces. And so this analysis will begin with the home space, and then consider the school space, examining how the physical, social and embodied aspects of these spaces interact with what we have come to call 'cyberspace'.

Students' computer use at home

In Hong Kong apartments are small. The average floor space per person is 7.10 square meters (as opposed to 20 in Singapore and nearly 16 in Tokyo) (Chan et al., 2002). In most of the households we visited computers were placed not in children's rooms, but in the living area of the apartment where family members congregated to eat meals, watch TV, play mahjongg and converse (Figures 7.1 and 7.2 which show opposite ends of the same living space). Use of

FIGURE 7.1 Jason's living room (view A)

the computer was often shared among family members, with children being the primary users.

Thus, when they are operating their computers, the *discourses in place* towards which young people's attention is typically directed exist not just in the circumference of the screen. They also include family conversations and activities taking place around them in which they have various levels of involvement, as well as other media in the environment, such as written texts like newspapers, magazines and school textbooks, and other electronic media such as telephones, radios and television sets. Four students in the study were asked to install webcams and to take movies of themselves using their computes. What is striking about these movies is the amount of time their gaze is *not* on the computer screen but directed at something else in their immediate environment. In a total of 738 minutes of webcam data, students were looking *away* from their screens for 198 minutes, more than a quarter of the time they were seated in front of their computers.

The amount of attention they gave to these discourses in material space varied widely depending on the activities they were engaged in online and the activities that were taking place in the physical space. The initiation of an interaction by a co-present other (e.g. a parent or sibling), the ringing of their mobile phone or the start of their favourite television program sometimes took their attention briefly away from their screens. Often though, they were able to participate in family conversations and activities, chat with friends on the telephone and attend to what was going on on TV without taking their attention away from their screens. In other words, the demands made by discourses in place more often than not make operating a computer for these students a *polyfocal*

FIGURE 7.2 Jason's living room (view B)

activity. By polyfocal I mean not that they were able to focus on many things at exactly the same time, but that their attention shifted rather rapidly among multiple activities in a complex cognitive and social dance (Jones, 2009).

Even when students' computers were isolated in their bedrooms, the demands of their immediate physical environments persisted, with computer use often accompanied by television watching, phone conversations and the occasional intervention of family members. In fact, students' rooms were typically even more 'media rich' than their family living rooms (Steele and Brown, 1995), equipped with various portable media like ipods and mobile phones, and with walls plastered with photos, posters, maps and other texts – a visual expression of their polyfocal attention (Figure 7.3).

Just as the physical environment normally offered multiple foci of attention, the space of the students' computer screens was normally not treated as a single focus of attention, but a series of overlapping and interested foci, with different programs open in different windows and multiple tasks being performed at once. Students regularly combined 'doing homework' with web-browsing, engaging in multiple instant messaging conversations, reading and contributing to message boards, online diaries or blogs, writing and drawing on 'flash boards', visiting chat rooms, downloading and sharing (mostly pirated) music, videos and software through websites and peer to peer applications, and playing online games. The discourses in place of students' home computer use, then, created a series of overlapping and interested spatial and interactional contexts

FIGURE 7.3 Kitty's bedroom

across which practices were polychronically (Hall, 1959) distributed over a wide array of activities at once, with multiple tasks in progress simultaneously. Practices were almost always parts of 'event complexes' in which attention was distributed over various online and offline spaces, making it difficult to discuss one particular practice in isolation, or sometimes even to understand what constituted a practice, where a practice began and ended. When asked how much time they spent on instant messaging in a particular week, for example, most participants in our study could not answer, saying things like: 'How do I know? The program is on all the time'. These practices were also often interconnected, with offline conversations 'resemiotized' (Iedema, 2001) into words and symbols in chat windows, phone conversations, blog entries, exchanges of files from one computer to another, online gaming sessions or homework assignments.

The presence of computers also altered the *interaction order*, both in the immediate spaces of students' homes and in the wider geographical spaces of their neighbourhoods and city. Despite concerns that adolescent computer use isolates young people from their families (DeGaetano, 2004; Lau and Au, 2002), research has shown that the actual situation is much more complicated. For example, in a recent survey of over 200 families in Korea, Lee and Chae (2007) found that while respondents perceived computer use as resulting in declines in family time, they did not perceive a negative affect on family communication. In fact, communication around computer use and co-use by family members was seen to improve family communication.

This was also borne out in our own observations. Not only did our participants frequently communicate with family members *while* using computers and often used computers together with parents and siblings (to play games, shop or search for information of mutual interest), computers also afforded children (who usually knew more about them than their parents) opportunities to assume 'identities of expertise' in their families (Holloway and Valentine, 2003). Adolescents were often called upon to assist their parents in dealing with technical problems and to help them with online tasks such as paying bills and investing in stocks, activities in which, in the absence of computers, adolescents are not normally included.

At the same time, computers were also used by our participants as 'boundary objects', allowing them to shield certain activities from their parents, giving them a sense of 'privacy' heretofore impossible in such cramped living arrangements. An instant messaging conversation with a friend or romantic interest, for example, is much easier to conceal from co-present others than a phone conversation. The best thing about ICQ (a popular instant messaging program), one participant noted, is that 'no one will know what we are talking about and doing in ICQ'. Thus, computer mediated communication functioned as what Leander (2005) has called a 'boundary practice' – a practice which facilitates the management of boundaries (and identities) between different social worlds (home, school, shopping centres, circles of friends), enabling users to extend the territory upon which they could act into realms in which parents and siblings had no access and could not police. While this fact sometimes caused some consternation among parents who wondered what their children were doing online, they also saw some benefits: rather than forcing students out of the home, computers allowed students to engage in activities and relationships they did not wish to share with their parents without leaving the physical proximity (and safety) of their families.

Computers also have a profound effect on the way these students operate in the physical/social spaces that extend beyond the walls of their crowded apartments. Perhaps the biggest error in approaches which bifurcate physical space and cyberspace and conclude that computers isolate students from the physical world (see for example Kraut et al., 1998; Kroker and Weinstein, 1994) is that they ignore the fact that the vast majority of people with whom students communicate online are people (friends, classmates, relatives) with whom they regularly have face to face interaction, sometimes on a daily basis. Nearly all research that has looked in detail at this relationship has found that the vast majority of people who engage in computer mediated communication regard it as an extension of their 'real-life' social interactions rather than as separate from them, that, far from propelling users into 'cyberspace', the effect of CMC is more often to ground them more firmly within their existing material communities and circumstances (Hamman, 1998, 1999; Holloway and Valentine, 2003; Orleans and Laney, 2000).

Similarly, observations of our participants made it clear that rather than isolating them from the physical world it expanded their immediate sense of physical space as they populated their computer screens with interactions with friends and classmates most often residing in close geographical proximity. IM contact lists constituted social gatherings in which interactants enacted 'presence' on multiple computer screens located throughout geographical space, gatherings which, although 'virtual' in nature, most often had important consequences in the physical world. At the same time, computers again acted as 'boundary objects', helping users better manage their social relationships. The discourses in place of IM interfaces, for example, provided various affordances and constraints for managing social and relational spaces and distributing attention through them, allowing users to modulate their presence through adjusting their online 'status', indicating, for example that they were free for chat, busy or temporarily away from their computers or choosing to be 'visible' or 'invisible' to selected parties.

In many ways computer mediated communication was not so much about 'communicating' for our participants as it was about distributing and attracting social attention. As online and offline interactions and relationships blended and interactants played with the new media's unique ability to convey who was directing attention towards whom, computer mediated communication came to reflect the attention structures of interaction orders that extend over online and offline spaces. IM contact lists and strategies for managing them, for example, resemiotize aspects of students' social relationships: who's in; who's out; who is more deserving of attention; who gets assigned 'invisible'.

The attention structures inscribed in the discourses in place and enacted in social relationships interact with and affect the attention structures that develop in the historical bodies of users. Our participants had years of practice in distributing attention over multiple interactions and tasks. These attention structures, which they take for granted, are perhaps best understood by looking at historical bodies where they have not been developed: those of their teachers. One teacher, for example, described her experience engaging in IM interactions with her students like this:

> It was a mixture of feelings. I was very busy and almost unable to handle the chaotic situation when about ten dialogue boxes appeared on the screen simultaneously. My fingers were trembling and I didn't know which one to click on . . . my students said that I was a 'low B' (not very intelligent) in handling the confusion that the IM messages had created.

Students, however, were more accustomed to the multi-tasking which computers not only enabled but almost required. One participant claimed:

> I have no trouble studying and memorizing things, chatting with my friends and playing online games. I think it works quite well. Faster. As I have to think while playing games. I have already started thinking, thinking how to type. My brain is already functioning. So it is faster and easier for me to study.

These polyfocal attention structures in the historical bodies of these students are stored not as information, but as intuition as, knowledge 'built into the movements, bodies and unconscious ways of thinking (users) have built up through repeated practice' (Gee, 2003: 110). It is the 'embodied' nature of home computer use that makes the attention structures that it develops so different from those that develop around the 'disembodied' and abstract information that is often part of school-based learning.

When engaging in IM conversations or playing online games, students felt that their attention was always situated in clear material and social contexts (Gee, 2003; Tynes, 2007). The management and focus of attention had constant and immediate consequences on the 'physical' world of the game or the social world of their peer groups in ways that it did not in many school-based practices like doing 'exercises', writing essays or taking examinations. Users were involved in 'embodied stories' (Gee, 2003), and the 'embodied' quality of practices like 'fragging' (i.e. killing) an opponent in an online game or arguing with one's boyfriend over IM were palpable.

Students' computer use at school

The ways computers are integrated into school-based literacy practices for these students created very different orientations towards physical space than those observed in their homes. For one thing, most school-based literacy practices – and the policies that inform them – promote fundamentally different expectations about attention. Far from the polyfocal orientation discussed above, students in school were expected to pay attention to only one thing at a time, and for longer periods. This monofocal orientation is enforced by the *panopticon* style settings (Foucault, 1977) of traditional classrooms in which the physical environment, social relationships and the habitual practices of participants channel attention towards the teacher. Conventions for gaining and granting attention are also built into the interaction order of classrooms, which include conventions like teachers electing students for attention or students inviting it by raising their hands. Attention giving or attention seeking outside of this rather strict economy is seen as disruptive.

'Multimedia Learning Centers' (MMLCs) were established in the territory's secondary schools to enhance interactive and experiential learning, but despite the Hong Kong government's enthusiastic commitment to making IT an integral part of teaching, computer-equipped classrooms remain underused (Hong Kong Dept. of Education, 2001) for many of the reasons related by teachers in the beginning of this chapter. In particular, teachers feel that the presence of computers is a 'distraction' from learning. Consequently, many of the teachers we talked to avoided using these facilities. When asked what she thought the purpose of the MMLC was in her school, one student replied, 'I think the main purpose of it is to show it to parents on parents' day'. When they did use these facilities, teachers usually worked to design activities in which students used computers in the most restrictive ways possible if at all. Another student remarked:

> It's like the classroom. The only difference is that we have a computer in front of us. Sometimes, she may type something outside and we see. She controls our computers. We only see. You can never use the computer throughout the class. We only sit and see.

The particular lesson I will analyze here involved secondary 3 (grade 9) students in an English class. The class used the MMLC about once a fortnight in response to a regulation imposed by the school administration. Usually these forays to the MMLC involved working through exercises on a multimedia CD-ROM called *Planet English*, filling in online grammar exercises, watching movies or practising 'speaking' (which usually meant pronunciation). On the occasion of our observation, the students were instructed to read a passage from their textbooks into a microphone and then listen to it through their computers. At the end of the lesson the teacher played back some students' attempts for the class to discuss.

In this class students sat at long tables arranged in rows on either side of a central aisle, each seat fitted with a computer, monitor, keyboard and mouse. The teacher's desk and computer were situated in the front of the room. In other words, the *discourses in place* in the form of the layout of the class mirror almost exactly the arrangement of the traditional *panopticon* classroom. At the same time, however, the ability of the teacher to use this layout to monitor students was limited by the computer screens, which shielded students from scrutiny, making it necessary for the teacher to situate herself in the aisle to see what they were doing (a position that made it impossible for her to make use of the computer monitoring system on her own screen at the front of the class). Furthermore, penetrating the rows of computers to reach students farther away from the aisle was nearly impossible (Figures 7.4 and 7.5).

FIGURE 7.4 MMLC – view from rear

FIGURE 7.5 MMLC – view from front

Another important discourse in place in this classroom was the text that the students were meant to recite: a passage from their print textbook about pandas. Unlike the texts students were accustomed to interacting with online, this printed text was linear and monologic. In this particular activity, students were primarily engaged with the text on a phonological level – the text was treated as a collection of symbols to be transformed into sounds; the meaning of the text was inconsequential. For most of the lesson, the majority of students' gazes were directed down at this text, which they had to hold in their hands because the desk space in front of them was taken up by their computer monitors (Figure 7.6).

In contrast, the aspect of the discourses in place which normally one would expect to be central in such settings, the text displayed on the computer screen, here is also practically inconsequential. Students' screens showed simply an interface designed to look like the controls of a tape recorder (Figure 7.7).

FIGURE 7.6 The textbook

FIGURE 7.7 The computer screen

Perhaps the most striking aspect of the discourses in place in this situation is that they had very little to do with one another; the meaning of the room filled with computer equipment, the meaning of the teacher's movements throughout the room, the meaning of the text students were reading, and the meaning of the words and symbols on their screens appeared to be totally divorced from one another. The actions participants were meant to take with these discourses in place were disconnected from the meanings expressed in the texts themselves, and seemed to have little to do with the way such discourses are used to take actions in 'real' social practices (where we do not normally read to our computers).

Rather than being used for practices computers are used for in their everyday world, in this and other lessons we observed, computers were appropriated into 'old-literacy' practices, turned into tape recorders, written texts and fill in the blank exercises. Thus, the spaces constructed by computers were domesticated and 'rewired' by conventional pedagogical discourses (Leander, 2005). One of our participants remarked, 'we have listening in MMLC. But it has nothing to do with computers'. Another put it perhaps most succinctly when he said simply, 'Our teacher uses computers to teach book stuff'.

The interaction order in this situation was based chiefly on surveillance. The teacher's physical and virtual monitoring of activities helped give shape to the students' attention as they performed or resisted performing (Figures 7.8 and 7.9) the assigned task. The task dictated that they interact only with the teacher or with themselves in the form of a recording of their own voice.

Through this analysis I do not mean to dismiss the pedagogical value of recoding and listening to one's pronunciation, nor am I trying to suggest that interesting and interactive lessons which keep students 'on-task' cannot be performed in physical spaces like these. In fact, that is what they are designed for.

Figure 7.8 MMLC

FIGURE 7.9 MMLC

This cannot happen, however, as long as practices in these rooms attempt to impose attention structures from traditional classroom spaces and traditional literacy practices that fundamentally contradict the orientations towards space characteristic of computer mediated communication.

Educational activities which fail to recognize and exploit this kind of interaction are fundamentally 'out-of-synch' with the discourses in place and the interaction orders implicit in the technology and with the attention structures students have built up in their historical bodies through years of using computers.

Conclusion

The point I have tried to make in this chapter is that physical space is primarily a social achievement. It is not just a matter of material objects (like computers) or of individual cognitive processes, but a product of the interaction among the material, social and psychological worlds of social interactants. The problem of attention in such physical spaces as these classrooms is not the fault of the individuals, and not the fault of the computers, but the result of a complex nexus of overlapping and competing attention structures in the discourses in place, the interaction order, and the historical bodies of participants which are reflected in broader discursive formations around architecture.

Attention structures not only work to orient us towards different aspects of space; in very fundamental ways they shape our social identities and social relationships. The actions that we perform with others create the spaces that we inhabit with them, and the ways we orient towards space makes some actions more possible and some less possible. The monochronic orientation towards space evidenced by the teachers and parents in this study seems to lend itself to more transactional exchanges in which computers are constructed as a means for transferring information (knowledge, money and goods), whereas the more polychromic orientation evidenced by students lends itself to more relational exchanges in which social formations are established and maintained and computers are seen primarily as a means of communication and social networking (Thurlow, 2007). As homes and schools become increasingly media rich (Livingstone, 2002), the competing attention structures associated with these media increasingly characterizes relationships between young people and adults. Spaces in which competing attention structures overlap are sites of social struggle in which people reproduce or resist particular social positions. Fairclough (1992) argues that in cases where different situations create the need for diverse positionings; people either accept and modify their behaviour to cope with each setting or they struggle and contest for change. For the MMLC students in this study, one strategy for contesting the positioning imposed on them was to simply 'switch off' their attention in much the same way their teachers had 'switched off' their computers in attempts to combat distraction. This disconnect, which pervades physical spaces (home vs school), textual spaces (the generic practices of textbooks vs those of new media texts), and social spaces (interpersonal relationships vs institutional relationships), creates a vicious circle of disengagement, disinterest, frustration and distrust. If new technologies are to be used effectively in educational settings, governments, school authorities and teachers must appreciate that simply creating access to hardware and software is not enough: materials and lesson design must also integrate an understanding of how the uses of technologies emerge from the everyday discourses and practices of the people who actually use them.

References

Chan, H. W., Tang, B. S. and Wong, W. S. (2002), 'Density control and the quality of living space: A case study of private housing development in Hong Kong', *Habitat International*, 26(2), 159–175.

Danet, B. and Herring, S. C. (eds) (2007), *The Multilingual Internet: Language, Culture, and Communication Online*. New York: Oxford University Press.

DeGaetano, G. (2004), *Parenting Well in a Media Age: Keeping Our Kids Human*. Fawnskin, CA: Personhood Press.

Fairclough, N. (1992), *Discourse and Social Change*. Cambridge: Polity Press.

Foucault, M. (1977), *Discipline and Punish*. New York: Pantheon Books.

Gee, J. P. (2003), *What Video Games Can Teach Us about Learning and Literacy*. New York: Palgrave Macmillan.

Hall, E. T. (1959), *The Silent Language*. Garden City, NY: Doubleday.

Hamman, R. B. (1998), 'The online/offline dichotomy: Debunking some myths about AOL Users and the effects of their being online upon offline friendships and offline Community'. Unpublished MPhil. Thesis, University of Liverpool.

—(1999), 'Computer networks linking network communities: A study of the effects of computer network use upon pre-existing communities'. http://www.socio.demon.co.uk/cybersociety/ (accessed 15 July 2005).

Haraway, D. (1991), 'A cyborg manifesto: Science, technology, and socialist-feminism in the late twentieth century', in D. Haraway, *Simians, Cyborgs and Women: The Reinvention of Nature.* New York: Routledge, pp. 149–181.

Healy, J. (1998), *Failure to Connect: How Computers Affect Our Children's Minds and What We Can Do About It.* New York: Simon and Schuster.

Hembrooke, H. and Gay, G. (2003), 'The laptop in the lecture: Effects of multitasking in learning environments', *Journal of Computing in Higher Education,* 15(1), 1–19.

Herring, S. C. (ed.) (1996), *Computer-mediated Communication: Linguistic, Social and Cross-cultural Perspectives.* Philadelphia, PA: John Benjamins.

Holloway, S. L. and Valentine, G. (eds) (2003), *Cyberkids: Children in the Information Age.* London: Routledge.

Hong Kong Department of Education (2001), 'Preliminary study on reviewing the progress and evaluating the information technology in education projects'. http://www.ited.ed.gov.hk/Documents/ITEd_Report/FinalReport_v3.0_web.htm (accessed 15 July 2005).

Iedema, R. (2001), 'Resemiotization', *Semiotica,* 137(1/4), 23–39.

Jensen, P. S., Mrazek, D., Knapp, P. K., Steinberg, L., Pfeffer, C., Schowalter, J. and Shapiro, T. (1997), 'Evolution and revolution in child psychiatry: ADHD as a disorder of adaptation', *Journal of the American Academy of Child & Adolescent Psychiatry,* 36(12), 1672–1679.

Jones, R. (2005), 'Sites of engagement as sites of attention: Time, space and culture in electronic discourse', in S. Norris and R. Jones (eds), *Discourse in Action: Introducing Mediated Discourse Analysis,* London: Routledge, pp. 141–154.

—(2009), 'Inter-activity: How new media can help us understand old media', in C. Rowe and E. Wyss (eds), *New Media and Linguistic Change,* Cresskill, NJ: Hampton Press, pp. 11–29.

Katriel, T. (1999), 'Rethinking the terms of social interaction', *Research on Language and Social Interaction,* 32(1–2), 95–101.

Kraut, R. E., Patterson, M., Lundmark, V., Kiesler, S., Mukhopadhyay, T. and Scherlis, W. (1998), 'Internet Paradox: A Social Technology that Reduces Social Involvement and Psychological Well-being?', *American Psychologist,* 53(9), 1017–1032.

Kroker, A. and Weinstein, M. A. (1994), *Data Trash: The Theory of the Virtual Class.* New York: St. Martin's Press.

Lanham, R. A. (1993), *The Electronic World: Democracy, Technology and the Arts.* Chicago: The University of Chicago Press.

Lau, K. and Au, W. K. (2002), 'Use of computers and family life of tertiary students in Hong Kong', in *Computers in Education, 2002. Proceedings. International Conference Vol. 1,* pp. 494–498.

Leander, K. (2005), 'Home/schooling. Everywhere: Digital literacies as practices of space-time', Symposium conducted at the Annual Meeting of the American Educational Research Association. Montréal, Canada.

Lee, S. J. and Chae, Y. G. (2007), 'Children's internet use in a family context: Influences on family relationships and parental mediation', *CyberPsychology and Behavior*, 10(5), 640–644.

Lefebvre, H. (1991), *The Production of Space*. Cambridge, MA: Blackwell.

Livingstone, S. (2002), *Young People and New Media*. London: Sage.

Norris, S. and Jones, R. (eds) (2005), *Discourse in Action: Introducing Mediated Discourse Analysis*. London: Routledge.

Orleans, M. and Laney, M. C. (2000), 'Children's computer use in the home: Isolation or sociation?', *Social Science Computer Review*, 18(1), 56–72.

Schmidt, R. (2001), 'Attention', in P. Robinson (ed.), *Cognition and Second Language Instruction*. Cambridge: Cambridge University Press, pp. 3–32.

Scollon, R. (2001), *Mediated Discourse: The Nexus of Practice*. London: Routledge.

—(2005), 'The rhythmic integration of action and discourse: Work, the body, and the earth', in S. Norris and R. Jones (eds), *Discourse in Action: Introducing Mediated Discourse Analysis*. London: Routledge, pp. 20–31.

Scollon, R. and Wong Scollon, S. (2004), *Nexus Analysis: Discourse and the Emerging Internet*. London: Routledge.

Steele, J. and Brown, J. D. (1995), 'Adolescent room culture: Studying media in the context of everyday life', *Journal of Youth and Adolescence*, 24(5), 551.

Thurlow, C. (2006), 'From statistical panic to moral panic: The metadiscursive construction and popular exaggeration of new media language in the print media', *Journal of Computer Mediated Communication*, 11, 667–701.

—(2007), 'Fabricating youth: New-media discourse and the technologization of young people', in Sally Johnson and A. Ensslin (eds), *Language in the Media: Representations, Identities, Ideologies*. London: Continuum, pp. 213–233.

Turkle, S. (1995), *Life on the Screen: Identity in the Age of the Internet*. New York: Simon and Schuster.

Tynes, B. M. (2007), 'Internet safety gone wild: Sacrificing the educational and psychosocial benefits of online social environments', *Journal of Adolescent Research*, 6, 575–584.

Winn, M. (2002), *Plug-in Drug: Television, Computers and Family Life* (25th Anni. edn). Camberwell, Australia: Penguin Books Australia Ltd.

Chapter 8

'A Latino Community Takes Hold': Reproducing Semiotic Landscapes in Media Discourse

Thomas D. Mitchell

In this chapter, I examine how an article in the *Pittsburgh Post-Gazette* came to characterize or rather mischaracterize the Latino community in a neighbourhood about 2.5 miles from downtown Pittsburgh.[1] As the only feature article on Latino immigrants living in Beechview, this article by Diana Nelson Jones was framed in a way that (over)emphasized conflict between 'longtime' and new residents – even though it strived for objectivity by providing a variety of perspectives. In effect, the Jones article represents a familiar discourse of fear about Latino immigrants on the part of the 'traditional' residents, even reproducing such a discourse through the use of the two most common metaphors that Otto Santa Ana (2002) found to negatively portray immigration in his study of public discourse about Latinos in California: immigration as an 'invasion' and/or immigration as a 'flood'.

The Jones article supported the idea that the Latino population in Beechview was substantial and rapidly increasing and represented non-Latino residents' reactions to these new immigrants as fearful. This created an impression of the neighbourhood that is inconsistent with the actual numbers that the census and other sources give, numbers that were also mentioned in the article itself. In other words, there is a discrepancy between the reported size of Beechview's Latino population, on one hand, and the way this population is represented in the media, as growing and substantial enough to produce fear on the part of non-Latino residents. Subsequent *Post-Gazette* articles sustain the link between Latino immigrants and this specific Pittsburgh neighbourhood, referring to Beechview as having a 'strong Latino presence' ('Latin Chic', 2006) and as being 'a growing Spanish-speaking enclave' (Fitzpatrick, 2005). As in the Jones article, however, when these journalists cite census figures, the numbers indicate the Latino population is in fact relatively small. If the largest estimate of the Beechview Latino population is no more than 5 per cent of the total, why, I wondered, do journalists choose to represent the situation as they do?[2]

I argue in this chapter that there are at least three (likely interrelated) reasons. First, there are circulating discourses, both local and non-local, that position immigration as a threat and which effectively constrain how immigrants can be represented. Second, journalistic practices and genre expectations constrain what reporters can write and how. Third, I would also like to propose that the semiotic landscape of Beechview – its visual and aural dimensions – as experienced by journalists like Jones may lead them to think of the immigrant population as being more significant, more substantial than it actually is. To this end, I decided to spend time myself in the spaces at the centre of Jones' and others' reporting about the immigrant community of Beechview.

Attitudes about immigrants are invariably shaped by local people's experiences of and with them (Blommaert et al., 2003). In the context of media production, this can hold true not only for the journalist's sources, but also for the journalist herself. The contribution this chapter seeks to make is to show that in order to understand media representations of immigrants, we need to supplement text-based analyses of media discourse with ethnographically-oriented research about how reporters might experience the spaces and places of immigration in the course of their work. Paying attention to the semiotic landscape experienced by the producers of media discourse gives us a way of understanding a key part of the 'text production' aspect of the discourse practice (Fairclough, 1992, 1995) of news reporting that may be overlooked in analyses of news texts in isolation. To this end, I start by examining the underlying journalistic values, actors and structures that shape the particular instance of news making at the centre of my study.

Framing the problem: Media discourse about the place/s of immigration

Teun van Dijk (1991) argues that analyzing media discourse is of great importance because of how it can shape public opinion and create perceptions that become widely held (pp. 226–227). The way journalists describe events, individuals and groups creates identities and influences social relations. Particularly important is the selection of the news actors whose opinions and observations contribute to the shape of the world created by the story. It has been noted that an ideal of objectivity operates as an 'occupational ideology' of the press (Roshco, 1975: 41), and thus journalists often feel compelled to include voices of opposing news actors.

The case-study article I focus on here, which appeared in July 2005 with the title 'In Beechview, a Latino Community Takes Hold', reflects an attempt at the ideal of objectivity in this way. The news actors to whom the journalist gave voice were representative of non-Latinos and Latinos in nearly equal number. The article's 'accessed voices' (Hartley, 1982: 111) were a white native Pittsburgher who owned a Mexican grocery with her Mexican husband; a Roman Catholic priest who had occasionally given Mass in Spanish in Beechview; an employee from a bank near Beechview; a postal worker; the owner of a business in Beechview who had emigrated from Italy 26 years previously; the president of the Beechview Merchants Association (BMA); an unattributed 'some' who, given a voice both by author, Jones, and the president of the BMA, were representative of the non-immigrant residents; and a Mexican immigrant resident of Beechview. The priest, the Italian business owner, and the Mexican immigrant were all characterized as being positive about the new immigrant community.

Perhaps the journalistic ideal of objectivity contributed to Jones' framing of the story in a way that is typical of 'conflict-saturated' news (Cappella and Jamieson, 1997: 9). As van Dijk (1986) notes, focus on conflict and controversy is common in the media: 'The news media do not passively describe or record news events in the world, but actively (re)construct them' with a 'special focus on negative, conflictual . . . events' (p. 204). Instead of portraying the new immigrant community by focusing solely on its members and giving voice to as many segments of it as possible, Jones emphasized tensions between Latino and non-Latino residents. In the analysis that follows, I show that the way she established the story's lead was also consistent with the representation of the neighbourhood given by the president of the BMA, the only directly quoted representative of the longtime residents. Therefore, the constraints of her profession seem to have dictated that the article be structured in a way that foregrounded negative consequences of immigrants' arrival.

The article can be divided into five main sections. The headline comprises the first section. The second (Paragraphs 1–3) may be characterized as the lead and its elaboration. In these paragraphs, the overall structure of the article is outlined: there are conspicuous Latino immigrants in Beechview and they are recipients of both animosity and support. The third section (Paragraphs 4–11) provides evidence of Latino immigrant growth. The fourth section (Paragraphs 12–17) gives accounts of community member reactions to the new immigrant population. The final section, which I do not discuss here, is a 'human interest' story that provides details of the experience of the aforementioned Mexican immigrant living in Beechview.

The headline: Invasion

Multiple analyses of news discourse (e.g. Bell, 1991; van Dijk, 1987) have emphasized the importance of headlines. News headlines frame an event in a way that is meant both to attract readers' attention and to summarize the story's content. While the journalist who writes a piece may have no control over the headline, it is someone's (likely a subeditor's) subjective expression of the story's main point. The headline, like the lead, 'forms the lens through which the remainder of the article is viewed' (Bell, 1991: 152). According to van Dijk (1987), headlines frequently portray ethnic minorities in a negative light (p. 245) and, I suggest, the Jones article is no different.

In the headline, 'In Beechview, a Latino Community Takes Hold', an unfortunately negative portrayal is foregrounded. As Santa Ana (2002) points out in his own analysis of media depiction of Latinos in California, military metaphors that refer to the arrival of immigrants as an invasion are prevalent in news discourse. The phrase 'takes hold' has a negative meaning potential, evaluating immigrants' arrival through a discourse of fear with respect to cultural change that is attributed to non-immigrant residents in the article. The use of this arguably martial metaphor positions the article as taking the perspective of the (threatened) longtime residents.

The phrase 'takes hold' carries the 'semantic implication' (van Dijk, 1991: 69) that the Latinos are claiming territory that belongs to the non-Latino residents. Plants and weeds (the latter also observed by Santa Ana [2002: 89] as a negative metaphor referring to Latinos) also take hold. It is especially notable that the headline's author chose this metaphor rather than a straightforwardly positive one, like 'a Latino Community Flourishes'. Instead, the headline immediately portrays this community as outsiders with a grip on something that might not be theirs. As a result, even though the article provides a variety of perspectives, including an extended profile of a Mexican resident who ends the article on a positive note ('We want to be a part of Beechview'), the lens through which readers initially view the article positions immigrants in a negative way.

An outline of conflict

The lead paragraph of the Jones article, in typical journalistic fashion, serves as an abstract for the rest of the article (Bell, 1991; van Dijk, 1991) by establishing the main theme of conspicuous cultural change:

Paragraph 1

If it weren't for the vacant storefronts along Broadway Avenue in Beechview, a Mexican restaurant and two small Mexican stores might not stand out. As it is, Maya, Tienda La Jimenez and La Azteca attest to change afoot in one of Pittsburgh's most traditional neighborhoods.

Note the listing of the names of the businesses in the second sentence, which do not add any new factual information. Instead, stating the three Spanish names recontextualizes them (Blommaert, 2005), adding a 'new metapragmatic frame' (p. 254) in which to interpret them. Rather than identifying the shops (it has to be inferred that Maya is the restaurant and the other two the stores), the choice to reproduce their names suggests that Spanish is effacing English in Beechview.

Even though the change in the neighbourhood is still relatively limited (one restaurant and two 'small' stores), it is potentially threatening: change is 'afoot', as if it were animate, agentive and bound to continue. The Spanish language refers metonymically to the immigrant community, which is changing the face of this 'traditional' neighbourhood. The use of 'traditional', an unattributed evaluation, evokes the perspective of white, non-immigrant residents. (As we will see below, it is ambiguous whether an Italian immigrant qualifies as a 'traditional' community member.) A threat to 'tradition' (often perceived as undesirable) is construed here in terms of language shift: Spanish is the symbol of (undesirable) change. Regardless of surrounding vacancies, it is quite probable that for Mexican residents of Beechview, the businesses Jones mentions do not 'stand out' at all; by implying that they do, Jones frames the situation from the non-immigrant residents' perspective.

In the next paragraph Jones elaborates on the idea that the Mexican businesses 'stand out':

Paragraph 2

> And stand out they do, for good and ill. Samantha Franco has heard derogatory references to Mexicans in the store she owns with her husband, Saul Jimenez, and some in Beechview say they haven't dined at Maya because they see too many Mexicans inside.

The 'they' in the first sentence refers anaphorically to the businesses and cataphorically to Mexicans, and thereby confirms the metonymic link between the three businesses and the Latino population as a whole. The 'ill' effects of their being conspicuous are the provocation of verbal abuse from other members of the community, the fear they produce among some of these residents, and a loss of potential customers for the restaurant owners due to this fear. Thus the first news actor, apparently included to speak from the perspective of the Latinos (given that she is the co-owner of a Mexican grocery), is not quoted as saying something positive about the new immigrant community. Rather, she is used to give evidence of the divisions that exist. In fact, Franco is not even a Latina, although her husband is Mexican, but rather a white native Pittsburgher.

Jones makes an unattributed assertion that a nameless 'some' (perhaps the same people who make the 'derogatory references') are reluctant to eat at the Mexican restaurant because there are 'too many Mexicans inside'. The effect of giving voice to this ambiguous and nameless 'some' is to create the impression that they represent the common opinion of the 'traditional' residents of Beechview. Attributing these opinions to an undefined neighbourhood collective carries a different implication than if Jones were to have attributed this position to a single source, named or not.

Since Paragraph 2 seems to be about how Mexicans stand out 'for ill', we might expect the next to turn to how they stand out 'for good'. However the third paragraph does something else:

Paragraph 3

> But there also is support for the neighborhood's most rapidly growing minority, which recently petitioned for a Spanish-language Mass they can walk to. St. Catherine of Siena Church on Broadway is obliging.

Here a reader might expect evidence of a positive impact that Latinos have had on the neighbourhood (such as, for example, increased vitality of the business corridor). However, the idea of standing out seems to have been left behind. Rather, Jones contrasts the lack of support from 'some' community members with the support that a local church has contributed by providing a space for a Mass in Spanish.

Evidence of growth

The fourth paragraph begins the segment of the text in which Jones provides evidence of the immigrant community's growth:

Paragraph 4

> In just a few years, Latinos – mostly Mexicans – moving into Beechview have created the most concentrated Latino population in the city, according to several sources. This is a watershed moment for Pittsburgh, where the Latino presence, small by any U.S. large-city standards, has grown steadily but never established an enclave. Jim Bryce estimates the population to be 'several hundred, at least, just in Beechview', based on the names he recognizes as Latino on mail he delivers for the U.S. Postal Service.

Paragraph 5

> Luis Lomas, PNC Bank's outreach manager to the Latino community for the past 2 1/2 years, said his demographic information shows Beechview's concentration has taken the lead since the last census.

In Paragraph 4, Jones implies that Beechview might be (on its way to becoming) the city's first Latino enclave. She does so by asserting that it has the 'most concentrated Latino population,' and then commenting that although the city has never before established an enclave, 'this is a watershed moment for Pittsburgh'.

Note Jones' choice of the word 'watershed'. The word connotes a turning point, but literally means a ridge of high ground that separates two river systems. The most prevalent metaphor that Santa Ana (2002) found was the 'immigration as dangerous waters' metaphor, one that he held to 'transform aggregate individuals into an undifferentiated mass quantity' (p. 76). 'Watershed moment' may be understood to imply that Pittsburgh is on its way to being flooded with Latinos. Here, again, we see the constraints of prior discourse acting on the way in which immigrants are portrayed; Jones does not represent the immigrants as threatening, per se, but she draws on and reproduces language that positions immigrants in this way. Interestingly, van Dijk (1987) noticed the water metaphor's recurrence as well: 'An even more effective and stereotypical way to emphasize numbers or masses are the frequently used 'flood' metaphors' (p. 372).

Jones directly quotes a postal worker, Jim Bryce, and cites PNC Bank's outreach manager to the Latino community, Luis Lomas. She apparently uses them as sources for informal census data since the last official census was conducted 5 years earlier. Jones notes that the 2000 census reported 147 Latinos out a total of 8,772 residents in Beechview and quotes Lomas as saying that the 'number has at least doubled since then'. She also quotes the priest who gives Mass in Spanish as saying the 'numbers continue to grow'. Later, in Paragraph 18, she cites the visibility of Latin-American foods at the Foodland supermarket as further informal evidence of a cultural shift: 'Even Foodland is playing to the growing market'.

As mentioned earlier, the largest estimate of the Latino population Jones cites is no more than a few hundred, or around 5 per cent of the total population. Yet she dedicates a significant segment of the article to showing that this growing population is evidence of cultural change, claiming that 'this is a watershed moment'. There seems to be a discrepancy between the numbers Jones cites and the impression of the Latino population she creates through her descriptions and the perspectives of news actors she chooses to include.

Community member reactions

In Paragraph 13, Jones shifts from providing evidence of the immigrant population growth to giving the reactions of Beechview community members. First, she quotes Palmo Cicchino, 'who himself emigrated from Italy 26 years ago'. He has a very positive impression of the new immigrants, praising them for their work ethic and desire to 'improve their lot,' in contrast with opinions expressed two paragraphs later:

Paragraph 16

Some longtime residents are far from excited about the new immigrants. Don Bell, president of the Beechview Merchants Association, said residents at a recent Weed and Seed meeting 'expressed concern about the rapid influx of Mexicans, of the illegals who have no rights and can be easily exploited, and issues such as over-occupancy and health code violations'. Someone asked, 'How do we know there aren't ads in grocery stores in Mexico that say "Move to Beechview,"' he said.

Paragraph 17

Concerns rise more easily when you have a commercial street that is 'moribund,' he said. When for food you have two Mexican grocery stores, a Mexican restaurant and a Foodland, he said, 'it's like, "Whoa, what's happening? It's rapidly going in one direction."'

Here the definition of 'traditional', as it was used in Paragraph 1, is fleshed out, since we can assume that the longtime residents are the ones who make Beechview a traditional neighbourhood. Cicchino may be interpreted as not qualifying as a 'longtime', and hence 'traditional', resident because he was born in Italy. As such, Jones presents the positive opinion of just one non-Latino Beechview community member, an immigrant himself, and makes no indication as to whether there are other non-Latinos, especially longtime residents, who share his perspective.

She proceeds to the idea that 'some' of the residents are 'far from excited about the new immigrants,' reinforcing the implication (from Paragraph 2) that anti-immigrant sentiment is the majority point of view. The stereotypical representation of Mexican immigrants as violators of health codes may be interpreted to be a strategic marginalization, much like the strategy discussed by Modan (2002) of elites who characterize as filth those who threaten the spatial order of their neighbourhood (p. 489). This quotation contributes to the sense of tension between the traditional and new residents. It also serves to bolster the unstated implication that the cultural change in Beechview is more threatening than the numbers indicate.

Don Bell's word choice in the phrase 'rapid influx' is consistent with the already noted 'immigrants as dangerous waters' metaphor described by Santa Ana (2002). In Paragraph 17, he says, 'It's rapidly going in one direction'. He is talking about the fact that there are two Mexican groceries and only one Foodland, but 'it' arguably refers to the neighbourhood in general, suggesting it is going in the wrong direction. Jones' paraphrase of Bell's comment in the first sentence of Paragraph 17 is nearly the same idea that is expressed in the lead: commercial property vacancies cause Mexican businesses to stand out, or, for Bell, cause concern to rise 'more easily'. Allan Bell (1991) describes how journalists, having gathered information, must figure out how to organize it: 'Focusing a story is a prime preoccupation of the journalist. Until a journalist finds what to lead a story with, the story remains unfocused' (p. 152). It is plausible that Don Bell's comments were influential in the crafting of Jones' lead.

In summary, even though it does not advocate this position, the article frames the community of Beechview in terms of a conflict in which the immigrants are conspicuous invaders, and the non-immigrant residents are negatively disposed towards Latinos. The article's lead, and as a result, its headline, focus the story for the reader in this way. By reproducing the metaphors of dangerous waters and invasion and emphasizing tensions between the Latino and non-Latino residents, the article contributes to the discourse of fear that is attributed to the latter. Finally, the longtime residents' fear and the amount of evidence presented about the Latino community's growth seem to be at odds with the demographic data being reported.

Intertextual relations: A link between Beechview and Latino immigrants 'takes hold'

Articles linking Mexicans and Beechview began appearing in 2004, 2 years before the Jones article. The first, published in February 2004, reporting on the owners of a Mexican grocery, states that Beechview has a 'small, but growing Mexican population' and that the 'tienda [Mexican grocery] has become a gathering spot for Mexicans' (Thomas, 2004). An article from May 2004, discussing ethnic food and culture in Pittsburgh, refers to Beechview in a very similar way: 'In the southern city neighbourhood of Beechview, you can stop into a tiny grocery called the Tienda de Jimenez that is one of the gathering places for growing numbers of Mexican immigrants' (Batz, 2004).

Following the Jones (2005) piece, an article in the Business section (Fitzpatrick, 2005) claimed that, although levels of immigration to the Pittsburgh area were generally low, there were some indications of an increase: 'There are reports of a growing Spanish-speaking enclave in Beechview'. Whether this journalist (who does not name the sources of these reports) is referring to Jones' article or not, a connection between Latinos and Beechview has clearly achieved some media traction.

One of the Lifestyle section articles, 'Latin Chic' (2006), is a review of a book about Latin food and décor. The lead attempts to make a local connection and provide evidence for how in vogue Latin culture is nation-wide:

> Even here in Pittsburgh, a city notoriously underpopulated by Hispanics, the Spanish-speaking community has increased dramatically in recent years. Two new tapas restaurants have opened, neighborhoods like Beechview have a strong Latino presence. (p. S-14)

As we see, Beechview's 'strong Latino presence' is provided as evidence that Pittsburgh does in fact have a 'dramatically' growing Spanish-speaking community. In the other article from the Lifestyle section (Batz, 2006), the author writes about increased 'Hispanic offerings' at grocery stores around the city.

He notes, 'In Beechview, where many Mexicans have settled, the Foodland store has an end-of-aisle display'.

Given that articles in the Business section and the Style section (which have different purposes and intended audiences) each make reference to Beechview (and no other neighbourhood), a link between Latino immigrants and this specific place clearly seems to have taken hold. The language of these articles, which report Beechview as having a growing enclave and a Spanish-speaking population that has 'increased dramatically', contributes to the sense that the Latino population there is larger than 'several hundred'. It is notable that this population is described as 'small, but growing' in the first article, and then characterized as an 'enclave' and as having a 'strong' presence in articles after the Jones (2005) feature news story.

'Too many Mexicans'? The mediatization of a semiotic landscape

The media representation I have outlined, in comparison with the census data from 2000, clearly indicates a discrepancy between the reported size of the Latino population in Beechview and the size of the population imagined in the discourse that portrays it. Jones' (2005) article, while citing informal sources that report a population size of at least several hundred, suggests, both through her language and the language of those she interviewed, that there is a greater 'presence' than just 4 or 5 per cent. Likewise, other accounts in the *Post-Gazette*, like 'reports of . . . an enclave' (Fitzpatrick, 2005), indicate a larger population than the reported estimates. I have already suggested two possible reasons for this apparent overrepresentation of the Latino population: nationally and locally circulating discourses that represent immigration as an unstoppable threat, and journalistic conventions that require presenting events in terms of negativity and conflict. Both these factors are widely discussed in the literature on media discourse. I would like now to turn to a third possible reason for the *Post-Gazette*'s negative framing of Beechview by considering the ways reporters might have experienced the semiotic landscape of the neighbourhood and its Latino population.

As a way to start thinking about the role of the semiotic landscape in shaping media discourse, I collected data on the visual and aural landscape of Beechview. This data allowed me to supplement ideological and generic explanations for the representation of immigrants with a more phenomenological explanation of a kind that is frequently missing in the work of critical discourse analysts and other media discourse scholars. Humanistic geographers have theorized the relationship between space and place and recognize that there is a phenomenological link between the two concepts: 'what begins as undifferentiated space becomes place as we get to know it better and endow it with value' (Tuan, 1977: 6). Through interaction with a neighbourhood, a person comes to have a 'sense of place' that is based on accumulated experiences, both sensory and intellectual, with aspects of the landscape like landmarks, buildings, signs, sounds and smells. As Johnstone (2004) suggests, 'Those who are interested in what physical environment and political boundaries mean to people need ways of finding out about particular people and particular meanings' (p. 75). Analysis of semiotic landscapes offers a way of systematically describing how an individual comes to experience a place. In the case of the media representation of Beechview and its immigrant population, such analysis provides a supplementary account of the discursive practices involved in producing the (problematic) newspaper reports I have considered above.

As Adam Jaworski and Crispin Thurlow suggest at the start of this volume, a semiotic landscape is 'any . . . visible inscription made through deliberate human intervention and meaning making'. In this same vein, recent research (cf. Gorter, 2006) has focused on *linguistic* landscapes in cities where two or more languages are in competition with each other for prominence. This research follows Landry and Bourhis (1997) by attempting to draw conclusions about the sociolinguistic context of an area based on such factors as how often each language appears on official (government) signs as opposed to private signs, the order and size in which each language is represented when signs contain multiple languages, and whether these signs communicate translations or different information in the different languages. Discrepancies in the presence/absence and/or prominence of different languages on official and non-official signs in multilingual contexts has been used to draw conclusions about (a) power relations between groups in a community, (b) how identities are asserted within a community, and (c) how business owners expect to influence potential clients (Ben-Rafael et al., 2006). Research along the lines of the studies found in Gorter (2006) operates under the assumption that the *quantity* of signs in a language is directly proportionate to perceptions of the ethnolinguistic vitality of its speakers in a particular area.

However, not all linguistic landscape research points to such conclusions. Coupland (also in this volume) notes how the quantity/prominence of Welsh in the signage of Cardiff is indicative of a symbolic projection of the area's Welsh identity rather than the actual (small) number of Welsh speakers there. Likewise, my own discourse analysis of the *Post-Gazette* suggests that there is a discrepancy in Beechview between the perception of the Latino community's vitality and the numerical data that account for its presence. Quantifying (or analyzing the arrangement of) the written signs alone does not explain this discrepancy. Rather, it is necessary to consider how these signs are experienced, and by whom, in conjunction with other elements of the landscape. Silences, which can be understood to be expressed by vacant buildings that display no written language, may contribute to how an individual interacts with other dimensions of the semiotic landscape. Additionally, and as Scollon and Wong Scollon (2003) remind us, people moving around a landscape also contribute to it: 'As we walk we may be chatting with a friend. This friend and all of the others present are also signs in the place which we "read" in taking our actions' (p. 2). While I did not 'read' people as English or Spanish speakers based on their physical appearance, the study of sound adds yet another layer to this observation, such that the spoken words of those present in the semiotic landscape also impact our experiences of it. In this sense, I wanted also to take into account the different languages or varieties I heard while moving through Beechview. This proved to be a useful way to supplement conventional linguistic landscape data and gain a more robust sense of how an outsider might experience the neighbourhood.

I selected the Beechview business corridor for my site of study because it was the specific focus of the media discourse I analysed, and because it is the only area in the neighbourhood that has commercial enterprises grouped together.[3] Following Backhaus (2006), I approached signage as 'any piece of written text within a spatially definable frame' and counted each instance of signage 'as one item, irrespective of size' (p. 55). Given that all *official* signs in Beechview are in English, a comparison of official and private signage was not a suitable approach (see Kallen, this volume). All of the signs I discuss here are privately posted. The visual/textual data was collected in October 2006 and represents a 'snapshot' of this dimension of the Beechview semiotic landscape based on one particular day.

In order to characterize the textual/visual semiotic landscape, I collected data while standing in front of the local Foodland store over a 5-day period and while walking along the business corridor over 4 days. I collected data on different weekdays and different weekends with some variation in time of day. While doing this observational work, I also made a note any time I heard a language being used. Given the available data, I determined that the most revealing method of investigation would be to:

1. quantify business property occupation according to (a) vacancies, (b) Latino businesses and (c) non-Latino businesses.
2. quantify the total number of unofficial signs;
3. quantify the signs in Spanish, if any, which appear on non-Latino businesses;
4. quantify the signs on the Latino businesses according to whether they contain Spanish, English, or both;
5. quantify (a) the people I heard speaking Spanish, (b) the people I heard speaking English and (c) other instances of language use;

As a backdrop to my study of the linguistic/semiotic landscape, I started by considering property occupation along the business corridor, revealing that there were 7 vacant properties (see Figure 8.1), 4 properties housing Latino businesses, and 17 properties housing non-Latino businesses. I was unable to determine how many vacancies existed in July 2005, when Jones published her article, so I cannot say if the street was more or less 'moribund' in 2006 than it was in 2005.

FIGURE 8.1 Vacant storefronts in Beechview

In recording the visual/textual/linguistic landscape of Beechview, the business corridor contained a total of 399 signs, of which 385 (96.5%) contained only English. There were no signs that contained any Spanish on the storefronts of the non-Latino businesses. There was one sign that might be interpreted as directed to Spanish speakers posted on the glass at the entrance of the Foodland. It was an advertisement in English for a special Spanish Mass and procession (see Figure 8.2) at the local Catholic church. An identical poster was found on the door of three businesses operated by Spanish speakers, but in these instances the entire text appeared in Spanish (see, for example, Figure 8.4).

Of all the signs I recorded, only 14 contained any Spanish. The Latino businesses had comparable numbers of all-English and all-Spanish signs. The all-English ones ranged from the name of the establishment (Figure 8.3), to typical storefront communications like neon 'OPEN' signs, to notices about community activities. All-Spanish signs ranged from the name of the store (Figure 8.4), to advertisements for international calling cards, to the notices about the Spanish Mass just mentioned. One of the Mexican grocery stores was called 'Tienda Mexico City' (Figure 8.5, *tienda* 'store'), while the Mexico City restaurant's window (Figure 8.3) revealed its full name to be 'Mexico City Taquería' (see Figure 8.6). There is a mixing of English and Spanish in both of these names; the type of establishment is conveyed in Spanish, and the name, Mexico City, is in English, but obviously indexes a Spanish-speaking place. The CD/DVD store had just opened and did not yet have any name or signs displayed. The other grocery had a sign that read 'LA JIMENEZ LA JIMENEZ' to

FIGURE 8.2 Advertisement (in English) for a Spanish Mass (see colour plate section)

FIGURE 8.3 Mexico City Taquería

FIGURE 8.4 Tienda La Jimenez storefront

FIGURE 8.5 Tienda Mexico City storefront

identify it (Figure 8.4). Like the restaurant sign in Figure 8.6, the design of the La Jimenez sign also asserts a Mexican identity through its alignment with the colour scheme of the Mexican flag: the paint of the building is white, each 'LA' is red, and each 'JIMENEZ' is green.

FIGURE 8.6 Mexico City Taquería window paint (see colour plate section)

Finally, in investigating the aural dimension of the semiotic landscape of Beechview, I noted 14 people speaking Spanish and 63 people speaking English while I was standing in front of the Foodland store. While walking, I observed 13 people speaking Spanish and 50 people speaking English. The total number of people I heard speaking Spanish during my time in Beechview was 27 (19.3%). One element of the 'soundscape' not represented in this snapshot account came from the new, nameless store, which opened during the course of my fieldwork. It had outdoor speakers that played Latin music at high volume one Sunday afternoon. I was able to hear these sounds, which included Spanish lyrics, clearly while standing in front of the Foodland approximately one hundred yards away. It was a noticeable addition to the soundscape given that no other locale was playing music on that or any other day.

Representing (or misrepresenting) the semiotic landscape in media discourse

The presence of Spanish on signs in Beechview (3.5%) appears to be approximately proportionate to the reported size of the Latino immigrant community indicated by Jones' sources of informal demographic data. However, three broader aspects of Beechview's semiotic landscape are instrumental for understanding how someone like Jones might have experienced Latino immigration as more significant or more substantial. These, in turn, help partly explain why the *Post-Gazette* coverage might on the one hand create the impression that there are more than just a few hundred Latinos in Beechview and, on the other hand, contribute to the generally negative framing of immigration in US media discourse.

First, looking at the number of Latino businesses (14.3%) in relation to vacant storefronts (25%) and non-Latino businesses (60.7%) suggests that any journalist would very likely notice the Latino 'presence' in the neighbourhood as she walked through the business corridor. By going into the neighbourhood and calculating this ratio myself, I can imagine how Latinos might be perceived to 'stand out' when almost one in five of the occupied storefronts were Latino-operated. While Jones' article mentioned the significance of the vacancies, a walk through the neighbourhood adds a level of understanding that may not be gained from reading the article alone. Second, the fact that there are two *tiendas* within a half mile of each other, which might suggest a demand for the goods these businesses carry exceeding the needs of only 'several hundred' people, can again only be properly understood moving through the semiotic landscape oneself. Lastly, with nearly 20 per cent of the people I heard speaking Spanish, it is possible to imagine that the aural landscape (or soundscape) of the neighbourhood shaping a journalist's sense of the place. When one actually experiences Beechview's business corridor as a *lived* space (cf. Lefebvre, 1991) it certainly *looks* and *sounds* as if it has a significant 'Latino presence'.

Taken together, the findings from my investigation of semiotic landscape suggest that a reporter visiting the neighbourhood could understandably imagine that there is a significantly larger Spanish-speaking population than census data or informal estimates claim. In addition to circulating discourses about immigration and the conventions of journalistic writing, there is thus a third reason why a reporter like Jones might be lead to represent or (inadvertently) misrepresent the Latino population in a place like Beechview in a way that belies the actual numbers. It is in this way, that I hope also to have shown how semiotic landscape research (the *geosemiotics* which Scollon and Wong Scollon, 2003, write about) may be profitably integrated with text-based analyses by linking representations of place in discourse with individuals' experiences of place. Semiotic landscape research is certainly a useful way of broadening our understanding of the processes of textual production.

Acknowledgements

I would like to thank Barbara Johnstone, Beth Mitchell, Kay Mitchell and Mark Thompson for their helpful feedback and guidance on previous versions of this chapter. I am also grateful to Adam Jaworski and Crispin Thurlow for their editorial help in preparing the chapter for publication.

Notes

[1] Pittsburgh, a post-industrial city, has attracted relatively few immigrants in the past few decades. According to the most recent census data, the population of 'persons of Hispanic or Latino origin' was 1.3 per cent (U.S. Census Bureau, 2000). The *Pittsburgh Post-Gazette* is the city's largest and oldest newspaper. Between February 2004 and October 2006, nine *Pittsburgh Post-Gazette* articles mentioned Beechview in connection with its growing Latino immigrant population. Four letters to the editor responded to Jones' feature article.

[2] Part of the Latino population that is unaccounted for in both census and informal demographic data could be attributed to undocumented immigration, but none of the journalists reports such an idea.

[3] This area is about 0.5 miles long, stretching from just north of the intersection of Broadway Avenue and Hampshire Avenue to the intersection of Broadway Avenue and Belasco Avenue. There are a few more business locations along a 0.3 mile stretch on Broadway further south, but this is not considered part of the business corridor. I base this assessment on what I have learned at community planning meetings and on the quote from Don Bell in Paragraph 17 of the Jones article.

References

Backhaus, P. (2006), 'Multilingualism in Tokyo: A look into the linguistic landscape', in D. Gorter (ed.), *Linguistic Landscape: A New Approach to Multilingualism.* Clevedon: Multilingual Matters, pp. 52–66.

Batz Jr., B. (2004, May 16), 'Flavors of the world simmer: In region's ethnic culture', *Pittsburgh Post-Gazette,* p. Z-38.

—(2006, May 24), 'New flavor to savor: More grocery stores warm up to Hispanic food', *Pittsburgh Post-Gazette,* p. Lifestyle A-1.

Bell, A. (1991), *The Language of News Media.* Oxford: Blackwell.

Ben-Rafael, E., Shohamy, E., Amara, M. A. and Trumper-Hecht, N. (2006), 'Linguistic landscape as symbolic construction of the public space: The case of Israel', in D. Gorter (ed.), *Linguistic Landscape: A New Approach to Multilingualism.* Clevedon: Multilingual Matters, pp. 7–30.

Blommaert, J. (2005), *Discourse.* Cambridge: University of Cambridge Press.

Blommaert, J., DeWilde, A., Stuyck, K., Peleman, K. and Meert, H. (2003), 'Space, experience and authority: Exploring attitudes towards refugee centers in Belgium', *Journal of Language and Politics,* 2(2), 313–334.

Cappella, J. N. and Jamieson, K. H. (1997), *Spiral of Cynicism.* New York: Oxford University Press.

Fairclough, N. (1992), *Discourse and Social Change.* Cambridge: Polity Press.

—(1995), *Media Discourse.* London: E. Arnold of the Hodder Headline Group.

Fitzpatrick, D. (2005, December 4), In Pittsburgh, the welcome mat is out to immigrants, problem is, not enough people are coming', *Pittsburgh Post-Gazette,* Business Section.

Gorter, D. (ed.) (2006), *Linguistic Landscape: A New Approach to Multilingualism.* Clevedon: Multilingual Matters.

Hartley, J. (1982), *Understanding News*. London: Methuen & Co.
Johnstone, B. (2002), *Discourse Analysis*. Malden: Blackwell.
—(2004), 'Place, globalization, and linguistic variation', in C. Fought (ed.), *Sociolinguistic Variation: Critical Reflections*. Oxford: Oxford University Press, pp. 65–83.
Jones, D. N. (2005, July 21), 'In Beechview, a latino community takes hold', *Pittsburgh Post-Gazette*, p. A-1.
Landry, R. and Bourhis, R. Y. (1997), 'Linguistic landscape and ethnolinguistic vitality: an empirical study', *Journal of Language and Social Psychology*, 16, 23–49.
Latin chic. (2006, February 6), 'Latin chic', *Pittsburgh Post-Gazette*, p. S-14.
Lefebvre, H. (1991), *The Production of Space*. Cambridge, MA: Blackwell.
Modan, G. (2002), '"Public toilets for a diverse neighborhood": Spatial purification practices in community development discourse', *Journal of Sociolinguistics*, 6(4), 487–513.
Roshco, B. (1975), *Newsmaking*. Chicago: University of Chicago Press.
Santa Ana, O. (2002), *Brown Tide Rising: Metaphors of Latinos in Contemporary American Public Discourse*. Austin: University of Texas Press.
Scollon, R. and Wong Scollon, S. (2003), *Discourses in Place: Language in the Material World*. London: Routledge.
Thomas, L. (2004, February 22), 'Here in Beechview', *Pittsburgh Post-Gazette*, p. G-12.
Tuan, Y.-F. (1977), *Space and Place: The Perspective of Experience*. Minneapolis, MN: University of Minnesota Press.
U.S. Census Bureau (2000), 'State and county quickfacts'. http://quickfacts.census.gov/qfd/states/42/4261000.html (accessed 25 October 2006).
van Dijk, T. A. (1986), 'Mediating racism: The role of the media in the reproduction of racism', in C. Neuwirth (ed.), *Argumentation*. New York: McGraw-Hill, pp. 202–215.
—(1987), *Communicating Racism*. Newbury Park: Sage.
—(1988), *News as Discourse*. Hillsdale, NJ: Lawrence Erlbaum Associates.
—(1991), *Racism and the Press*. London: Routledge.

Chapter 9

Silence is Golden: The 'Anti-communicational' Linguascaping of Super-elite Mobility

Crispin Thurlow and Adam Jaworski

Signalling new freedom for some, globalizing processes appear as uninvited and cruel fate for many others. Freedom to move, a scarce and unequally distributed commodity, quickly becomes the main stratifying factor of our times. . . . A particular cause for worry is the progressive breakdown in communication between the increasingly global and extraterritorial elites and the ever more 'localized' rest.

Z. Bauman, 1998, pp. 2–3

As the single largest international trade in the world, there is no one whose life remains unaffected by tourism – be it those people privileged enough always to tour or people who are only ever the 'toured'. Nor is tourism merely an important economic activity. Scholars in fields such as anthropology, sociology and cultural studies have for some time been undertaking detailed analyses of the social and cultural practices by which tourism is represented, organized and experienced (e.g. Franklin and Crang, 2001; Morgan and Pritchard, 1998; MacCannell, 1983; Selwyn, 1996; Urry, 2002). In particular, *critical* tourism research usually seeks to understand tourism as a major cultural industry and to demonstrate its role in establishing ideologies of difference and relations of (unequal) power. Indeed, tourism seldom merely reflects the socioeconomic order but is instrumental in organizing and reorganizing it (e.g. Lash and Urry, 1994). It is undoubtedly a significant force in the reorderings of global capital.

There is in fact a striking complicity and circularity in the relationship between tourism and globalization. A core assumption underpinning the discourses of both tourism and globalization is that of the promise of the 'global village' and the transformational potential of encounters with the Other. Just as tourists are often encouraged to think that the very act of travel and encountering cultural Other guarantees a broadened horizon and greater intercultural understanding, one of the major premises and justifications of globalization is the assumption of an increased, 'cosmopolitan' tolerance for diversity and the harmonious integration of peoples (cf. Hannerz, 1996). As such, while tourism is commonly viewed as a manifestation of globalization, it simultaneously justifies itself in terms of the ideological aspirations of globalization. These two discursive formations thus work hand-in-hand to establish many of the same cultural mythologies and economic inequalities. Increasingly, both are also realized as semiotic projects as much as economic ones.

As a major service industry – particularly in the richer countries of the 'West' – tourism has undergone (and helped perpetuate) the major shift by which service-oriented economies in general render goods more discursively mediated and increasingly *semioticized* (cf. Fairclough, 1999; Lash and Urry, 1994). In fact, tourism, like marketing and advertising, is a supremely semiotic industry. Not only does it entail face-to-face (or more mediated) forms of visitor–host interaction, but the ultimate goods traded and purchased (by tourists) are the prefigured images of holiday brochures and postcards, as well as holiday memories (e.g. snapshots) and their narrative enactments. Central to this semiotic activity are fantasies and performances of 'going native', notions of adventure, and the promise of meeting new peoples, cultures and sites. Material goods such as souvenirs, artefacts and snippets of language formulae brought back from foreign trips are all useful props in the enactment of these performed narratives (Morgan and Pritchard, 2005) and they serve as an extension of the tourist gaze (Urry, 2002) which, transformed subsequently into the 'tourist haze', in turn mythologizes the destination, the experience and tourism itself.

It is in this sense also that tourism – like globalization – can be viewed as a key identity resource for members of post-industrial, late-modern societies (Thurlow and Jaworski, 2003; also Giddens, 1991). Just as global mobility is characterized by the movement of elites, so too do elites in turn characterize themselves as elite by their global mobility and by their reference to it in talk and in writing. Once again, tourism and globalization are inherently and dialectically complicitous. And discourse is implicated in them both.

The discursivity of elitism

Numerically and, to some extent, descriptively, the notion of 'elite' is never easily defined. It is far easier – and, we suggest, more accurate – to examine elite status as a *structure of feeling* (Williams, 1977): 'a cultural hypothesis, actually derived from attempts to understand . . . affective elements of consciousness and relationships . . .' (pp. 132–133). This feeling gives rise to discourse whereby an elite identity is *enacted*; in other words, it is talked into existence and otherwise semiotically achieved. In these terms, our take on elitism is akin to Bourdieu's (1984) sociological analysis of social distinction and taste. We are also particularly keen to distinguish *elitism* as a discursively achieved (or, more likely, *attempted*) identity and subject position from *elite* where, as it has typically been discussed

FIGURE 9.1 'Where those who've got it go'

in social scientific literatures (e.g. Carlton, 1996), it is usually conceived of as a structural, social category describing those who rule or lead as a function of their material wealth or political power. Our preferred sense of elitism as something interactionally and semiotically realized means that we are less concerned with any objective or descriptive categorization of elite groups *per se*, and more with individual subjectivities and processes of (self-)attribution by which people may appeal to the notion or 'ideal' of an elite status.

Elite identities are thus not only material or actual; they are also ideological and aspirational. In other words, they are hegemonic and normative ideals (cf. Gramsci, 1971; Butler, 1990) in relation to which many people, regardless of wealth or power, position themselves or are persuaded by others to position themselves. And this is always achieved discursively; that is, through desirable, highly controlled representations and displays of the signifiers of status, and at the same time by repressing other unmediated forms of contact between privileged and non-privileged groups – between the rich and the poor, for example. Language and discourse are thereby employed in the *fabrication* of elite mythologies which uphold the physical, social, cultural, symbolic and economic marketplace (for a case-study example, see Thurlow and Jaworski, 2006). Which is certainly not to imply that all elitist enactments are equal or successful, or that, over time, everyone benefits equally. Nonetheless, assigning elite behaviour only to the obviously rich and powerful overlooks two things. First, social hierarchies are mutually established; hegemonic order is maintained through the constant promotion and uptake of symbolic or material markers of privilege and status (cf. Gramsci, 1971). Second, any assumption that elitism is done only by elites also tends to obscure wider global inequalities by which all 'Western' consumption patterns are arguably *de facto* elitist. For example, it can be argued that all tourism, all travel-for-leisure, is elite – be it vacationing on Mustique, touring Italy with the kids, partying on the Costa del Sol, or back-packing through Thailand. It is for this reason, that much of what we are examining here we deliberately distinguish as *super-elite* travel.

Following on from the idea of *elite* as a discursive accomplishment – a social process rather than some essentially fixed, personal attribute – we are interested in the way that elite subjectivities and feelings are structured and enacted by what Rampton (2003: 68) calls 'processes of symbolic differentiation' and through stylized performances of class identity. Accordingly, we consider the conscious enactment and explicit representation of elitism in terms of identificational adjustments and interpersonal alignments. For us, elitism entails a person's orienting – or being oriented – to some ideological reality and/or its discursive representations in order to claim exclusivity and/or superiority on the grounds of knowledge, authenticity, taste, erudition, experience, insight, access to resources, wealth, group membership or any other quality which warrants the individual to take a higher moral, aesthetic, intellectual, material, etc. ground against 'the masses' or 'the people'. In Jaworski and Thurlow (2009), for example, we examine the ways speakers/writers in selected print media take an elitist *stance vis-à-vis* their readers/viewers, the public at large and other social actors. In Thurlow and Jaworski (2006), meanwhile, our focus was on the *stylization* of elite identities by others – specifically, the range of semiotic resources (or rhetorical strategies) used by airline marketers to create elite identities for their Business Class and frequent-flier passengers. What we examine in our chapter here is yet another semiotic resource by which these elite identities are nowadays being discursively accomplished: silence.

The (meta)pragmatics of silence

The most typical characterization of meaningful silence is that of absence of words when communication is assumed to be taking place, although silence can also be identified in situations when words are actually spoken allowing silence to be treated as gradable on a scale from most to least silent forms rather than an all or nothing linguistic category (cf. Tannen and Saville-Troike, 1985; Bilmes, 1994; Jaworski 1993).

Against this conceptual backdrop, we take Halliday's (1978) broad classification of the functions of language and other semiotic systems as a basis for organizing the functions of silence in communication: *ideational, textual* and *interpersonal.* The ideational function of silence can be associated with the realization of a range of pragmatic or illocutionary acts such as refusals, rejections, requests, commands and so on (cf. Saville-Troike, 1985), as well as with the *negative* acts of referentiality such as secrecy, withholding information, censorship, taboo and so on. In its role as a contextualization cue, silence may also perform the textual function of framing talk or giving it coherence. For example, a shift from the 'literal' to 'performative' frame may be signalled by an extended pause before someone starts reciting a poem (cf. R. Bauman, 1977), which is equivalent to the conductor raising his/her baton and eliciting a moment of silence in a concert hall before the orchestra starts playing a symphony.

Interpersonal silence, meanwhile, operates at the vertical dimension of power and control, being predominantly found in situations of extreme power differential (cf. Braithwaite, 1990), and as a potent resource for challenging, defying and subverting established power relations (e.g. Gilmore, 1985). As far as the horizontal dimension of distance, silence may be a marker of extreme detachment, such as between strangers (Saville-Troike, 1985) or extreme closeness between intimates (Jaworski, 1998). In this sense, silence is not to be avoided as 'awkward', 'alarming' or 'dangerous' and replaced by small talk. Instead, silence may be a highly desirable index of closeness and involvement on the one hand, and freedom from imposition on the other. These contrasting and seemingly contradictory functions of silence offer another good illustration of Nessa Wolfson's (1988) bulge theory which we return to shortly.

This distributional view of silence is useful in that it accounts for the prevalence of (small) talk in contexts marked by the relative lack of clearly defined status roles in interaction. Having said that, it is also possible to associate the ritualized, ceremonial, scripted notion of small talk and its relative low semantic relevance with the use of silence. In his well-known paper on silence among Western Apaches, Basso (1972) demonstrated silence to be the dominant linguistic form in socially ambiguous situations, situations where the identity of focal participants is unclear, and in moments of 'transition' from one social state to another (see also Braithwaite 1990; Jaworski, 1993). There is a clear link here with the notion of silence as characteristic of liminal or liminoid social spaces (Turner, 1977).

In this chapter, we are primarily concerned with two interlocking, meta-level uses of silence: (1) as a semiotic resource represented linguistically and visually in high-end advertising contributing to the 'global semioscape' (Thurlow and Aiello, 2007) of luxury tourism; and (2) as our own key metaphor (Jaworski, 1997) in theorizing the social consequences of these commercial representations of social space. Silence is, it seems, a key marker of both luxury and social status.

Silence and (social) space in luxury tourism

This chapter is accompanied by a sister publication (Thurlow, Gendelman and Jaworski, in prep.) where our dataset is analyzed with a more specific focus on *spatialization* – the representation and cultural production of space/place.

FIGURE 9.2 'Speechless'

In writing these two pieces together, however, it has become apparent that space and silence are two semiotic resources that work almost symbiotically to realize the kind of social exclusion upon which contemporary notions of class inequality are predicated (cf. Low, 2001). Throughout, the deployment of silence and space is coupled with a number of other markers of super-elite lifestyle (e.g. haute cuisine, butlers, spa treatments, luxury brands – as in 'luxurious Givenchy Spas' and 'Jack Nicklaus Signature Golf Courses'); it is also accompanied by hyperbolic claims to the exclusivity of the experience on offer, by flattery, and by synthetic personalization (cf. Fairclough, 1989) of the implied traveller – for example, tag-lines like 'An invitation to the most exclusive club on earth' or 'Fai un regalo alla persona senza la quale non saresti nessuno. Te stesso' (English: 'give a gift to the person without whom you'd be nobody: yourself'). The pseudo-poetry of the copy also evokes a 'new-age' spirituality throughout ('Let our endless ocean views inspire peace [*sic*] and rejuvenation'; and, elsewhere, 'Where you can bathe your soul in the clear, warm waters'), while also leveraging the cultural capital of an educated, flowery lexicon ('. . . there is a place where time is told by the changing of tides and luxury blends perfectly with nature').[1]

But it is not this elitist content alone which marks these ads as distinctive from other discursive styles and practices in tourism. Print and broadcast representations of mainstream ('mass') tourism are replete with quotations and snippets of local languages (in the form of code-crossing), metapragmatic comments about local ways of speaking, reports of interactions between tourists and hosts, images of signs, 'ethnic' music, and so on. This kind of *linguascaping* (Jaworski et al., 2003) offers tourists another mode for pre-visualizing and consuming the tourist destination in the form of an aural/linguistic 'gazing' (Urry, 2002). However, while one of the *raison d'êtres* of tourism is to meet new people, to learn about new cultures, etc., tourism advertising sometimes offers silence as the key mode of linguascaping destinations. In the case of super-elite, luxury tourism advertising, this silencing of the tourist experience is almost absolute and the usual tourist linguascape is effectively reversed. In some cases, silence is very explicitly and obviously invoked as with the typographic muffling of 'noise' and language in Figure 9.3a/b, as well as Figure 9.2's play on 'speechless' or the main tag-line in Figure 9.4 ('Discover a secret world where silence is the only sound on earth').[2] For the most part, however, the semiotic production of silence is more subtle.

Reversing the tourist linguascape

To start, one recurrent feature of our corpus is the noticeable absence of signage on buildings and other architectural locations which would otherwise anchor these spaces as specific, bounded places (Figure 9.5). Although the degree to which place is specified does vary, for the most part photographic representations of the spaces depicted are typically decontextualized and generic. Along these lines, one visual resource frequently employed is the depiction of isolated, 'natural' landscapes, once again to leverage the sense of exclusivity (Figure 9.6). In some cases these references are made explicitly ('secluded beaches' and, in Figure 9.1, 'unspoiled islands'), at other times they are implied visually and linguistically (see Figures 9.1 and 9.4). These 'virgin', pre-linguistic places work to produce a sense of silence through their being similarly – and purportedly – unlabelled, unnamed and 'unclaimed'. Finally, what is perhaps most striking about these advertisements is their genre-defining representation of uncannily depopulated spaces which are, in communicative terms, silenced by default. Without people to do the talking there can obviously be no talk!

The representation of an absence of words is also mirrored by the relative lack of copy in the advertisements – a technical feature we return to in a moment when we consider material codes and other design choices. For now, however, we want to consider the six other silencing tactics (or semiotic resources) we see repeatedly in our dataset, ones which do not rely solely on the absence of (printed) verbal communication for their metapragmatic silencing effect. These six, overlapping silencing tactics are typical of those in our whole dataset (see Note 1) but are also demonstrated multiple times in the examples we have been able to reproduce here. Any one advertisement almost always deploys two or more of these six semiotic resources.

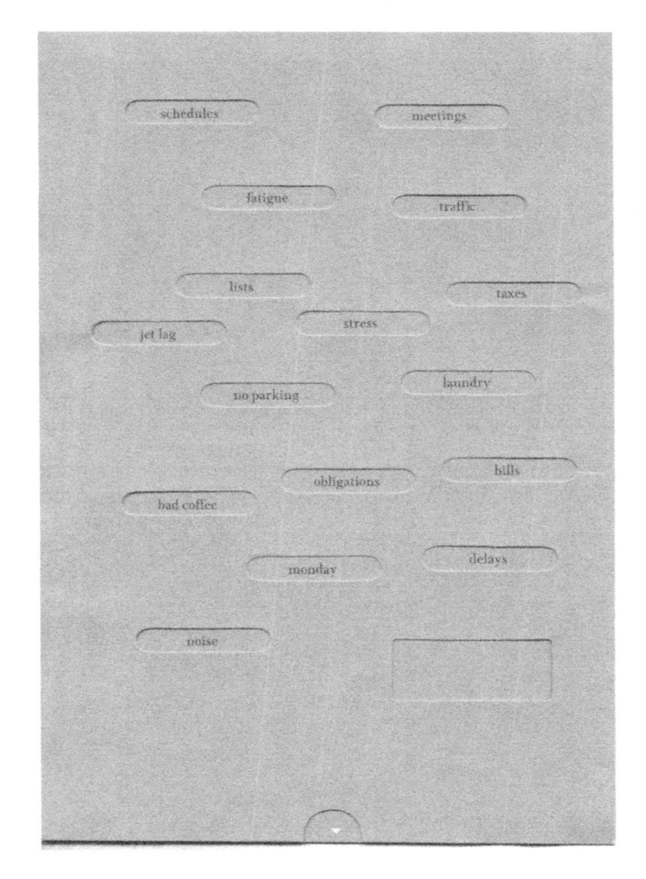

Figure 9.3a and b 'This is how it should feel'

FIGURE 9.4 '. . . where silence is the only sound on earth'

1. Lexicalization and metaphorization

As we say, some advertisements make explicit appeals to 'silence' and 'peace', while in other places we find metaphoric references to mythologically non-linguistic or at least tranquil, other-worldly places (or states of being) drawing heavily on quasi-religious referents, e.g. 'paradise', 'heaven', 'sanctuary', 'halo', 'dream' (cf. Jaworski and Thurlow, 2009). See, for example, the Spanish ad (Figure 9.7) which, beneath a fabricated starry sky, promises '. . . despertar a un sueño' ('wake into a dream'). See also 'paradise' in Figure 9.1 and Figure 9.5's playful tag-line 'The most magnificent place you can get into without a halo'. At other times, narrative copy implies the *speechless* experience of luxury or of touristic landscapes as, for example, in 'breathless', 'breathtaking' (Figure 9.11) and 'it will take your breath away'. By the same token, the relative absence of voices and of noise more generally is suggested also through references to tourists being able to hear sounds which may otherwise be inaccessible to them in their 'normal' noisy environments and in the fast pace of life: the 'breeze', the 'soothing

FIGURE 9.5 'Ultra exclusive. Absolute privacy. Beyond attentive.'

and calming sound of the sea' and 'the faint sound of your beating heart'. In Figure 9.8, meanwhile, 'serenity' is achieved by 'letting the world crash around you'. This quintessentially touristic escapism is clearly also the conceit which underpins the double-entendre of Figure 9.2's 'speechless'.

Finally, although less evident in the examples we've selected here, the typical privileging of the visual in tourist texts – e.g. the invitation to gaze upon exotic spaces, luxurious services and beautiful people – we notice a more embodied, sensory experience being promoted in luxury tourism advertising. The dominance of the visual and aural is, it seems, also being off-set by explicit and implicit references to touch (e.g. massages on the beach), texture and smell. The latter, of course, being a commonly signifier of class status (Carlisle, 2001; Douglas, 1966).

2. Non-interactive represented participants

Given their scarcity, represented participants (after Kress and van Leeuwen, 1996) are typically depicted in one of three combinations: an interaction between a

FIGURE 9.6 'A trip dedicated to me' (see colour plate section)

tourist and a local person (often a servant), a romantically implicated tourist couple (only ever a man and a woman), or an individual tourist (usually a woman). In each case, these represented participants are silenced differently.

Disengaged servers: The quality and attentiveness of service which is a key discourse in all service-industry advertising has a certain intensity in luxury tourism advertising (See Figure 9.5's 'Beyond Attentive'. Elsewhere, we find 'Luxuries, amenities and services that EXCEED EXPECTATIONS' and '. . . be pampered by our attentive staff'). Nonetheless, service workers (e.g. waiter, masseuse, guide) in our dataset are seldom present and, if they are, never shown talking with tourists. The guest is there to be pampered and indulged and, it

FIGURE 9.7 'Wake into a dream'

appears, being spoken to potentially impinges on this freedom. In some instances, this host–tourist status differential is also established through the visual decentring and thus interactional marginalizing of the server (see Figure 9.9). It is this general sense of represented disengagement which works to silence the seemingly othered local person and, consequently heighten the sense of quietude of the advertisements.

All of this is less surprising when understood as an expression of social distance. In this regard, Nessa Wolfson (1988) comments on the relatively reduced social compulsion (or inclination) for status unequals to produce talk in a number of key social situations (e.g. speech acts such as complimenting, inviting, thanking). Her argument is that, for status unequals and intimates alike, social distance is seen as relatively fixed and parties have a clearer sense of where they stand in relation to each other. Like Victorian children, therefore, the tourist workers/servers should be seen but not heard. In fact, what strikes us about luxury labour is that it is always 'visibly invisible' – the product of the labour must be evident but the act of labour and/or the labourers themselves must not

FIGURE 9.8 '. . . letting the world crash around you'

(cf. also Sherman, 2007; Thurlow and Jaworski, submitted). It is this which explains, in part, the unseen hands behind the immaculate lawns and beaches (Figures 9.8 and 9.4) and carefully assembled sun-loungers (Figures 9.1, 9.8 and 9.10). It also explains, in Figure 9.10, the neatly rolled towels on which a flower has been meticulously positioned. If labour/ers is/are displayed this is usually for particular effect, as with the performance of a uniformed, dedicated 'butler' in Figure 9.9 – compared with the staged dinner in Figure 9.4.

Silent intimates: As is typical of many tourism representations, our dataset contains many images of all-White (with one exception to date), man–woman couples in intimate interaction with each other (e.g. Figures 9.4, 9.8, 9.9 and 9.12).

FIGURE 9.9 'Service'

In keeping with Wolfson's speech behaviour framework, these represented participants are just as unlikely to be depicted in conversation. More often than not, the couples are shown simply holding hands, gazing lovingly into each other's eyes, relaxing on the beach, etc. It is precisely the silence of these moments which conveys their intimacy and their romance. These heteronormative tourist 'bubbles' (cf. Smith, 1977) are certainly removed from the company of others.

Solitary tourists: Perhaps the most obvious implications of silence – as the absence of talk – are to be found in the many depictions of single represented participants (e.g. Figures 9.6 and 9.11). The underlying promise of these solitary depictions

Figure 9.10 '. . . the most exclusive club on earth'

is of course that of exclusivity but one which carries the added promise that guests/visitors will be undisturbed – whether by crowds of other tourists or, in some cases, by having anyone sitting next to them. This is the same conceit we have found in the elitist textual practices of airline frequent-flyer programmes (Thurlow and Jaworski, 2006) where business/first-class passengers are seldom shown sitting next to anyone (or at least at a 'safe' distance). Where solitude is often, in popular Anglo-American terms, associated with desolation and loneliness, in this case it seems to function as a maker of glamour and privacy – of being left alone – and of territorial ownership/control. As with fly-on-the-wall documentaries and most cinematic texts, the noisy production of these images (and all the images in our dataset) is conveniently concealed – no directors, no camera people, no make-up artists and so on. Which brings us to our next silencing resource.

3. Disengaged viewing participants (i.e. readers)

Central to a social semiotic analysis is the understanding that images are never merely passive representations but are instead modes of social (inter)action produced by/between the image's creator, the represented participants (i.e. the people in the image) and the *viewing* participants (i.e. the person or people seeing the image) (Kress and van Leeuwen, 1996; Jewitt and Oyama, 2001). These relationships parallel those established in face-to-face interaction, and may be framed to lesser or greater degrees by *social distance* (e.g. a close up or long shot), *power* (e.g. low-angle or high-angle shot) and *involvement* (e.g. direct or indirect gaze). With regards to our luxury travel advertising, and related to the depiction of solitary represented participants, viewing participants are seldom invited to interact or 'communicate' with represented participants by engaging in mutual gaze (Kress and van Leeuwen's, 1996, 'demand images'); instead, they are positioned voyeuristically – as silent onlookers. As such, passivized 'offer images', where the gazes of the represented and viewing participants do not meet (Kress and van Leeuwen, 1996) such as Figures 9.11 and 9.12 avoid any implied interaction between the reader of the advert and the characters in the adverts themselves. This 'non-interactive' relationship is perhaps manifested most explicitly in frequent depictions of a lone woman facing or orienting away from the viewer, allowing/inviting the reader to put him-/herself in the position of the tourist gazing at both the represented woman and the open vista she is gazing upon.[3] This 'rear view' perspective is a very common visual trope in tourism advertising and one which, as Messaris (1997) notes, not only evokes the sexualized, escapist mythologies of tourism but which is also very reminiscent of nineteenth-century Romantic landscape paintings. In thinking about the material practices of reading (a travel magazine, for example), we are also reminded that this too is typically an unspoken, solitary process. As such, the entire interactional frame of the advertising is silent.

4. Inactivity, stillness and 'empty' spaces

Sticking with a similar kind of material (or technical) code like the embodied practice of reading just mentioned, it is worth noting that photography itself 'freezes' moments and necessarily renders motion still. The very act of textual representation is itself, therefore, one which both stills and silences. Nonetheless, the stillness of represented scenes is also more semiotically explicit than this; for example, through the consistent depiction of undisturbed water – whether in swimming pools (e.g. Figures 9.8 and 9.12) or in the sea (e.g. Figures 9.1, 9.2,

9.6 and 9.9) – coupled with sharp reflections cast in swimming pools (e.g. Figures 9.7, 9.10 and 9.11). These reflections also work in tandem with the luxurious connotations of polished, shiny surfaces (e.g. lights reflecting on floors) we see elsewhere in our research.

It is the more general 'emptying' of represented spaces and typographic spaces which signifies in turn the uncluttering of the tourist locations depicted. These unfussy spaces are thereby rendered quiet. As we have already suggested, silence is just as likely to be achieved through the complete absence of people. Although the presence of human characters is occasionally implied (see below), what is most unusual about these images of luxury tourism are the eerie rows upon rows of unoccupied deck chairs (Figure 9.8), the ghostly empty swimming pools (Figures 9.7, 9.8 and 9.10), and the noticeably uncrowded beaches (e.g. Figure 9.1, 9.2 and 9.6). This human geography is mirrored also through the depiction of vast, open physical terrain – most especially of sea, but also sometimes of mountains and other 'natural' landscapes.

One other common visual motif – and one related also to the absence of people – is the depiction of apparently abandoned chairs, sandals, books, drinks or items of clothing. These indexical signs or 'quotations' of prior and out-of-frame activity work to highlight or intensify the sense of inactivity, idleness and rest. These 'raptured' spaces are somehow rendered even quieter as a result – see, for example, Figure 9.1 (the unoccupied deck chairs) or in Figure 9.7 (the abandoned towel or bathrobe).[4] In other adverts (not shown here), we find a snorkel and flippers left on the shoreline, or two half-drunk glasses of wine and a bathrobe dropped on the steps of a jacuzzi; these scenes invite one to imagine tourists now relaxing on the beach following a diving session or interacting passionately (and noisily?) in their hotel room. A sense of energy spent or of post-coital calm is fostered. Inactivity is, of course, itself relative and is sometimes communicated also through direct and indirect references to temporality; for example, the stopping of time, the deceleration of tempo and a relaxing of pace. In Figure 9.2, the image is anchored as 'a place where time is told by the changing of tide', while the words/experiences eclipsed in Figure 9.3a and 9.3b include 'schedules', 'jet lag' and 'delays'. Although not necessarily true of delays, this *chronotopic* framing (cf. Bakhtin, 1981) relies on the understanding that 'fast' signifies busy, and 'slow' signifies leisurely, still or, again, tranquil.

5. The silence of nature

Just as the 'raptured' spaces mentioned above can be sequentially conceived of as silences following earlier activities, the silence of nature in luxury tourist adverts is primeval, pre-existing and only waiting to be tamed, to be occupied by the elite traveller. It is as if this untouched land is in the process of being discovered, conquered and turned into landscape under the tourist gaze. The pre-linguistic and un-named exists outside of social time and space. For example, in the best tradition of colonial exploration and conquest, the copy of an Australia.com advertisement (not included here – see Note 1) says in large, bold letters superimposed on a long shot of a beach/seaview with a lone couple walking in a distance: 'HAVE YOU EVER named an island after yourself?' This type of neocolonial fantasy also has the interesting effect of reversing the usual tourist transformation of *spaces* into *places* by rendering otherwise known, named *places* into generic, unidentifiable *spaces*.

One way the silence of nature – which is to say its being nonverbal/pre-verbal and peaceful – is coupled with the silence of inactivity lies in the frequent depiction of sunsets (e.g. Figures 9.4 and 9.9). In literal terms, of course, the setting of the sun brings with it the close of the day's activities and the falling of nocturnal peace. For many, sunsets commonly carry the meaning potential of serenity and calm, being the typical object of a romantic, solitary tourist gaze (Urry, 2002). The horizon, with its even line, likewise creates a heightened sense not only of space – i.e. as far as the eye can see – but also of equilibrium and calm. Indeed, horizonal lines or perspectives are common in our larger dataset and in the examples we reproduce here (see Figures 9.1, 9.2, 9.4, 9.6, 9.9, 9.10, 9.11 and 9.12). The relative absence of (tempestuous/changeable) weather is of course a key feature in the 'sun-sand-sex' trope that runs through so much tourism discourse. However, it takes on an added significance in the context of luxury tourism discourse as yet another silencing resource.[5] In keeping with the sense of calm and order created by sunsets, horizons and clear skies, recall that we also see throughout our dataset the uncanny stillness of water – in the 'empty' swimming pools (Figures 9.7, 9.8, 9.10, 9.11 and 9.12) as well as the seascapes (Figures 9.1, 9.2, 9.6 and 9.9).

This kind of strategic 'landscaping' works together with another semiotic resource we have been struck by in our ethnographic research: the production of luxury through spatial, material, symbolic and interactional order/orderliness (Thurlow and Jaworski, submitted). In this case, it is the measured juxtaposition of ordered and un-ordered (disordered?) spaces which works to instil – and accentuate – a similar sense of tranquility. For example, in Figure 9.8, the manicured lawns, symmetrically planted palms and regimented sun-loungers mark themselves off from the open sea, breaking onto a rocky outcrop. In Figure 9.13, meanwhile, waves break gently on an unnaturally smooth beach. Importantly, this type of ordered landscaping also echoes the meaning potentials of neocolonial 'virgin territories' and of 'visibly-invisible labour' mentioned already. The implied traveller is promised here a chance to step into an untouched, undisturbed, unspoiled space, be it a hand-swept beach, rearranged sun lounger, or an empty pool. It is as if no-one else has been there before. The image of the elite tourist is not only to be alone in the paradise but the first ever to get there. It starts to become clear why the infinity pool, with its deliberate, self-conscious boundary marking, has become so emblematic of contemporary luxury (in the examples here: Figures 9.10, 9.11

and 9.12). While the so called 'negative edges' create the spacious illusion of these pools' extending to the horizon, the illusion also draws attention to itself so as to leverage the frisson of an *enclavic* order (we return to this idea in a moment).[6]

6. Multimodal design

Finally, we return to material/technical codes to consider some of the different design choices which enable a visual 'texturing' of silence. One striking example here is the design of typographic text (or copy); specifically, the use of small, 'discrete' lettering which connotatively corresponds to the paralinguistic

FIGURE 9.11 'A little harder to get to.' (see colour plate section)

expression of low volume and whispering. By the same token, in Figure 9.4 the fluid, undulating copy suggests a particular lightness typical of smoke or mist, and corresponds with the supposedly whispered words of the man into the woman's ear. A similar softness of the curved line is to be found across our data-set in the shapes of the beach shores and islands (Figures 9.2, and 9.6), edges of the swimming-pools (Figures 9.10 and 9.11), architectural and landscape features (the lawn in Figure 9.8, the arches in Figure 9.9), and the framing of the main photographic images (Figure 9.8 again). These examples of visual *rhyming* (i.e. the repetition and mirroring of design choices) also work at a more abstract level to instil a sense of coherence and order.

FIGURE 9.12 'One & Only' (see colour plate section)

Other typographic features work to produce a sense of understated luxury and elitism through the connotation of italic or calligraphic typefaces with notions of tradition (i.e. fountain pens) and personalized attention (i.e. handwriting) – in particular, see Figure 9.2. The quietness of typographic text is sometimes achieved also through its minimization in the context of a large, open textual space (e.g. Figures 9.6 and, especially 9.11). Indeed, one visual resource deployed for similar effect is that of framing (Kress and van Leeuwen, 1996); in this case, written (i.e. verbal) text is often clearly separated or removed from images (i.e. the pictures of places) by the use of frame lines and other features of spatial layout – see, for example, Figure 9.9 and to some extent Figure 9.10. Even the 'speechless' imposed on the beach in Figure 9.2 finds itself somehow isolated. Similarly, the idealizing slogans of many ads float above the main picture – in the picture but not of the picture. This 'de-voicing' of the represented spaces not only leaves the tourist landscape free of any signage but also arranges the design of the advert itself so that the 'clutter' of copy does not encroach on the pristine visual image.

One design feature which also helps to produce a sense of absence, calm and inactivity (or lack of busy-ness) is the use of colour in the ads.[7] We suggest that the dominant colour scheme used in these examples is that of 'tranquility' but one which is achieved not simply through connotative significations of hue. The *saturation* of colours in the ads works more subtly; it is neither exaggerated (as in the 'vulgar' intensity of signage and beach toys of the mass-oriented seaside holiday resort) nor very soft and pale. Thus, displaying high naturalistic modality, these images evoke a sense of tenderness, while also exuding a sense of exuberance which is further accentuated by the pervasive bright red swimming costume of the women in Figures 9.6 and 9.11. By contrast, the exceptionally unsaturated colours in Figure 9.12 render the image as low in naturalistic modality but quite high in abstract modality, symbolizing the general *ideal* of (in)activity in a type of resort rather than one of the particular locations listed at the bottom of the page (i.e. The Bahamas, Dubai, Maldives, Mauritius, Mexico). The choice of black and white draws on the connotations of 'classic' and/or traditional while also metaphorically transposing the notion of distinction to the One&Only chain of resorts through its being distinguished from the colour of most other advertisements.

The relatively undifferentiated palette of the dominant blues, greens and whites corresponds to and draws its symbolic value of associative quietude by mirroring the views of uninterrupted sky and water, of manicured lawns and palm tops, and of smooth sandy beaches.[8] Colour co-ordination – as another mode of visual rhyming – is a typical semiotic design feature of visual images in contemporary, global print media (Kress and van Leeuwen, 2001) and we see the same means of maintaining textual coherence in our dataset. For example, the lettering in Figure 9.1 draws from the blue of the parasol and turquoise green of the sea, while the logo and the swimsuit in Figure 9.6 are the same red. However, one colour which appears to 'hold' for many of the adverts in our sample is white. Apart from the red swimsuits of the women, the most common colour of the clothes of the represented participants in our whole dataset is white. While it may be the light, practical colour for warm summer days, it is possibly also the impractical, labour-intensive, high-maintenance colour of luxury. Tourists' white clothes are then also 'echoed' in white furniture, table cloths, carpets, and other accessories (see Figures 9.1, 9.4, 9.8, 9.9, 9.10) – not to mention the iconic white-sand beaches (e.g. Figures 9.1, 9.2 and 9.6).[9] A more cultural-historical (or iconographic) interpretation of this particular aesthetic preference might also point to the almost imperceptible resonance with the Whiteness of the represented participants themselves (cf. Dyer, 1997).

'Speechless': Silence, exclusivity and 'anti-communication'

> *The bourgeois subject continuously defines and re-defines itself through what it marks as 'low' – as dirty, repulsive,* noisy, *contaminating. Yet the very act of exclusion is constitutive of its identity.*
>
> *Stallybrass and White, 1986: 191; emphasis ours*

The conceits of both tourism and advertising are multiple, and some more familiar than others. That the world is sublimely White, heterosexual and beautiful. That the weather is always perfect. That visitors/guests are the only ones (that matter). That servers/servants never make themselves noticeable. That hotel swimming pools are always empty. That pristine beaches and virgin islands are there to be discovered. That absolute silence exists. An absolute silence for the absolutely wealthy.[10] So too is the repertoire of semiotic resources used in luxury tourism advertising – of which the commodification of silence and social space are just two – remarkably limited; many of the same discursive narratives and iconographic tropes are repeated over and over again. At times, it has felt as if we could easily produce one of these adverts ourselves, knowing the semiotic formula as we do. Nor is this solely or simply an Anglo-American textual-discursive practice. It is interesting to see how, as the luxury market rapidly expands, the same visual genre is establishing itself as part of the 'global semioscape' – a globalizing aesthetic produced through the formal and informal circulation of symbols, sign systems and other meaning-making practices (Thurlow and Aiello, 2007: 308). We see evidence of this in the random sample of Italian and Spanish ads in our dataset (e.g. Figures 9.6 and 9.7). Just three short extracts from three commercial travelogues also reveal how this 'reclassifying' of silence is being taken up more widely and by no means limited to the multimodal texts of magazine advertising. In extracts 1 to 3 below, we find very much the same commentary being invoked to represent, respectively, 'the most luxurious ship ever built' (*The Sunday Times* travel section, 28 March 2004), the 'palace-hotel' of an Indian maharajah (*Saturday Guardian* travel section,

11 March 2006), and a Four Seasons hotel in Tokyo (*Holland Herald* – KLM's inflight magazine, May 2006) (all emphasis added):

Extract 1

The atmosphere is *hushed*, orderly almost reverent. You're inhabiting a thing of extraordinary craft and beauty, and somehow the message comes across that you should behave accordingly. *It's a bit like being in church.*

Extract 2

You won't find monogrammed bath towels here, or menus, or indeed any sign [sic] *at all that this is anything but a private residence.* To stay at Ahilya . . . is to be welcomed as a guest of royalty. . . . *After the feverish activity of my last few weeks in India, I can't get over the silence. Straining my ears, I can make out nothing but the gentle patter of water as a gardener tends to the flowers below my window.*

Extract 3

A spirit-lifting simplicity of design and *decadent degree of luxury* . . . The location, next to Tokyo Station in the Marunouchi business district and the edge of glitzy Ginza, couldn't be livelier, but *triple-glazing means the rooms are silent.*

We begin to understand better how silence has become such a key semiotic resource in promoting luxury travel when we consider some of the more general principles by which tourism and tourist spaces are commonly organized. Not unlike other aspects of social role enactment or identity formation, tourism is always a performance and every performance needs a particular 'stage' or 'theatre'. In this regard, Tim Edensor (2001) distinguishes the performative nature of tourists' behaviour based on their habitus (Bourdieu, 1984); that is, their bodily dispositions grounded in and reproducing the divisions of class, ethnicity, gender, sexuality, etc. from the types of contexts or spaces which generate shared expectations of what should be seen or done. Inevitably, both these determinants of the tourist performance are inextricably linked, and the high-status end of travel spaces represented in our data calls for specific performances of tourism in which class, ethnicity, gender and sexuality are highly codified characteristics of the implied social actors.

Two general types of 'stages' for tourist performances are invoked by Edensor: 'enclavic' spaces and 'heterogeneous' spaces. The former are heavily policed at the edges to prevent their permeability, and within to ensure conformity to institutionally imposed rules (e.g. the dress code). These spaces are carefully planned and managed in the interest of maintaining high standards of cleanliness, superior service, specific décor and atmosphere, and to reduce any ambiguity of their function or purpose. 'Shielded from potentially offensive sights, sounds and smells, these "environmental" bubbles provide in-house recreational facilities, including displays of local culture' (ibid.: 63). On the other hand, heterogeneous tourist spaces are multifunctional and 'weakly classified', with unclear and porous boundaries between the public and private spheres, random mixture of style and design, where tourists and hosts mingle. 'In some ways, heterogeneous spaces provide stages where transitional identities may be performed alongside the everyday enactions of residents, passers-by and workers' (ibid.: 64).

As enclavic spaces, super-elite, luxury tourism spaces are designed precisely to minimize disturbance – literal, psychic, political – and the effect or goal is to eschew any transformative intercultural potential that lies in disturbance or in the challenge of the unexpected. Indeed, this mode of travel makes an apparently decisive – and unapologetic – move away from the mythology of intercultural contact which traditionally permeates tourism discourse (Favero, 2005; Thurlow & Jaworski, 2010). At a time when Urry (2002) and others (e.g. Jacobsen, 2003; Pezzulo, 2007) are commenting on the growth of so called alternative tourisms (e.g. eco-tourism, heritage tourism) and the rise of internationalized travel, the arch 'bubble tourism' (Smith, 1977) of luxury travel is expanding exponentially. And, in the context of luxury travel, even the eco-tourism must be luxurious.[11] In these luxury spaces, any 'adventure' must be safe and comfortable, any spontaneity must be planned and coordinated. Not surprisingly, communication too must be brought into line, which brings us back to silence.

Metapragmatic uses of language and communication are always ideological since it is through our delimitation of language boundaries, evaluation of language varieties, structures and use that we inevitably make manifest our subject positions, allegiances and patterns of power and dominance (Silverstein, 2001/1981; Schieffelin et al., 1998; Jaworski et al., 2004; Thurlow, 2006). For example, Gal and Irvine (1995) demonstrate how '[a]rguments about language were central in producing and buttressing European claims to superiority of the metropolitan bourgeoisie over "backward" or "primitive" others, whether they were residents of other continents, other provinces, or other social classes' (p. 967). Such linguistic differentiation continues to be indicative of 'self-evident' and 'natural' (naturalized) divisions between national and ethnic groups, genders, social classes and so on. The way people view and represent linguistic differences map onto their understanding, classification and evaluation of social actors, events and activities which they find significant, and to the formulation of their preferred worldviews (ideologies) (Gal and Irvine, 1995: 970; Silverstein, 1979; Woolard and Schieffelin, 1994).

That silence is a power-filled communicative resource is, perhaps, not altogether surprising. Nor is it remarkable, as Peter Stallybrass and Allon White (1986) comment in the quote above, that noise and the absence of noise are markers of class status. The wealthy and privileged have always sought to isolate themselves from the masses, to remove themselves from the throng. Confusingly, however, we often also speak (in literal or metaphoric terms) of oppressed groups being 'silenced' or 'voiceless'. This is a claim which, after all, sits at the heart of Cheris Kramarae's (1981) Muted Group Theory (see also Mark Orbe's, 1998, application of these ideas to racialized inequalities). By contrast, in the case of luxury travel it is the privileged who are seeking out – or being encouraged to seek out – silence. Importantly, however, it may not be silence per se which is sought but rather being able to *choose* silence as a means of establishing social space, securing exclusivity and performing distinction. The privilege of exclusivity – its frisson – lies in being able to decide if and when one wants to be excluded or to have others excluded. Or, at least, believing that one is able to make this choice.

Not surprisingly, therefore, the performance of plenty and of plentiful choice is everywhere in luxury tourism (cf. Thurlow and Jaworski, submitted) – a choice which may or may not actually exist. Indeed, the discourse of tourism – and especially luxury tourism – is riddled with paradox and oxymoron: Safe adventures; Planned spontaneity; Genuine fakes; Extraordinary ordinary; Casual elegance; Exotic familiarity; Affordable exclusivity; Contemporary tradition. Perhaps the two most overarching oxymoronic tensions in luxury tourism are 'tailored choice' and 'controlled disorder'. In fact, we have shown before that choice and control appear consistently to be the two key markers or values of high status nowadays (Thurlow and Jaworski, 2006; see also Schwartz, 2004). These are the quintessential, illusory objects of contemporary desire.[12] It is, we believe, in the service of choice and control that silence as/for social space is co-opted. This in turn allows an ordering of the unordered, the managing of the liminal, the unfamiliar, the unknown, the unpredictable, and the appearance choice where there really is none. It's the putative Fordist choice: you may have any colour you want provided it's black!

Like the stories of everyday life, the veracity (or validity) of the promotional claims of luxury travel advertising is largely unimportant. The power of these claims lies in their ability to establish aspirational ideals or 'regimes of truth' about travel, about luxury, about status and social distinction – and to persuade us of their truth rhetorically through performative reiteration (e.g. infinity pools), superlatives (e.g. 'the most magnificent place', 'the world's best cruise liner'), narrative detail (e.g. 'more than three miles of white-sand beaches', rolled towels), aphoristic copy ('A hotel is where you stay. Montage is where you live.'), and so on. What makes this type of luxury advertising far more worthy of our critique is that it also promotes an elitist discourse which says as much about the shaping of the aspirational desires and lifestyles of the not-so-rich and the poor as it does about the actual leisure activities of the really or absolutely rich. In truth, the really rich have moved onto bigger and better and more exclusive things.[13] In the meantime, the intertextual discourse of tourism, globalization, luxury and communication continues to establish and promote its new or revised markers of distinction and privilege for everyone. It also normalizes the very notion of class status itself. Silence is thus not simply a feature of super-elite lifestyles but a semiotic resource by which anyone may style themselves or being stylized as elite.

Drawing boundaries between talk and silence and vesting them variably with a potential for power or powerlessness, sublime or corrupt mediation of meaning, or expression of honesty and dishonesty, has been equally loaded with ideologizing religious movements (R. Bauman, 1983), ethnic groups (Scollon and Scollon, 1990) and so on. Such deployment of metapragmatic and representational silence (and talk) finds a particularly fertile ground in privileging some social actors as silent by choice, while disadvantaging and discriminating others by depriving them of voice – silencing (Bilmes, 1994; Jaworski, 1993; Theismeyer, 2003). In each case, silencing is associated with extreme power differential and access or denial of economic, cultural and symbolic capital. In the case of our data, the two represented groups – the implied favoured, Western, White (often male), tourists, and the implied disenfranchised, poor, non-White locals depicted in the role of servants – both seem to occupy liminal zones outside of 'normal', social time and space. Both groups are thereby *othered*: the former as detached elites occupying the safety of the somewhat 'unreal' gated communities of luxury hotels, while the latter are pushed to the margins of legitimacy and visibility – occupying the same regulated spaces but only to police their boundaries and maintain their orderliness.

In the case of luxury tourism, what we therefore see is silence being fiercely (re)incorporated into the bourgeois imagination. The super-rich – and the bourgeoisie on their tails – are on the move again and looking for ways to redefine and distinguish themselves anew. It seems that travel, silence and communication are being (re)classed in the process – and precisely at a time when just about everywhere else everyone else is being compelled into talk, into believing that (good) communication is reducible to (more) talk (Cameron, 2000; Jaworski and Sachdev, 2004; Thurlow, 2001). In luxury tourism meanwhile, elite status is clearly being predicated on (the promise of) being free of – excluded from – both the babble of locals and the drivel of the masses but, increasingly, also from the drone of other/lesser elites. This marks a reversal of the usual linguascape of tourism. The repeated absence of signage, of people, of talk and other human interactions in our data is consistent with what we see as an increasingly 'anti-communicational' or rather anti-interactional ethos in super-elite mobility and in the lifestyles of the (absolutely) wealthy in general. Which is not to say that silence is non-communication (see our discussion on the metapragmatics of silence above). Nor is it to imply that communication-as-talk is necessarily a good thing – certainly it is no panacea for social ills (cf. Cameron, 2000). Nonetheless, the intense semiotic production of silence in luxury tourism advertising appears to encode an elitist ideology of segregation and isolationism which is, we think, more troubling. The hegemonic sway of this anti-communicational mindset or lifestyle is rendered all the more desirable to the aspirational classes through its being (re)semioticized as a mark of distinction and cosmopolitanism. As such, silence as an elitist resource becomes both a manifestation and production of the 'breakdown' in communication which, according to Zygmunt Bauman (1998, quoted at the start of our chapter), increasingly divides 'global and extraterritorial elites and the ever more "localized" rest'.

Acknowledgements

Crispin is indebted to the Simpson Center for the Humanities (University of Washington) for a 2007/2008 *Society of Scholars* research fellowship which enabled him to complete this chapter. We are grateful to Crispin's colleagues Ron Krabill and Craig Jeffrey for their insightful comments and to Paul Ford for his help with preparing our online database of luxury tourism advertising. Our work together was also enabled through funding from the Leverhulme Trust (grant no. F/00 407/D) to the Centre for Language and Communication Research, Cardiff University, for a larger project on Language and Global Communication.

Notes

[1] In addition to the examples reproduced here, the rest of our dataset of luxury tourism advertising is available online here: http://faculty.washington.edu/thurlow/spaces/index.html.

[2] These three advertisements (for *Westin Hotels & Resorts*, *Cap Cana* and *The British Virgin Islands*) are some of the most recent additions to our dataset. Perhaps the semiotic value of silence is becoming even more codified and conventionalized? Ironically, for all its promise of silence, Figure 9.4's copy actually includes some reported speech – although even this is 'whispered'.

[3] With very few exceptions, solitary figures are women which is, of course, consistent with the gendered nature of both advertising discourse and of tourism discourse.

[4] A similar effect of visual silence has been noted by Kwiatkowska (1997) in her analysis of the René Magritte painting *L'homme au journal*, which consists of four identical panels representing a man sitting at a table in a room and reading a newspaper, except that the man and the newspaper are 'missing' from the top right and the two bottom panels.

[5] This is less apparent in the examples we show here, where the skies are actually not cloudless (see Figures 9.1, 9.2, 9.4, 9.6, 9.9, 9.10 and 9.12) as they are in Figures 9.5 and 9.11. Certainly, though, what weather there is tranquil and one or two gentle clouds might even serve to accentuate and legitimate this.

[6] Because of their technical design, infinity pools are expensive to build and to maintain. Interestingly for the current analysis, an added effect of their fountain-like design is the increased stillness of the water. For more information, see this Wikipedia entry: http://en.wikipedia.org/wiki/Infinity_pool (accessed 27 August 2009).

[7] The following discussion is based largely on the discussion of the affordances of colour in Kress and van Leeuwen (2001).

[8] The almost imperceptible blending of colours of the water and sky (see Figures 9.1, 9.6, 9.11 and also 9.12), also creates near-perfect monochromes

reminiscent of the blue 'void' paintings by Yves Klein alongside other traditions of 'silent' monochrome painting (Lippard, 1981; Hafif, 1997).

[9] At the symbolic level, expansive white is also often associated with ultimate silence. As the Russian Suprematist painter Kasimir Malevich declared in 1919, white is 'the true, real conception of infinity' (cited in Gage, 1999: 247).

[10] For the distinction between *absolute* and relative wealth see www.i-needle.net (accessed 27 August 2009).

[11] In this regard, we are thinking of the kind of 'adventure cruising' offered by high-end tour operator Ambercrombie and Kent – for more, see www.i-needle.net (accessed 27 August 2009) which 'documents insane manifestations of the chasm between the unforgivably poor and the unjustifiably rich'.

[12] Ironically, as Barry Schwartz (2004) notes, there's a point at which endless, uncontrolled choice simply becomes a burden, an inconvenience.

[13] Hence the need for luxury tourism – as with other luxury products and services – to be constantly escalating their superlative rhetoric; for example, *The Mansion*'s (Figure 9.5) characterization of itself in terms of 'Ultra exclusive. Absolute privacy. Beyond attentive.' Or *Cap Cana*'s (Figure 9.2) claim to be 'the world's next great destination' (see Thurlow and Jaworski, 2006).

References

Bakhtin, M. (1981), *The Dialogic Imagination* (M. Holquist [ed.], Translated by C. Emerson and M. Holquist). Austin: University of Texas Press.

Basso, K. H. (1972), '"To give up on words": Silence in Western Apache culture', in P. P. Giglioli (ed.), *Language and Social Context*. Harmondsworth: Penguin, pp. 67–86.

Bauman, R. (1977), *Verbal Art as Performance*. Prospect Heights, Illinois: Waveland Press.

—(1983), *Let Your Words Be Few: Symbolism of Speaking and Silence among Seventeenth-Century Quakers*. Cambridge: Cambridge University Press.

Bauman, Z. (1998), *Globalization: The Human Consequences*. Cambridge: Polity.

Bilmes, J. (1994), 'Constituting silence: Life in the world of total meaning', *Semiotica*, 98, 73–87.

Bourdieu, P. (1984), *Distinction: A Social Critique of the Judgement of Taste*. Translated by R. Nice. Cambridge, MA: Harvard University Press.

—(1991), *Language & Symbolic Power* (J. B. Thompson [ed.], Translated by G. Raymond and M. Adamson). Cambridge: Polity Press.

Braithwaite, C. A. (1990), 'Communicative silence: A cross-cultural study of Basso's hypothesis,' in D. Carbaugh (ed.), *Cultural Communication and Intercultural Contact*. Hillsdale, NJ: Lawrence Erlbaum, pp. 321–327.

Butler, J. (1990), *Gender Trouble: Feminism and the Subversion of Identity*. New York: Routledge.

Cameron, D. (2000), *Good to Talk? Living in a Communication Culture*. London: Sage.

Carlisle, J. (2001), 'The smell of class: British novels of the 1860s', *Victorian Literature and Culture*, 29(10), 1–19.

Carlton, E. (1996), *The Few and the Many: A Typology of Elites*. Aldershot: Scolar Press.
Douglas, M. (1966), *Purity and Danger: An Analysis of Concepts of Pollution and Taboo*. New York: Praeger.
Dyer, R. (1997), *White*. London: Routledge.
Edensor, T. (2001), 'Performing tourism, staging tourism: (Re)producing tourist space and practice', *Tourist Studies*, 1(1), 59–81.
Fairclough, N. (1989), *Language and Power*. London: Longman.
—(1999), 'Global capitalism and critical awareness of language', *Language Awareness*, 8, 71–83.
Favero, P. (2007), 'What a wonderful world!': On the 'touristic ways of seeing': The knowledge and the politics of the 'culture industries of otherness', *Tourist Studies*, 7(1), 51–81.
Franklin, A. and Crang, M. (2001), 'The trouble with tourism and travel theory', *Tourist Studies*, 1(1), 5–22.
Gage, J. (1999), *Colour and Culture*. London: Thames and Hudson.
Gal, S. and Irvine, J. (1995), 'The boundaries of languages and disciplines: How ideologies construct differences', *Social Research*, 62, 967–1001.
Giddens, A. (1991), *Modernity and Self-identity: Self and Society in the Late Modern Age*. Cambridge: Polity.
Gilmore, P. (1985), 'Silence and sulking: Emotional displays in the classroom', in D. Tannen and M. Saville-Troike (eds), *Perspectives on Silence*. Norwood, NJ: Ablex, pp. 139–162.
Gramsci, A. (1971), *Selections from the Prison Notebooks*. New York: International Publishers.
Hafif, M. (1997), 'Silence in painting: Let me count the ways', in A. Jaworski (ed.), *Silence: Interdisciplinary Perspectives*. Berlin: Mouton de Gruyter, pp. 339–349.
Halliday, M. A. K. (1978), *Language as Social Semiotic: The Social Interpretation of Language and Meaning*. London: Edward Arnold.
Hannerz, U. (1996), *Transnational Connections: Culture, People, Places*. London: Routledge.
Jacobsen, J. K. S. (2003), 'The tourist bubble and the Europeanisation of holiday travel', *Tourism and Cultural Change*, 1(1), 71–87.
Jaworski, A. (1993), *The Power of Silence: Social and Pragmatic Perspectives*. Newbury Park, CA: Sage.
—(1997), '"White and white": Metacommunicative and metaphorical silences', in A. Jaworski (ed.), *Silence: Interdisciplinary Perspectives*. Berlin: Mouton de Gruyter, pp. 381–401.
—(1998), 'The silence of power and solidarity', in *Fallen Sons: Studia Anglica Posnaniensia*, 33, 141–152.
Jaworski, A and Sachdev, I. (2004), 'Teachers' beliefs about students' talk and silence: Constructing academic success and failure through metapragmatic comments', in A. Jaworski, N. Coupland and D. Galasiński (eds), *Metalanguage: Social and Ideological Perspectives*. Berlin: Mouton de Gruyter, pp. 227–244.
Jaworski, A. and Thurlow, C. (2004), 'Language, tourism and globalization: Mapping new international identities', in S. H. Ng, C-Y. Chiu and C. Candlin

(eds), *Language Matters: Communication, Identity, and Culture.* Hong Kong: City University Press, pp. 297–321.
—(2009), 'Taking an elitist stance: Ideology and the discursive production of social distinction', in A. Jaffee (ed.), *Perspectives on Stance.* New York: Oxford University Press, pp. 195–226.
Jaworski, A., Coupland, N. and Galasiński, D. (eds) (2004), *Metalanguage: Social and Ideological Perspectives.* Berlin: Mouton de Gruyter.
Jaworski, A., Thurlow, C., Ylänne-McEwen, V. and Lawson, S. (2003), 'The uses and representations of local languages in tourist destinations: A view from British television holiday programmes', *Language Awareness,* 12(1), 5–29.
Jewitt, C. and Oyama, R. (2001), 'Visual meaning: A social semiotic approach', in T. van Leeuwen and C. Jewitt (eds), *Handbook of Visual Analysis.* London: Sage, pp. 134–156.
Kramarae, C. (1981), *Women and Men Speaking: Frameworks for Analysis.* Rowley, MA: Newbury House.
Kress, G. and van Leeuwen, T. (1996), *Reading Images: The Grammar of Visual Design.* London: Routledge.
—(2001), *Multimodal Discourse: The Modes and Media of Contemporary Communication.* London: Arnold.
Kwiatkowska, A. (1997), 'Silence across modalities', in A. Jaworski (ed.), *Silence: Interdisciplinary Perspectives.* Berlin: Mouton de Gruyter, pp. 329–337.
Lash, S. and Urry, J. (1994), *Economies of Signs and Spaces.* London: Sage.
Lippard, L. (1981), 'The silent art', *Art in America,* 55, 58–63.
Low, S. M. (2001), 'The edge and the center: Gated communities and the discourse of urban fear', *American Anthropologist,* 103, 45–59.
MacCannell, D. (1999), *The Tourist: A New Theory of the Leisure Class.* Berkeley: University of California Press.
Messaris, P. (1997), *Visual Persuasion: The Role of Images in Advertising.* Thousand Oaks, CA: Sage.
Morgan, N. and Pritchard, A. (1998), *Tourism, Promotion and Power: Creating Images, Creating Identities.* Chichester: John Wiley and Sons.
—(2005), 'On souvenirs and metonymy: Narratives of memory, metaphor and materiality', *Tourist Studies,* 5(1), 29–53.
Orbe, M. P. (1998), *Constructing Co-cultural Theory: An Explication of Culture, Power, and Communication.* Thousand Oaks, CA: Sage.
Pezzullo, P. C. (2007), *Toxic Tourism: Rhetorics of Travel, Pollution, and Environmental Justice.* Tuscaloosa: University of Alabama Press.
Philips, S. U. (1972), 'Participant structures and communicative competence: Warm Springs children in community and classroom', in C. B. Cazden, V. P. John and D. Hymes (eds), *Functions of Language in the Classroom.* New York: Teachers College Press, pp. 370–394.
Rampton, B. (2003), 'Hegemony, Social Class and Stylization', *Pragmatics,* 13(1), 49–83.
Saville-Troike, M. (1985), 'The place of silence in an integrated theory of communication', in D. Tannen and M. Saville-Troike (eds), *Perspectives on Silence.* Norwood, NJ: Ablex, pp. 3–30.

Schieffelin, B. B., Woolard, K. A. and Kroskrity, P. V. (eds) (1998), *Language Ideologies: Practice and Theory*. New York: Oxford University Press.

Scollon, R. and Wong Scollon S. (1990), 'Athabaskan-English interethnic communication', in D. Carbaugh (ed.), *Cultural Communication and Intercultural Contact*. Hillsdale: Lawrence Erlbaum, pp. 259–286.

Schwartz, B. (2004), *The Paradox of Choice: Why More is Less*. New York: Ecco.

Selwyn, T. (ed.) (1996), *The Tourist Image: Myths and Myth Making in Tourism*. Chichester: John Wiley and Sons.

Sherman, R. (2007), *Class Acts: Service and Inequality in Luxury Hotels*. Berkeley, CA: University of California Press.

Silverstein, M. (1979), 'Language structure and linguistic ideology', in P. R. Clyne, W. F. Hanks and C. L. Hofbauer (eds), *The Elements: A Parasession on Linguistic Units and Levels*. Chicago: Chicago Linguistic Society, pp. 193–247.

—(2001), 'The limits of awareness', in A. Duranti (ed.), *Linguistic Anthropology: A Reader*. Oxford: Blackwell Publishers, pp. 382–402. (Original work published in 1981).

Smith, V. L. (1977), 'Introduction', in V. L. Smith (ed.), *Hosts and Guests: The Anthropology of Tourism*. Philadelphia: University of Pennsylvania Press, pp. 1–14.

Stallybrass, P. and White, A. (1986), *The Politics and Poetics of Transgression*. London: Methuen.

Tannen, D. and Saville-Troike, M. (eds) (1985), *Perspectives on Silence*. Norwood, NJ: Ablex.

Thiesmeyer, L. (ed.) (2003), *Discourse and Silencing: Representation and the Language of Displacement*. Amsterdam/Philadelphia: John Benjamins.

Thompson, J. B. (2000), 'The globalization of communication', in D. Held and A. McGrew (eds), *The Global Transformations Reader: An Introduction to the Globalization Debate*. Cambridge: Polity Press, pp. 202–215.

Thurlow, C. (2001), 'Talkin' 'bout my communication: Communication awareness in early adolescence', *Language Awareness*, 10(2&3), 213–231.

—(2006), 'From statistical panic to moral panic: The metadiscursive construction and popular exaggeration of new media language in the print media', *Journal of Computer Mediated Communication*, 11(3), 667–701.

Thurlow, C. and Aiello, G. (2007), 'National pride, global capital: A social semiotic analysis of transnational visual branding in the airline industry', *Visual Communication*, 6(3), 305–344.

Thurlow, C. and Jaworski, A. (2003), 'Communicating a global reach: Inflight magazines as a globalizing genre in tourism', *Journal of Sociolinguistics*, 7, 581–608.

—(2006), 'The alchemy of the upwardly mobile: Symbolic capital and the stylization of elites in frequent-flyer programmes', *Discourse & Society*, 17(1), 131–167.

—(2010), *Tourism Discourse: Language and Global Mobility*. Basingstoke: Palgrave Macmillan.

—(submitted), Elite mobilities: The semiotic landscapes of luxury and privilege. Submitted to *Visual Communication*.

Thurlow, C., Gendelman, I. and Jaworski, A. (in prep.), 'Elite imaginations: The visual spatialization of luxury and privilege in super-elite tourism discourse'.

Turner, V. (1977), 'Variations on a theme of liminality', in S. Moore and B. Myerhoff (eds), *Secular Ritual*. Amsterdam: Van Gorcum, pp. 36–52.

Urry, J. (2002), *The Tourist Gaze* (2nd edn). London: Sage.

Williams, R. (1977), *Marxism and Literature*. Oxford: Oxford University Press.

Wolfson, N. (1988), 'The bulge: A theory of speech behavior and social distance', in J. Fine (ed.), *Second Language Discourse: A Textbook of Current Research*. Norwood, NJ: Ablex, pp. 21–38.

Woolard, K. and Schieffelin, B. (1994), 'Language ideology', *Annual Review of Anthropology*, 23, 55–82.

Chapter 10

War Monuments and the Changing Discourses of Nation and Soldiery

Gill Abousnnouga and David Machin

Each day many of us will pass a war monument in our city, town or village without paying it much particular attention. It is simply part of the landscape of where we live. On occasion we may have taken a more careful look, reading the inscriptions and looking up at the pose and facial expression of the depicted soldier if it has the form of a statue. We may have thought briefly of the great loss and sacrifice mentioned on the inscription. Even if we considered ourselves to be pacifist, the monument may have inspired a moment of sadness, respect or dread at what those commemorated suffered.

Historians have discussed these monuments, these routine features of our everyday lives, as objects of collective mourning. These are ways that populations remember and pay respect to the soldiers who have given their lives on their behalf. In this chapter we take a different view. In his classic work, *Banal Nationalism,* Billig (1985) described the way that the nation and nationalism are concepts that are fostered, legitimized and maintained not so much through overt propaganda, but through mundane everyday processes and features particularly in the mass media: the weather map which will have political boundaries marked; sport, where a collective 'we' battles against the other; in history books and movies where nations, only relatively recently constructed since the eighteenth century, appear timeless and eternal populated by a single monolithic people. In the case of monuments we find one such mundane reminder of this collective spirit, this imagined common national unity and purpose. But in the case of monuments this fostering of nationalism serves in the first place as a legitimization of militarism.

As we have shown elsewhere (Abousnnouga and Machin, 2008) the great majority of war monuments we find in our everyday landscapes were deliberate attempts by governments, terrified of rising socialism during and just after World War I, to give a sense of meaning to the war, to distract from issues of social class and exploitation (Laybourn, 1997; McKibbin, 1974). It is clearly documented that in Britain, for example, many workers' movements were perceived by the authorities as being all too aware of the way that the ruling classes across Europe had profited well from the war while many millions of working-class men, many unaware at that point of national identities, were sent to die meaningless squalid deaths (Mosse, 1990). In this sense these earlier monuments were meant to be everyday semiotic devices to legitimize war and the idea of national unity in the face of evident exploitation and inequality, placing these at the heart of our towns and cities, making this commemoration a background feature of our everyday landscapes. At the time of monument building it was common to find cartoons depicting young soldiers being crucified by a group of fat privileged European elite. What if these had been used as the model for the monuments to be placed in our public places?

Since the large scale war monument building of the early twentieth century new monuments have been erected to commemorate other subsequent wars or to commemorate those not formerly remembered in earlier wars. For example, in 2007 in London's Hyde Park a memorial was erected in memory of the soldiers of New Zealand who died in World War II (see Figure 10.8). In many cases the names of soldiers 'fallen' in later conflicts are simply added to existing monuments. On the national cenotaph in London's Whitehall, for example, names include soldiers killed in World War II and Iraq. On state specified days of remembrance we can see all of these monuments used for official collective mourning where authority figures may appear with heads bowed, where national flags are waved and where nationalist music is played. However there are some crucial differences in the monuments built across the one hundred years from World War I. We can see this immediately in the inscriptions which shift from a lexis of 'sacrifice', 'God' and 'Country' to 'fallen', 'those who never returned' and even 'who gave all for freedom'. Clearly, while we might argue that these monuments still serve to legitimize militarism, this is done through different discourses. And, as we explore in this chapter, as well as linguistic differences, we find important visual differences, that, like the changes in linguistic choices, reveal on the one hand changing attitudes to war, soldiery and nation, but which at the same time are able to maintain discourses that could not be articulated through language.

In this chapter, using multimodal discourse analysis, we show that over the past one hundred years war monuments have been a systematic attempt by the authorities to use specific visual semiotic resources to disseminate and legitimize particular discourses of war, to communicate particular values, identities, goals and motives, placing these in everyday public spaces. We believe that these visually realized discourses have been a crucial part of justifying the deaths of millions of young men around Europe, occupation of territories and oppression of civilians around the world in the interests of the ruling elite. But unlike the linguistic choices we find on inscriptions, the visual/physical semiotic choices we find on monuments realize discourses only ambiguously. Importantly, this has allowed for the communication of meanings, kinds of identities, actions and values that would have appeared odd, inappropriate or even ludicrous had they been articulated as written inscriptions. This has permitted older discourses to persist that would certainly not be acceptable if realized linguistically. We analyse a sample of eight monuments erected at different times in order to reveal these processes.

Methodology

In this chapter, the model for analysis we use has four levels. At the first level we draw on the semiotics of Roland Barthes' (1973) classic two-step analysis: denotation and connotation, but wish to switch the emphasis normally given to the two levels of analysis.

On one level, images can be said to document. In other words they show *particular* events, *particular* people, places and things. Or, in semiotic terminology, they *denote*. So asking what an image denotes is asking: Who and/or what is depicted here? In terms of our monuments we can say that they might denote a soldier, a gun, or simply a rock. This is an important and often undervalued level of analysis as there is a tendency to jump to the next level below. Close attention *describing* to what is depicted, as we will show, is a crucial first step.

Other images and designed objects will still depict particular people, places, things and events, but to get general or abstract *ideas* across. They use them to *connote* ideas and concepts. So at the second level of analysis we ask what ideas and values are communicated through what is represented, and through the way in which it is represented. At this level we look at features and characteristics of the soldier, objects or forms that are depicted. At this level we can begin to get a sense of the kinds of identities, actions and values that are being communicated.

It is this second level of analysis that is often given priority over the first. This is due to two reasons. First, in our academic culture the act of analysis is given greater esteem than that of description. Second, since there can be no neutral denotation, as Barthes (1973) pointed out, it seems less worthwhile to invest considerable energy in this level. Any image, feature or object will connote something for us. Even everyday objects such as a tree or car carry meanings, for example of nature or of success, respectively. But without this first level much can be missed. We can draw this out with an example from linguistics. When we listen to a political speech we might be aware that the speaker has managed to give a particular spin on a set of events, but it is for a linguist, with their careful attention to the detail of the way that language is used, to show exactly *how* they have done this. This is why we need to be attentive to denotation. This is particularly important if we are to be able to show how the finer semiotic choices of war monuments connote discourses along with their associated values, identities and activities.

Central to attending to denotation, used successfully by Barthes (1973), and which is characteristic of the best work of Kress and van Leeuwen (1996, 2002) and van Leeuwen (2005), is the commutation test. This derives from a process of linguistic substitution used by the Prague structuralists (e.g. Jakobson and Halle, 1956), which can be used to isolate important signifying qualities. So as we make our observations, we can hypothetically change features or qualities, replacing them with others, or removing them completely and consider what kind of difference this makes. Van Leeuwen (2006) used this technique in his analysis of the meaning potential of typefaces. This allowed him to show how designers could draw on a number of features such as 'tall' versus 'stocky', which could mean 'elegant' as opposed to 'cumbersome', or alternatively 'pompous' and 'unstable' versus 'grounded' and 'stable'. When analysing monuments we can, for example consider the meaning of solidity by imagining the same monument being hollow, and so on for other features and dimensions.

Our second level of analysis is metaphorical association. This was the basis of the inventories created by Kress and van Leeuwen (1996) which they took from Arnheim (1969) who argued that visual communication is steeped in 'experiential associations' (p. 117). He explains that 'human beings are naturally aware of the structural resemblance uniting physical and non-physical objects' (p. 118). For example, if a person said 'I was this far away from hitting him' and made a gesture with their hand indicating a small distance between their finger and thumb, they are making an association between physical distance and emotional feeling. In the case of a tall, slim typeface, as opposed to a short, stocky one, we have physical experience of objects in the world that carry such features and qualities. The meaning potential of these can be used as semiotic resources in the design of images and objects as we will show as regards monuments. We can ask, for example, whether it is tall or short, angular or rounded, raised up or at ground level, hollow or solid. These can then be thought of in terms of our experiential associations.

Our third level of analysis draws our attention to the fact that features of images or objects can have meaning not due to any obvious metaphorical association but because of symbolic meanings that have become buried. Panofsky (1972) pioneered an approach to considering the origins of the symbolic meaning of art, what has been called 'iconology'. He realized that objects, animals, persons, postures and abstract shapes were used in art to symbolize particular people, values and behaviours. These had become conventions, established over time and the origins of the meaning may have become buried for contemporary viewers. This symbolism can be found, Panofsky thought, also in the very form of layout and choice of materials. These he said could 'reveal the basic attitude of a nation, a period, a class, a religious or philosophical persuasion' (1970: 7). In other words, we need to trace the meaning of form, objects and materials used in monuments to understand their cultural and ideological meanings. Why would a sculpture use bronze rather than stone or plastic, and why a thick rather than slim base? Why do some figures stride forward and others stand still? In this sense we need to use historical documents to help us to establish the meaning potentials of denoted features and qualities.

Our fourth level of analysis rests on the assumption that the most productive way to approach the use of semiotic resources that we have described above is by remaining faithful to the core assumptions of Critical Discourse Analysis (CDA) to which both Kress and van Leeuwen (see references above) have contributed extensively. In CDA, the broader ideas communicated by a text are referred to as discourses (van Dijk, 1993; Fairclough, 2000). These discourses can be thought of as models of the world, in the sense described by Foucault (1977), which can include kinds of participants, behaviours, goals and locations (van Leeuwen and Wodak, 1999). These discourses project certain social values and ideas and in turn contribute to the (re)production of social life. In CDA texts are analysed in terms of the details of the linguistic choices that they contain as these allow the analyst to reveal the broader discourses that are realized. Before the groundbreaking work of Kress and van Leeuwen's *Reading Images*, discourse analysts had focused on the way that discourses were realized through the linguistic mode. But Kress and van Leeuwen showed how we could systematically analyse the way that this happens visually through photographs, pictures and visual designs. Therefore, discourses, along with their values, participants, action settings, etc., can be connoted by both linguistic and visual choices. As we can study lexical and grammatical choices in language to reveal discourses so we can study choices of visual semiotic resources. This kind of approach can also allow us to describe what kind of resources are available to visual designers and show how these can be used to persuade and to legitimize.

We apply our model of analysis to a sample of eight monuments from our ongoing research. These monuments were built at different times and represent different wars. The first four are earlier monuments commemorating World War I, and the rest a range of more contemporary monuments. We show how choices of visual semiotic resources realize different discourses of the meaning of war and of nation. We begin with an analysis of the iconography of the monuments in turn and then move on to analyse form (size, positioning, materials, shape, etc.).

Analysis

Iconography of monuments

The iconography of war monuments includes an analysis of objects, persons and poses. We begin with the Cardiff national World War I memorial erected in 1928 (Figure 10.1). Typical of many monuments built in this period the structure represents a post-war return to architectural styles that connoted ideas of strength and high ideals and thinking. The sources of these were found in the

FIGURE 10.1 Cardiff National Memorial

idealized empires of Egypt, Greece and Rome. On the Cardiff monument, we find references to the Acropolis with columns and pilasters. A number of columns are used to create a portico which is a sort of entrance porch common to these classical structures. Such monuments also reflect the classical style by having complete symmetry to connote elegance and balance. Designers of these monuments often wrote of the styles having a 'civilizing effect' (Troost, 1942) through references to classicism. Up to the mid 1920s when many of the World War I monuments were built, there was a fashion in Art Deco which drew heavily on classicism. This can often be seen in the use of obelisks and other ancient Egyptian features.

While inscriptions on these early monuments referred to death as sacrifice to God and country, visually we find something that is not articulated linguistically. The deaths of young men in a colonial war are here represented through a discourse of classicism with its high ideals and philosophy, its perfect balance and association with Greek and Roman gods. As in many other examples of this type, the soldier in the Cardiff memorial is represented as a beautiful god found in the statues of classical architecture (Figure 10.2). He is depicted standing in an athletic, graceful stretch, with his face completely symmetrical unlike real faces, giving him an otherworldly feel.

On some monuments, as in the Machine Gunner monument in London, neo-classical figures themselves were used (Figure 10.3). Here, a neo-classical statue of David holding Goliath's sword stands flanked by two machine guns that have been draped in wreaths. In fact the public themselves were frequently

Figure 10.2 Soldier on Cardiff memorial

Figure 10.3 Machine Gunner monument, London

unhappy with these representations (Mosse, 1990; Quinlan, 2005). While the authorities built such monuments out of concern for a backlash from the working classes, often the visual choices were seen as a further insult.

On the Cardiff monument we find much religious iconography. There is the symbolism of the wreaths that were adopted into Christianity from ancient Greece as a symbol of victory and redemption (see also the wreaths on the Machine Gunner monument). The wreaths on the Cardiff monument are held up in offering to dolphins and a winged figure. In Christian art dolphins are symbolic of the resurrection (Ferguson, 1942). The winged figure holds swords used to connote victory (Quinlan, 2005). Such symbolism was all explained to the public at the time of the unveiling although during these events there would often be heckling and throwing of medals.

Figure 10.4 shows the World War I monument in Abertillery, South Wales. This particular figure has two significant features: the soldier is depicted as striding forward and with his hat removed from his head. This striding is important in the sense of him not standing still showing fear, nor running in panic or aggression. E. M. Viquesney, a highly influential monument designer in the United States, wrote of the importance of portraying the soldier striding confidently and purposefully through no-man's land. He felt that this would capture the spirit of 'quiet certainty' (Little, 1996). Bourke (1996) discussing a similar monument at Llandudno, Wales shows how the committee, while planning its design wanted 'no suggestion of callousness or brutality associated with war' (Book of Remembrance, Colwyn Bay War Memorial 1914–1918, [Colwyn Bay, 1922], cited in Bourke, 1996: 228). We see a similar lack of aggression,

Figure 10.4 Abertillery monument

Figure 10.5 Artillery monument, London

although a slightly different pose in the case of the London Artillery monument (Figure 10.5). Here the soldier stands at ease, legs apart. Along with his powerful bulky appearance this connotes quiet confidence and power. Notably in photographs of artillery men on the Somme, where they appear lost and bedraggled, many of them simply drowning in the mud or wasting away with disease, they do not appear so mighty.

Also characteristic of poses in the early war monuments was the removal of hats as in Figure 10.4. Again we have reference to Christian art where the bare head has the symbolic meaning of revealing oneself to God, which requires considerable purity. The removal of the helmets can also connote invulnerability, which is also connoted by the serene yet distant facial expressions carried by the soldiers.

It is important to note, in the tradition of CDA, we can ask what kind of participants in war are excluded from the war monuments. There are no dead or mutilated civilians, for example. Very few women and children or families are represented and in the rare examples the innocent who were protected are depicted. The actual effects of war on bodies and society are not depicted. In fact, across Europe and the United States proposals for anti-war and pro-peace war monuments depicting war through association of cruelty, death and destruction have been frequently unsupported by the authorities (Michalski, 1998). One good example is Käthe Kollwitz's proposed design for a statue of kneeling grief-stricken parents in Belgium. It is only more recently that monuments have begun to be built to commemorate the role of women in war and the peculiar nature of this will be the subject of a later paper. Nor do we commemorate the role of the weapons' manufacturers. Even in 1918, a political advisor noted the contrast between the devastated working-class communities and 'the enormous profits being made by businessmen who were involved in the manufacturing of goods for the war while living in the safety and comfort of home' (Rudy, 1918: 551).

On these early monuments the soldiers do not look at the viewer. In their analysis of gaze, Kress and van Leeuwen (1996) suggest that it is useful to think about the way that images can be thought of as fulfilling linguistic speech acts as described by Halliday (1978). He argued that when we speak we can do one of four basic communicative acts: we can offer information; offer services or goods; demand information; demand goods and services. In each case, there is an expected response possible. Kress and van Leeuwen show that while there are four speech acts there are two kinds of image act: 'offer' and 'demand'. These are useful for thinking about the way that the soldiers depicted in monuments interact with the viewer.

In demand images, the subject looks at the viewer whose presence is acknowledged and who is therefore addressed and required to respond. Of course the kind of demand that is made will depend on other factors such as facial expression, or posture. So, for example the subject through looking sad may demand that we feel pity.

In offer images the subject does not look at the viewer and the viewer remains unacknowledged. Kress and van Leeuwen (1996) suggest that we are encouraged to look at the scene or individual solely as onlookers or as voyeurs. In such a case the viewer is offered the scene as information available for scrutiny.

In the case of the Cardiff, Abertillery and London Artillery statues the soldiers do not look at the viewer. Therefore they make no demand nor expect a response through gaze. Rather they tend to look upwards, forwards to the horizon, or downwards in mourning. The image acts realized by gaze here are offers where the viewer can simply view the soldier as information. It is clear that it would have been problematic for angry working-class families to have seen the statues looking back at them, demanding a response. What would this response have been? In his description of how working-class people in Britain were feeling during this period, Arnot (1967) quotes Lloyd George, who spoke of 'a deep sense not only of discontent, but of anger and revolt, amongst the workmen against the war conditions' (p. 150). In this context, characterized by a revolutionary spirit across Europe, it was important that the depicted soldiers remained in the fantasy realm of classical mythology disengaged from their onlookers.

The Yomper monument (Figure 10.6) was erected in 1992 to commemorate the British Royal Marines who fought in the Falklands/Malvinas War 1982. The figure is very different in terms of pose and gaze. Compared to the earlier monuments he is depicted in a more realistic battle context, ready for action. He appears stern and focused, although not necessarily aggressive as he holds his gun almost gently, taking a small step rather than, say, striding. This suggests not rage but concentration and determination.

FIGURE 10.6 The Yomper from the Falklands/Malvinas War, Eastney, Southsea nr Portsmouth

Boorman (2005) describes the pose of the Yomper, the figure laden with equipment, as one of the enduring images of the Falklands War. It is pertinent that iconic images do not have to capture anything of the nature and politics of the war. In fact the war itself was an odd one for many British people at the time – the protection of an old colony, a group of sparsely inhabited islands just off the coast of Argentina. At the time, promoted by the then Prime Minister Margaret Thatcher, it encouraged a wave of nationalism particularly in the media, distracting from much of the ongoing civil unrest as her government challenged workers' movements against the dismantling of public services and privatization of heavy industry. One of the authors, living in the north of Britain at the time, recalls the disgust shown to the war and nationalism by family members who worked in the industries and communities under threat. A decade after the war, Thatcher herself unveiled the Yomper, while many of the working-class communities never recovered.

As a war, this conflict did not create the same kind of devastation in British communities and was fought by a small professional army far away. In this sense, it was less difficult for the Yomper memorial to reference battle itself as opposed to the earlier figures who held wreaths or stood guard. Nevertheless these professional soldiers were sold to the public as 'our boys' defending our national interests.

As with the earlier figures, the Yomper looks not at the viewer but upwards and to the horizon, in fact out to sea from where the marines originally departed for the war to much flag waving – unlikely in current times. The gaze carries the metaphorical meaning of up as being emotionally up, or up in terms of higher values. But additionally the soldier looks to the right as we look at him. The meaning potential of this can be illustrated using Kress and van Leeuwen's (1996) account of the meaning of left and right in visual communication (p. 188).

Kress and van Leeuwen (1996) show how left and right have always carried important cultural meanings. When we look at a time line, in Western culture, it generally runs from left to right. This could be due to the way that we read from left to right and also the way that language builds on information. Kress and van Leeuwen describe such structures in language as 'given' and 'new' structures. In speech, we begin with something that is already known and then move onto information we wish to impart. The given is the accepted, or at least what we offer as accepted, and the new is the possible, the as yet contested (p. 188). In images, given and new also applies. In adverts, we might find a photograph of a beautiful woman on the left, a given of beauty, and on the right a new product, a new route to achieve beauty. Often in interviews, we find the interviewer placed on the left so that we identify with them. In photographs, people depicted looking to the left seem to be looking backwards to the past, whereas those depicted looking to the right appear to be looking forward to the future, to the new, the possible, rather than the given. The Yomper looks to the right, to the possible. He also looks slightly upwards, which is positive. He was the visual realization of the discourses promoted by Thatcher who promised a return to a strong nation, its armies sailing off to protect colonies as in days of old. Yet also this is a soldier who has volition. He looks forwards and is an individual, rather than a member of a mass army. To mark this individuality and to humanize him, the Yomper is based on a photograph of an individual and identifiable soldier.

In the case of the Yomper, there is no reference to classicism and no religious symbolism. As we will see when we look at further dimensions of analysis, it is important that soldiery and war have become closer to the everyday on certain levels, while maintained as distinctive on others. In these more contemporary cases, the figures of soldiers do not represent high ideals in the manner of classical civilization, nor are they merged with Christian meanings. Yet they still maintain their distance by not engaging with the viewer and therefore requiring nothing of us.

In Figure 10.7, we see the monument to Merchant Seamen in Cardiff Bay. The monument combines the frame of a boat as if run ashore with a face on the

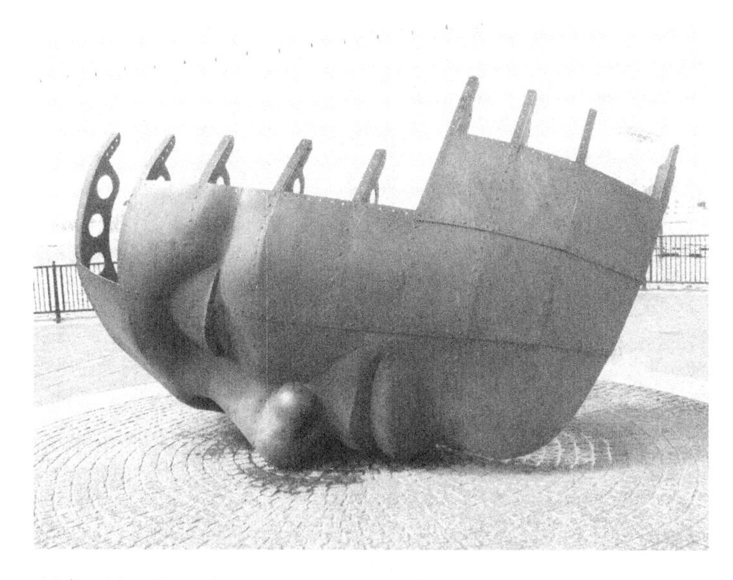

FIGURE 10.7 Merchant Seamen monument, Cardiff Bay

hull of the ship. It lies flat in a circle which carries the inscription. Here we find a return to classism – a broken statue from the Acropolis or a Roman courtyard. A face rendered in perfect clean lines and symmetry as in classical sculpture. For some of the viewers of the monument, interviewed by the authors, it was mindful of classicism through the mythology of seafaring films such as *Jason and the Argonauts*. Like the classicism of World War I statues, the face is restful, asleep, an absence of suffering. The face is not pressed and flattened into the ground but rests easily, and importantly also looks slightly to the right, to the new and the possible. But unlike earlier monuments, the solidity of stone and the raising into the 'ideal' through pedestals is not present. We will discuss the meaning of this shortly.

In Figure 10.8, we see the monument erected in Hyde Park, London to the soldiers from New Zealand who fought in World War II, unveiled in 2006. The monument is comprised of 16 bronze pillars that lean slightly forwards connoting movement and determination. Machin (2007), drawing on semiotic work from comics and animation, discusses the meaning potential of the oblique rather that vertical or horizontal lines. Oblique lines can mean dynamic and changing. A vertical line can seem proud, whereas a horizontal line seems passive and timeless (p. 84). Yet it is interesting that this dynamic movement, as the figures descend in a group from the slope of the grass, are represented simply as abstract figures and not as humans. In the spirit of monuments not representing aggression, a more realistic representation of 16 soldiers moving in this manner would not have been permissible. Abstracted in this way the meaning is diluted. Each of the pillars, when seen from above is a Christian cross.

FIGURE 10.8 New Zealand monument, London

So these aggressively moving forms do so as Christian entities, signalling upwards to the sky, to God.

The pillars also carry facts and general cultural information about New Zealand, for example, the 'iconic' New Zealand fern leaf and 'traditional' Maori carvings. This helps also to dilute the sense of the aggression as it connotes 'learning', 'education' and 'cultural inter-communication'. The monument was in fact developed by the Ministry for Culture and Heritage in consultation with the Ministry of Foreign Affairs and Trade. The designer Paul Dibble spoke of the monument allowing British people to learn something of the relationship between the two countries. Yet the discourse of war and nationalism remains. A soldier's identity remains bound up with ideas of nation and heritage. And what exactly do we learn about the relationship between the two countries?

The formation of the pillars, according to the designer, also resembles that of the New Zealand All Blacks rugby team when they perform the *haka*, their pre-match ritual. Discourses of nationalism, reified ancient history and sport are all seamlessly drawn upon.

FIGURE 10.9 Contemporary World War II soldier, Portsmouth

Finally, Figure 10.9 shows a statue of a World War II soldier in Portsmouth, UK, unveiled in 1997, one of very few designed by women sculptors. This particular sculpture is different from earlier ones for a number of important reasons that we will come to shortly in our discussion of form. Here we wish to speak only of posture.

The soldier is exhausted and sad; he encourages pity and generosity rather than awe or respect. This is important in a time where people have become generally less tolerant of soldiery. Perhaps through making him appear more contemporary, more like 'one of us', even handsome, but certainly not god-like in the fashion of some earlier monuments, the statue attempts to bring people back on the side of the soldier who suffers and gives, rather than the powerful soldier of the Falklands, or the classical figures from World War I.

The meaning of form in monuments

Of course monuments, not unlike photographs and paintings, communicate in large part due to their form and presence, although to this we can add their three-dimensional nature (O'Toole, 1994). In this section we consider the meaning potentials of height, size, solidity and angularity.

Height

The height that a statue is positioned in relation to the viewer has important meaning potential. The Abertillery figure, as was common at the time, is raised up on a pedestal. Others, such as in the Cardiff World War I monument, are raised up by standing on the steps, or 'crepidoma' of the main structure. Van Leeuwen (2005) has discussed the metaphorical associations of height. We generally associate height with status, as in 'upper class'. We often kneel before royalty, or sit lower than those of higher status. We also associate height with loftiness of ideals, although this can have a negative connotation where we say someone has 'their head in the clouds'. The opposite of this is a person who can be said to be grounded and down to earth. It is from these associations that Kress and Van Leeuwen (1996) suggest that we think of that which is placed at the top of visual compositions as the 'ideal', whereas that placed at the bottom is the 'real' (p. 193). So in an advertisement a beautiful woman might appear in the ideal as the fantasy, and the product in the real at the bottom. From this we can think about statues such as the Abertillery as being placed into the ideal, as being higher than the real, the everyday. The figure is raised up several metres so that the viewer is literally at his feet. Typically in World War I monuments soldiers depicted as classical gods, in peaceful yet determined poses were raised into fantasy. We can imagine the difference in meaning if we put a statue of a soldier either on a pedestal of 1m or 10m, or if they were placed at ground level, or even in a small hole.

In the later monuments, the Yomper and the New Zealand monument, we can see that the figures are no longer placed in the ideal. The Yomper is on a very slight base. He is only slightly in the ideal, but there is not the same distance between him and the viewer at ground level. The New Zealand pillars are at ground level. So as well as the move away from Christian iconography, the soldiers have become more real, more grounded; they are no longer placed in the ideal.

Jewitt and Oyama (2000) show that when an image positions the viewer as looking up at a person then the viewer has a less powerful position. Looking down at the person in the image gives the viewer power. In the older World War I monuments, the viewer always looked up at the soldiers as is still the case with the Yomper (Figure 10.6). But the World War II soldier in Figure 10.9 is at eye level with the viewer, which is achieved by putting him on a small pedestal, since he is shown sitting. In this way, we see him as an equal. As with the other more contemporary monuments, he is both grounded, although raised slightly, and is in a vulnerable pose.

In some contemporary monuments as in Figures 10.7 and 10.8, the viewer is encouraged to move among the features. On the one hand, soldiers cease to be ideal. But on the other hand, we can understand this as part of a broader change in the way that the public are encouraged to experience rather than look at heritage and art. Karp (2006) has discussed the way that interactive museums and sites of living heritage, for example, are a part of a kind of cultural tourism related to increased mobility of globalization as tourists travel to sample packaged cultures and histories of the world. Karp and Lavine (1991) also describe a drive where public displays, such as in museums have to be lively and people-friendly places which 'implicate' audiences. Monuments can become not only sites of mourning but of learning and may even tend towards the quasi artistic and curious, with instructions on how to understand complex symbolism. Newer monuments often point out that they are arranged so that they catch the sun's rays on a certain day, or that they align with certain stars, or face a city far away. All this is about the veracity of the experiential. The designer of the New Zealand monument specifically stated that it 'invites personal engagement by visitors – to read, touch, and contemplate'. Karp and Lavine (1991) warn about the way that there is often the assumption that we can learn complex histories by walking among static objects. And Kirshenblatt-Gimblett (2006) also states a concern that the discourses of heritage are generally diplomatic, conservative and celebratory. Muan (2006) urges that we ask what gets excluded and displaced in such experiencing.

Size

While the Yomper is not significantly raised up into the ideal, due to his lack of pedestal he is very large. The metaphorical association of size with importance allows the soldiers to be literally much larger than life. The World War I figures were taller than a human figure by only about half a meter, so they were not greatly larger than an average viewer. We can imagine the meaning potential of a soldier the size of a giant or conversely a small one the size of a doll. If we look around the world at very big statues we find these generally represent dictators. Examples are the figure of Saddam Hussein attached to the Ishtar Gate in Baghdad in the 1980s. Kruk (2008) has discussed the outsized statues of Stalin in the Soviet Union that were meant to symbolize not so much the man himself but the collective communist spirit. Michalski (1998) describes the use of such massive monuments as part of a 'ruler's cult' (p. 197). The Yomper is around 4m tall and appears as a giant. In contemporary times it would be less likely to see more monuments of this size.

In contrast, the soldier in the World War II monument, according to the designer, is the same size as an average man. As has been mentioned above, he is only raised on a pedestal enough to bring him to eye level, he is in a pose that shows him exhausted and lost – he is humanized, all of which allows the viewer to identify with him more than was the case with the older monuments. In these times of increased cynicism towards the conflicts our governments wage, we are taught to identify with rather than blame our soldiers.

Angularity

Van Leeuwen (2006) in his discussion of typefaces describes the meaning potential of angularity versus curvature. The significance of these may be based on experiential and cultural associations with round or angular objects. Roundness can mean 'smooth', 'soft', 'gentle', 'emotional'. It can also mean 'fluidity', 'ease' and 'organic'. In contrast, angularity tends to be associated with 'harsh', 'technical', 'masculine', 'objectivity'. These may be positively or negatively evaluated.

In some of the monuments, we find a stress on roundness. The classical architecture of the Cardiff memorial while using clean lines emphasizes curvature. The Merchant Seamen monument, while partly representing a ship is particularly round in its forms. In the New Zealand monument we find an emphasis on angularity. These shapes signify a sense of harshness and aggression. Yet it is important that the pillars represent aggressive soldiers only symbolically. The discourse of aggression, of soldiers acting in a warlike manner in a group, is mitigated by the symbolic nature of the form. Kress and van Leeuwen (1996) have suggested that we can think about such processes as being akin to the way truth is communicated in language. In language we have modals for indicating levels of truth or commitment to a state of affairs. For example, we can say something is 'possible' rather than it is 'certain'. We can say 'we should' as opposed to 'we will'. In each case the first is less committed to truth. In visual communication too we can look for the way that modality is decreased through reduction in articulation of details, in objects or surface realization. We can ask how much what we see is articulated in the manner we would expect in everyday life. This is a continuum with a decrease of detail on the one hand and an increase on the other.

In World War I statues there is a decrease in articulation of detail of clothing and faces. For Kress and van Leeuwen (1996) this would mean that truth or 'modality' is lowered and that therefore these are not realistic representations. Of course this would seem obvious. But we have to take the next step and consider in what ways the detail has been reduced. In some statues detail is smoothed away to give a beautiful roundedness. We find this on the World War I Artillery monument (Figure 10.5). On other statues it is replaced by blurring and rough lines. One example is the case of the Will Lambert project for the Revensbrück Concentration Camp where the articulation of detail is reduced by a texture of blurring. The sitting World War II soldier (Figure 10.9) has reduced detail and slight blurring of features. All of these are less real, or lower in modality, for example than the Yomper who is realized with a high articulation of detail. Where we have blurring we have metaphorical blurring of certainty and knowledge of clarity of vision. The World War II soldier appears to be a contemporary man in look, and build and how his uniform fits him. Yet the blurring also distances us from him and communicates his symbolic role, and the difficulty in knowing the truth for him, a truth not always told, although perhaps less so than in the case of the Holocaust memorial just mentioned.

In the case of the New Zealand monument (Figure 10.8), all detail of the figures has been removed. They are represented only as pillars in the form of the cross. Machin and Thornborrow (2003) have suggested that such low modalities have often been typical of the way that fairly tales, bible stories, or contemporary women's magazines are able to nevertheless communicate more serious messages about the social world. The lowering of modality allows certain aspects, identities and actions to be more easily exaggerated or suppressed. It also allows symbolic elements to do greater work, freed from the anchors of context. In this sense the New Zealand monument, freed from representing actual soldiers, is able to deal with aggression, soldiers moving in formation to attack.

Solidity

We can ask the basic question of the solidity of the monuments, which can also have important metaphorical associations. For example, what would the difference be between a statue of a soldier realized through a metal framework rather than solid bronze? Van Leeuwen (2005) suggests that if we can see the core of three dimensional objects, this may suggest vulnerability, or accessibility indicating a degree of openness or transparency where we are able to see the internal goings-on. For the most part statues of soldiers are represented as solid. They are not vulnerable, and we are not encouraged to look beneath the surface. This may seem an obvious observation since of course most public monuments are solid. But this is precisely because they are generally used to depict solidity of character, a single uncomplicated view of a figure to be revered, rather than analysed.

In the case of the Merchant Seamen monument (Figure 10.7) we do not find solidity. We are able to see inside and it is made of relatively thin metal sheeting. A boat could have been represented giving a more solid durable form. In this case the classicism of the monument, unlike that of the World War I monuments is not combined with solid immovability. The fragility of those involved in the war is communicated. The same fragility can be seen in the thinness of the metal used for the New Zealand pillars. While they appear as aggressive, they also appear as less than immovable. In both cases the power of empire and its cause is not present. The logic and unity of the armed forces represented through materials and iconography in the World War I monuments has been replaced with some degrees of empathy and fragility that would not have been possible immediately after the loss of a huge part of the population and when many of those remaining were unsupportive of the government.

Conclusion

While this chapter has drawn on an analysis of a small number of British war monuments, and while we are currently in the processes of gathering images and information on a large corpus of monuments, we can try to make a number of conclusions about the changing discourses that we have found realized. The participants in war that have been commemorated through monuments since World War I have remained predominantly the soldiers, rather than civilian victims or those who profit from war, and this has largely remained celebratory. However, some of the discourses realized by the monuments and the way viewers have been positioned as regards these figures have changed. Early monuments represented the power and immovability of nation and empire and the higher ideals of war and sacrifice through classical styles and idealized figures. Aggression, wounding and fear were not represented. Later monuments showed soldiers becoming more real than ideal. It seems that the British public is no longer likely to worship the soldier in the same way. This has also meant that soldiers might be represented in actual scale rather than larger than life. In the case of the Yomper however a huge increase in size and detail suggested temporary resurrection of the power of nation and empire and the cult of soldiery. Other monuments have moved towards the abstract and began to symbolize warfare though complex references and cultural heritage markers. War monuments are no longer necessarily placed in central public places in towns and villages but deliberately appear as attractions often positioned as tourist/learning sites, and discourses of militarism, are collocated with those of sport and mythical heritage. War becomes another resource for tourism and consumerism as local councils attempt to draw people to the locality. As the nation state has weakened, we have been encouraged to humanize soldiers and support them as ordinary simple people as wars themselves have become more difficult to explain away in nationalist terms. But it is clear that monuments which encourage us to see militarism and warfare as mundane, acceptable parts of our societies' conduct continue to form parts of the everyday semiotic landscapes of our cities.

References

Abousnnouga, G. and Machin, D. (2008), 'The visual institutionalisation of discourses in war monuments', in A. Mayr (ed.), *Language and Power: An Introduction to Institutional Discourse.* London: Continuum, pp. 115–137.

Arnheim, R. (1969), *Visual Thinking.* Berkeley: University of California Press.

Arnot, R. P. (1967), *South Wales Miners = Glowyr De Cymru: A History of the South Wales Miners' Federation.* London: Allen & Unwin.

Barthes, R. (1973), *Mythologies.* London: Fontana.

Billig, M. (1995), *Banal Nationalism.* London: Sage.

Boorman, D. (2005), *A Century of Remembrance: One Hundred Outstanding British War Memorials.* Barnsley, South Yorks, UK: Pen and Sword Books Ltd.

Bourke, J. (1996), *Dismembering the Male: Men's Bodies, Britain and the Great War.* London: Reaktion.

Fairclough, N. (2000), *New Labour, New Language?* London: Routledge.
Ferguson, G. (1942), *Signs and Symbols in Christian Art*. London: Oxford University Press.
Foucault, M. (1977), *Discipline and Punish: The Birth of the Prison*. London: Penguin Books.
Halliday, M. A. K. (1978), *Language as Social Semiotic: The Social Interpretation of Language and Meaning*. Baltimore: University Park Press.
Jakobson, R. and Halle, M. (1956), *Fundamentals of Language*. The Hague: Mouton & Co.
Jewitt, C. and Oyama, R. (2000), 'Visual meaning: A social semiotic approach', in C. Jewitt and T. van Leeuwen (eds), *Handbook of Visual Analysis*. London: Sage, pp. 134–56.
Karp, I. (ed.) (2006), *Museum Frictions: Public Cultures/Global Transformations*. Durham, NC: Duke University Press.
Karp, I. and Lavine, S. D. (1991), *Exhibiting Cultures: The Poetics and Politics of Museum Display*. London: Smithsonian.
Kirshenblatt-Gimblett, B. (2006), 'World Heritage and Cultural Economics', in I. Karp (ed.), *Museum Frictions: Public Cultures/Global Transformations*. Durham, NC: Duke University Press, pp. 161–203.
Kress, G. and Van Leeuwen. T. (1996), *Reading Images: The Grammar of Visual Design*. London: Routledge.
—(2002), 'Colour as a semiotic mode: Notes for a grammar of colour', *Visual Communication*, 1, 343–368.
Kruk, S. (2008), 'Semiotics of visual iconicity in Leninist "monumental" propaganda', *Visual Communication*, 7, 27–56.
Laybourn, K. (1997), *The Rise of Socialism in Britain*. London: Sutton.
Little, C. (1996), *A Comprehensive Guide to Outdoor Sculpture in Texas*. Texas: University of Texas Press.
Machin, D. (2007), *Introduction to Multimodal Analysis*. London: Arnold.
Machin, D. and Thornborrow, J. (2003), 'Branding and discourse: The case of *Cosmopolitan*', *Discourse & Society*, 14, 453–506.
McKibbin, R. (1974), *The Evolution of the Labour Party 1910–1924*. London: Oxford University Press.
Michalski, S. (1998), *Public Monuments: Art in Political Bondage 1970–1997*. London: Reaktion Books.
Mosse, G. L. (1990), *Fallen Soldiers: Reshaping the Memory of the World Wars*. New York: Oxford University Press.
Muan, I. (2006), 'Musings on museums from Phnom Penh', in I. Karp (ed.), *Museum Frictions: Public Cultures/Global Transformations*. Durham, NC: Duke University Press, pp. 257–285.
O'Toole, M. (1994), *The Language of Displayed Art*. London: Leicester University Press.
Panofsky, E. (1970), *Meaning in the Visual Arts*. Harmondsworth: Penguin.
—(1972), *Studies in Iconography: Humanistic Themes in the Art of the Renaissance*. Oxford: Westview Press.
Quinlan, M. (2005), *British War Memorials*. Hertford: Authors OnLine Ltd.
Rudy, C. (1918), 'Concerning Tommy', *Contemporary Review*, 113, November, 545–52.

Troost, G. (ed.) (1942), *Das Bauen Im Neuen Reich*. Bayreuth: Gauverlag.
Van Dijk, T. A. (1993), 'Principles of critical discourse analysis', *Discourse & Society*, 4, 249–83.
Van Leeuwen, T. (2005), *Introduction to Social Semiotics*. London: Routledge.
—(2006), 'Towards a semiotics of typography', *Information Design Journal + Document Design*, 14, 139–55.
Van Leeuwen, T. and Wodak, R. (1999), 'Legitimizing immigration control: a discourse-historical analysis', *Discourse Studies*, 1, 83–119.

Chapter 11

Building the Nation, Writing the Past: History and Textuality at the *Ha'apala* Memorial in Tel Aviv-Jaffa

Elana Shohamy and Shoshi Waksman

The central 'text' of this chapter is a monument commemorating a particular chapter of Jewish migration to Palestine between 1934 and 1948, known as the *Ha'apala*, when migration was otherwise restricted by the British Mandate. The monument is a tourist and leisure spot situated in a central location on the Tel Aviv waterfront next to major international hotels, embassies, shopping centres, restaurants and a promenade frequented by local and international visitors. The monument is located in an area redesigned in 2003, formerly known as *The London Garden*. According to Eliav Nachlieli, one of the designers of the site interviewed (13 February 2006) for the purposes of this study, the monument represents a plan to 'bring back' the *Ha'apala* and embrace it as a central theme in the creation of national collective memory. The construction of the monument was supported financially by several institutions (e.g. the municipality of the city of Tel Aviv) and private donors (including some *Ha'apala* participants) as part of a wave of initiatives to design historical and national tourist sites in Israel.

From immigration to tourism: The places of nations

Since the nineteenth century, immigration has been a major ideological theme and a rationale for the establishment of the state of Israel. Especially within the Zionist ethos, immigration has had a pivotal role in manifesting the ideology of creating a homeland for Jews and was a major enterprise in founding and sustaining the state. Immigration gained a special momentum after the Balfour declaration in 1917 when the right to establish a homeland in Palestine was established and it continued throughout the years of the British Mandate (1917–1948). While the idea of a Jewish state was not shared by all Jewish communities internationally, the events of the World War II and the Holocaust led to a broad consensus in that respect, and immediately after the foundation of the state of Israel in 1948 this consensus was further anchored in the *Law of Return* which granted Israeli citizenship to all Jewish and only Jewish immigrants. The only other ethnic group granted citizenship status in Israel were Arabs residing in Palestine at the time of the creation of the state of Israel (currently approximately 20% of the population). All other non-Jews were not welcomed, nor are they welcomed still, facing difficulties and hardship when seeking to make Israel their permanent home (see Shohamy and Kanza, 2009 for details).

By imposing a strict quota on the Jewish migration to Palestine, the British attempted to maintain a demographic balance between the Jews and Arabs, as agreed in the Balfour declaration. Yet, Jews from the *Yishuv* (e.g. those living in Palestine at the time) were eager to bring to Palestine large numbers of Jews in order to create a numerical advantage as justification and rationale for the establishment of a sovereign, independent Jewish state with a clear Jewish hegemony over the Arabs (cf. Kimmerling, 2004). Thus, the quotas which were established by the British were viewed by the *Yishuv* as a major obstacle to the creation of an independent Jewish state; it was during that time that several Jewish organizations, in Palestine and elsewhere, fostered mass migration of Jews to Palestine against the restrictions of the British authorities in illegal ways. It is estimated that about 120,000 Jews, mostly refugees from and survivors of the World War II, attempted illegally to enter Palestine by boats with the loss of approximately 3,000 lives. Some of those who were caught were held by the British authorities as prisoners in camps in the neighbouring island of Cypress (see Figure 11.1 as displayed on the *Ha'apala* site).

FIGURE 11.1 Jewish immigrants in prison camps in Cypress (taken from the *Ha'apala* site)

It is within this broader, historical and political context that the *Ha'apala* site was conceived and constructed. It is a materialized text which narrates an important chapter of Jewish migration and the role these immigrants played in the establishment of a collective ideology of the nation state. It is also a tourist site.

Contemporary tourism is one of the key domains in which nations construct their discourses of national identity and unity. For example, as stated by Pretes (2003), '[h]egemonic discourse of nationalism may manifest itself in tourism sights . . . encouraging tourists to embrace national goals' (p. 126). It is through tourist spaces such as commemorative monuments that all national tourist organizations promote national ideologies and foster national identities (Green, 2002; Scarles, 2004; Waitt, 1997). But tourist sights/sites of great national importance are also 'consumed' by local and international visitors alike producing as a result, varying types of meanings. For example, Greenspan (2005) demonstrates how the memorial space of Ground Zero (former site of the World Trade Center in New York) is shaped as either 'local' or 'global' through the dynamic interaction of different types of visitors interacting in and within the site.

The targeting of potentially diverse groups of tourists, or 'post-tourists', promoting 'alternative' types of tourism, 'special interest' tourism, ecotourism, heritage tourism, and so on, leads to a multitude of tourist experiences and interpretations of tourist sites (Light, 2000). Likewise, national commemoration sites allow multiple reading positions to be adopted by tourists, despite the deployment of specific semiotic resources and the manipulations of the visitor's gaze towards a specific interpretation of the site by its authors and ideologues (Amir, 2006; Azaryahu, 1995; Feldman, 2003; Hatuka, 2008). Specifically, we want to consider here how national commemoration sites like the *Ha'apala* memorial are of great relevance for exploring the ways in which national ideologies are represented for different groups of visitors – global and local – through the deployment of the dominant histories, accounts and myths creating imagined national consensus and unity (Amir, 2006).

The *Ha'apala* stories: Text, memory, identity

The narrative of the *Ha'apala* is displayed on the 'windows' of two sculptures of stylized boats which contain documentary photographs from the *Ha'apala* years along with texts describing the chronology of events (Figure 11.2). On one side of the site, a bronze sculpture was erected consisting of six undulating pillars bearing engraved lists of the names of the boats which participated in the *Ha'apala* migration act, along with the number of people who survived and those who died on their way to Palestine (Figure 11.3).

Figure 11.2 One of the boats with embedded texts and pictures

Figure 11.3 The memorial pillars

Figure 11.4 The site embedded in the Tel Aviv tourist area

As has been mentioned, the site is part of a busy pedestrian promenade, a major tourist area of international hotels, entertainment sites, bars and restaurants which attract both local and international visitors (Figure 11.4).

The opening written text in one of the 'windows' (Figure 11.5) affirms the public narrative of the *Ha'apala* in both Hebrew and English. This 'meta-text' contains a summary of the main storyline and also the rationale for the site's construction. It specifically states that, in 1917, the British Government declared the need to establish 'A national home for the Jewish people in Palestine' and renounced its commitment to the Jews by restricting immigration to Palestine. Therefore, the Jewish refugees with the help of the Jewish Zionist movements and especially during the years of the Holocaust found 'illegal' ways to immigrate to Palestine, thus paving the way to the establishment of the state of Israel.

FIGURE 11.5 The meta-text of the *Ha'apala*

The display includes about 20 fragments of combined Hebrew texts and photographs. These elaborate the ideas presented in the meta-text by referring to specific events and anecdotes. Four main, complementary themes of national ideology and immigration emerge from these items: (1) ownership of the space; (2) reinforcement of a collective identity; (3) shared traumatic past as a basis for shared national future; and (4) recruitment of the private for the public. In what follows, we demonstrate how these themes are discursively organized and how they position different groups of tourists, based on the beliefs and stereotypes of their relationship to the national ideology.

Theme 1: Ownership of the space, and redefinition of others

One of the most apparent themes in the texts is the redefinition of the complex relationship between the *Yishuv* (the Jews residing in Palestine at the time and managing self-governing institutions) and the British Mandate. As it has been noted, the *Ha'apala* monument is situated in an area known as *The London Garden*, a site originally constructed in 1942 as a token of identification of the residents of Tel Aviv with the British people during the Blitzkrieg. While there was a strong feeling of identification with the British people in Palestine, especially during the war, the *Ha'apala* monument presents the British as traitors and oppressors who intervened to prevent the establishment of a Jewish state. The wording of the meta-text explicitly accuses the British Government of having 'Renounced its commitment to the Jews and restricted the immigration (Aliyah) to Erez Israel'. The only reminder of the site's previous function (and name) is a small plaque placed at the entrance to the garden, separate from the displays on the boats, it reads as follows in both Hebrew and English:

> The London Garden was inaugurated in May 1942, and dedicated to the City of London – as a token of identification of the inhabitants of Tel-Aviv with the British Nation, who suffered from severe intensive German bombing at the time of the 'Blitz' during the Second World War.
>
> In 2003, Atarim Corp. initiated and developed a parking lot for 500 vehicles, and on its upper level a new garden, for the pleasure and enjoyment of the public.

This reorientation clearly acts as a mechanism for gaining ownership of the space both literally and figuratively.

Some of the texts and the photographs displayed in the *Ha'apala* memorial (not reproduced here) portray the British soldiers as visually the 'Other' (van Leeuwen, 2008): brutal, insensitive to suffering, confused and easily manipulated. They are depicted holding guns, with their backs turned to the camera as they antagonistically face the crowded ships overloaded with Jewish refugees.

The location of the *Ha'apala* memorial/site – together with its written and visual displays – delivers a very simplified version of the British–Jewish relations at the time. There is no mentioning of their important relationship as allies during World War II and the complex relationship between the British and the Jewish *Yishuv* in Palestine, especially the sensitivity of dealing simultaneously with the Jewish and the Arab populations. Another excluded narrative is the existence of the Arabs who were living in Palestine at the time of the *Ha'apala* migration – people whose existence and welfare the British were responsible for protecting. Palestinian Arabs are deleted, or erased, from the *Ha'apala* story as it is memorialized at the *Ha'apala* site – no texts, no photographs. It is as if they do not 'belong' to the story. The redefinition of the British as (only) antagonistic soldiers and the total exclusion of the Arabs in all parts of the site both serve to appropriate and claim the space and the story for the Jews as the sole legitimate actors.

Theme 2: Reinforcement of collective identity

The second theme that emerges from the site is that of national identity, group solidarity, collective belonging, national consensus and unity. Specifically, a number of photographs represent celebratory moments of 'togetherness' in joy and happiness, for example enacted in such group activities as dancing, singing and physical exercise (Figure 11.6). Other facets of 'togetherness' are based on images of shared suffering and solidarity between the *Yishuv* and the refugees – such as the anti-mandate demonstration in Figure 11.7.

FIGURE 11.6 *Hora* dancing

FIGURE 11.7 Demonstration against the British Mandate

The Hebrew texts describe specific anecdotes and events related to the images shown, offering explicit examples of the solidarity between the *Yishuv* residents and the refugees.

Theme 3: Shared traumatic past as a basis for shared national future

A special place for the creation of a sense of national ideology is reserved for the experience of the Holocaust as a shared traumatic past and the ultimate rationale for the need to establish a sovereign homeland. According to the theory of cultural trauma, traumatic events serve as an important basis in fostering collective identities (Tota, 2006). In the *Ha'apala* site, representations of the Holocaust are established linguistically and visually in different ways. For example, in the meta-text (see Figure 11.5 above), visitors are told: 'In the years 1939–1944 when World War II and the Holocaust raged on and swept all over Europe . . . the natural reaction of the Jewish people and the surviving refugees was to fight these restrictions . . .'

The texts that follow elaborate on this central idea. Tellingly, Jewish refugees are labelled using two different but complementary Hebrew definitions: *Palyt* ('refugee') and *Maapil* ('illegal migrant during the *Ha'apala* period'). These two terms are used alternatively in the monument which renders equivalent the notion of the refugee as a Holocaust survivor and the *Maapil* heroically seeking to immigrate to Palestine.

Theme 4: Shared national future recruitment of the private for the public

Finally, the reinforcement of collective national ideology is related to the personal stories appropriated in the represented texts and images. For example, some of the pictures displayed show glimpses of personal, even intimate, moments in the lives of the immigrants, such as in the photo of women napping and resting on a deck of a ship (Figure 11.8), or, in an image not shown here, of a baby in a cradle. Yet, these personal moments are more 'stadium' than 'punctum' in Barthes' (1982) terms, since they are 'recruited' into the immigration collective ideology by the captions that accompany – or anchor – the pictures. Figure 11.8, for example, is anchored by the following caption (in English translation): 'On the deck of the Ataratu ship', with no mention of the people represented. Similarly, the baby in a cradle is referred to simply as 'a young *maapil*'.

A similar effect is created by the inscriptions on the memorial wall (Figure 11.3), where the names of the *boats* are engraved while there is no mention of the names of the people who died on their way. By focusing on the boats and not

FIGURE 11.8 Private moments on a boat

the people, the *Ha'apala* site prevents any intimate acts of reading the names, acting more as an object of mourning and not as a mourning place. Once again, what is represented and memorialized in the *Ha'apala* site is a collective memory of acts of national ideologies or mythologies rather than an intimate memory of individual acts and/or personal stories.

Placing the reader: Different tourists, different stories?

Given the multiple themes of national ideology delivered on the *Ha'apala* site we will now show how the linguistic and visual resources of the site narrate the nation in ways which distinguish among groups of tourists who may visit the site. These differentiations are based on the categorizations described earlier in the chapter where national ideology in Israel is based on an ethos of the need to recruit Jewish immigrants. Since the main theme of the *Ha'apala* site is the promotion of national ideology, and given the various themes mentioned above, we will show how the resources used perpetuate these categories. Specifically, we are interested in those tourists who 'belong' and who can relate to this national(ist) ideology, either as residents of the state or as potential immigrants, and those tourists who are non-Jewish and who would be unwelcome immigrants, but who are needed in order to provide support and legitimacy for the existence of a Jewish state.

The first group of tourists addressed by the site are clearly the 'locals' – residents of Israel and, especially, of Tel Aviv-Jaffa. It is clear from the prevalent use of the Hebrew language (except in the meta-text), that the messages of national ideology are targeted at those with sufficient proficiency in Hebrew to begin with. This observation is consistent with Eliav Nahlieli's comment in his interview with us: 'Our intention was to direct the messages of the site to a local audience' (Interview, 13 February 2006). It is clear that, for local Jewish–Hebrew speakers, there is a vast repertoire of representations and resources from which the meaning of the dominant themes of the site can be interpreted. These include the location of the site, the texts and photographs, and the hegemony of Hebrew. All of which mark the local Jewish Israeli tourist as the main consumer of the messages of national ideology delivered at the site.

Other tourists visit the site as well, of course. English, a major language of international tourism (Shohamy and Gorter, 2009), complements Hebrew in the bilingual construction of the meta-text at the entrance of the site (Figure 11.5). For this second group of tourists there are very limited linguistic resources made available on the site, further information is available to them through the photos which are left to be interpreted without understanding the Hebrew texts and captions which anchor them. Thus, international English speaking visitors rely on their interpretation of the site through reading the meta-text and gleaning whatever remaining details from the photos meant to enhance a sense of tourist 'objectivity' (cf. Mellinger, 1994). The visible hegemony of Hebrew, however, also conveys a sense of exclusion for international visitors positioned as outsiders, observers of the site, and not as part of the addressed community. Having said that, the meta-text still delivered its message of a victimized and just society in need of a sovereign state – a message recruits international visitors as sympathetic supporters.

Upon analysing the English version of the meta-text, a third group of addressees emerges: Jewish visitors from abroad, particularly from the Unites States of America. The meta-text appears to contain multiple lexical items likely to be transparent only to *Jewish* international tourists, what Benor (2009) refers to as 'Jewish English'. The most salient word here is 'HA'APALA' (the ideological term in Hebrew for the illegal migration), written in capital letters at the top of the meta-text, followed by others: 'Eretz Yisrael', a Biblical reference to the 'Land of Israel', a term which is widely used among Jews living in the 'Diaspora', rather than 'the Land of Israel', 'Aliya', referring to 'immigration' in the sense of 'going up' (literally, moving up to a 'higher' place). All those coined and coded terms which are likely to be familiar to the wider society of Jews only provide a message of belonging to the Jewish community, irrespective of their knowledge of Hebrew. These words mark Jews from abroad as a special (and probably preferred) group of international tourists. In terms of the ideologies transmitted via this 'inside language', the use of the word '*Ha'apala*' as 'immigration' avoids the term 'illegal' migration.[1] In choosing these words, there is an attempt to appropriate meanings constructed – even those in English – via the linguistic codes within the English script. Thus, the use of an ideologically charged immigration lexicon establishes boundaries between different groups of tourists: Jewish vs. non-Jewish, with the former being the in-group.

Lastly, it is also possible to identify a fourth group of tourists that, by their absence from the text, actually have a strong presence. This is, of course, Israeli Arabs. These people played an important part in the *Ha'apala* narrative since they were living in Palestine at the time and were the main reason leading to the British restricting the immigration of Jews so not to violate the demographic balance. They are, however, not referred to in the texts of the site; in fact, they are totally excluded from it. Their non-existence is made evident by the absence of the Arabic language anywhere on the site even though Arabic is an official language in Israel and the first language of Arabs living in Israel. This exclusion of Arabic occurs also in spite of a 1999 Supreme Court decision which stipulates the need to use Arabic in public places in mixed cities such as Tel Aviv-Jaffa (see Shohamy, 2006, for more on this).

Conclusion: Building the nation, (re)writing the past

> *The question is not whether we should or should not preserve the past, but what kind of past we have chosen to preserve.*
>
> *Urry, 1999: 212*

The *Ha'apala* memorial was built to tell a story about the building of a nation. To remember – and to remind – people of a particular moment in Israel's (Jewish) history. It is a highly ideological, materialized text situated in a central tourist space. Strategically, its messages differentiate between different groups of tourists whose investments in the historical, national and emotional narratives are clearly different: the insiders (local and international) and the outsiders. The different 'reading' positions delivered to these groups are based on specific views, stereotypes and categorizations of each group of visitors and the site is intended to legitimate, sustain and justify the narrative of a Jewish state while representing an imagined national consensus.

Yet, several questions emerge based on this type of particular writing/promotion of the past. First, what is the value of sites that deliver categorical messages to address specific groups? It remains to be seen if the *Ha'apala* memorial is 'successful' in accomplishing its main function of conveying an overarching story of the building of Israel. Most likely, the story/ideology of the *Ha'apala* (site) is not activated for all tourists, all the time and in the same way (Shohamy and Waksman, 2009). By the same token, to what extent is the design of the memorial effective and/or appropriate in the current era? Nowadays, tourists arrive at tourist sites with vast amounts of prior knowledge made available to them through multiple channels (e.g. television, the internet, tourist brochures). Light (2000) notes that there has been a significant change in the nature of tourism and especially with regards to commemoration sites. In fact, both Feldman (2003) and Greenspan (2005) call for more 'open', less controlled tourist sites which can work against semiotic closures, enabling tourists to find different, even contradictory, voices and meanings. In spite of the different ways it addresses different audiences, the *Ha'apala* site presents a capsule of historic 'truth' which might not appeal to contemporary tourists who are exposed to so many diverse sources of information and multiple points of view. Promoting such homogenous tourist narratives may result in visitors objecting to 'being fed' and/or indoctrinated.

Another question that needs to be raised relates to the very options that exist in designing sites for writing (i.e. presenting and commemorating) historical periods in a way that will appeal to various tourists groups. For instance, what range of voices and narratives exist which might increase transparency, visibility and dialogicality? Even more, what voices are there in opposition to the authoritative interpretation of 'official' history? The particular writing of history – the semiotic resources deployed – in *Ha'apala* site 'close off' many potential readings and experiences, in favour of one dominant 'voice' and 'face' of immigration. This (fore)closure crafts and establishes a collective, mono-vocal story (or memory) of nation building with clear, unambiguous contours and with no questions asked. We would suggest that the deletion of alternative and personal voices in the *Ha'apala* site may actually serve to undermine the commemoration, precisely because it reduces the potential for a mass of interested tourists to feel invited – to share, debate and rethink the personal and collective stories embedded in the site. Alternative stories might just as easily have included the choice Jews had to immigrate to other countries and not to Palestine or Israel; the conflicting attitudes of the *Yishuv* towards the *Ha'apala*; the dilemmas faced by the Jewish immigrants when deciding 'where to go', as well challenging the notion of a Jewish state as the best/only solution for anti-Semitism.

One striking feature of the *Ha'apala* site is the way it appears to have been designed to differentiate between various, pre-determined groups of visitors/tourists. These sorts of closed characterizations of tourists, however, further restrict access by some, those viewed as outsiders, while enabling the entrance for those who are considered to belong, the insiders. The marking of such defined boundaries between groups of tourists is artificial, stereotypical and clearly imposed; it does not reflect the contemporary reality of more fluid, more hybrid communities of tourists in which endless possibilities and combinations of transnational identities exist. As such, it is a telling oversight of the *Ha'apala* memorial that English is the only non-Hebrew language used. Other languages would have allowed individual tourists to construct their own meanings and to find other ways of interacting with the site – to have enabled the site to become a space of even greater negotiation, discussion, remembering.

It is important to realize that memorializing sites like the *Ha'apala* do not exist in a vacuum. They are anchored in a political ecology which invariably entails bureaucracies of inclusion and exclusion. In many ways, tourist sites are just extensions and manifestations of these bureaucracies. By the same token, however, it is through the development of educational policies for cultivating critical views of ideological sites and practices that categorical differentiations between insiders and outsiders can be challenged and questioned. Thus, tourist sites like the *Ha'apala* may also fulfil an important educational role in the implicit and explicit policies of nations and their problems.

Note

[1] It should be noted that the term 'illegal' migration is rarely used in the Hebrew version to refer to the 'Ha'apala'; rather it is constructed as immigration in heroic terms, like pioneers or pilgrims.

References

Amir, T (2006), *Life Saver Typology of Commemoration in Israel – Architecture and Society* [Brochure].Translated by T. Amir, Israeli Pavilion, the 10th Venice Biennale.

Azaryahu, M. (1995), *State Cults: Celebrating Independence and Commemorating the Fallen in Israel, 1948–1956*. Beer Sheba: Ben Gurion University. (in Hebrew).

Barthes, R. (1982), *Camera Lucida*. London: Fontana.

—(1985), 'Rhetoric of the image', in R. Barthes, *The Responsibility of Forms*. Translated by R. Howard. New York: Hill and Wang, pp. 21–40.

Benor, S. B. (2009), 'Do American Jews speak a "Jewish language"? A model of Jewish linguistic distinctiveness', *Jewish Quarterly Review*, 99(2), 230–269.

Feldman, K. S. (2003), 'The shape of mourning: Reading, aesthetic cognition, and the Vietnam Veteran Memorial', *Word & Image*, 19(4), 296–304.

Green, G. L. (2002), 'Marketing the nation: Carnival and tourism in Trinidad and Tobago', *Critique of Anthropology*, 22(3), 283–304.

Greenspan, E. (2005), 'A global site of heritage? Constructing spaces of memory at the World Trade Center site', *International Journal of Heritage Studies*, 11(5), 371–384.

Hatuka, T. (2008), *Revisionist Moments: Political Violence, Architecture and Urban Space in Tel Aviv*. Tel Aviv: Resling.

Kimmerling, B. (2004), *Immigrants, Settlers, Natives*. Tel Aviv: Am Oved Publishers.

Light, D. (2000), 'An unwanted past: Contemporary tourism and heritage of communism in Romania', *International Journal of Heritage Studies*, 6(2), 145–160.

Mellinger, W. M. (1994), 'Towards a critical analysis of tourism representations', *Annals of Tourism Research*, 21(4), 756–779.

Pretes, M. (2003), 'Tourism and nationalism', *Annals of Tourism*, 30(1), 125–142.

Scarles, C. (2004), 'Mediating landscapes, the processes and practices of image construction in tourist brochures of Scotland', *Tourist Studies*, 4(1), 43–67.

Shohamy, E. (2006), *Language Policy: Hidden Agendas and New Approaches*. London: Routledge.

Shohamy, E. and Gorter, D. (eds) (2009), *Linguistic Landscape: Expanding the Scenery.* London: Routledge.

Shohamy, E. and Kanza, T. (2009), 'Language and citizenship in Israel', *Language Assessment Quarterly,* 6(1), 83–88.

Tota, A. L. (2006), 'Public memory and cultural trauma', *Javnost – the Public,* 13(3), 81–94.

Urry, J. (1999), 'Gazing on history', in D. Boswell and J. Evans (eds), *Representing the Nation: Histories, Heritage and Museums.* London: Routledge, pp. 208–232

van Leeuwen, T. (2008), *Discourse and Practice: New Tools for Critical Discourse Analysis.* New York: Oxford University Press.

Waitt, G. (1997), 'Selling paradise and adventure: Representations of landscape in the tourist advertising of Australia', *Australian Geographical Studies,* 35(1), 47–60.

Chapter 12

Faces of Places: Façades as Global Communication in Post-Eastern Bloc Urban Renewal

Irina Gendelman and Giorgia Aiello

We start from the straightforward premise that façades are important discursive spaces. Commonly defined as the 'face' or outward appearance of a building, façades are typically decorated with ornamental or architectural detail that distinguishes them from the other sides of a building (Harris, 1993). The façade thus becomes a key discursive element of any architectural design since it plays a role in how the building itself and the location of the building are to be perceived and experienced. While it is the case that a façade is designed intentionally to communicate a particular message, it is also a text that conglomerates across time and through genres which may include but are often beyond the intent of the architect. In this way, the façade is a communicative event that tells stories through its changing materiality, representing the building and its contents, but also the particular ideologies and power dynamics of the city in relation to its inhabitants and broader economic and political processes.

Of course, the use of architecture for the display of power is neither surprising nor new. Façades are key instruments of representation in totalitarian regimes, often explicitly referring to iconography as an instrument of propaganda. For example, the Nazis in Germany and the Fascists in Italy, inspired by classical Roman architecture, used its imagery as a backdrop for parades and other political spectacles, deliberately dwarfing the crowd into faceless supporters (Lasswell and Fox, 1979; Lasansky, 2004). When Russia's Peter the Great founded St Petersburg as a 'Window to the World', he sought to distance himself from what he saw as a backwardness of isolationist Russia and to signal to Europe his allegiance to the West by Europeanizing not only the faces of his subjects (ordering the men to shave their beards) but also the faces of the city.[1] Later, Stalin added his own monumental and largely symbolic architecture to the city. Stalinist architecture came to be recognized as a method through which the Soviet state communicated authority to its citizens (Tarkhanov and Kavtaradze, 1992).

With the rise of US capitalism, façades have more recently begun to embellish less grandiose, vernacular structures such as the decorated shack described by Venturi, Brown and Izenour (1977). Reminiscent of a Hollywood set, this edifice is characteristic of buildings in Las Vegas or American roadside attractions, where the architecture itself is irrelevant and completely dependent on the façade. Typically, an otherwise unremarkable structure is decorated with highly visible signage, meant to be seen from a distance and from a moving vehicle. As was the case with totalitarian architecture, these vernacular façades are actively deployed as semiotic resources for the achievement of both ideological and material ends.

It is against this general backdrop that we focus in this chapter specifically on the ways in which façades nowadays come to be deployed as semiotic resources in the context of advanced or so called global capitalism, with a particular concern for the fast-changing urban landscape of a selection of cities that have only recently entered the 'global marketplace'. These and other urban centres are increasingly part of economies that transcend their local or national boundaries, and are thus also dependent on global capital. As a growing number of cities around the world participate and compete in the global marketplace, the spectacle of the city is more than ever a significant economic tool. The richness of exchanges and cultural production that occur within the – physical and/or imagined – boundaries of the city is also an ideal setting for communication research.

By looking at façades, our intent is to promote an approach to examining cities not as collections of different modes of communication – e.g. images, languages, scripts, sounds, etc. – but instead as forms of communication in their own right. More broadly, in turning to the city as a 'laboratory' for communication research, we are not only interested in the types of communication that take place *in the context of* urban space; rather, we are especially drawn to the study of *space as a medium of communication*. In their work on tourism, Jack and Phipps (2005) highlight the importance of taking materiality seriously in the study of any form of symbolic exchange. Until recently, they claim, scholars focusing on material culture have tended 'to concentrate on the action of exchange rather than on the objects themselves' (p. 30). In a similar vein, we view building façades as material objects that play an important role in the symbolic production of cities.

In relation to this last point, Anderson (1983) writes that historicized buildings become artefacts that act as material resources for constructing a national identity. He explains that imagined communities are cultivated through the process of reconstructing (and we argue also renovating) monuments, plotting them on maps, producing technical reports about them, reproducing their images in glossy books, printing them on tourist literature and further through a 'general logoization' (p. 182) in the market (such as printing names and images on t-shirts, stamps, soda bottles, etc.). This process helps nations define the otherwise nebulous sense of nationhood for its citizens as well promote its cities as unique destinations to the rest of the world. At the same time, the global economy leaves its own imprint on the façades. While the logoization of historic buildings helps brand cities as historic centres, the buildings themselves are also branded by globalist imagery. Furthermore, anonymous urban dwellers sometimes irreverently 'de-face' the sanctioned faces of façades, defying official designs and adding to the imperative of façade management.

(Con)texts and methods: Post-Eastern Bloc façades in the global economy

In 2003 St Petersburg celebrated its 300th anniversary, with more than 40 foreign government leaders – including the US President George W. Bush and British Prime Minister Tony Blair – invited to attend the elaborate celebrations that had been planned for May 27. This was also to be three days before the G8 summit which was also hosted by the city. The makeover that was planned for the city in the run-up to this anniversary offers a striking example of the key role played by symbolic capital (Bourdieu, 1991) – and especially the visual symbolic capital embodied by cityscapes – in the material/financial context of global capitalism. According to a BBC reporter, just days before the anniversary teams of construction workers were 'restoring buildings to something like their former glory' (Parsons, 2003). The buildings being restored were overwhelmingly located along Nevsky Prospekt, 'once the most famous avenue in the Russian Empire' and renovation meant that it was mainly the pastel coloured façades that were 'resurfaced and repainted' (Parsons, 2003). In combination with funds from both local and international entrepreneurs aimed at protecting world-famous landmarks such as the Hermitage Museum, the central government allocated 'more than $1bn to lift the city's sagging cheeks and jowls' (Parsons, 2003).

The case of St Petersburg stands out as a prime example of the economic and political stakes involved in the spatial (re)presentation and (re)organization of contemporary cities in the context of globalization. However, it is also important to note that a number of post-communist cities have experienced a marked uptake in local and global attention paid to their cityscapes. With the growing inscription of former Eastern Bloc economies and, in particular, urban agglomerates into the global economy, former Eastern European nations have become increasingly concerned with image-building and self-promotion.[2] In this context, for example, cities like Dresden and Warsaw have been increasingly preoccupied with the renovation of their city centres as a way not only to improve infrastructure for their inhabitants, but also to provide attractive environments for global commerce. Most recently, Romania has become heavily invested in the visual appearance of its cities.[3] Between 2003 and 2006, 100 foreign investors set up their operations in Sibiu, and in 2004 the Romanian government applied for UNESCO World Heritage Site status to be conferred to the Transylvanian city's historic city centre. In 2007, Sibiu was also the first post-communist city to become a designated 'European Capital of Culture' on the basis of criteria such as its ability to bring a common European cultural heritage to the fore while also maintaining a diverse and distinctively local identity (see Aiello, 2007; Aiello and Thurlow, 2006).

With post-communist European cities such as the ones just mentioned so recently (and so aggressively) competing for global capital, and as a way to illustrate our discursive approach to the city, we now turn to urban building façades in the rapidly changing post-Eastern Bloc.[4] While our approach to collecting the data for this study was by no means aimed at creating a systematic archive of examples from across Central and Eastern Europe, we did choose to focus on several post-communist urban settings that are currently undergoing similar processes of urban change and renewal. St Petersburg is the main site of our current inquiry; however, much of what we have observed in St Petersburg is echoed, recontextualized and therefore also reinforced in other cities such as Dresden, Warsaw and Sibiu – all prime examples of the increasing construction, commodification and overall globalization of the 'iconosphere' (Porębski, 1972; Chmielewska, 2005, this volume), that is the visual urban landscape of cities. With numerous photographs collected in St Petersburg, Dresden, Warsaw and Sibiu between June 2006 and March 2007, we set out to analyse the ways façades work as power-laden semiotic resources for transforming these cities into global competitors. We see how this transformation is taking place on the very surface of cities. In the process, logos and images of consumption are replacing communist propaganda, while new governments and corporations are investing in – and, quite literally, branding – the reconstruction and 'beautification' of historic centres once destroyed, run-down and covered in soot. As such, the façades performatively establish the stage for a certain experience of the city.

Our approach to the city and its façades is heavily informed by the key principles of *multimodality* (cf. Kress and van Leeuwen, 2001) and *indexicality* (cf. Scollon and Wong Scollon, 2003). Multimodality helps us understand façades as an arrangement of various modes of communication. We are particularly interested in the visual composition of linguistic text, images and design as they are superimposed or juxtaposed with one another into the semiotic landscape. Indexicality, meanwhile, allows us to explore the meanings that these visual dimensions of façades gain through their location in particular places. Ultimately, we are interested in how meaning can be understood and interpreted given the complex visual form of façades and their particular emplacement in specific locations. In doing so, we ask: What are some of the key semiotic resources that can be found on post-communist cities' building façades in the wake of globalism? In addition, what are the meaning potentials realized by different indexical and multimodal arrangements of these key semiotic resources? Finally, what do these meaning potentials tell us about the complex power dynamics that underlie and shape the global economy?

Analysis: Key semiotic resources and meaning potentials

Our analysis takes us first to two key semiotic resources, namely *referencing* and *layering* which we see at work across the images of façades we collected. We then examine the meaning potentials offered by different arrangements of these resources, with a specific focus on the management of different, and at times competing, identity appeals to the global(ist) gaze.

Referencing

Façades often deploy literal or stylistic references that contribute to establishing a relationship with the viewer. These references may be shaped by the specific people/events or styles deployed on the façade but may also vary greatly depending on the spatial and temporal (i.e. indexical) circumstances in which the viewer 'takes in' the façade. While literal references point to specific people and events that are most often directly related to the powerful institutions and regimes that erected a given façade, stylistic references operate at the level of the cultural cachet associated with given decorative and architectural elements. In both cases, however, referencing is a semiotic resource that actively relies on specific kinds of denotation – be it the representation of given people and events or decorative and allegorical elements that are typical of a specific style of art or architecture – to direct the viewer to secondary meanings (or connotations) associated with the status or cachet of what is represented. This is not unlike what Eco (1986) defines as the (always shifting) relationship between the primary and secondary functions of architectural forms. While both literal and stylistic references may have relatively stable primary (or denotative) meanings, their secondary (or connotative) meanings depend both on the circumstances of their production and reception, or social usage.

As an example of these ideas, in Figure 12.1 the bas-relief memorial plaque (left) hangs over column-like vertical grooves that exaggerate the height of the building, stylistically referencing Roman architecture. Their vertical continuity gives the building a rational magnitude stripped of flamboyant detail that was frowned upon by the Soviet state.[5] The plaque also displays a realistic portrait of Aleksei Kosygin with linguistic text below, anchoring the image by describing Kosygin as a 'prominent leader in the Communist party and the Soviet government'. This plaque features literal, but by no means ideologically innocent, references through visual style, imagery and language to people and events in Soviet history. It turns an ordinary building wall into a patriotic sign, which quite literally educates Soviet citizens. Cultural landscapes (such as memorials and monuments) are a form of archiving or preserving information in space and time as a way to communicate it to the public and to shape collective memory for particular goals (Foote, 2000). However, this particular memorial plaque, and other such plaques of Communist leaders sprinkled across the city, rest in liminal spaces. They no longer serve the original goals of the Soviet state, yet remain on the walls throughout the city as quasi-denotative signs of a bygone

Figure 12.1 Soviet-era bas-relief plaque, St Petersburg, Russia

era (i.e. they literally signify the regime in which they were created and deployed) but still uncertain of their current role as memorials, propaganda and, by now, perhaps, Soviet kitsch.

While Soviet façade decorations served to indoctrinate the Soviet Citizen, the Greek demi-gods appearing along the freshly repainted pink façade of Beloselsky-Belozersky palace (Figure 12.1, right), appeal to another collective consciousness. Atlantes holding up Corinthian columns were inspired by the Greek myths of Atlas holding up the sky on his shoulders. In contrast to the Soviet imagery, sought to display simple visual vocabulary that could be understood by the uneducated peasants (coming into the city from rural farming collectives), these façades' references to classical styles of architecture and mythological representation were designed for the Russian aristocracy, those educated to read the artistic language of Greco-Roman mythology (Tarkhanov and Kavtaradze, 1992). The pink palace was commissioned by its noble owners to mirror the tzar's architect Bartolomeo Rastrelli's design of the Stroganov Palace on the opposite side of the canal. In the most recent efforts to renovate the city for St Petersburg's 300th anniversary, the palace was repainted and returned to what was deemed a colour most true to its origins – another stylistic reference to pre-Soviet 'high culture'.

Referencing, it must be stressed, is not static but can shift over time. What was once deployed as a literal reference may become a stylistic reference in its own right or simply the referent itself may change. For example, the imagery that once referenced Greek mythology and a Western aesthetic now references high culture and imperial Russia. By the same token, the Soviet-era representation of political events and leaders may now have become a stylistic signifier of a certain (Russian, socialist) aesthetic, rather than a direct reference to those events and leaders worthy of recognition and memorialization. What is more, the juxtaposition of layers can also alter the referencing of façades.

Layering

In many instances we observe multiple layers of façades that are superimposed over one another. Scollon and Wong Scollon (2003) describe layering as a form of inscription that is characterized by 'add-ons' and which is accomplished by 'attaching the sign at the top of the other one where it is clearly *not* part of the original semiotic design' (p. 136). In particular, they emphasize the temporary nature of added layers such as 'For Sale' and 'Now Open' signs and, conversely, also the 'authenticity' of the more permanent façade layers on which these signs are placed. From an analytical standpoint, layering as a semiotic resource is not tied to any specific form or material, but can instead be realized in various and even multiple modes. In this sense, façade layers can reveal multiple meanings in diverse forms and also at varying times. For example, we see how façades themselves may act as a canvas for political expression through layering. In the days leading up to the G8 summit in St Petersburg, we recorded numerous graffiti written across freshly cleaned façades in high-traffic areas of the city. The lettering was large and bold and seemed to communicate to a global audience in its various languages, as in the Russian 'G8 against the world' or the English 'G8 Kills' and 'Bush Fuck Off'.

To take another example, Figure 12.2 reproduces one version of a stencilled graffito found throughout the city at the time. In this case, it is located on the

FIGURE 12.2 Graffiti on the wall of a public market, St Petersburg, Russia

façade of a popular public market and appears itself to have incited discourse. The stencil references a famous Soviet slogan 'Lenin shows the path to Communism'. It is a mix of writing in Zulu and Russian and some graphic images. The Zulu text *Lenin ubonisa indlela yenkululeko* 'Lenin shows the path to freedom' is rendered in smaller Russian wording below 'Lenin shows the path'. On the right, there's a silhouetted image of Lenin with his arm extended (as if 'showing the path') and below is more Russian wording as if continuing the slogan: 'against the rule of corporations'. A (former) DDR coat of arms featuring a hammer, compass and sheaves of wheat appears at the bottom left position, invoking and reinforcing the socialist imagery and a radicalized working-class ideology. The contents, choice of languages, and the 'iconic' imagery of the stencil align its author(s) with the Soviet-era, pro-communist ideal of class struggle and solidarity with the colonized peoples of Africa, and the alliance of farmers and workers in their struggle against corporate imperialism for an egalitarian society.

In response, someone lacking a marker scratched out the image of Lenin. A third author wrote 'fish' in Russian, pointing to the slogan and above 'smell it', implying that the slogan is rotten. Here the layers of old ('pro-communist') and new ('anti-communist') ideologies compete for space on the wall. While the sprucing up of the façades was accelerated for St Petersburg's 300th anniversary and the G8 summit, the same façades also served as surfaces for defiance against the intrusion of global capitalism. This defiance was not only expressed via the content of graffiti, but also through the act of defacing the cleaned façades themselves. At the same time, the discourses that were taking place on the façades speak of a new era where public political dissent is possible, where Russians can call 'Lenin's path' rotten and where, this time, communist propaganda is relegated to the marginalized realm of graffiti.

Both referencing and layering are most often deployed in multimodal arrangements, which are realized through a variety of materials and visual and linguistic cues. In fact, these two key semiotic resources are most often simultaneously at work. Specifically, both referencing and layering are frequently found in semiotic arrangements that actively manage different identity claims and meaning potentials along the local/global continuum. In this regard, the main meaning potentials in the façades that we observed can be divided into three main categories: reconstructing the past; fashioning a canvas for global commerce; and balancing the local and the global.

Reconstructing the past

As an attempt to recover the distinctive features of its urban centre, the city of Dresden has used building façades to reconstruct its historic imagery. After World War II, the Soviets had left Dresden's rubble in the middle of the city as a memorial to the devastation of war.[6] In the 1990s, since the collapse of the

FIGURE 12.3 A restored façade (left) hiding ruins (middle); canvas reproduction of a façade hides construction (right), Dresden, Germany

Soviet regime and Germany's reunification, Dresden saw one of Europe's largest reconstruction projects in the rebuilding of its monumental eighteenth-century baroque cathedral, Frauenkirche. By 2005, the cathedral was re-erected at the cost of US $217 million, becoming a major tourist destination and a symbol of Dresden's historic and cultural past (Clayton and Russell, 2001). During the continued construction of surrounding buildings in the cathedral plaza, canvas murals of old German façades hung over entire buildings.

In Figure 12.3, the photograph that we shot on a trip to Dresden in 1991 shows a Soviet-era façade, the only restored part of the bombed building. The façade (left) is a layer, an illusion of an edifice, hiding the rubble behind it (middle). In 2006, we photographed a reproduction of a similar façade (right) that hides – by means of layering – the new construction beneath it. Both times, despite the World War II destruction and the new construction, the façades serve as a material link – both a literal and stylistic form of referencing – to the pre-war history of the city. These temporal layers underscore the function of the façade as a 'face'. There is no authentic or real face, just the changing layers that reference particular truths (or lies) in particular places in time. The canvas murals veiling new construction, like the structures veiling World War II destruction, work as Dresden's theatrical 'set' of history. This type of (re)construction of architectural trophies (Urry, 2005) sheds the unpleasant memory of World War II and references a more glorious time. It serves not only to reinvigorate a national identity, but also allows the city to compete on a global scale with other European cities endowed with historic architecture.

Often, the developers of post-communist cities display urgency about costly symbolic renovation projects that seem to supersede broader social concerns. In Sibiu, we were struck by the apparent abyss that ran between the relatively small historic centre and its immediate surroundings.[7] While the city centre was

FIGURE 12.4 Renovated façades, Sibiu, Romania

perfectly manicured – its historic pre-communist buildings' façades had been repaired and repainted (Figure 12.4) in sight of the city's year as a designated European Capital of Culture in 2007 – the rest of the city was replete with decaying façades of old buildings, missing sidewalks, mud, dust and enormous potholes. As an act of referencing, the repainting of Sibiu's historic façades in their 'original colours' (though much brighter than the rest of the city) points to the privileging of a limited set of narratives. Ultimately, in communicating itself to the international and local public alike, Sibiu's main focus was on the physical appearance of its city centre as an active reference to high culture and its (pre-communist) past, to the extent that the City Hall would not allow much European Capital of Culture publicity to be displayed in public space, and on building façades in particular.[8]

Fashioning a canvas for global commerce

As Eastern Bloc cities are scrambling to revive the faces of their buildings, some façades are invoked as a canvas for advertising, thus achieving a double goal of cleaning up a façade and capitalizing (literally) on a previously untapped resource: façade space as a commodity. Steps away from the Palace of Culture and Science (Stalin's highly controversial 'gift' to Warsaw in 1952), a drab apartment building in Warsaw is almost entirely covered up by a colourful advertisement. The billboard is the epitome of a capitalist reframing of the formerly communist Czech(oslovak) product, a Škoda car, draped over a Soviet-era dingy brown façade (Figure 12.5).

FIGURE 12.5 Car advertisement on a Soviet-era building, Warsaw, Poland (see colour plate section)

While the renovation, and even complete reconstruction, of distinctively 'historic' (i.e. pre-war, pre-Soviet) residential buildings to their 'original' state serves as a means for building national pride and attracting the profits of global commerce, tourism and investment, Soviet-era façades are often converted into canvases for corporate communication. In this case, layering is used to cover rather than highlight the façade's 'original' work of referencing. Not unlike Venturi et al.'s (1977) decorated shed, these façades are used as means for the spectacular consumption of superimposed, market-driven and, therefore, also mutable markers of global capitalism. In her work on the branded landscape of contemporary Warsaw, Chmielewska (2005) points out that city buildings covered in gigantic corporate banners become pure vehicles, or 'mere scaffolding' (p. 364), for commercial branding. Ultimately, the placement and *em*placement of brands across sites and formats is part and parcel of corporations' strategic 'creation of a metatextuality for themselves through ad campaigns' (Danesi, 2006: 105). This is by no means a recent phenomenon. As Danesi (2006) writes:

> Already in 1892, the Coca-Cola Company spread its logo across the US, painting it as a mural on walls, displaying it on posters and soda fountains where the drink was served, and imprinting it on widely marketed, common household items (calendars, drinking glasses, etc.). (p. 105)

In relation to this last point, Chmielewska (2005) too emphasizes the distinctive and weightier nature of displaying global brands and logos 'on a specific

FIGURE 12.6 A Coca-Cola ad with Hermitage façade, St Petersburg, Russia (see colour plate section)

building or in a significant place' (p. 358) rather than on generic, freestanding, billboards.

It is no accident, then, that the Winter Palace, a quintessentially historic façade in St. Petersburg, has been used in a Coca-Cola ad campaign placed on a soda cart on Nevsky Prospekt (Figure 12.6). In this case, however, it is not the brand that is physically positioned on the façade, but rather the image of the façade that is imported into the ad, where the silhouette of a sideways bottle of Coca-Cola is layered and quite literally 'filled' with the museum's image. The Cyrillic tagline on the ad reads 'the value of tradition' and, in doing so, it cleverly capitalizes on the choice of Russian language and the familiar image, at once, to localize and to globalize itself. The Winter Palace's façade is used as a logo in a double sense. On one hand, it is reproduced as a logo via everyday objects (here on a coke bottle and on a vending cart), emphasizing the palace as a national monument within the nation's visual landscape. This logoization acts to link the imagination of Russianness with the façade, now a metonymical reference for Russia and a visual resource for further branding. The tagline anchors the image, by making this link explicit – the imagery of the building stands for tradition, tradition is valuable and Coke values it. The ad uses the branded façade as a resource to localize itself, mitigating the effects of what might otherwise be antithetical to the imaginations of a traditional Russia.

Balancing the global and the local

It is important to emphasize not only that advertising displays 'rely on images of the historical landmarks of the city' (Chmielewska, 2005: 364), but also that historic façades themselves are at times subject to branding. In this regard, some of the façades we observed show an active balancing of global and local identities in the pursuit of globalist ends.

The tensions between localization and globalization are especially visible in the vernacular visual forms of urban façades. One Polish building we saw, for example, displays a blue and white sign in bold lettering above its storefronts that reads *Polonia* ('Poland' in Latin) and below, a red and white awning of a bar is branded by Coca-Cola (Figure 12.7). The layered façade of this now-defunct cinema (see *kino* in faded lettering on either end of the Polonia sign) is more complex than this, however. Thanks to the other Polish-language signage and graffiti, we know we are in Poland, yet it is primarily the banner that anchors its national identity most obviously. With only the global branding of the Coke signs and the graffiti (in itself a global genre), this photograph would be difficult to place. Closer inspection reveals that the Coke awning too is one minute localized (by the Polish *[za]piekanka* 'cheese on toast' and *Mini Smak* 'Little Taste' – although the *Mini* is itself a borrowing from English) and the next globalized (*pitakebab*). Along the same lines, the Coke-branded vending machine is also localized with its own façade which shows a well-known iconic statue in Warsaw. Juxtapositions such as this are common. In Warsaw, a three-story banner ad for a global brand of chocolate bars shows three layers of façade. A trompe l'oeil candy banner ad 'hangs' over a photographic reproduction of a historic façade. The entire ad, itself, hangs over the actual façade that is covered with graffiti and dirt (Figure 12.8). The work of façade restoration is done

FIGURE 12.7 Local-global façade, Warsaw, Poland

FIGURE 12.8 Building covered with composite banner façade, Warsaw, Poland (see colour plate section)

by the advertisement, which references a clean neoclassical style of 'high culture', gaining a symbolic cachet not otherwise afforded by graffiti and dirt. The result is the representation of what the local façade should look like and perhaps will look like if the global market is allowed its way. As described earlier, the temporary veil of global advertising often hides the old dilapidated façades in need of renovation, sometimes in exchange for funds to pay for the renovation of the veiled building.

Potemkin Villages: Façades and/as global communication

According to lore, when the Russian Empress Catherine the Great visited the desolate Crimea, her general, G. A. Potemkin (who had just conquered Crimea) erected elaborate façades of houses along the path taken by her carriage. These façades hid the run-down peasant dwellings and gave the empress an impression that she was travelling through vibrant villages. By doing this, Potemkin embellished his own accomplishments. This story, whether legend or history, speaks to the visual power of a façade. The term *Potemkin Village* is now a common figure of speech, referencing a false front or a superficial fabrication intended to deceive the observer and to hide an undesirable fact or condition (Merriam-Webster, 2003).

Because of the prominence of façades as urban texts, they are the first to get erected, polished up or covered up in the management of urban identity. At the same time, Eastern European cities do not simply represent themselves to the world but are subject to a global imperative. In the same way that Potemkin was not simply exercising his will over the villagers but working under the pressures of imperial expectations, post-communist cities *must* position themselves in relation to, and appeal directly to, the global gaze. The production of post-communist façades is a delicate dance between overt commodification, efforts to preserve a unique local identity, and, at the same time, the marketing of that identity through a performance of 'staged authenticity' (MacCannell, 1999).

Indeed, there seems to be a division of labour between building façades from different eras and the symbolic import of both pre-Soviet and Soviet façades is equally exploited for its global capital. In the process, pre-Soviet façades are recontextualized as historic, authentic and therefore also worthy of global attention through the very act of renovation and the display of preservation (such as in the canvas murals reproducing the 'original' appearance of the façade). On the other hand, Soviet-era façades – and specifically those of residential or otherwise 'anonymous' buildings – may simply need to be hidden away when too run-down or actively refashioned into 'screens' and 'windows' for global consumption. As such, façades do not necessarily offer accurate renditions of any given local reality; they can instead be seen as (visual) texts realizing imaginative meanings that are to be attached to the city.

In exploring façades as a genre of global communication, we mean to illustrate the ways in which they can be read, offering some tools for reading in identifying key semiotic resources such as *layering* and *referencing*. We have also considered how these resources combine with specific contexts to produce a range of meaning potentials pertaining to the different identity claims that are deployed across façades. While we have proposed some tools for reading façades, it is important to stress that their meaning potentials are not fixed and are continuously changing over time and need to be read anew and within new contexts. Ultimately, urban building façades may be regarded as key visual interfaces between global capital and the gaze of investors, tourists and locals alike, much in the same way as scholars define branding. Brands are both 'an *interface* between producers and consumer' (Lury, 2004: 48) and 'a form of immaterial capital' (Arvidsson, 2006: 7). By means of designing and organizing semiotic material in such a way that it can be used as 'immaterial capital', brands literally become symbolic currency for material profit. In addition, as Lury (2004) states, logos are the 'face' of branding, in that – while the brand in itself is 'intangible or incorporeal' – a logo is what 'makes the brand visible' (p. 74). Along the same lines, the visual discourse of cities (of which façades are a part) can be considered currency for the (more or less) successful acquisition of symbolic capital in the global marketplace.

Just as in the post-industrial and transnational contexts of the global economy exchanges of semiotic 'goods' have a tremendous impact on the shaping and consolidation of cultural, political and economic realities (Lash and Urry, 1994), façades are a crucial, yet understudied component of the global symbolic realm. Façades help us understand the competing ideologies and discourses in the production of cities. In order to compete in the global market, the former Eastern Bloc is required to conform to the conflicting standards and expectations of the global consumer, be it a local one or an outsider such as a tourist. The global consumer, on one hand, may expect a recognizable authenticity of something unique to the locale such as Communist relics and historical monuments. On the other hand, they may also anticipate a generic Europeanness and overall 'Westernness', including the qualities associated with 'world-class' cities – such as clean façades, familiar brands, English language and easy access to Coca-Cola. All the while, in many of the post-Eastern Bloc cities, as major funds are allocated towards restoring façades, there is a preponderance of homeless citizens, most often the elderly who can't afford to buy food with their now worthless pensions left over from the communist era.

Acknowledgements

We are grateful to Adam Jaworski and Crispin Thurlow for their expert and kind guidance, editing help and encouragement with this chapter.

Notes

[1] Peter the Great hired Bartolomeo Rastrelli, an Italian-born architect, to design the Winter Palace in the city centre. Rastrelli designed several palaces among many in the nearby area of the city centre. St Petersburg's centre is known for its mixture of baroque, neoclassical and rococo styles.

[2] For example, in the wake of the 2004 and 2007 inclusion of ten post-communist countries into the European Union, in recent years countries such as the Czech Republic, Bulgaria and Estonia have hired designers and communication firms to brand their nation by means of logos, slogans and communication campaigns aimed at tourists and investors (Alda, 2006; Bolin, 2006; Kaneva, 2006).

[3] Romania is one of the newest entries into the European Union and a country with a historically shaky economy, even when compared to other post-communist countries.

[4] We refer to the Eastern Bloc as a geo-political territory that emerged during the Cold War, became insular and diverged from the Western Bloc in politics, economy and culture. Since the collapse of the Soviet regime, the Eastern Bloc became more widely referred to as Central and Eastern Europe.
[5] This modernist building was constructed as a bank in 1915 and became a Textile Institute in 1930 under the Soviet regime.
[6] Dresden was severely bombed by the Allied Forces at the end of World War II. The controversial bombing destroyed the city's baroque city centre and killed thousands of civilians.
[7] Interestingly, the renovation and even brand-new construction of key infrastructure such as city roads, the train station square and the airport were subordinated to the restyling of Sibiu's 'face' – quite literally – for the acquisition of international symbolic capital, in the guise of recognitions such as the European Capital of Culture and the UNESCO World Heritage site titles, and consequently also of cultural cachet in the global tourist marketplace.
[8] A choice that is opposite to the public communication trends of most 'western' European Capitals of Culture.

References

Aiello, G. (2007), 'The appearance of diversity: Visual design and the public communication of EU identity', in J. Bain and M. Holland (eds), *European Union Identity: Perceptions from Asia and Europe.* Baden-Baden: Nomos, pp. 147–181.

Aiello, G. and Thurlow, C. (2006), 'Symbolic capitals: Visual discourse and intercultural exchange in the European capital of culture scheme', *Language and Intercultural Communication*, 6(2), 148–162.

Alda, K. (2006, February 22), 'Branding the Czech Republic: Beyond the "backward"', *Prague Post.* Retrieved 19 March 2007, from LexisNexis database.

Anderson, B. (1983), *Imagined Communities: Reflections on the Origin and Spread of Nationalism.* London: Verso.

Arvidsson, A. (2006), *Brands: Meaning and Value in Media Culture.* London and New York: Routledge.

Bolin, G. (2006), 'Visions of Europe: Cultural technologies of nation-states', *International Journal of Cultural Studies*, 9(2), 189–206.

Bourdieu, P. (1991), *Language and Symbolic Power* (J. B. Thompson [ed.]). Cambridge: Harvard University Press.

Chmielewska, E. (2005), 'Logos or the resonance of branding: A close reading of the iconosphere of Warsaw', *Space and Culture*, 8(4), 349–380.

Clayton, A. and Russell, A. K. (2001), *Dresden: A City Reborn.* Oxford: Berg.

Danesi, M. (2006), *Brands.* New York and London: Routledge.

Eco, U. (1986), 'Function and sign: Semiotics of architecture', in M. Gottdiener and A. P. Lagopoulos (eds), *The City and the Sign: An Introduction to Urban Semiotics.* New York: Columbia University Press, pp. 55–87.

Foote, K. E. (2000), 'To remember and forget: Archives, memory, and culture', in R. C. Jimerson (ed.), *American Archival Studies: Reading in Theory and Practice.* Chicago: The Society of American Archivists, pp. 29–46.

Harris, C. M. (1993), *Dictionary of Architecture and Construction.* New York: McGraw-Hill.

Jack, G. and Phipps, A. (2005), *Tourism and Intercultural Exchange: Why Tourism Matters.* Clevedon: Channel View Publications.

Kaneva, N. (2006), 'Marketizing national identity after communism: The case of *Branding Bulgaria*', Symposium conducted at the 2006 AEJMC Convention, San Francisco, CA.

Kress, G. and van Leeuwen, T. (2001), *Multimodal Discourse: The Modes and Media of Contemporary Communication.* New York: Oxford University Press.

Lasansky, D. M. (2004), *The Renaissance Perfected: Architecture, Spectacle, and Tourism in Fascist Italy.* University Park, PA.: Pennsylvania State University Press.

Lash, S. and Urry, J. (1994), *Economies of Signs and Space.* London: Sage.

Lasswell, H. D. and Fox, M. B. (1979), *The Signature of Power: Buildings, Communication, and Policy.* New Brunswick, NJ: Transaction.

Lury, C. (2004), *Brands: The Logos of the Global Economy.* London and New York: Routledge.

MacCannell, D. (1999), *The Tourist: A New Theory of the Leisure Class* (3rd edn). Berkeley: University of California Press.

Merriam-Webster, Inc. (2003), *Merriam-Webster's Collegiate Dictionary.* Springfield, MA: Merriam-Webster.

Parsons, R. (2003, May 26), 'St Petersburg gets lavish face-lift', *BBC News.* http://news.bbc.co.uk/2/hi/europe/2937744.stm (accessed 18 April 2008).

Porębski, M. (1977), *Ikonosfera.* Warsaw, Poland: PWN.

Scollon, R. and Wong Scollon, S. (2003), *Discourses in Place: Language in the Material World.* London: Routledge.

Tarkhanov, A. and Kavtaradze, S. (1992), *Stalinist Architecture.* London: Laurence King.

Urry, J. (2005), 'The complexities of the global', *Theory, Culture & Society,* 22(5), 235–254.

Venturi, R., Brown, D. S. and Izenour, S. (1977), *Learning from Las Vegas: The Forgotten Symbolism of Architectural Form.* Cambridge, MA: The MIT Press.

Chapter 13

Semiosis Takes Place or Radical Uses of Quaint Theories

Ella Chmielewska

Increasingly, we deal with places and their artefacts through visual interfaces, through pictures and representations. We saturate places with images, veil them with display screens and banners, we cover them in inscriptions and annotations. This intense visuality of places is not only manifest in the proliferation of images but also in the heightened visibility of language. The aggressive presence of texts in the visual field disrupts the opposition of text and image confounding theoretical approaches from visual studies, and upsetting the assumptions of linguistics. It calls for new methods for 'reading' the complex semiological landscapes.

No matter how places are produced, used, viewed and represented, however, their presence extends beyond our field of vision and their meaning exceeds the interpretive powers of our language. We confront places in their physicality and from our discreet corporeal positions. We do not simply decode collections of signs; we are *immersed* in the landscapes made of objects and surfaces whose material presences and discrete locations are as consequential to semiosis as their messages. This landscape is not merely 'viewed' or 'read' but actively perceived by the subject *implaced* within her semiotic sphere.

While acknowledging the work on visual semiotics, semiotic landscape and multimodality (Kress and van Leeuwen, 1996; 2001) and on 'discourses in place' (Scollon and Wong Scollon, 2003), this chapter steers into a different, if adjacent, territory. Rather than exploring meaning-making practices, modalities of discourse and types of semiotics, it focuses on the material objects of semiosis and on specific places where meaning is manifest. Grounded in Edward Casey's notion of *implacement* as a condition of inhabitation (1993), the chapter points to sources centred on the concern for context and material surface: the largely unknown (in the English-speaking scholarship) theory of language by Karl Bühler (1934/1990) and often neglected work on perception by James J. Gibson (1966). This is not, however, an attempt at 'looking back', but rather 'looking around' – a procedure most fitting for examining the complex sphere of meaningful surfaces, or the *iconosphere* (ikonosfera) defined by Mieczysław

Porębski (1972) as an entirety of the visual sphere (Chmielewska, 2005). This 'looking around', or *glancing* to follow Casey's (2007) validation of this exploratory mode, departs from the trajectory defined by the dominant semiological *gaze,* and the acknowledged theoretical positions that privilege arbitrary signs. Instead, it foregrounds the surface where meaning is articulated.

In centring on place and specificity, the discussion proceeds along two interrelated tracks. The first, presented in a textual form, points to new radical uses of some overlooked theoretical material. The second, integrating the parallel visual argument, posits a paradoxical figure of a complex tourist/observer confronting her cultural constructions of semiotic landscapes in two distinct locations. The text and the images are connected by a purposefully subjective account, where a hyphenated 'Westerner', an East-European-born urban explorer inflected by interest in place and visuality, revisits Warsaw and confronts the (unfamiliar) 'Chinese city.' Focussing on the specificity of context, this discussion reveals the problematic of positionality and language in elaborating semiotic landscapes, the 'constant unease between effort at self-positioning and the language and knowledge available for us to write these into culture' (Rogoff, 2000: 15). It aims at highlighting the potential of a close reading (Chmielewska, 2005: 354) of discreet *place–scapes* (Casey, 2007: 164). At the same time it also emphasizes the continuing challenge of placing visual material in the epistemological position traditionally reserved for the written text.

The (semiotic) object talks back

Saussurian semiology implies the arbitrariness of signs, and semiotic methodologies typically focus on meanings and codes that are unquestionably abstractable, that can be detached from the materiality of sign objects and moved into language-based analysis. Positioning the inquiry within Peircean semiotics potentially allows for more nuanced examination of the visual, but does not necessarily change the tenuous position of the object. Peirce's triad is widely employed in visual methodologies, where signs are presented as partly iconic, indexical and symbolic (Elkins, 2004; Scollon and Wong Scollon, 2003). As Elkins explains, Peircean sign signifies mimetically, is 'affected' by its object, and denotes by convention; it 'contains' itself, then, is related to its object, and 'is interpreted to represent an object' (Elkins, 2004: 6, 12). The focus here is clearly on the sign, its function and nature, and the object is left outside any scrutiny. It may be telling that Elkins in his explication resorts to 'the rudimentary diagram of perspective' (p. 12) and in doing so he further detaches the sign from its object. While implicating the position of the viewer, he frames the concept as an image, with the object locked into a double representation: a sign representing an object, and a specific drawing convention representing the sign representing the object (p. 13).

But objects, beside their capacity of being represented, take space and take place, their surfaces implying varied sensory experience(s). They mark the surrounding landscapes and in-form places, necessitating elaboration of the role of materiality and specificity in semiosis. It may be useful, then, to turn to those few theories of language and perception that explicitly recognized the object and its context as a locus of meaning. Bühler's theory of language (1934/1990) foregrounds the 'significative exchange' tied to the deictic field of the sign, the sign's physical context and its related 'environment of things' (p. 182). Gibson's 1966 theory of perception, pointing to affordances of objects, stresses the surface marking as the basis of making meaning visible. Both theories explicitly account for the position of the (actively perceiving) viewer, the particularity of context, and the surface as generative of meaning. Both acknowledge the topo-sensitivity (Eco, 1979) of artefacts, challenging the semiotic theories that programmatically detach the sign from the site of its signification, at best allowing for an indexical function and focus on the *image of* an object, not the *object itself* with its material condition and its related set of meanings.

Bühler (1934/1990) posits that every language sign, far from being arbitrary, is context-dependent, 'ideationally harmonized with what is named by it' (p. 180). He positions the object, the sender and the receiver in a communicative triad constituted by their overlapping fields of meaning: deictic, expressive and triggering. The 'significative exchange' then is not about coding/decoding of information, but rather centred on the complex reconfigurations of semiotic interdependencies (p. 182).

Taking off from Bühler's triadic conceptualization of the dynamic communicative process and the spatio-temporal circumstance of the meaningful action (p. 2), We suppose the 'receiver' of environmental information who does not merely respond to abstracted stimuli, but deals with places from her specific location and follows a particular approach to the material surfaces by which she is affected. She actively searches for, organizes, classifies and selects information *while* moving among, around objects, in relation to their surfaces, to changing points of *surface attachment* or *implacement.*

An implaced, or topo-sensitive sign derives its meaning from its particular positioning. This type of sign most vividly manifests the tensions between the visible language sign, its presence on the material surface, and its location within the substantial context. Drawing the designating field into the sphere of meaning of a sign is critical for understanding a whole array of signs and objects that saturate the immersive visual landscape (from graffiti through logos and road signs, billboards and monitors, to urban screens or road blocks). For Bühler (1934/1990), the visible attachment of the sign to its object indicates an ideational condition and the specific bond with context; it demarcates the semantic functions of signs, with every sign designating 'a well-defined place in physical space and thus an environment consisting of things' (p. 184). Bühler's deictic triad, a semiotic 'shifter' of 'here-now-I' underpins this dynamic and reciprocal relationship (p. 117).

In their concept of semiotic landscape Gunther Kress and Theo van Leeuwen (1996) link verbal and visual signs through the actions of the sign maker and the context of sign production (p. 15). They take marking and materiality as critical for semiosis (p. 230). In order to deal with the visual and material aspects of language Roy Harris (1995) attends to the semiological function of the surface and the complex properties of the graphic space of language signs (p. 113). The concept so central to Harris' integrationalist theory and to Kress and van Leeuwen's notion of semiotic landscape had been comprehensively treated a few decades earlier in the work of Gibson (1966) where landscape is considered a 'persistent arrangement of surfaces', a layout where the surface is 'a precondition of vision' (p. 307). Gibson takes displays and representations as interventions into 'pre-existing surfaces' that convey structures of information. The surface as a 'boundary between the organism and its environment' informs both the object and its context (p. 101). For Gibson, the surface is not superficial – it is a meaningful interface between the object and the medium. It constitutes part of the object, part of the place to which it belongs and the key *object* of our attention in the 'serious business of perceiving the world' (Gibson, 1982: 278). Surface rigidity gives support and constancy to things. It gives the landscape its stability (1966: 8–10).

The observer perceives and comprehends the 'world of surfaces' dynamically, and the 'optical information consisting of invariants' (Gibson, 1982: 278) is crucial for her positioning, orientation and meaningful behaviour (p. 235). Casey (2007) emphasizes that it is a glance, not the sustained gaze, that 'has a genius for surfaces' (p. 139). The landscape, then, as an aggregate of meaningful surfaces demands a specific kind of 'reading.' Already in 1926 Walter Benjamin called for a radically different deciphering of the radical (re)positioning of the observer/reader *vis-à-vis* the urban text – the reader's body dynamically immersed among the variegated surfaces of perceivable texts demanded a vertical reading (Ward, 2001: 138). The collections of urban texts Benjamin navigated were not examined through any sustained engagement of his gaze, rather they were probed by glances, momentary sightings of (visual) quotations (Casey, 2007: 226–229). In his discussion of the glance as a probe and a deictic device, Casey upholds Benjamin's intuition as well as Gibson's sustained theoretical engagement with the surface and its directional perception (2007: 146–149). His phenomenological account validates Gibson's elaboration of the landscape and directionality (Gibson, 1966: 68) as well as, indirectly, Bühler's attention to deictic markers and their condition of surface attachment (Bühler, 1934/1990: 180–181).

The critical 'where'

Every urban sign, each billboard or display screen is a semiotic object whose material presence indexes and informs both the visual context and the specific physical location. Whether the content of its message is generic or place-specific, its location creates a discrete condition of semiosis. Even if the particular marker is universally understood and can be easily 'decoded', the place it designates is not merely indexed (referenced or pointed at) but charged with specific meaning. The codes themselves are locally bound. Place forms a particular 'where' that is, as Michel de Certeau (1988) claims, 'marked by someone or something' (p. 108). Or as Mariusz Tchorek (1966/1986) suggested, a place is a felt and meaningful presence whose critical 'where' creates 'a sudden gap in the approach to the world' (Borowski et al., 1986: 54). This gap – a tension, an absence of the expected – is an opportunity to 'face' the place on its own terms and seek alignment with its uniqueness, to endorse the viewer's topo-sensitivity. While for Tchorek (2000) place inherently contains the (potential) 'other', for MacCannell (2001), the presence of the other's gaze creates an 'opening in the cultural unconscious' (p. 36).[1] The gap is also a danger of appropriation, approximation, an exposure to imposing what we already know or what we desire *for* the place, or for our position in it. While bringing about a chance of insight, the gap then also poses a risk of disregard or subjugation.

Our focus on place necessitates an inquiry into *topo-semiotic* condition of signs and an attention to the correspondence between material and spatio-temporal articulations, visual (re)presentations and linguistic presences. Topo-sensitivity is not equivalent to indexicality. The first is centred on the sign-object, the latter on the relationship within the sign system. While 'in place meaning of signs' have attracted methodological elaboration in the form of *geosemiotics* (Scollon and Wong Scollon, 2003), Eco's (1979) term seems more apposite for my discussion. Topo-sensitivity implies reciprocal engagement between a sign and its place, as well as discrete attachments of the sign-objects. To focus on place means a shift of attention from the mode of viewing or representing and systems of referencing and positioning to the object itself. To focus on *topo-semiosis*, We need to allow the presence of material objects and surfaces into the signifying field.

This turning towards the sign-object potentially unsettles the common theoretical grounding used for studying complex phenomena such as tourism, often preoccupied with the all-knowing gaze fixed upon the viewed object from the position of power. The privilege of gaze as an analytical tool, locates the modalities of authority along the straight 'line of vision' and the single-point perspective. Similarly, grafting the hegemonic concepts of semiology into any space of analysis immediately 'others' the object under consideration, immobilizing it under the imposed theoretical gaze (Kress and van Leeuwen, 1996). The notion of the 'second gaze' accounts for the visual engagement of the host, though not necessarily for all the glances, glimpses, darting stares directed at the 'tourist' herself (MacCannell, 2001; Jaworski et al., 2003). And what about the (possible) agency afforded to the objects under scrutiny? Those objects that 'may open a window in structure, [offer] a chance to glimpse the real' (MacCannell, 2001: 36).

Whether examining places from a position of control or vulnerability, one actively seeks invariants, recognizable signs and known patterns of meaning (Gibson, 1966: 284). When faced with ambiguous traces and signs, one resorts to strategies of approximation, reading familiarity into visual events. In the rapidly globalizing world, signs of the familiar are plentiful: the green logo of Starbucks, an English phrase, the shape of a known trademark. The more alien the surroundings, the stronger these recognizable signs stand out in an undifferentiated landscape. They act as orienting markers, signposts that allow to create and negotiate the space of familiarity within the foreign territory (Bühler, 1934/1990: 93). By disrupting the singular 'Western' position of the observer, we can productively complicate the picture. Now, the inflections of vision can potentially come from some Other present in the semiotic field: the host potentially affecting the gaze of the tourist (Jaworski et al., 2003: 158), or other language(s) known to the observer, the *Logos* modulated by migration into the global English and into the sphere of Western imagery and thought habit (Chmielewska, 2005). Navigating this semiotic landscape, the theorist is never mute. His (*sic!*) *accent grave* mercilessly reveals its local roots, the specific (linguistic) point of attachment (Barthes, 1997).

Kress and van Leeuwen (1996) emphasize their departure from the semiotic tradition that privileges verbal signs and assigns a subservient role to the image (p. 16). To foreground the motivated sign they distance themselves from Roland Barthes and Parisian semiology. But Barthes inadvertently provides an argument for a critical distance to the theoretical assumptions of hegemonic semiology. His gaze was never abstract and detached but strongly rooted in the specific language and its assumptions. Immersed in his language, preocupied with re-presenting, while pointing out meaningful details, he superimposed the conceptual system of *his langue* on the potential for discovery of a place (1983). In Bühler's (1934/1990) semiotic triad, Barthes (the sender) repositioned for our viewing the object he observed, the *japonaise* constructed out of significant elements that triggered his perception (his *jouissance?*) (1983).

Walter Benjamin, on the other hand, was acutely aware of his spatio-cultural position of the 'attentive European' (Gilloch, 2002: 166). His call for a recalibrated reading and his insistence on locating the reader's body within the variegated surfaces of perceptible texts suggest a potential for a radical repositioning of the point of theoretical attachment and the particular place of analysis. While Berlin inspired Benjamin's proposal for revised ways of reading, it was Moscow who, questioning the Parisian strategies of the 'banal tourist', forced him, as Gilloch points out, to re-learn strategies for dealing with urban surfaces (2002: 164–6). Though Benjamin credited Moscow for demanding from its reader the 'intimacy with objects' (as cited in Gilloch: 167), he failed to account for the city's 'semiosphere' (Lotman, 1984) thus manifesting the limits of his logo-centric vision. Yuri Lotman's 'semiosphere' reminds us of the semiotic tradition positioned in this (geo-semiotic) blind spot. Porębski's 'iconosphere' constitutes an adjacent theoretical development (Chmielewska, 2005). Each posits a *complex semiotic entity* rather than a singular sign as a unit of meaning. The notion of 'semioscape' recently proposed by Thurlow and Aiello (2007: 154) complements Porębski's concept with its emphasis on visual semiosis while also addressing the necessarily 'poli-factorial' (Lotman, 1984) or multimodal (Kress and van Leeuwen, 2001) objects and agents of semiosis that are particularly relevant to the analysis of place.

Today, radical demands for 'deployment of new vocabulary' (Gilloch, 2002: 168) come from places whose surface displays seem particularly aggressive: freed from centralized political control, or loosened from the ideological authority post-socialist cities of 'Eastern Europe' and the fast changing cities of China.[2] These are also spaces where the 'Western' gaze and its resonant (Parisian) accent could be productively disrupted by the attention to the graphic space of language(s) and the local specificity of diacritical marks. Today, urban landscapes of Eastern Europe and China, challenge the hegemonic understanding of visibility and graphic demarcation of language signs, potentially provoking re-examination of the relationship between the sign and its context. Both force the tourist/theorist to confront the conceptual and linguistic stereotypes of spatial practices and related theories. The East European city offers a fruitful territory for exploring the relationship between a graphic mark, its sound, and the complexity of changes in the global semiotic landscape (Chmielewska, 2005). The Chinese city provides the urban reader with a different challenge: the graphic space of language is highly visible there (Harris, 1995: 20), so the relationship between 'image' and 'word' would necessarily take on a different role in the 'discourses in place' (Scollon and Wong Scollon, 2003).

Kress and van Leeuwen (1996) confirm these geo-cultural blind spots by singling out two cultural territories, 'Eastern Europe and some parts of Asia', where advertising (and the related tension between words and image) was apparently introduced 'relatively recently' (p. 12).[3] Rather than disputing this claim, we take it as a deictic marker for our discussion and follow the insufficiently exotic, abject European Other as a potent source of reflection on semiotic landscapes (Chmielewska, 2005). we situate this theorist-tourist in the place where the mere dismissal of diacritical marks makes the language look familiar 'enough.' Instead of abiding by the singular Parisian gaze, we allow for an account from a complex marginal position whose (linguistic) grounding lies outside the privileged Western cultural terrain and further direct this (already conflicted) mode of looking towards the unfamiliar non-Western landscape of another Other: China.

In considering these territories, we cannot ignore their ideological 'Easterness': the lingering othering through geo-political positioning. Its former political aura taints the designation 'Eastern Europe' with hues, at times, similar (to a degree) to those used for China: both spaces, though in different ways, are blemished by communism. Rather than viewing these cultural and linguistic spaces as necessarily explained by the established Western theories, we regard both as potential sources of insight (Chmielewska, 2005; Wasserstrom, 2007). These two territories have been obscured by the political separation and different developments of the ideological uses of words and images, different traditions of 'reading.' These are the two spaces across which this specific 'tourist' moves, revisiting the contemporary (post-socialist) Warsaw, observing the familiar and interpreting the new, and encountering for the first time the Chinese city in its newly acquired (state)capitalist garb.

Placing the gaze

Immersed in the urban semiotic array, the gaze of this tourist is on the move, unstable, self-conscious. It may be assertive when she pauses to make a judgement, to contemplate a view, to scrutinize an object, to stare at something that caught (and held) her eye. Its engagement is continually corrected by peripheral vision. Its sharpness is calibrated by changing perspectives and positions of her mobile (physical and cultural) body. Her gaze is accompanied (aided, subverted, or superseded) by her glancing, by quick surface probing, momentary engagements with shapes, patterns, textures and objects. Itself visible, exposed, her sight is inflected by glances of others, deflected by darting stares caught within her field of vision (or a viewfinder), even those blocked, ignored, unacknowledged, or those imagined, anticipated, desired (Casey, 2007: 147). Her sighted agency is conflicted, mediated by inverted commas: not a model figure of the Western *flâneur* whose amblings along the Parisian boulevard can be applied equally well to a walk through a Beijing street, Warsaw's Jarmark Europa, or Vieux Montréal.[4] Neither is it an overly confident Barthesian gaze that forces the difference into a possessive construct of a singular image. When she explores an unknown city she is not constructing a new domain of signs, she is immersed in the environment of semiotic objects with their volumes, materialities, textures, surfaces, agencies and histories. She may not know how to 'read' their properties, how to access their codes, she may even fail to notice them, but there are no empty spaces or 'empty signs' there (Barthes, 1983): every fragment is saturated with meaning.

In her looking, our tourist is dynamically engaged with *places*. Her field of vision is populated with bodies and events that do not neatly configure along the lines of perspective converging in one-point of her 'tourist gaze.' Rather, they rudely invade her personal space, obfuscate and deter her focus, fragment her momentarily confident stare into side glances. These intrusions are not merely visual, they are noisily acoustic, unsettlingly spatial, palpably tactile. The concept of the tourist gaze fails this hyphenated-Western viewer in the vast hyper-commercial post-socialist space of Warsaw's Parade Square. And it fails her as well, though in different ways, in the tight and crowded semiotic landscape of a Beijing market, where the chants of the insistent merchants' are deceptive as they are not about vision: *loo-kah-loo-kah-chee-poh-chee-poh!*

The expanse of the Parade Square in Warsaw, even though now broken up by road blocks, parked cars and commercial structures, remains spatially oppressive. This is not a place for the *flâneur*'s stroll, nor taking in the views. Navigating among objects in one's course, staying balanced on the Square's uneven surfaces, one combats the intimidating distance. The space remains totalitarian. Now domesticated, stripped of ideological power, its monstrous landmark maintains its spatial dominance. Still commanding this space, it apprehends the tourist's glances interfering with her observations. It directs and subjugates her gaze. With the blank stares of its monumental figures it induces a sense of disquiet.

Beijing market is unsettling in different ways. It places the tourist on display. The calls of the merchants control her glances forcing her into a state of heightened awareness of the deictic powers of her own looking. Even a momentary glance might be intercepted as an indicator of (commercial) interest. She intently tries not to 'loo-kah' then, not to engage with the vigilant gazes of the merchants tracking her glances and attaching them to (potentially desired) objects in her field of vision. Every look is imminently consequential. It is directed by incantations, gestures and postures. The pace, the modality of movement among the stalls, the proximity of objects, bodies and voices, the ways of looking and strategies of averting the gaze, the alertness to the space saturated with glances and deictic objects, the entire multimodal cacophony 'invites displacement' (Bühler, 1934/1990: 163).

When revisiting Warsaw, this diasporic tourist cannot shed her knowledge and memories of the place as she knows it from studying its cultural histories, and as she desires it to be since having been born there weighs her down with a sense of personal investment. Having lived in the place at times gives her an access to specific moments of place-memory. She notices changes in relation to her past visits and overlays them onto the larger patterns of familiarity. She registers details the habitual 'viewer' may fail to see, and she brings into her viewing assertions based on what she has lived elsewhere. Familiarity with the representations of this place inflects her viewing, and her glance cannot stop at the surface but penetrates the material, excising meaning out of traces, constructing the semiotic landscape out of patterned fragments. Moving in the space of Warsaw, she relies on her knowledge of the city's *iconosphere* – the entirety of its signs, images, markers – and the *Corpus Inscriptionum* of the place (Sulima 2002; Chmielewska, 2005). She is simultaneously reassured, enthused and stifled by it; hypersensitive to varied layers of meaning she is compelled to see obscure semiotic layers and read historical references into signs.

When visiting a Chinese city for the first time, her perception is vigilant and supple, taking in minute details and zooming out to longer views. Everything is new and noteworthy. Few familiar signs are spotted quickly and with joyful bemusement, their context and placement scrutinized. Known Chinese signs (drawn from her 'vocabulary' of five written characters) are identified with considerable pride in her 'competence.' They form tenuous links to (desired) understanding and they quickly construct a concrete, if unstable, 'image' of the place. Just as Kevin Lynch (1984/2007) insisted, this image is not a mere 'mental map,' it is an array of orienting elements, their familiarities connected into a certain narrative path, facilitating the *wayfinding* through the new environment of foreign signs. The first Chinese city (Beijing) instantly becomes emblematically 'Chinese' as it forms a certain semiotic hinge for visual and symbolic interpretative practice. Subsequently visited, Nanjing and Shanghai, are nuanced by the impressions from the first, formative visit. Also, places become quite different when explored with a guide (a sinologist colleague or a local student) and when ventured into alone, when relying on her own conspicuous linguistic inability – a specific condition for viewing in which the visual is not inflected by the verbal.[5]

The moment this tourist focuses on the specific, her attention already sets a frame for understanding, her look ceases to probe the surface and turns into a penetrating gaze. The moment she singles out a visual event for scrutiny, it becomes a visual pronouncement. And here, the necessary selection of adequate representative images for this discussion forms a narrative quite different from the one experienced *in situ*. Once 'presented' within this chapter, fitted into a set of formal requirements it constructs a new 'discourse in place.' The observed landscape becomes abridged to minimal visual statements, set within the new context of viewing.

Two screens, two surfaces

The images offered here are a visual reflection on the semiotic landscape of two differently defined and differently observed places. One is a singular place, the city of Warsaw, heavily mediated by the specific interest and knowledge of the author/tourist. The other can be indexed by named sources of visual discovery (Beijing, Nanjing and Shanghai), but the images themselves obscure place specificity: they demonstrate what this particular tourist selected in her viewfinder as strikingly 'Chinese,' arresting because of the tension between difference and familiarity.

Each pair of images is representative of a phenomenon known from the global stage: large advertising screens and small surface interventions. Gigantic screens ubiquitous in East European and Chinese cities manifest the scale of the economic and political change as well as the local vulnerability to the pressures of the market. The screens are 'Western' in their form: they announce the arrival of 'global' modes of advertising, and they colonize local landscapes, paradoxically furnishing a visible 'proof' for claims that advertising had never before existed in these cultural terrains (Kress and van Leeuwen, 1996: 12). Small individual interventions into the urban surface (inscriptions and stencils) are manifestations of the local, individual hand, though for the tourist they inscribe themselves as well into the global imagery already saturated with various styles and techniques of graffiti.

This visual sample underscores the methodological difficulty here. Even in the carefully constructed typology, the selection process is based on presuppositions that already frame possibilities of interpretations. If the criteria for the choice of pictures are based on the traditional epistemological dichotomy of text and image, the visual can only be posited as an illustrative material. It may be meaningful in its evidential role, but is ultimately subservient to the textually rendered proposition, necessarily subjugated to the role of an emblematic case study, significant merely as a tool for showcasing the argument. And the viewing of these selected images is of course different from the modes of seeing the actual scenes *in situ* so the reader is alerted here to Bühler's elaboration of semiotic attachment (1934/1990: 180) and Gibson's differentiation between immediate and mediated perception (1966: 267).

The city of Nanjing is draped in large advertising screens that separate the streets from construction and demolition sites. The scene drew the attention of this tourist not only because of its ascetic quality – a large expanse of whiteness contrasting with aggressive colours of the adjacent screens – but also because of the deictic figures of the three workers. Like The Three Graces, they preside over an open 'channel of communication' where the material of networking and wiring of the global communion is literally put in place. The relationship between the global communication network and the Chinese film is striking. Our tourist 'reads' this banner in relation to known cinematic images, her fascination with the graphic qualities of Chinese writing, and in the context of the city's demolition hidden behind the gloss of the screen. The significance of the image on the screen is derived from the specific siting as the city is being redrafted by the very forces that are courted with the cinematic spectacle. The Chinese copy of the advert is obscure to our tourist so she approximates the visual message to the codes she knows: taking the language signs as graphic forms, reading their colours and composition. She 'reads' the image without the interference of language. This lack of semiotic layers is revealed when she subsequently learns the character for 'red' central to the image. The screen itself creates a barrier between the viewer and the dramatic urban changes. She does not know what building is being demolished behind the screen, or what is the public discourse surrounding a particular project envisioned for the site. Her reading is *surface deep*, it deals with the specificity by way of semiotic approximation.

The image from Warsaw also shows a large urban screen, but here the vinyl sheath covers a specific structure reducing it to a scaffolding. Located at the major intersection in the city centre, the building forms the superior exposition site. Though hidden, it is not insignificant in this display; it is needed as a referent, its façade exposed through the veil. The building's obscured neglect, shared by all architecture of Warsaw's 'socialist modernity,' contributes to the significance of the screen. The image carries a curious message: *Precz z wolnos´cia˛* ('Out with Freedom'). The display recalls home-made banners from the times of political protests, and it works on the memory of the official displays along the traditional route of parades that punctuated the urban space behind the Iron Curtain with messages of ideology, faces of leaders and party slogans (Chmielewska, 2005). Those messages, however, were synchronized with the calendar of official events. Now, the display is a permanent condition. Replicating the façade, 'projecting' its documentary-like black and white image, the banner also references heritage regulations requiring the adverts to represent building's details. The building has been a signpost for a decade. While all previous displays were easily identifiable, now, no brand name accompanies the banner. Our tourist doesn't know what this visual intervention is about. Her anticipation is heightened. As Bühler would suggest, the advert has created a 'psychological compulsion' and the impact of the subsequent image relies on the viewer's anticipation of the next visual event (1934/1990: 180). Through its intertextual complexity, in recreating the surface no longer visible behind the screen, the display marginalizes the building further, denying it even the agency of representing itself. The display also trivializes the gestures of protest. The emoticon [;)] inserts further irony, contemporizing the slogan by referencing the global language of text-messaging.

The walls along tight streets of Shanghai's traditional neighbourhoods are marked by clusters of stencils and inscriptions. Without any guidance this tourist cannot make sense of the markings. She cannot read them, though she could identify parts of the messages: each stencil or an inscription containing a string of numerals. She is attracted to the aesthetics of the markings, to the textures and the randomness of compositions. Her visual references come from street art. These markings though, she finds out, are advertisements for small trades and services – each carrying a (business) phone number. The markings then are not individual expressions of rebellion, but manifestations of a capitalist spirit. As an intervention into the Chinese political and economic context these are subversive gestures, calling cards of individual entrepreneurs, ephemeral visual offers left on equally precarious surfaces of the neighbourhoods. To this tourist, another constellation of stencils photographed in a small street in Nanjing may look similar to those seen earlier in Shanghai. These ubiquitous tags of the new economic reality of the Chinese city are distinct in each place, and they need to be read in the context of the specific urban morphology and other markings: most significantly, the ominous character spelling out the ultimate surface manipulation, the impending demolition.

The inscription on a wall in Warsaw looks like a rebellious graffiti: a quick scribble and a tag, an apparent defacement of the building's surface. The words spell out: CHOŁD POLEGŁYM, 'Homage to the fallen'. The interlocked letters P and W stand for 'Polska Walcząca' (The Fighting Poland), a symbol of the underground army during the World War II (and of the 1944 Warsaw Uprising) and later, before 1989, a symbol of political defiance. This tourist had seen this particular mark when it first appeared in this place just before the 60th anniversary of the Uprising. The word 'homage' (hołd) is misspelled here personalizing the message. The missive is carefully placed: this is exactly where one of the barricades stood in 1944. The message is not offensive to the place; its graffiti format is apposite – rendered in the tradition in which this 'tag' functioned, as a symbol of opposition. Such act of writing would have carried a heavy penalty both during the Nazi and Soviet occupations. The form then adds gravity to the message. Today, the joined letters PW appear everywhere in Warsaw: commemorated in stone, rendered in bronze, used as a playful logo for the new Museum of the Uprising and marking the Museum's merchandise. 'Cool' and domesticated, it is no longer invested with the strength of subversion or danger. Although this scribble is not a sign of rebellion but commemoration, because of the illegal and expressive nature of its form, by materializing risk and subversion, it stays true to its message – paying homage to the Insurgence and the city.

In each of these cases, the image and its reading rely on the reader's knowledge of the context outside the frame, the specific spatial, material and cultural array as well as the language and the setting of display. Without considering their surface conditions, these are merely images: they do not form semiotic landscapes but mere snap-shots of a 'tourist view': each taken for its aesthetic value, general illustrative qualities. If collected as visual artefacts that 'represent a place', they may reveal more about the viewer than about the locality. The knowledge of the *iconosphere* of the place, of the local discourses, allows the viewer/reader an access to the city and its signs, to the understanding of the elements of the landscape. But that knowledge simultaneously obscures the immediate visual effect that places make, shifting the reflection from the surface to the underlying circumstance, the surrounding context. Semiotic landscape of each place is thus articulated in both types of inspection. It is not a fixed entity, but a matrix of meaningful surfaces dynamically configured for each locale.

Coda

Places are complex and immersive environments with persistent and substantial presence in our field of vision, our language(s), memories and knowledge(s). Whether we experience them as tourists or as locals, whether we view them *in situ* or from afar through some mode of re-presentation, places necessitate specificity of analysis. A close, topo-sensitive reading they require productively complicates abstracting theories and generalizing assumptions. This attention to the particular surface (dia)critically engages with text and image, but is focused on the place of their interaction rather than on their positioning and antagonisms. It invites unfashionable and/or forgotten theoretical and methodological tools, and is intent on crossing the disciplinary boundaries.

Bühler's (1934/1990) notion of *deictic field* allows for regarding elements of semiotic landscapes in their multiple linguistic and graphic forms. Its focus on contextual dependence of signs facilitates accounting for the sphere of meaning inscribed in the sign's material setting and its specific placement; the very site of display. Gibson's (1966) differentiation between the mediated perception of images and immediate experience of meaningful surfaces corroborates Bühler's communicative triad emphasizing the active role of objects in significative practices.

Taking up the problematic of place, attachment, context and surface questions the traditional privilege afforded to the arbitrary signs. Considering *semiosis in situ* potentially engages with (both linguistic and pictorial) signs in their relation to the surface of display, the materiality of context, and the attributes of multi-sensory fields that topo-sensitive signs necessarily occupy. Reflecting on specificity of place rehabilitates the role of perception in semiosis opening up the limited and static theoretical models of vision onto experience, immersion and the materiality of meaningful objects, onto surfaces that inform, constitute or surround each event of our encounter with semiotic landscapes.

Semiotic landscape is not a fixed image, a picture set within a rigid frame. It is a dynamic layout of surfaces and objects. While crowding our field of vision, objects and their surfaces remain programmatically neglected in semiotic theory and in much of visual studies. Addressing visual research, Irit Rogoff (1998) postulates the 'possibility of engaging with all texts, and images and other stimuli and frameworks we encounter, of breaking down the barriers of permissible and territorialized knowledge' (p. 23). This possibility needs to include some overlooked or simply older approaches that in systematic ways and with considerable rigour already prepared a remarkable ground for critical engagement with the basic precepts we routinely employ in contemplating the visual.

We need to, as well, bear in mind the dynamic dimensions of our *implacement*. The position from which we (visually and corporeally) confront places is continually augmented by our mobile gazes and quick glances, and by numerous itinerant lines of visions that intersect, interfere and interact with the surrounding landscape. This position cannot be unproblematically examined as abstracted, nor as statically Western. Involving both spatial and temporal dimensions, topo-sensitive signs become increasingly salient to the analysis of the fast changing visual landscapes of contemporary cities. The close reading of the physical context demands attending to the process of dynamic perception (Gibson, 1966) to mobility and multimodality (Kress and van Leeuwen, 2001) of the visual field, with *implacement* implying the immediate and the immanent in addition to placing (emplacement) (Scollon and Wong Scollon, 2003).

We engage with places and their incessant visual chatter in ways which cannot be accounted for by positioning us as mere viewers armoured with a directed and fixed all-powerful stare. Our movements rely on familiarity with the surroundings, memory of multisensory events, and an anticipation of experiences. Our making sense of the semiotic landscapes depends on our abilities to navigate within the palpable surfaces. Our visual experience is as much embodied (dependent on our kinaesthetic abilities, body memory and spatial competences) and it is tongue-tied (reliant on language, names, linguistic and conceptual mapping). It is informed by our corporeal relating to objects. John Urry (2003), taking into account the condition of globalization, has augmented his elaboration of the 'tourist gaze' by adding the notions of corporeality, thus allowing the viewer perceptual potentials of a performative body, 'body-as-seen' (p. 5). The earlier theoretical position then was modified by the changing geo-cultural circumstance of the mobile gaze and further nuanced by considering the 'second gaze' and 'a process of reflexive engagement, where hosts and tourists jointly construct each other's subjectivities' (MacCannell, 2001; Jaworski et al., 2003: 36). Still, we need to push the notion of visual engagement with semiotic landscape even further by attending to the object of our looking, the place itself.

The place demands tactile attentiveness to topography and surfaces, a corporeal engagement with its 'concrete particulars' (Gilloch, 2002: 165), and an intimacy of objects. Its multifaceted condition requires a dialogic and sensorial engagement; an *im*mersion within the meaningful sphere of 'multimodal

discourses' (Kress and van Leeuwen, 2001), within 'poly-factorial' spectacles and events. Our presence *in* place is never static; it involves 'mediated coordination' (Bühler, 1934/1990: 216) of significative exchanges and active explorations of the environmental information (Gibson, 1966: 186).

If we understand an object merely through its images (representation) we inevitably lift it from its context and abstract its surface(s), consequently disregarding a possibility of meaning present in the very attachment of the sign to place, a condition of attachment of its attributes and its position within the material surround. Familiar and persistent in our field of vision, clearly speaking to signification of the surface, context and language, implaced signs objects, have a potential for radically challenging the language-image (word-picture) dyad and substantially unhinging the remarkably conservative grounding that underpins theoretical approaches to the visual. To consider meaning *in situ* we need to radically situate our inquiry: allowing for our distinct positions, discourses surrounding the particular locale and their specific linguistic and symbolic contexts, the singularity and subjectivity of the place. It is in the complex *here-now-I* that *semiosis takes place.*

Notes

[1] I am grateful to Adam Jaworski for probing the notion of 'a gap' and suggesting to consider 'the second' gaze.

[2] 'Eastern Europe' is a problematic historical and geo-political construct. See Katarzyna Murawska-Muthesius on the construction(s) of this notion (2004).

[3] Kress and van Leeuwen (1996) note the semiotic revolution attempted in the early years of the Soviet Union, and compare the 'changing role of distribution between language and image' *then* to the current developments in the globalizing world (p. 27). The role of the visual in constructing the new 'semiotic order' *then* (and *there*?) and *now* (and *here* – in the West?) would certainly need more elaboration and accounting for the influences of Russian (and East-European) intellectual tradition on Western semiotic thought together with positioning the cultural and linguistic territories of various 'Easts' in relation to the 'Western notions of literacy' (p. 20).

[4] The reference to Montréal is meant to add complexity to the tourist by positing her as a hyphenated Canadian whose East-European cultural identity has been significantly mediated by her intimacy with complex (post-colonial) spaces.

[5] My guide within the Chinese semiotic landscape has been Joachim Gentz (University of Edinburgh). My Cicerone in Nanjing was Guan Hong Liang, in Beijing, Cordula Hunold (Göttingen) and Walter Wang, and in Shanghai, Jie Chen.

References

Barthes, R. (1983), *The Empire of Signs.* Translated by R. Howard. New York: Hill & Wang.

—(1997), 'Semiology and the urban', in N. Leach (ed.), *Rethinking Architecture: A Reader in Cultural Theory.* London and New York: Routledge, pp. 166–172.

Borowski, W., Ptaszkowska, A. and Tchorek, M. (1986), 'Foksal gallery documents', *October*, 38, 52–62.

Bühler, K. (1990), *Theory of Language: The Representational Function of Language*. Translated by D. F. Godwin. Amsterdam, The Netherlands: J. Benjamin. (Original work published in 1934).

Casey, E. S. (1993), *Getting Back into Place: Toward a Renewed Understanding of the Place-World*. Bloomington and Indianapolis: Indiana University Press.

—(2007), *The World at a Glance*. Bloomington and Indianapolis: Indiana University Press.

Chmielewska, E. (2005), '*Logos* or the resonance of branding: A close reading of the *iconosphere* of Warsaw', *Space and Culture*, 8(4), 349–380.

de Certeau, M. (1988), *The Practice of Everyday Life*. Berkeley: University of California Press.

Eco, U. (1979), *Theory of Semiotics*. Bloomington: University of Indiana Press.

Elkins, J. (2004), 'What does Peirce's sign theory have to say to art history?', *Culture, Theory & Critique*, 44(1), 5–22.

Gibson, J. J. (1950), *The Perception of the Visual World*. Boston: Houghton Mifflin.

—(1966), *The Senses Considered as Perceptual Systems*. Boston: Houghton Mifflin Company.

—(1982), *Reason for Realism*. New York: Laurence Erlbaum.

Gilloch, G. (2002), 'Benjamin's Moscow, Baudrillard's America', in N. Leach (ed.), *The Hieroglyphics of Space: Reading and Experiencing the Modern Metropolis*. London and New York: Routledge, pp. 164–184.

Harris, R. (1995), *Signs of Writing*. New York: Routledge.

Jaworski, A., Ylänne-McEwan, V., Thurlow, C. and Lawson, S. (2003), 'Social roles and negotiation of status in host–tourist interaction: A view from British TV holiday programmes', *Journal of Sociosemiotics*, 7(2), 135–163.

Kress, G. and van Leeuwen, T. (1996), *Reading Images: The Grammar of Visual Design*. London and New York: Routledge.

—(2001), *Multimodal Discourse: The Modes and Media of Contemporary Communication*. New York: Hodder Arnold.

Lotman, Y. (1984), 'O semiosfere', *Sign System Studies*. (*Trudy po znakovym sistemam*), 17, 5–23.

Lynch, K. (2007), 'Reconsidering the image of the city', in M. Carmona and S. Tiesdell (eds), *Urban Design Reader*. Amsterdam, The Netherlands: Elsevier, pp. 108–113.

MacCannell, D. (2001), 'Tourist agency', *Tourist Studies*, 1, 23–37.

Murawska-Muthesius, K. (2004), 'Welcome to Slaka: Does Eastern (Central) European art exist?', *Third Text*, 18(7), 25–40.

Porębski, M. (1972), *Ikonosfera*. Warszawa: PWN.

Rogoff, I. (1998), 'Studying the visual culture', in N. Mirzoeff (ed.), *The Visual Culture Reader*. London and New York: Routledge, pp. 14–26.

—(2000), Terra Infirma: *Geography's Visual Culture*. London and New York: Routledge.

Scollon, R. and Wong Scollon, S. (2003), *Discourses in Place: Language in the Material World*. London: Routledge.

Sulima, R. (2002), *Antropologia codzienności*. [Anthropology of the everyday] Kraków: Wydawnictwo Uniwersytetu Jagiellońskiego.

Tchorek, M. (2000), 'Birth of Place, Place of Birth', manuscript, essay presented at the Center for Contemporary Art, 11 November 2000. Warszawa: Fundacja Tchorek-Bentall.

Thurlow, C. and Aiello, G. (2007), 'National pride, global capital: A social semiotic analysis of transnational visual branding in the airline industry', *Visual Communication*, 16(3), 305–344.

Urry, J. (1990), *The Tourist Gaze*. London: Sage.

—(2003), 'Globalising the tourist gaze', Dept of Sociology, Lancaster University. Retrieved from http://www.lancs.ac.uk/fass/sociology/papers/urry-globalising-the-tourist-gaze.pdf (accessed 27 August 2009).

Ward, J. (2001), *Weimar Surfaces: Urban Visual Culture in 1920s Germany*. Berkeley: University of California Press.

Wasserstrom, J. N. (2007), 'Is global Shanghai "good to think"? Thoughts on comparative history and post-socialist cities', *Journal of World History*, 18(2), 199–234.

Index

FIGURE 1.5 Hairdresser in English, Irish and Polish, Rathmines

FIGURE 1.7 Polski Imprezki, near O'Connell Street

FIGURE 2.3 Isle of Man Fire and Rescue Service vehicle (2006)

HEALTH SERVICES

Shirveishyn Slaynt

Public Notice

Emergency Doctor Service

For the Health of the Nation – Cour Slaynt yn Ashoon

The present emergency GP service will change in two respects from 1st April 2003.

First, the present service, which applies to the patients of all GPs except patients registered with the Ramsey, Laxey and Port Erin group practices, will be extended to include those patients and thus become an all-Island service.

Second, responsibility for operating the service passes from MannDoc (a GP run co-operative) to the Primary Health Care Division of the Department of Health and Social Security.

The emergency GP service operates when your GP surgery is closed. If you have a medical condition that isn't life-threatening but cannot wait until the surgery opens, you should telephone your usual doctor's surgery and a recorded message will inform you of the number to call to speak to the doctor on duty.

The duty doctor will offer you medical advice over the telephone or advise you to attend a consultation at the out-of-hours surgery. In exceptional circumstances, the doctor may arrange a home visit. The out-of-hours doctor's surgery, based at Noble's Hospital is not a drop-in service and patients should note that they **will not** be seen by the duty doctor without an appointment.

The service is available from 6pm to 8am Monday to Friday, with 24-hour cover over weekends and bank holidays.

If you have chest pain or a life-threatening emergency you should always call 999.

Isle of Man Government

DEPARTMENT OF HEALTH AND SOCIAL SECURITY

Rheynn Slaynt as Shickyrys Y Theay

FIGURE 2.5 Manx Department of Health leaflet (2005)

FIGURE 4.2 Sign nailed to a roadside fruit and vegetable stall

FIGURE 4.4 Hand-painted sign on external wall of a restaurant

Figure 4.6 Large billboard poster for Air Jamaica (on a main highway)

Figure 4.8 Large billboard poster on a main highway

Figure 6.1 Graffiti, Sydney

Figure 6.2 Stencil Art, Melbourne

FIGURE 6.6 And the Word Became Flesh

FIGURE 8.2 Advertisement (in English) for a Spanish Mass

FIGURE 8.6 Mexico City Taquería window paint

FIGURE 9.6 'A trip dedicated to me.'

FIGURE 9.11 'A little harder to get to.'

Figure 9.12 'One & Only'

Figure 12.5 Car advertisement on a Soviet-era building, Warsaw, Poland

Figure 12.6 A Coca-Cola ad with Hermitage façade, St Petersburg, Russia

FIGURE 12.8 Building covered with composite banner façade, Warsaw, Poland

Made in the USA
Middletown, DE
06 April 2019